Cultural Ways of Worldmaking

Concepts for the Study of Culture

Edited by
Doris Bachmann-Medick · Horst Carl · Wolfgang Hallet
Ansgar Nünning

Editorial Board
Mieke Bal · Hartmut Böhme · Sebastian Conrad · Vita Fortunati · Isabel Gil
Lawrence Grossberg · Richard Grusin · Hans Ulrich Gumbrecht
Ursula Heise · Claus Leggewie · Helmut Lethen · Christina Lutter
Andreas Reckwitz · Frederik Tygstrup · Barbie Zelizer

1

De Gruyter

Cultural Ways of Worldmaking

Media and Narratives

Edited by
Vera Nünning · Ansgar Nünning · Birgit Neumann

in collaboration with
Mirjam Horn

De Gruyter

ISBN 978-3-11-048603-2
e-ISBN 978-3-11-022756-7
ISSN 2190-3433

Library of Congress Cataloging-in-Publication Data

Cultural ways of worldmaking : media and narratives / edited by Vera Nünning, Ansgar Nünning and Birgit Neumann ; in collaboration with Mirjam Horn.
    p. cm. -- (Concepts for the study of culture ; 1)
ISBN 978-3-11-022755-0 (alk. paper)
1. Mass media and culture. 2. Language and culture. 3. Culture in literature. 4. Discourse analysis, Narrative. 5. Creation (Literary, artistic, etc.) I. Nünning, Vera, 1961- II. Nünning, Ansgar. III. Neumann, Birgit.
P94.6.C795 2010
302.23--dc22

2010016943

Bibliografische Information der Deutschen Nationalbibliothek
Die Deutsche Nationalbibliothek verzeichnet diese Publikation in der Deutschen Nationalbibliografie; detaillierte bibliografische Daten sind im Internet über http://dnb.d-nb.de abrufbar.

© 2010 Walter de Gruyter GmbH & Co. KG, Berlin/New York

Gesamtherstellung: Hubert & Co. GmbH & Co. KG, Göttingen

∞ Gedruckt auf säurefreiem Papier

Printed in Germany

www.degruyter.com

Preface and Acknowledgements

Taking as its point of departure Nelson Goodman's theory of symbol systems as delineated in his seminal book *Ways of Worldmaking*, this volume gauges the possibilities and perspectives that the worldmaking approach offers as a model for the study of culture. Its main objectives are to explore the usefulness and range of the approach ushered in by Goodman for the study of culture and to supplement Goodman's philosophy of worldmaking with a number of complementary disciplinary perspectives, literary and cultural approaches, and new questions. It focuses on three key issues or concepts for coming to terms with ways of worldmaking and their interdisciplinary relevance and ramifications, viz. (1) theoretical approaches to ways of worldmaking, (2) the impact of media on ways of worldmaking, and (3) narratives as ways of worldmaking. The volume serves to demonstrate how the choice of media and narratives affects the worlds that are created and how these worlds are established as socially relevant. It also illustrates the extent to which worldmaking is imbued with cultural values and is thus inevitably implicated in power relations.

This collection of essays emerged from an international symposium on "Ways of Worldmaking: Narratives, Archives and Media" held by the European Summer School in Cultural Studies (ESSCS) in July 2007 in Giessen and Heidelberg. The symposium gauged the possibilities and perspectives that the worldmaking approach offered for the interdisciplinary study of culture. All the articles were commissioned for this volume and most of them represent substantially revised versions of the keynote lectures and other selected papers given. As hosts of the ESSCS we are particularly grateful to the other members of the steering committee: Steven Connor from the London Consortium, Thomas Elsaesser and Jaap Kooijman from the Amsterdam School for Cultural Analysis, Frederik Tygstrup from the Copenhagen Doctoral School in Cultural Studies, and Knut Stene Johansen from the Norwegian Graduate School of Literary Studies, for the excellent collaboration and the dedicated promotion of a European platform for the development of interdisciplinary approaches to the study of culture. We should also like to thank all the colleagues and doctoral students who have participated in the ESSCS in and since 2007. The support of the European Commission and the wonderful venue of Castle Rauischholzhausen contributed greatly to the success of the conference.

The editors would also like to express their gratitude to all people involved in the process of designing and preparing this volume. Particular thanks are due to our colleague and co-editor Birgit Neumann, who did a splendid job throughout the editing process. We are very grateful to Mirjam Horn for her highly valuable assistance in carefully copy-editing the articles and formatting the manuscript as well as for her unflagging attention to detail; to Simon Cooke and Joanna White for valuable help in linguistic matters; and to our assistants Nele Gerkens, Dominique Lerch, Natalie Krümmelbein, Katharina Schwertfeger, and Anna Weigel for their additional support in checking bibliographical references and formatting. Cooperating with the wonderful team at de Gruyter, especially Dr. Heiko Hartmann and his successor Dr. Manuela Gerlof, has been, and is, a great pleasure. Thanks to their great dedication, interest in the projects, and thoughtful responses, it is a privilege as well as pleasure for any scholar to publish with what is an exemplary academic press.

Giessen/Heidelberg, April 2010
Ansgar Nünning and Vera Nünning

Table of Contents

ANSGAR NÜNNING and VERA NÜNNING: Ways of
Worldmaking as a Model for the Study of Culture: Theoretical
Frameworks, Epistemological Underpinnings, New Horizons 1

I. THEORETICAL APPROACHES TO WAYS OF WORLDMAKING

STEVEN CONNOR: 'I Believe That the World' 29

HERBERT GRABES: Three Theories of Literary Worldmaking:
Phenomenological (Roman Ingarden), Constructivist
(Nelson Goodman), Cognitive Psychologist (Schank and Abelson) 47

BEN DAWSON: Worldmaking as Fate 61

FREDERIK TYGSTRUP: The Politics of Symbolic Forms 87

II. MEDIA AS WAYS OF WORLDMAKING

BIRGIT NEUMANN and MARTIN ZIEROLD: Media as Ways of
Worldmaking: Media-specific Structures and Intermedial Dynamics . . 103

KNUT OVE ELIASSEN: Remarks on the Historicity of the
Media Concept 119

STEPHEN SALE: Do Media Determine Our Situation? Friedrich
Kittler's Application of Information Theory to the Humanities 137

ULRIK EKMAN: Irreducible Vagueness: Augmented Worldmaking
in Diller & Scofidio's *Blur Building* 149

MATTHEW TAUNTON: Worlds Made of Concrete and Celluloid:
The London Council Estate in *Nil By Mouth* and Wonderland 175

III. NARRATIVES AS WAYS OF WORLDMAKING

ANSGAR NÜNNING: Making Events – Making Stories – Making Worlds: Ways of Worldmaking from a Narratological Point of View . . 191

VERA NÜNNING: The Making of Fictional Worlds: Processes, Features, and Functions 215

INGER ØSTENSTAD: Literary Worldmaking 245

CAROLINE LUSIN: Writing Lives and 'Worlds': English Fictional Biography at the Turn of the 21st Century 265

HANNA BINGEL: Fictional Narratives and Their Ways of Spiritual Worldmaking: (De-)Constructing the Realm of Transcendence in *City of God* by Way of Metafiction and Multiperspectivity 287

ELISABETH WÅGHÄLL NIVRE and MAREN ECKART: Narrating Life: Early Modern Accounts of the Life of Queen Christina of Sweden (1626-1689) 307

RENÉ DIETRICH: Seeing a World Unmade, and Making a World (Out) of Remains: The Post-Apocalyptic Re-Visions of W.S. Merwin and Carolyn Forché 329

Notes on Contributors 355

Ways of Worldmaking as a Model for the Study of Culture: Theoretical Frameworks, Epistemological Underpinnings, New Horizons

ANSGAR NÜNNING and VERA NÜNNING

1. Ways of Worldmaking Shaping Cultures (and vice versa): Theories, Media, Narratives

One might as well begin with the observation that in the age of globalisation and today's media society, more than ever before, people find themselves surrounded by many worlds and many more worldmakers. No matter whether we switch on the television or the radio, use the internet, go to a museum, do research in an archive, listen to a lecture, political speech or a story told by a friend, we are always faced with a variety of worlds made by human beings using language or other symbol systems. Recent years have seen an increasing interest across many disciplines in the question of how exactly worlds are made and how the relation between worldmaking and orders of knowledge can be described. This testifies to the fact that the question of ways of worldmaking is of great importance not only in philosophy, but in the arts, humanities, social sciences, and in society at large. Since a wide array of symbol systems, modes of organisation, media and social practices are involved in making worlds, however, it is anything but easy to come to terms with what Nelson Goodman called "worldmaking." What is needed is a flexible, wide-ranging and interdisciplinary approach that takes into account different kinds of world models, and different processes of producing them.

Nelson Goodman's theory of symbol systems as delineated in his seminal book *Ways of Worldmaking* arguably provides such an approach. When Goodman coined the felicitous term 'ways of worldmaking,' he managed to highlight the fact that we are faced with a multiplicity of conflicting worlds or world-versions and that there are no 'givens.' According to Goodman, it is "by means of multiple symbol functions and systems we create and comprehend the worlds we live in" ("Routes" 132). Goodman's theories and writings are "far-ranging with topics including aesthetics, epistemology, philosophy of science, and philosophy of language" (Carter 251). He provides detailed analyses of different types of symbols and of the symbol systems of the various art forms (see Goodman, *Languages*) as well as philosophy, with which he was primarily concerned, but he was also interested in other ways of worldmaking, e.g. those of the sciences and everyday discourse (see Goodman, *Ways*).

Goodman proceeds from the assumption that the world we experience is always already made from other worlds: "Worldmaking as we know it always starts from worlds already on hand; the making is a remaking" (*Ways* 6). His main aim is to examine "the processes involved in building a world out of others" (7). Though he denies having attempted any comprehensive or systematic survey, he does provide a perspicacious account of some of the most important processes that go into worldmaking, viz. composition and decomposition, weighting (i.e. emphasis or ratings of relevance), ordering (and reordering), deletion and supplementation, and deformation (see Goodman, *Ways* 7–17; for an excellent concise summary, see Herman, "Narrative Ways" 77–79). Goodman also raises a number of questions that are as crucial for anyone interested in the study of culture—or cultures, for that matter—as for the philosopher: "In just what sense are there many worlds? What distinguishes genuine from spurious worlds? What are worlds made of? [...] What role do symbols play in the making? And how is worldmaking related to knowing?" (*Ways* 1).

This volume, however, is devoted neither to a philosophical discussion of these questions nor to an exegesis of Nelson Goodman's theory of symbols nor to an illustration of the reception and impact that his influential works have had (see Berka). Its main objectives are rather to explore the usefulness and range of the approach ushered in by Goodman for the study of culture and to supplement Goodman's analytical philosophy of worldmaking with a number of complementary disciplinary perspectives, approaches, and questions. Although the very terms of the titles of Goodman's two most famous books—*Languages of Art* (1976) and *Ways of Worldmaking* (1992)—clearly signal that "the limited attempt to produce a comparative theory of symbols has become a global project" (Mitchell 29), his "neutral comparative study" (Goodman and Elgin 31) of symbol systems is arguably not as global as the title *Ways of Worldmaking* may suggest. On the one hand, there are indeed "More Ways of Worldmaking" (Hernardi, "Guest Editorial") than those scrutinised by Goodman. On the other hand, Goodman himself excluded quite a number of areas and issues that are of great interest for the study of culture. As W.J.T. Mitchell has shown, "[t]here are three basic subject areas that Goodman routinely excludes from his system: values, knowledge, and history" (Mitchell 24).

These three subject areas are, of course, of paramount importance for anyone interested in the study of culture, impinging as they do on our cultural ways of worldmaking, our collective identities, and our scholarly practices.

Therefore this volume not only intends to emphasise and illustrate the great usefulness of Goodman's approach, but also attempts to expand, supplement, and amplify the framework conceived by Goodman in *Ways of Worldmaking* and reconceived by him and Catherine Elgin in *Reconceptions in Philosophy and Other Arts and Sciences* (1988). To this end the present volume seeks to include other ways of worldmaking than those Goodman focussed on and to explore how these are related to questions of contexts, culture(s), history (or histories), functions, and values, i.e. to issues that Goodman excluded, but that cultural ways of worldmaking are inevitably embedded and involved in. While Goodman was mainly concerned with devising "a synchronic, systematic map of the fundamental rules and types that operate in all symbolic behavior, in any language, culture, or moment in history" (Mitchell 24), i.e. in universal aspects of worldmaking as a "universal science" (25), most of the chapters in this volume focus on how ways of worldmaking operate in particular cultural, literary and historical contexts, taking in both synchronic and diachronic issues as well as the question of what functions specific ways of worldmaking fulfil in each case and in varying cultural contexts. In so doing, they expand the worldmaking approach, deliberately focussing on issues that lie beyond the scope of Goodman's project.

Useful concepts for exploring the question of how ways of worldmaking and cultures mutually impinge on each other are the notions of media and narratives, which have come to the forefront of interdisciplinary research, but which have not yet been thoroughly explored as ways of worldmaking (see Bruner, "Self-Making"; Herman, "Narrative Ways"). This volume focuses on three key issues or concepts as a starting point for exploring cultural ways of worldmaking and their interdisciplinary relevance and ramifications, viz. (1) theoretical approaches to ways of worldmaking, (2) media as ways of worldmaking, and (3) narratives as ways of worldmaking.

The articles in Part I of this volume discuss a number of theoretical approaches to ways of worldmaking which not only serve to complement Goodman's constructivist approach (see section 2 below) by contrasting it with other theories but also to illuminate key concepts and the politics of symbolic forms. Steven Connor addresses a number of fundamental issues surrounding the question, 'what is a world?', focussing on the ways in which 'the world' can come into being, while also giving a brief history of the concept of 'the world.' Comparing three theories of literary worldmaking, Herbert Grabes puts Goodman's approach into perspective by looking at the similarities and differences between Goodman's constructivist position, Roman Ingarden's phenomenological theory, and Schank and Abelson's cognitive psychological approach. Ben Dawson's essay explores the ways in which Hegel's early work remains important in responding to the constructivist and pluralist epistemology that underlies Goodman's approach. Frederik Tygstrup focuses on one of the issues that Goodman (and Ernst Cassirer) largely ignore, namely the politics of symbolic forms. The construction and reconstruction of symbolic forms, Tygstrup shows, is a privileged mechanism of worldmaking as it transforms heterogeneous data into a more or less coherent world, a universe centring around the lived experiences of human agents trying to come to terms with their communal environment. What Tygstrup and the other articles of this section illustrate is the extent to which worldmaking is imbued with cultural values and thus inevitably implicated in power relations. The transformation of contingent data and experiences into a meaningful and socially significant world has wider political and ethical implications. What is at stake is the power of processes of worldmaking to turn chaotic data into culturally significant truths, the evidence of 'facts,' and thus to include them in a shared world of ideologies and certainties. It is because any and every constructed world serves particular interests that it is so important to defend the plurality of worlds against the desire of homogenisation. From this perspective, politics, i.e. the struggle for the power to define truth, is essentially a negotiation of the diverse forms of worldmaking.

Another one of the lacunae in Goodman's account concerns the role of media, medialisation and the dynamics of pre- and remediation (see Bolter and Grusin; Grusin; Erll) as important factors that have shaped, and continue to shape, our ways of worldmaking. As Schmidt has convincingly shown, all our ways of constructing or fabricating world-models are thoroughly shaped by the conditions of mediality (see *Systemflirts*). Part II of this volume ("Media as Ways of Worldmaking") is therefore devoted to exploring the impact of media on our ways of worldmaking. Though Goodman's theories can readily be applied to new media, the latter have also generated new ways of worldmaking that deserve to be studied in detail. Goodman does mention some media in passing, while even devoting a whole chapter to "The Sound of Pictures" (see *Languages* ch. II) and two shorter chapters to music and musical quotation respectively (see Goodman, *Languages* ch. V.2; *Ways*, ch. III.3). He did not, however, pay any sustained attention to the role of media as ways of worldmaking. Media not only provide means of communication, but they also shape cultural processes and our understanding, and fabrication, of reality. Given the fundamental impact media have on ways of worldmaking, the question of how medial forms structure our world-models constitutes a central research area in a variety of disciplines.

The chapters of Part II of this volume explore different aspects of the intricate relationship between media and worldmaking: Birgit Neumann and Martin Zierold focus on media-specific structures and intermedial dynamics, stressing that the power of individual media to create and perpetuate world models relies as much on media-specific forms as on their inter- and transmedial adaptations. In this view, worldmaking is an ongoing, dynamic and open process in which the same messages, contents, forms, and values are represented again and again in diverse media. Knut Ove Eliassen adds an important historical dimension to the study of media as he explores the historicity of media concepts, showing that the semantics of the term 'media' orders and indeed produces the very epistemology of the field 'media studies.' Because the term 'media' does not function independently of the technologies and practices it denotes, nor of the institutions that uphold it, Eliassen raises the fundamental question of whether 'media' is indeed an adequate term to analyse the technologies that formatted and shaped worlds in the period before the term received its present meaning. The historicity of media concepts raises important methodological questions and stresses the necessity of context-sensitive approaches to ways of worldmaking which can cross the border between textual formalism and historical contextualism. Some of these methodological challenges that arise when analysing the medial configurations that support our ways of worldmaking are addressed in Stephen Sale's contribution. Analysing the constitutive role that communications media play in cultural production, Sale explores the potentials of applying Friedrich Kittler's information theory to the humanities. The essays by Matthew Taunton and Ulrik Ekman offer in-depth case studies which further investigate the relation between media and worldmaking, providing concrete examples from architecture and multimedia art respectively. Taunton's paper problematises Goodman's constructivist notion of worldmaking by exploring the construction of the London council estate; and Ekman's contribution discusses how the artistic-architectural project 'Blur Building' uses new media and information technology so extensively that it ultimately challenges any notion of a given sense of 'the world.' Hence, the contributions gathered in Part II share an interest in how the choice of media affects the worlds that are created and in how these worlds are established as socially relevant worlds. Because worlds are always made from other worlds, the articles indicate the necessity of a dynamic turn in media studies. Behind this shift lies, among other things, the idea that individual media are always part of the social circulation of meanings, truths, and ideas: Worlds as such are never fixed once and for all, but are something that has to be made, processed, and circulated time and again in different media via concomitant processes of inter- and transmedial translation.

Like media, narratives are also of fundamental importance for the ways in which we make sense of the world and our experiences. As the chapters in Part III of this volume ("Narratives as Ways of Worldmaking") serve to demonstrate, narratives are at work in processes such as identity formation, ordering experiences, remembering and negotiating values, and fabricating storied versions of 'the world.' Although narration can be viewed as a universal practice, the way narratives are formed is culturally and historically variable. The articles in Part III explore such issues as the socio-historical dimension of narratives, the interrelation between narrative and personal and cultural identity, and narrative as a means of negotiating, constructing, and deconstructing knowledge, norms, values, and worlds, both in literary texts and in biography and historiography. Ansgar Nünning gauges the complexity of narrative worldmaking, i.e. of the procedures and processes through which happenings, occurrences, or incidents become meaningful events, stories, and storyworlds. He discusses the various procedures which are involved in narrative worldmaking, e.g. selection, deletion, abstraction, hierarchisation and ratings of relevance, configuration, ordering, and emplotment, and the choice of point of view and the arrangement of perspectives. What he stresses is that the worldmaking potential of narratives depends as much on symbolic forms and formal strategies as on their correspondence to the culturally available schemata, metaphors, and plots that contemporary society lives by. The complexity of worldmaking is also at the heart of Vera Nünning's contribution which focuses on the specific processes that are involved in the construction of narrative and fictional worlds. Vera Nünning explores to what extent the five processes identified by Goodman—namely composition and decomposition, weighting, ordering, deletion and supplementation as well as deformation and reshaping—are involved in the making of fictional worlds. Though these processes indeed inform fiction, Vera Nünning argues that they are not the only principles that should be considered if one wants to understand the specificity of fictional worlds. She therefore discusses eight additional features which are relevant to fictional worldmaking. Inger Østenstad also addresses a number of fundamental issues concerning literary worldmaking, focussing on both the strategies that literature can employ to construe worlds and the social processes in which literary texts are caught up and in which they play a role. The specificities of literature are addressed in Caroline Lusin's article, in which she analyses the narrative processes involved in the writing of fictional (auto-)biographies and shows that literature opens up a space in which world- and identity-making are self-consciously laid bare. Because each event and every single life, as also highlighted in the contribution by Elisabeth Wåghäll Nivre and Maren Eckart, is open to different interpretations, narratives always point to what is not told, to an underlying system of alternative stories. Literary texts, then, are essentially ambiguous, indeterminate, and complex, providing a space for experimenting with alternative ways of world- and identity-making, and it is this complexity of literature which can make readers aware of their own strategies of worldmaking as well as the norms that guide these strategies. Literature, as Hanna Bingel shows, can articulate what had been latent in culture. Exploiting the properties of narrative in a way that no longer emphasises continuity and coherence, but depicts a world of disunity and fragmentation, literature can even work at 'unmaking' worlds, as René Dietrich's essay shows. In sum, the contributions of this part of the volume show that literature, while being closely linked to other media and discourses, is a very specific form of worldmaking: It is a practice of worldmaking that allows readers to experience 'the world' differently. Literature can couple coherent representations of the world, of objects, moral messages, and human agency with a self-conscious reflection of ways of worldmaking. Through this paradoxical structure it exposes the normativity of the construed worlds and engages us in an open process of negotiation of our own strategies of worldmaking.

By focussing on the reciprocal relationship between cultures and ways of worldmaking, the articles also examine the functions that the ways of worldmaking of media and narratives fulfil within cultures and theories. Goodman's approach has managed to throw a great deal of light on how symbol systems shape or indeed make worlds. He was mainly concerned with the question of how symbol systems make a world, but he did not dwell on the equally interesting questions of how a world, or a culture, makes or shapes its symbol systems (see Maine 46), and of what functions different kinds of worldmaking fulfil. It is in part this deficit that the articles in this volume seek to address.

What Nelson Goodman said of the modes of organisation and worldmaking can be applied equally well to all of the phenomena and processes that the study of literature, the media and culture at large is concerned with: "they are not 'found in the world' but *built into a world*" (Goodman, *Ways* 14). Time and again Goodman emphasises that "myth, art, language, and science are thus symbols not in the sense of mere figures that refer to some reality by means of suggestion and allegory, but in the sense of agents each of which produces and posits a world of its own" ("On Capturing" 8). Worldmaking is thus "not a passive and imitative but a dynamic and productive operation" (9). Like metaphors, ways of worldmaking should be regarded as "A Mechanism of Creativity" (see Turner and Fauconnier). Let us therefore turn our attention to the constructivist premises that provide the epistemological underpinnings of Goodman's approach to the questions involved in worldmaking.

2. The Epistemology of Worldmaking: Constructivist Premises of the Worldmaking Approach

In order to outline the epistemological issues involved in the notion of 'ways of worldmaking,' it is useful to introduce some of the theoretical insights of constructivism, which constitute the epistemological premises that lie behind the worldmaking approach. Goodman's comprehensive theories of symbol systems and ways of worldmaking proceed from constructivist (or constructionist) assumptions (see Spree). Bruner, for instance, refers to "Goodman's constructivism" ("Self-Making" 77), Carter observes that "Goodman's philosophical theories embrace nominalism, constructivism, and a form of radical relativism" (251), and Goodman himself speaks of his "skeptical, analytic, constructionalist orientation" (*Ways* 1). Therefore it might be useful to provide a brief summary of what has been labelled 'constructivism,' or 'radical constructivism,' which is still an open and interdisciplinary discourse rather than a rigid or fully developed theory (see Schmidt, *Der Diskurs*), in order to outline the epistemological underpinnings of the notion of ways of worldmaking.

Challenging any positivist or realist conception of reality, the roots of constructivist thinking go back to a tradition in which reality is held to be constructed, not given—i.e. to the epistemological arguments of Vico, Berkeley, Hume, Kant, Wilhelm von Humboldt, Ernst Cassirer, Gregory Bateson, and Jean Piaget, to name but a few of the thinkers in the history of philosophy who would deserve a place in a genealogy of constructivism. Relying on empirical research in neurophysiology, the biology of cognition, and cognitive psychology, what has come to be called 'radical constructivism' (see Glasersfeld, "Introduction") proceeds from the assumption that human beings do not have access to an objective reality and that they cannot know anything that lies outside their subjective cognitive domain. Their processes of cognition therefore do not merely copy features of the external reality; individuals rather generate subject-dependent constructs or versions of their world through their verbal descriptions. Worldmaking is thus conceived of as an activity or process that actively constructs patterns and versions rather than merely representing them: "Recognizing patterns is very much a matter of inventing and imposing them," Goodman (*Ways* 22) observes. Goodman's constructivist approach to languages of art and ways of worldmaking is based on, and entails, a "demolition of the copy-theory of representation" (Mitchell 29).

A constructivist theory of cognition thus relinquishes what can be called 'metaphysical or ontological realism' and develops an epistemology "in which knowledge does not reflect an 'objective' ontological reality, but exclusively an ordering and organisation of the world constructed by our experience" (Glasersfeld, "Introduction" 24). In the processes of perception and cognition that make up his or her construal of world-models, the individual does not acquire knowledge of the 'objective' properties of the world but projects a construction of the world that 'fits' the data received by the senses. Constructivism is radical in that it no longer conceives of knowledge as reflecting or being concerned with an objective ontological reality. Rejecting the notion "that representations are or could be pictures, replicas, copies of an experiencer-independent ontic world" (Glasersfeld, "Facts and Self" 437), constructivism emphasises the central role the human observer plays in all cognitive processes (see Schmidt, *Systemflirts* 21-35).

In the constructivist framework underlying the theory of ways of worldmaking, therefore, facts neither have 'real' or 'natural' existence nor do they constitute objective properties of an observer-independent world (for a discussion of the cultural history of the fact see Poovey). Instead, facts and world-versions are conceptualised as intellectual constructs that result from an observer's cognitive processes and that are constituted by the human observer himself rather than given. Emphasising that theories and models of culture are not isomorphic representations of reality, but that they are the only reality that is accessible to human beings, constructivism thus echoes Cassirer's and Goodman's view that facts and structures are not inherent in reality but shaped by symbolic forms of the mind, as the title of the respective chapter of Goodman's *Ways of Worldmaking*—"The Fabrication of Facts" (91–107)—serves to emphasise. Elgin summarises Goodman's, and her own, view on that matter:

> What facts there are is a function of the symbol systems we develop. That is, we participate in the creation of the facts by creating symbol systems with the capacity to represent those facts. In Goodman's terminology, we create worlds by creating, refining, and manipulating symbols. (Elgin, "Sign" 20)

Rather than essentialising facts as something that is ontologically given or pitting facts against theories, Goodman emphasises that they are mutually interdependent:

> Facts [...] are theory-laden; they are theory-laden as we hope our theories are fact-laden. Or in other words, facts are small theories, and true theories are big facts.

> This does not mean, I must repeat, that right versions can be arrived at casually, or that worlds are built from scratch. We start, on any occasion, with some old version or world that we have on hand and that we are stuck with until we have the determination and skill to remake it into a new one. Some of the felt stubbornness of fact is the grip of habit: our firm foundation is indeed stolid. Worldmaking begins with one version and ends with another. (*Ways* 96–97)

Like later proponents of radical constructivism, Goodman conceptualises 'worlds' or world-versions as a human contrivance, as heuristic and abstract models constructed by the philosopher, ordinary human being, or theorist for understanding cultural or historical phenomena. In other words, there is no such thing as a given world—the only thing we can ever have access to are culturally shaped world models or versions. Time and again Goodman reminds his readers that we "cannot test a version by comparing it with a world undescribed, undepicted, unperceived" (*Ways* 4), that "truth cannot be defined or tested by agreement with 'the world'" (17), and "that truth must be otherwise conceived than as correspondence with a ready-made world" (94). Hilary Putnam, too, emphasises "that there is no such thing as *comparing* any version with an 'unconceptualised reality.' [...] All we have is comparison of versions with versions" (Putnam 611).

It is because of this 'man-made' character of world versions and of the inaccessibility of an 'unconceptualised reality' that it seems appropriate to shift our attention from the correspondence theory of truth to the activity of model building, to the modes of organisation that go into worldmaking, and to the exploration of the role that symbolic ways of worldmaking and frames of reference play in trying to come to terms with cultural phenomena. According to Goodman and other constructivists, the correspondence theory of truth does not offer any clear conception of the relationship between discourses or descriptions and a world beyond discourse, let alone of truth conceived of as a correspondence between the two (see Ullian). "The faults of *truth* are many and grave," Goodman and Elgin observe:

> Construed as correspondence between discourse and the readymade world beyond discourse, it runs into double trouble: there is no such world independent of description; and correspondence between description and the undescribed is incomprehensible. (154)

Therefore Goodman turns the reader's attention to the frames of reference, emphasising that the latter "belong less to what is described than to systems of description" (*Ways* 2). For Goodman, 'truth' is always relative to such frames of reference, systems of description and to versions: "so truths can conflict, by belonging to conflicting right versions" (Ullian 57). 'Truth' is therefore not absolute, but relative, in that "'true' marks some trait of observation sentences" (59). In Goodman's constructivist framework, truth, like knowledge and certainty, "must forever be excluded as absolute error," as Mitchell (25) rightly observes.

The informing principle of a constructivist view of the world, therefore, is the "substitution of the concept of fit (and its dynamic corollary, 'viability') for the traditional concept of 'truth' as a matching, isomorphic, or iconic representation of 'reality'" (Glasersfeld, "Interpretation" 209). In the last chapter of *Ways of Worldmaking*, tellingly entitled "On Rightness of Rendering," Goodman discusses the question of what "standards of rightness" can be applied when one compares competing versions or "Worlds in Conflict" (*Ways* 109–10). He discusses a number of such standards and criteria that can be adduced. In the case of theories and models, these include e.g. "the cogency and compactness and comprehensiveness, the informativeness and organizing power of the whole system" (19). Other criteria that might be considered as 'standards of rightness' or yardsticks that allow us to compare conflicting versions are utility, credibility, probability, coherence, deductive and inductive validity, i.e. conformity with rules of inference or with principles that codify practice, respectively, rightness of categorisation (see *Ways* 122–27), and, last, but certainly not least, "efficacy in worldmaking and understanding" (129). Following Goodman, most constructivists would agree that it *is* important to distinguish between better and less good world versions, "'better' not in the sense of objectively *truer* (a criterion discredited by the constructivist approach), but in terms of such criteria as rightness of fit, validity of inference, internal consistency, appropriateness of scope, and above all *productivity*" (McHale, *Constructing* 9).

These constructivist conceptualisations of cognition, facts, truth(s), and world-models as observer- and subject-dependent constructs can offer theoretically consistent and empirically well-founded solutions to many of the epistemological and methodological problems that have come to the forefront in recent discussions in philosophy, historiography, and literary and cultural studies. Within the framework of a constructivist theory of cognition and culture, subjectivity, perspectivity, relativity, selectivity, and constructivity should be accepted as methodological principles of any enterprise in the study of culture since they are ineluctable features of every act of perceiving and interpreting the data received by the senses. According to a constructivist point of view, cultural and scientific knowledge can never 'objectively' represent real events or cultural changes; knowledge rather pertains to methodological means historians and cultural theorists have evolved in order to select, interpret, and organise relevant data on the basis of their sources and their conceptual and discursive tools. The real events of the past and the facts of history are separated by an unbridgeable gulf which historiography, as the word itself implies, unsuccessfully tries to overcome through narrative (see White, "The Value"; *The Content of the Form*). A constructivist conceptualisation of historiography, reality, and worldmaking unequivocally emphasises that facts, history, and the world(s) are (wo)manmade and that our concepts and theories, too, are fabricated. This already serves to show that the worldmaking approach is indeed a global project, though it is arguably of particular relevance for a number of domains.

3. Domains and Functions of Worldmaking: Self-Making, Community-Making, Literary Worldmaking

These constructivist notions, which provide the epistemological underpinnings of Goodman's theories, pertain to a wide range of different domains of worldmaking. They range all the way from *Making Selves*, to borrow the subtitle of a seminal book by Paul John Eakin, to worldmaking at large. As we will try to show below, the question of ways of worldmaking is particularly important in the case of narrative fiction, other literary genres, and other artistic media in that they function as worldbuilding institutions, projecting alternatives to the world models that we generally regard as 'reality.' In addition, they often self-reflexively foreground and explore many of the epistemological questions involved in worldmaking.

Narratives in general are not only one of the most powerful ways of worldmaking, but also of 'self-making.' The main reason for this is that storytelling can generate real and possible worlds; narratives also exert performative power, i.e. they do not merely represent life, but they constitute and indeed 'form' life. Life itself, like reality, is pretty amorphous, chaotic, and contingent. When it is turned into a story, however, it is given form, structure, and meaning. Though most people would probably agree that narratives are of fundamental importance for the ways in which we make sense of our experiences and of our lives at large, the worldmaking capacity of stories and storytelling has not received the degree of attention that it arguably deserves (see Herman, "Narrative Ways"). In his pioneering account of the creation of an autobiographical self, felicitously entitled *How Our Lives Become Stories: Making Selves*, Paul John Eakin has shown that narratives are at work in processes like identity formation, ordering experiences, remembering and negotiating values.

However, although we frequently speak of 'self narratives,' 'life narratives,' 'storied selves,' 'narrative self-making,' or even 'narrating the self into existence,' the relation between the individual's experience, life or identity and its representation in narrative implied by these phrases is far from self-evident. Life, of course, is not a mere narrative and people exist regardless of whether they tell their story (see Eakin 99). Nonetheless, as narrative psychologists have demonstrated, narrative and identity seem to be so closely intertwined that they constantly feed into and mutually constitute each other. Indeed, the very possibility of identity is intimately tied to the notion of narrative and narrativity—not only as descriptive of the self but, more importantly, as fundamental to the constitution or construction of the subject (for a detailed account see Neumann and Nünning). We not only "organize our experience and our memory of human happenings mainly in the form of narrative" (Bruner, "Narrative Construction" 4); in fact, we also use narrative so ubiquitously as a way of self-making that we might come to the conclusion that the self is generated mainly through narrative. The potential of narratives to suggest and project a coherent identity does not, however, imply that the process of self-narration could ever be completed. Because every narrative self-account is itself part of a life, embedded in a lived context of interaction, intention, and ambiguity, there is always a next and different story to tell.

Moreover, when individuals try to make sense of their personal experience they tend to order it along the lines of literary genres or other text types. Genres themselves can thus be conceived of as important ways of self-making and worldmaking in that they provide the necessary and salient frames, scripts, and schemata for narrating coherent selves and building worlds. As Jerome Bruner and others have convincingly shown, the constructions of autobiographical selves are neither random nor merely personal but rely heavily on conventions and patterns that can be traced back to "fairly easily recognizable literary genres" (Bruner, "Self-Making" 68). Genres, just like metaphors, fulfil an important "forming function" (69) in that they shape the process of constructing selves. The stories we tell when we make our selves are obviously related to the events of our lives, but they "must also fit the requirements of narrative as a form of organizing experience" (70). Genre conventions thus exert a forming influence on life stories, which are embedded in the culturally available plots and values of the respective society. Serving as repositories of narrative models and schemata, genres provide a foundation for our sense of identity, while at the same time making us members of the community that generated the cultural models in the first place.

Narratives not only serve as the most important means of self-making, but they also contribute to what may be called 'community-making,' with genres serving as one of the interfaces between the making of selves and the making of communities. The main reason for this is that the narratives of our lives usually draw on the historically and culturally transmitted repertoire or archive of stories and plots, which serve as idealised models for the elaboration of our own experiences. Hinchman and Hinchman have pointed out that the "stories that individuals create often strike variations upon a repertoire of socially available narratives that, in turn, legitimise the community and guarantee its continued existence" (xvii).

Another important function of narratives and media is therefore their potential to generate or forge communities. As Bruner observes, "one important way of characterizing a culture is by the narrative models it makes available for describing the course of a life" ("Life as Narrative" 15). Narratives serve to make, and reinforce, communities; and arguably cultures can in turn be described as 'communities of stories' or 'narrative communities' in that they are characterised by a repertoire of stories, culturally available plots, and "culturally canonical accounts" (Bruner, "Self-Making" 70; "Self-Making" passim):

> Without doubt it is narratives that form the basis of collective, national memories and that constitute politics of identity and difference. Cultures should always also be conceived of as narrative communities which are distinguished from each other by their reservoir of narratives. (Müller-Funk 14; our translation)

Narrative genres in particular are central to the formation of collective identities and 'imagined communities' *sensu* Anderson for the simple reason that not only a nation but "any imagined community, is held together in part by the stories it generates about itself" (Arata 1). Media in turn serve to reinforce these narrative communities by disseminating culturally prevalent stories and plots as well as the values and norms the latter serve to reinforce and inculcate.

Though Goodman's approach is so wide-ranging that it lends itself to investigating the world-making practices of just any of the systems that one finds in a functionally differentiated society (i.e. the domains of politics, the economy, and law, as well as the arts, the humanities, and the sciences), it is arguably particularly important for what may for convenience sake be called 'literary worldmaking,' and thus for the study of literature and culture, for at least two reasons: first, as S.J. Schmidt already pointed our twenty-five years ago, literature is "the only place where the construction of world-models as such becomes thematic, and where this thematisation can bear upon all positions from ortho-models to remote fantasy worlds" (Schmidt, "The Fiction Is" 265). The same holds true for other art forms and media, which also self-consciously explore ways of worldmaking, while also enhancing our readiness to imagine and recognise alternative world-models or world-versions (see Hernardi, "Why Is Literature?").

Some literary genres in particular, e.g. science-fiction and revisionist historical novels, are world-building genres in that they project alternatives to the world-models that we know as 'reality' and that they conduct "extended, elaborate thought experiments" (Elgin, "Laboratory" 48): "A thought experiment is an imaginative exercise designed to determine what would happen if certain conditions were met" (47). In doing so, such literary genres often recirculate, recycle and reconfigure world-models already on hand, thus illustrating Goodman's claim that worldmaking "is a remaking" (*Ways* 6). Moreover, though their production and projection of new alternative world-models, they often foreground and flaunt their worldmaking practices, bringing the processes of worldmaking themselves to the fore (see McHale, "Science-Fiction").

The second reason why the worldmaking approach is particularly relevant for the study of literature and culture has to do with the fact that the 'objects' that literary and cultural studies investigate are not merely given or found in the real world, but are themselves constructed. Academic disciplines themselves can be conceived of as particular ways of worldmaking, as activities that construct the phenomena they, more often than not, purport merely to investigate. In his seminal book *Constructing Postmodernism*, Brian McHale makes an observation that is of crucial importance for anyone interested in coming to terms with the plurality of worlds and modes of worldmaking: "If literary-historical 'objects' [...] are constructed, not given or found, then the issue of *how* such objects are constructed, in particular the genre of discourse *in which* they are constructed, becomes crucial" (McHale, *Constructing* 3). This observation holds not only true for such literary-historical 'objects' as genres, periods, or artistic movements, but also for any cultural phenomenon we choose to investigate as scholars working in literary and cultural studies.

In sum, media, narratives, and other ways of worldmaking are important "cognitive tools, instruments of understanding" (Goodman, "On Capturing" 7–8). They not only play a key role in our daily efforts at self-making, but they also serve to forge communities. Literature and other art forms are of particular interest for studying culture(s) in the context of such an approach in that they serve to stage, thematise, and foreground the complex processes and ways of worldmaking, while at the same time conducting self-reflexive thought experiments in self- and worldmaking. That is one of the many reasons for the fact that the study of literature and other art forms can provide a great deal of insight into both ways of worldmaking and the study of culture.

The interrelationship between self-making and worldmaking on the one hand, and narratives, genres, and media on the other again underscores the point made above, viz. that ways of worldmaking do not just shape cultures and worlds, but that they are also shaped by them in that they inevitably use the respective culture's theories, concepts, genres, schemata, and stories to make selves, communities, and worlds. Since "autobiography (like the novel) involves not only the construction of self, but also a construction of one's culture" (Bruner, "Self-Making" 77), the study of genres like autobiographies, biographies and many others can afford valuable insights into the culture from which they originate. Just as the "requirements of a genre-linked narrative" (76) as a form of organising experience impinge upon the stories people tell about their lives, so do the conventions of particular ways of worldmaking shape the worlds that are projected by the media.

Particular media, genres, narratives, and other ways of worldmaking are as much an "expression of the culture" (74) as they are a means of shaping the respective cultures, and making the worlds, that we live in. It is the media genres, their conventions and formats, that determine what we regard as newsworthy or interest-worthy, and that provide the forms of organising e.g. 'the news' or the 'media events' (see Dayan and Katz), which we should never take for granted as 'givens' or take to be 'natural,' let alone mistake for a mere copy or neutral mimetic representation of events or of reality. Being inextricably intertwined with the cultures in which they are embedded, investigations of the multiple ways of worldmaking that we encounter in our contemporary media culture arguably provide a paradigm approach for the study of culture, as we will try to show in the final section.

4. New Horizons: Ways of Worldmaking as a Paradigm for the Study of Culture

Nelson Goodman's theory of symbols and the constructivist approach to ways of worldmaking he and his followers ushered in have opened up new horizons and fertile avenues of research for the study of culture in many ways. The notion of ways of worldmaking as briefly delineated above offers a highly flexible and productive framework that can fruitfully be adopted, expanded, and supplemented for the study of culture. Goodman's ambitious theory can arguably even serve as a paradigm model for the study of culture in that it is not only germane to his own main research domain, but is also relevant to a number of important recent approaches to the study of culture such as those outlined above. "Nelson

Goodman's constructivism arms one well to appreciate the complexities of self- and life-making," Bruner ("Self-Making" 77) observes. In the same vein, one might add that it also arms one well to explore the complexities of worldmaking that are involved in the wide array of symbol systems and social practices that are dubbed 'culture.'

First of all, Goodman's ardent defence of pluralism (see Goodman, *Ways* 4–5; Putnam), his constructionist (or constructivist) epistemology (see section 2 above) and his observation that there are many equally valid descriptions for any aspect of the phenomenal all tally well with recent developments in many fields of the humanities, especially with the prevailing spirit of anti-essentialism and constructivism (see McHale, *Constructing*; Schmidt, *Der Diskurs*). Like Goodman, the study of culture is mainly interested in processes rather than static products, in the diversity of conflicting descriptions and the multiplicity of cultural worlds, and in the question of what goes into worldmaking: "The movement is from unique truth and a world fixed and found to a diversity of right and even conflicting versions or worlds in the making" (Goodman, *Ways* x). Since the study of culture is concerned with such issues as different possible ways of reporting events in the media, conflicting versions of the past in contemporary memorial cultures, and the performative power of narratives and other symbol systems, the constructivist and pluralist character of Goodman's worldmaking approach is very much germane to it. An analysis of composition and decomposition, deletion and supplementation, deformation, ordering, weighting (see Goodman, *Ways* 7–17), and other formal devices for making worlds can all shed lots of light on both the question of what goes into making the cultural worlds that we live in, and the ideological implications and functions that particular ways of worldmaking serve to fulfil. Acknowledging that "worlds themselves may be built in many ways" (*Ways* 5), Goodman encourages us to explore how different ways of worldmaking impose structures, ascribe properties, and disseminate particular versions, views, and values that should never be taken for granted but rather analysed and critiqued for what they are: conflicting versions of reality rather than 'the reality' (see Steven Connor's article in this volume).

Second, while the two other universal sciences, structuralism and semiotics, have used language as their basic model, Goodman's theories of symbol systems have the added value for the study of culture that they pertain equally well to non-verbal and performative ways of worldmaking (see Mitchell 25). What Goodman's theories reflect is "the concern of a philosophical theory of representation" rather than that "of a linguistically based semiology" (Culler 17). A quotation from *Ways of Worldmaking* might serve to show just how wide-ranging Goodman's approach actually is: "Worlds are made by making such versions with words, numerals, pictures, sounds, or other symbols of any kind in any medium; and the comparative study of these versions and visions and of their making is what I call a critique of worldmaking" (94). The fact that his approach does not focus on language or verbal worldmaking alone, but is equally applicable to "pictures, sounds, or other symbols of any kind in any medium" makes it particularly useful for studying intermedial, multimodal, and performative mainfestations of contemporary media culture. Instead of conceiving of 'culture as text,' Goodman's approach allows the study of culture to include the wide array of signifying systems and practices that confront us in the domain we designate as 'culture.'

Thirdly, Goodman's approach has the great advantage of offering a "neutral comparative study" (Goodman and Elgin 31) of a wide range of symbol systems. Though it may be open to debate just how neutral any theory can ever be, his formal theory of symbol systems makes no ideological or normative stipulations, focussing instead on the ways symbols are organised and used. Moreover, it provides a flexible framework for comparative inquiry that is potentially applicable to a broad range of cultural activities, processes, and products, a "framework for the study of how worlds are constructed both in and outside of philosophy and other arts and sciences" (Hernardi, "Guest Editorial" 1). Goodman's detailed analysis of the symbol systems of "the various art forms according to their symbolic features affords the possibility of greater discrimination among the art forms of painting, music, literature, dance, architecture, and the other arts" (Carter 252). Though it is certainly true that "the symbol systems we devise are apt to differ greatly in structure and representational resources" (Elgin, "Sign" 15), both the questions raised by Goodman and the approach he developed for finding answers to them work equally well for a wide array of cultural ways of worldmaking, including literary genres and media, performative arts and rituals, and cultural institutions like museums or archives.

A fourth reason why the ways of worldmaking approach could serve as a model for the study of culture is thus its broad scope which opens up a wide range of possible applications to diverse fields of inquiry. Though Goodman has been taken to task for what critics have called the "totalizing ambition" (Mitchell 29) that is already highlighted in the very terms of the title of his book *Ways of Worldmaking*, the fact that "the limited attempt to produce a comparative theory of symbols has become a global project" (ibid.) enhances the range and applicability of his project. In their again tellingly entitled book *Reconceptions in Philosophy and Other Arts and Sciences*, Nelson Goodman and Catherine Elgin emphasise the broad range of disciplines and perspectives that their approach encompasses: "We work *from* a perspective that takes in the arts, the sciences, philosophy, perception, and our everyday worlds, and *toward* better understanding of each through significant comparison with the others" (Goodman and Elgin 164). Instead of pitting the arts, the humanities, and the sciences against each other, such an approach provides a useful framework for comparatively exploring similarities and differences with regard to their respective forms of worldmaking, which always serve as cognitive tools: "Underlying this approach is Goodman's belief in the cognitive nature of art, which invites consideration of the arts as partners with the sciences in the pursuit of understanding" (Carter 252). For anyone interested in the study of culture, this not only has an obvious appeal, but also serves a useful function in that it alerts us to the ubiquity of symbol systems and their performative power in generating worlds. Since "the use—that is, the fabrication, application, and interpretation—of symbols is centrally involved in all these fields" (Goodman and Elgin 164), a general theory of symbols and their functions has the added value of providing a common frame of reference, while at the same time serving as a rough yardstick for exploring commonalities and differences between the respective modes and ways of worldmaking involved in these different domains.

A fifth reason for the paradigmatic quality of Goodman's approach for the study of culture is that it shifts attention from 'culture' or 'cultural objects,' assumed to exist, ready to be examined, to the level of the concepts that we deploy to construct the objects of inquiry in the first place. If we cannot have access to an 'unconceptualised reality' (see Putnam 611), as Goodman and a host of other constructivists maintain, then the question of how such objects are conceptualised or constructed becomes the key issue. This question pertains both to the level of first-order observations by participants in the cultural field, and to the level of second-order observation by those engaged in the study of culture. On all levels of observation, human beings draw distinctions, name the phenomena that they distinguish, and deploy all the ways of worldmaking that Goodman himself distinguishes.

Last, but certainly not least, a sixth reason for why Goodman's theory of worldmaking arguably constitutes a model for the study of culture is that is has an important self-reflexive dimension that also applies in the arts, humanities, and sciences themselves. The different academic disciplines and cultures of research can also fruitfully be conceptualised as particular ways of worldmaking. Since all cultural domains and kinds of culture are conditioned by knowledge and shaped by ways of worldmaking, the concepts we generate and the methods we develop to construct our cultures of knowledge and research can also be regarded as ways of worldmaking. Since the specificity of different cultures of knowledge is not only grounded in the content of knowledge but also in the modality of its creation and transmission, it is imperative to extend the concepts of cultural knowledge and ways of worldmaking to include cultures of research and education. We should thus like to emphasise the very practical importance that the insights into cultural ways of worldmaking should have for any scholar, especially for those engaged in the study of culture. If it is indeed true that "we create and comprehend the worlds we live in" (Goodman, "Routes" 132) by creating symbol systems, then we should pay much more attention to the concepts, metaphors, narratives, theories and other ways of worldmaking that we devise, carefully refining and reconceiving them. Goodman's approach thus not only provides a productive framework for the study of media and narratives as particular ways, institutions or modes of worldmaking, but it also opens up innovative and rewarding avenues for the self-reflexive exploration of the generation of, and the differences between, academic cultures of knowledge and research. The same holds true for culture-specific signifying practices and conceptualisations, which are also mediated and even constituted by particular ways of worldmaking, which, more often than not, remain unacknowledged.

Goodman's approach is not only extremely fruitful for exploring the worldmaking power of the media and of narratives, but also for a wide array of diverse cultural practices, genres, and institutions. Although it might go without saying, we should like to emphasise that focussing on the worldmaking power of media and narratives does not, of course, pretend to exhaust the broad topic of ways of worldmaking. Though the worldmaking potential of such narrative genres as autobiographies, biographies, historiography, and travelogues may be particularly palpable, this performative power is by no means restricted to narratives. There is a wide range of other symbolic kinds and genres that play an important role as ways of worldmaking. These include, for instance, concepts, metaphors and other rhetorical devices as well as drama, performances, and rituals.

As far as other institutions besides media that are deeply involved in worldmaking are concerned, what immediately springs to mind are, for instance, archives and museums. The concept of the archive has been productively used in the past to describe and analyse how knowledge is stored and organised within a culture. Archives are constantly drawn upon to negotiate meaning in everyday lives as well as in the media. Both the concept itself and the question of how archives are organised and function as cultural ways of worldmaking, of preserving and generating order of cultural knowledge, deserve to be explored. As Anne Hawley has shown, museums are also extremely interesting ways of institutional worldmaking, reflecting as they often do both the world of their founders and the conceptual ideas of the current directors and curators.

What has also received comparatively scant attention is the prominent role that metaphors play in the ways in which we construe our various worlds, both our everyday world and the worlds and 'truths' that the sciences make (see Brown). Metaphors not only serve to shape prevailing views of culture and theory, metaphors are also at the same time shaped by the cultures and theories from which they originate (see Nünning, Grabes, and Baumbach). On the one hand, metaphors project structures onto cultural phenomena which defy direct observation, serving to make sense of them. They thus play a central role in shaping both culture and theory. On the other hand, metaphors are also moulded by both everyday cultural notions and by theories. As Zoltán Kövecses has convincingly shown, metaphors not only reflect prevailing cultural models, but they also fashion or even constitute cultural models. Like media, narratives and other ways of worldmaking, metaphors, too, play a constitutive rather than just reflective role in determining the perception of culture and theories, making worlds rather than just representing them. Far from being mere poetical or rhetorical embellishments, narratives, metaphors and other kind of symbolic forms arguably play an essential and constitutive role in cultural worldmaking. One might even go so far as to argue that they create the very realities they purport merely to describe: "changes in our conceptual system do change what is real for us and affect how we perceive the world and act upon those perceptions" (Lakoff and Johnson 145–46). Offering ways of organising complex experiences and historical changes into structured wholes (see Lakoff and Johnson 81), metaphorical concepts like evolution, improvement, or progress not only "provide coherent structure, highlighting some things and hiding others" (139), they are also capable of giving people a new understanding of the respective target domain, playing "a very significant role in determining what is real for us" (146).

In sum: Goodman's approach not only opens up a wide range of new avenues of exploration for the study of culture, it could arguably even be a (though not 'the') model for the study of culture, for the reasons outlined above. It alerts us to the multiplicity of worlds and the great diversity of competing versions that we are daily confronted with in our contemporary media society, while at the same time providing us with a set of useful cognitive and conceptual tools for coming to terms with the instruments, modes, and processes involved in cultural ways of worldmaking. Moreover, what Goodman has called "a critique of worldmaking" (*Ways* 94), i.e. "the comparative study of these versions and visions and of their making" (ibid.), can fruitfully be amplified and expanded by exploring the ideological and political implications, as well as the functions, of cultural ways of worldmaking.

We should like to conclude by observing that while the principles of human worldmaking identified and systematised by Goodman continue to prevail in many areas, new ways of worldmaking appear in e.g. the new media, which also subtly change older ways of making worlds. The best way to come to terms with what Bruner has called "The Narrative Construction of Reality" or what, following Goodman, we might call the 'symbolic construction, or making, of worlds' is arguably through an analysis of the wide range of combinable yet distinct ways of worldmaking that the arts and the media, as well as the humanities and the sciences, have developed. If the 'objects' that we explore when we study cultural phenomena are indeed constructed, not given or found, then—to quote Brian McHale once more—"the issue of how such objects are constructed, in particular the genre of discourse in which they are constructed, becomes crucial" (*Constructing* 3). And it is through a careful examination of the key concepts, metaphors, narratives, and other symbolic forms that we can gain an insight into the mechanisms of construction that are involved in our cultural ways of worldmaking. That, arguably, is the main reason why Goodman's constructivist approach is such a useful model for the study of culture, though his flexible framework can also benefit from some amplifications, applications, expansions, and reconceptions, as the chapters that follow attempt to demonstrate.

References

Anderson, Benedict. *Imagined Communities: Reflections on the Origins and Spread of Nationalism*. London: Verso, 1983.

Arata, Stephen. *Fictions of Loss in the Victorian Fin de Siècle*. Cambridge: Cambridge UP, 1996.

Berka, Sigrid. "An International Bibliography of Works by and Selected Works about Nelson Goodman." *Journal of Aesthetic Education* 25.1 (1991): 99–112.

Bolter, Jay David, and Richard Grusin. "Remediation." *Configurations: A Journal of Literature, Science, and Technology* 4.3 (1996): 311–58.

Brown, Theodore L. *Making Truth: Metaphor in Science*. Urbana/Chicago: U of Illinois P, 2003.

Bruner, Jerome. *Actual Minds, Possible Worlds*. Cambridge, MA/London: Harvard UP, 1986.

—. "Life as Narrative." *Social Research* 54.1 (1987): 11–32.

—. "Self-Making and World-Making." *Journal of Aesthetic Education* 25.1 (1991): 67–78.

—. "The Narrative Construction of Reality." *Critical Inquiry* 18 (1991): 1–21.

Carter, Curtis L. "A Tribute to Nelson Goodman." *Journal of Aesthetics and Art Criticism* 58.3 (2000): 251–53.

Culler, Jonathan. *Structuralist Poetics: Structuralism, Linguistics and the Study of Literature*. London: Routledge & Kegan Paul, 1975.

Dayan, Daniel, and Elihu Katz. *Media Events: The Live Broadcasting of History*. Cambridge, MA/London: Harvard UP, 1994.
Eakin, Paul John. *How Our Lives Become Stories: Making Selves*. Ithaca/London: Cornell UP, 1999.
Elgin, Catherine Z. "Sign, Symbol, and System." *Journal of Aesthetic Education* 25.1 (1991): 11–21.
—. "What Goodman Leaves Out." *Journal of Aesthetic Education* 25.1 (1991): 89–96.
—. "The Laboratory of the Mind." *A Sense of the World: Essays on Fiction, Narrative, and Knowledge*. Ed. John Gibson et al. New York: Routledge, 2006. 43–54.
Erll, Astrid. *Prämediation – Remediation: Repräsentationen des indischen Aufstands in imperialen und post-kolonialen Medienkulturen (von 1857 bis zur Gegenwart)*. Trier: WVT, 2007.
Eubanks, Philip. "The Story of Conceptual Metaphor: What Motivates Metaphoric Mappings?" *Poetics Today* 20.3 (1999): 419–42.
Glasersfeld, Ernst von. "On the Concept of Interpretation." *Poetics* 12 (1983): 207–18.
—. "An Introduction to Radical Constructivism." *The Invented Reality: How Do We Know What We Believe We Know? Contributions to Constructivism*. Ed. Paul Watzlawick. New York: Norton, 1984. 17–40.
—. "Facts and Self from a Constructivist Point of View." *Poetics* 18.4–5 (1989): 435–48.
Goodman, Nelson. *Languages of Art: An Approach to a Theory of Symbols*. 1968. Indianapolis: Hackett, 1976.
—. *Ways of Worldmaking*. 1978. Indianapolis: Hackett Publishing, 1992.
—. "Routes of Reference." *Critical Inquiry* 8.1 (1981): 121–32.
—. *Of Mind and Other Matters*. Cambridge, MA/London: Harvard UP, 1984.
—. "On Capturing Cities." *Journal of Aesthetic Education* 25.1 (1991): 5–9.
—. "Retrospections." *Journal of Aesthetic Education* 25.1 (1991): 97–98.
Goodman, Nelson, and Catherine Z. Elgin. *Reconceptions in Philosophy and Other Arts and Sciences*. Indianapolis/Cambridge: Hackett Publishing, 1988.
Grusin, Richard. "Premediation." *Criticism* 46.1 (2004): 17–39.
Hawley, Anne. "A Venerable Museum Faces the Future: Guided Tour through the Gardner and Its Director's Mind." *Journal of Aesthetic Education* 25.1 (1991): 79–88.
Heinen, Sandra, and Roy Sommer, eds. *Narratology in the Age of Cross- Disciplinary Narrative Research*. Berlin/New York: de Gruyter, 2009.
Herman, David. "Narrative Ways of Worldmaking." *Narratology in the Age of Cross-Disciplinary Narrative Research*. Eds. Sandra Heinen, and Roy Sommer. Berlin/New York: de Gruyter, 2009. 71–87.
Herman, David, Manfred Jahn, and Marie-Laure Ryan, eds. *Routledge Encyclopedia of Narrative Theory*. London/New York: Routledge, 2005.
Hernadi, Paul. "Guest Editorial: More Ways of Worldmaking." *Journal of Aesthetic Education* 25.1 (1991): 1–4.
—. "Reconceiving Notation and Performance." *Journal of Aesthetic Education* 25.1 (1991): 47–56.
—. "Why Is Literature: A Coevolutionary Perspective on Imaginative Worldmaking." *Poetics Today* 23.1 (2002): 21–42.
Hinchman, Lewis P., and Sandra K. Hinchman. "Introduction: Toward a Definition of Narrative." *Memory, Identity, Community: The Idea of Narrative in the Human Sciences*. Eds. Lewis P. Hinchman, and Sandra K. Hinchman. Albany, NY: State U of New York P, 1997. xiii–xxxii.

Kövecses, Zoltán. *Metaphor in Culture. Universality and Variation*. Cambridge: Cambridge UP, 2005.

Lakoff, George, and Mark Johnson. *Metaphors We Live By*. Chicago/London: U of Chicago P, 1980.

Maine, Barry. "Erich Auerbach's 'Mimesis' and Nelson Goodman's 'Ways of Worldmaking': A Nominal(ist) Revision." *Poetics Today* 20.1 (1999): 41–52.

McHale, Brian. *Constructing Postmodernism*. London: Routledge, 1992.

—. "Science-Fiction, or: The Most Typical Genre in World Literature." *Genre and Interpretation*. University of Helsinki. 11 June 2009.

Mitchell, W.J.T. "Realism, Ideology, and Ideology: A Critique of Nelson Goodman." *Journal of Aesthetic Education* 25.1 (1991): 23–35.

Movracsik, J.M. "Review: Ways of Worldmaking by Nelson Goodman." *The Journal of Aesthetics and Art Criticism* 37.4 (1979): 483–85.

Müller-Funk, Wolfgang. *Die Kultur und ihre Narrative: Eine Einführung*. 2002. Wien/New York: Springer, 2008.

Neumann, Birgit, and Ansgar Nünning. "Ways of Self-Making in (Fictional) Narrative: Interdisciplinary Perspectives on Narrative and Identity." *Narrative and Identity: Theoretical Approaches and Critical Analyses*. Eds. Birgit Neumann, Ansgar Nünning, and Bo Pettersson, with Simon Cooke, René Dietrich, Merja Polvinen, and Alexandre Segao Costa. Trier: WVT, 2008. 3–22.

Nünning, Ansgar, Herbert Grabes, and Sibylle Baumbach. "Metaphors as Ways of Worldmaking, or: Where Metaphors and Culture Meet." *Metaphors: Shaping Culture and Theory*. REAL – Yearbook of Research in English and American Literature 25. Eds. Herbert Grabes, Ansgar Nünning, and Sibylle Baumbach. Tübingen: Narr, 2009. xi–xxviii.

Poovey, Mary. *A History of the Modern Fact: Problems of Knowledge in the Sciences of Wealth and Society*. Chicago: U of Chicago P, 1998.

Putnam, Hilary. "Reflections on Goodman's 'Ways of Worldmaking.'" *The Journal of Philosophy* 79.11 (1979): 603–18.

Rosenberg, Jay F. "Review: Ways of Worldmaking by Nelson Goodman." *Noûs* 16.2 (1982): 307–11.

Ryan, Marie-Laure, ed. *Narrative Across Media: The Languages of Storytelling*. Lincoln/London: U of Nebraska P, 2004.

—. "From Parallel Universes to Parallel Worlds: Ontological Pluralism in Physics, Narratology, and Narrative." *Poetics Today* 27.4 (2006): 633–74.

Schmidt, Siegfried J. "Der Radikale Konstruktivismus: Ein neues Paradigma im interdisziplinären Diskurs." *Der Diskurs des Radikalen Konstruktivismus*. Ed. Siegfried. J. Schmidt. Frankfurt a.M.: Suhrkamp, 1987. 11–88.

—. *Systemflirts: Ausflüge in die Medienkulturgesellschaft*. Weilerswist: Velbrück Wissenschaft, 2008.

Schmidt, Siegfried J., and Helmut Hauptmeier. "The Fiction Is That Reality Exists: A Constructivist Model of Reality, Fiction, and Literature." *Poetics Today*, 5.2 (1984): 253–74.

Spree, Axel. "Goodmans 'radikaler' Konstruktivismus." *Kodikas/Code. Ars Semeiotica: An International Journal of Semiotics* 21.3–4 (1998): 321–31.

Turner, Mark, and Gilles Fauconnier. "A Mechanism of Creativity." *Poetics Today* 20.3 (1999): 397–418.

Ullian, Joseph S. "Truth." *Journal of Aesthetic Education* 25.1 (1991): 57–65.

White, Hayden. "The Value of Narrativity in the Representation of Reality." *Critical Inquiry* 7.1 (1980): 5–27.
—. *The Content of the Form: Narrative Discourse and Historical Representation.* Baltimore, MD/London: Johns Hopkins UP, 1987.
Wollheim, Richard. "The Core of Aesthetics." *Journal of Aesthetic Education* 25.1 (1991): 37–45.

I. Theoretical Approaches to Ways of Worldmaking

oxygen as a by-product. Human beings live off this vegetable pollutant, which they recombine with carbon, largely through the act of combustion known as respiration, and put back, in currently prodigious quantities, into the air.

Though Lovelock has acknowledged the influence of those scientists like Vernadsky, who saw the possibility of a systematic and integrated earth in which living and nonliving organisms would be treated as an inclusive whole, he has kept a sober and dignified distance from some of the loopier claims for the implications of the Gaia hypothesis. In particular, he has never embraced assertions of the progressive co-evolution of mind and *mundus*. Indeed, his most recent book, *The Revenge of Gaia* (2006), chillingly proposes that, far from being the integrating peak of co-evolution, man is well on the way to being dispensed with by an earth that is undergoing one of its rapid transitions to an inhospitably hot condition. Although he writes with passion of his love for the countryside of the West Country and with bitterness at its destruction, Lovelock sees no prospect of a peaceful truce in which human beings would learn the lesson of living in tune with nature, and be able to live in a condition of sustainable development. Rather, technological means must urgently be sought to mitigate the effects on the atmosphere of man's tenancy of the earth, nuclear power being the most egregiously and culpably neglected of these means. For what matters most is that there should be fewer humans: Lovelock calls for what in effect would be a cull, to reduce the population from over six billion to around half to one billion. For Lovelock, it is not a matter of human beings learning to tread more lightly upon the earth. Rather than returning to the land, the least injurious way to sustain the human population would be for nearly all human beings to live in dense urban masses, consuming the junk food they adore, which could be synthesised from the air or the effluents from nuclear power stations, rather than the products (whether organic or not makes little difference) of catastrophically overfarmed land (see Lovelock 170).

It is hard to know whether Lovelock's work belongs on the side of the growth of world consciousness or its retraction. While the Gaia theory has contributed hugely to a new synthesis of world and 'world,' his actual arguments suggest that the human world has no choice but undignified, sustainable retreat (Lovelock 8). The world can only be appeased by a standing aside of 'the world.' As Bruno Latour observed in a lecture given to the British Sociological Association, the war being waged by human beings on Gaia is truly a 'world war,' in a sense to which no previous conflicts really approximate: "Speak of a *World* War… Those of the 20th century were little provincial conflicts compared to the one that awaits us. Retreat, retreat! before it's too late and we lose everything" (Latour, "A

Plea for Earthly Sciences" 1). There is another feature of this war of 'the world' on the world to which Latour draws our attention:

> We will lose especially because this war against Gaia has one trait in common with that rather local fight ridiculously called the "War on Terror": it cannot be won. Either we come out on top of Gaia, and we disappear with her; or we *lose* against Gaia, and she manages to shudder us out of existence. (Ibid.)

In reality, we cannot win because it is no longer clear what winning this kind of world war could mean.

Ironically, the orderly retreat of 'the world' from the world can only be engineered by an increase in world consciousness. The strongest and most emphatic exponent of world consciousness in the last ten years has been Michel Serres. His previous work, governed by the figure of Hermes, had been concerned with the logic of unpredictable crossings and communications, often in the mode of a kind of minority, drawing attention to the exceptional, the unexpected, the anomalous, and the unassimilated, in a way which has occasionally endeared him to the supporters of micrological perspectives. But, for the last ten years, Serres's work has been taking a different turn. In this period, he has been trying to make good on his promise made to Bruno Latour in an interview from 1990 to try "to form, to compose, to promote—I can't quite find the right word—...a *syrrhèse*, a confluence not a system, a mobile confluence of fluxes. Turbulences, overlapping cyclones and anticyclones, like on the weather map" (Serres and Latour 122). The beginning of this process is perhaps to be found in his *The Natural Contract* (1995), but the decisive move to the universalist thinking that has characterised his recent work is taken in *Atlas* (1994). As its title suggests, this book is an attempt to provide a kind of *mappa mundi* for the modern world of communications. Serres had devoted much of his earlier work to the describing of patterns of interference, intersection, relation, and communication—describing his work as 'a philosophy of mixed bodies,' or a 'philosophy of prepositions.' A map of the modern world would need to render and make navigable a world that is no longer the inert background or arena of these movements, but is formed through them. If we are to construct a new understanding of the world, it will have to be through a mapping of movement, itinerary, trajectory. And this is because relations are no longer exceptions, especially in the world that we have constructed, but rather constitute the world. In a space formed out of mediations and relations, of passe-partouts and between-times, it is no longer possible to maintain the separation of different spaces—or the distinction between the local and the global. Later books extend Serres's attempts to intimate a map of global connections in *Atlas*. In these works, Serres candidly connects the making of a new kind of world with the emergence of a new kind of humanity, in 'hominescence.'

At the centre of *Hominescence* (2001) is what Serres calls "the greatest event of the twentieth century" (Serres, *Hominescence* 90), by which he means the end of agriculture as it had been practised up to this point. "The Earth, in the sense of the planet photographed in its globality by astronauts, takes the place of the earth, in the sense of the plot of ground worked every day" (ibid.). This condition is created by and reciprocally accelerates a "general humanisation of species" (Serres, *Hominescence* 92). The central section of *Hominescence*, entitled "The World," takes the measure of this new configuration of man in relation to the natural world. Serres sees this as a new domestication of nature, though it completes, rather than fundamentally contradicting, a process begun in the Neolithic period. In this process, the natural world is not literally enclosed in farms and zoos, but it is absorbed into knowledge: "[T]he Universe has become the farm of knowledge" (115). Such a prospect of a universal subordination of animals to the dominion of man may fill animalists with horror, but Serres insists that such a relation needs not of itself be dominative. Rather, now that nature has entered culture, a word which Serres insists on taking in its primary meaning, animals and human beings can enter into new relations of mutual cultivation, a reciprocally-defining dance of care, charm, and enchantment. Even more than this, as we "leave the farm and enter into the world" (144), we are in the process of constructing a new, collective body, borrowing and integrating the particularities of every species. Insofar as a species represents a certain inhabitation of a particular time and space, the construction of what Serres calls the "Biosom" (146) effects a synthesis of such times and places:

> If each species carves out a space-time, that is, a niche in the world to subsist in, or if, inversely, the spatio-temporal dimensions of each particular niche bring about the appearance of one or more species, as if they represented each grade or rung of this ladder, then the Biosom composes the global space-time, complex and intersecting, of the ensemble of living creatures in the world. (147)

2. Unworlding

Bruno Latour has characterised a paradoxical wrinkle in the history of globalisation:

> [W]hen the cartographer Mercator transformed Atlas from a distorted giant supporting the Earth on his shoulder into a quiet and seated scientist holding the planet in his *hand*, this was probably the time when globalization was at its zenith.

> And yet the world in 1608 was barely known and people remained far apart. Still, every new land, every new civilization, every new difference could be located, situated, housed, without much surprise into the transparent house of Nature. But now that the world is known, people are brought together by violent deeds, even if they wish to differ and not be connected. There is no global anymore to assemble them. The best proof is that there are people setting up demonstrations against globalization. The global is up for grabs. Globalization is simultaneously at its maximum and the globe at its nadir. There are lots of *blogs* but no globe. (Latour, "From Realpolitik to Dingpolitik" 27)

Once, there was a strong idea of the world without a corresponding experience of it. Once it was possible to imagine the world without being able to live it. Now we are forced to live in the world, and maybe also to live out the world, without being able, or without daring, to imagine it. We have become mundophobic, world-shy.

Latour here points to another tradition of worldthinking that attempts to effect the remission of 'the world.' Heidegger inherits from Hegel the conception of a relation between what he calls *Dasein*, which he is at pains to tell us is not necessarily to be identified with human existence and the worlding of the world. He as well inherits the sense that it is in some way the destiny of *Dasein* to concern itself with the worlding of the world. This is in contrast to animals, for example, which have a merely passive or reactive relation to their environments, or *Umwelte*.

But Heidegger marks the beginning of a difficulty or reluctance in the project of thinking the world. Heidegger, in *Being and Time*, sets out to try to grasp the "worldhood of the world" (63–148). Asking this question, Heidegger has already made something like a break, almost a breakthrough. For he newly assumes that being cannot be understood apart from its worldly condition and that this condition of having to be in a world is essential to it. Where much philosophical endeavour prior to Heidegger had assumed that the condition of belonging to the world was just that, a condition, attaching to but not an essential part of the nature of things and beings, Heidegger shows that the accident of being in the world is an essential accident, and as such is something to be grasped rather than abstracted away.

Worldhood must be understood because it is always presupposed in everything to do with *Dasein*. The world has thus already begun to advance upon understanding, calling to be understood, refusing any more to be simply set aside as a condition of things. Indeed, Heidegger's determination to try to find a way to think worldhood itself may be thought of as a crucial kind of explication, or of worlding, whereby the world comes into the world. But the specific way in which Heidegger insists that the world comes into the world means that it must also retreat from understanding. This is because, for Heidegger, the essential condition of the world is to be that in which everything that is in the world must have its being, it is to be the outside of everything that is inside it. It is for this reason that Heidegger's account of the world can predicate so little of it. *Dasein* is that form of existence that cannot but pose the worldhood of the world, even if that worldhood must in its essence remain withdrawn. The best that we can hope for is the achievement of *Gelassenheit*, which allows the in-the-worldness of the world to be disclosed without being grasped.

Heidegger's work has recently been subjected to extensive reworking in the work of Peter Sloterdijk, who has attempted in the three volumes of his *Sphären* (1998–2004) to update and particularise the unhelpfully dim view of technology taken by Heidegger. His way of doing this is to investigate the condition of insideness, or enfoldedness. Sloterdijk's *Sphären* trilogy reads human history—philosophical, religious, artistic, political, in terms of the elaboration of different kinds of spheres, or spaces of introversion. The first volume concentrates on 'microspherology,' the construction of the intimate and elementary spheres, typified by the simplest dyadic relations between the child and the womb, or mother. The second volume follows through the macrospherological evolution of larger, more inclusive, and metaphysical spheres, typified in imperial conceptions of the One World, or in Marshall McLuhan's notion of the global village. The third volume proposes, by contrast, that the modern world must be understood nonholistically, and in terms of a polyspherology which will take account, in a "multifocal, multiperspectival and heterarchical" manner, of the complex aggregations of different spheres that make up the world (Sloterdijk 23, my translation). Where the governing metaphor for microspherology is the bubble, and the governing metaphor of macrospherology is the globe, the aptest and most versatile metaphor for the polyspherological condition of the modern world is that of foam: "In place of the philosophical super-soap-bubble, of the All-Monad of the unitary world…there is a polycosmic agglomeration. This may be described as an assemblage of assemblages, a semi-opaque foam of world-making constructions of space" (63–64, my translation).

These ensphering, of various kinds and on different scales—that of the cell, the body, the womb, the city, the nation, the world—are always in part withdrawn from awareness and experience, precisely because they depend upon what is held to be given or latent. For Sloterdijk, the last and most recent environment is not in fact the solid world, but rather the atmosphere, the image of ensphering as such. The air which surrounds us is ubiquitous, abundant. But modernity is characterised by progressive stages of what Sloterdijk calls 'explizieren,' which we should probably translate as 'explicitation,' a 'making explicit,' rather than explication or simple explanation. By this, Sloterdijk means the making manifest of the complex support systems and dependencies that constitute man in his environment. Environmentalism itself, provoked by Jacob von Uexküll's development of the idea of the *Umwelt* (1909), is an example of the explicitation, which may be thought of as bringing the outside into perception.

Sloterdijk has read this era of explicitation as having two effects. One is that we come closer to the possibility of understanding the limits to our autonomy and the full extent of our ensphered condition. There is always, for human beings, a sphere, an *Umwelt*, in which we participate and which participates in us. The second effect is that we lose the vital sense of openness, or givenness. In a sense, we have lost the world in its givenness, the givenness of 'the world.' For explicitation makes it clear that not only might we depend on the air, but the air might depend on us. When we draw air into our sphere, when we enter an era of 'air-conditioning,' we must recognise the danger of asphyxiation, and Sloterdijk seems to share with Heidegger the sentimental memory of the implicitness of being-there, where the 'there' is always richly and abundantly given. But the process of explicitation not only makes known the grounds of our dependence on what lies outside us (most dramatically in the explication of the process of respiration at the end of the eighteenth century), but it also makes clear the extent of our entanglement—we might say, our convolvement—with the things that surround us. Explicitation makes it possible to understand and to regulate, even to transform what had previously been thought to be simply given; but by no means does it extricate us from that givenness. It may be possible to move into an explicitation of the process of explicitation itself, the result of which is a disclosure of a principle which must be regarded not as the opposite of explication, the fantasy of latency, but as its consequential contrary, namely the fact of implication. The opposite of the explicit may be the implicit; but the contrary of the explicit is the implicated.

In his *We Have Never Been Modern* (1993), Latour argued against modernity's defining self-conception of the split between nature and culture, or, as we might put it, between the world and 'the world.' In fact, he argues that there have only ever been "cultures-natures" (Latour, *We Have never Been Modern* 104), the bumpy, rutted, heterogeneous 'Middle Kingdom' of things that can be assigned securely neither to nature nor to culture, but are active mediators between them. In the work he undertook during the 1990s in the history of science and technology, Latour set himself the task, alongside others who identified themselves with actor-network theory, of following through the 'associology' of various hybrid objects of this kind.

Latour gives us important resources for understanding the nature of our implicatedness in and with the world. And yet Latour also insists that we must give up the validating idea of the 'one world' of nature, and recognise the multiplicity of the worlds that we inhabit. He even calls for a genuine 'war of the worlds' to replace the 'clash of civilisations,' which he sees as a phoney war, a war by the West or the Whites on behalf of the 'one world' of Nature and Reason against the rest. In fact, he argues, this 'one world' does not exist and has never existed. It is there to be made (and by war, or by war as a necessary prelude to an enduring peace). He therefore aligns himself with the point of view expressed by Isabelle Stengers in her *Cosmopolitiques*, first issued in seven volumes in 1997, and reissued in two volumes in 2003, that we need to give up the idea that the world constituted by scientific knowledge, and especially the 'master discipline' of physics, has final authority over the other worlds or frameworks of reality. She represents the cosmopolitical, in almost direct opposition to Kantian cosmopolitanism, as a deliberate defection from worldhood. As opposed to the Kantian view "that politics should aim at allowing a 'cosmos,' a 'good common world' to exist," she explained that "the whole idea of cosmopolitics is to slow down the construction of this common world" (Stengers, "The Cosmopolitical Proposal" 995). Though she appears to be happy to tolerate the abstract horizon or orientation constituted by the prospect of a 'common world,' she wishes to discourage, even perhaps to discredit, all efforts to speak in its name and borrow its authority:

> In the term cosmopolitical, cosmos refers to the unknown constituted by these multiple, divergent worlds and to the articulations of which they would eventually be capable [...] There is no representative of the cosmos as such; it allows nothing, demands no "and so ..." [...] As for the cosmos, as it features in the cosmopolitical proposal, it has no representative, no one talks in its name, and it can therefore be at stake in no particular consultative procedure. (Stengers 95–100)

Like Stengers and the other 'cosmopolitiques' she has encouraged (Soubeyran and Lolive), Latour scorns the 'tolerance' paradigm, but in fact his discourse belongs to an ecology or protectionism of plurality. He wishes for a war of the worlds to protect the possibility of a plurality of worlds, of the internal extraterrestrial, of an infinite intraterrestrial. His common world will, he believes, need to be constructed, and through war.

3. The Missing All

In truth, the worlds that Goodman describes are quite obviously the same kind of thing that we refer to when we use words like cultures, civilisations, mythologies, frames of reference, discursive regimes, idioms, games, rituals, clubs, cliques, clans, and gangs. The more verification we seem to lend Goodman's claims by multiplying examples of such worlds, the more those claims are in fact eroded.

The most important difference between what Goodman seems to mean by 'a world' and 'the world' is the following: A world is strongly determined but weakly determining. By contrast, the world is strongly determining but weakly determined. This must in fact be so. We have the impression that frameworks or states of affairs that we can strongly and exhaustively specify must be similarly strong or exhaustive in their effects. But this is a mistake. The very fact that these frameworks can be so strongly and persuasively specified, that their grammar is so readily legible, is what makes it impossible for them to contain us. We can step outside them precisely because we can see around them. In fact, once we have seen around them, we have in some way already stepped outside them. So a strongly determined world must be weakly determining.

The same is not true of the world, because the world is not totally specifiable. But this does not mean that we are less determined. Anyone who actually tries to complete Goldberg's achingly incomplete sentence 'I believe that the world' is using sleight of hand. It is not just the largeness and variousness of the world that makes it unspecifiable. It is because the world is an open necessity. There is no necessity for the world to be constituted in any way in particular, but it is absolutely necessary that it will come to be constituted in some particular way or ways that are always more finite than the current possibilities. This is the kind of indeterminate finitude that I think we can read out from Heidegger's conception of worldhood, though it is perhaps to anticipate what he might have said, had he ever written the second part of *Sein und Zeit*.

For the world is not merely a place—and this is another of the distinguishing features of 'the world' as opposed to 'a world.' World as *wer-ald*, the time of man, even the age of man, is always world-weary. No matter how many worlds there may seem to be, the point is that it will make no difference to us, because being in the world means only being able to have lived in one world. Of course one is able to choose, maybe constrained to choose, among many worlds. But one will have chosen only one, or only one conglomerate. The world is an issue of the future perfect. "The world was all before them," Milton (ll. 1537) writes of Adam and Eve. But the world is not a prospect; it is a retrospective construal, or the prospect of such a construal. This is the meaning of the definite article in 'the world.' The worldliness of the world is not the issue; the world is the 'the-ness' of the world. When he said that the world is everything that is the case, Wittgenstein was a little previous (like the world itself, perhaps): rather, the world is everything that will have been the case. To think the world is to give it the chance of having been.

We find the idea of the unity of the world a terrifying, even a terrorist concept. This is because unity, which used to sound like an augmentation—the joining together into one of the 'whole world'—now seems to us like the most brutal of reductions. The plurality of worlds, the possibility of the plurality of worlds, must, we feel, be defended from the desire of the imperialist and the desire of the terrorist alike, for they are the same desire, for there to be only one world. But perhaps Michel Serres is right when he points out the conservatism and defensiveness of the philosophy of the fragmentary:

> Let's take a vase or some object that is more solid, more constructed, larger. The larger it is, the more fragile it is. If you break it, the smaller the fragment is, the more resistant it is. Consequently, when you create a fragment, you seek refuge in places, in localities, which is more resistant than a global construction… Constructing on a large scale means moving towards vulnerability; thus, synthesis requires courage—the audacity of the frail. (Serres and Latour 120)

So the frothing paroxysms of worldmaking are perhaps not generative, as we would like them to be, but fiercely defensive, conservative, reductive. Perhaps they amount to something like the process that Wilfred Bion called "attacks on linking." This process is typical of what Klein called the 'paranoid-schizoid' phase of the young child, who splits the world up into good and bad objects, in order to defend itself against the anxious, melancholy acknowledgement that the good breast and the bad breast, the good mother and the bad mother, are the same thing (see Klein 61ff.).

'The world' has two dimensions or axes. One of them is number—the question of how many our world is to be, or how many sub-worlds it is going to allow. We fear that, if the world is reduced to one, it will necessarily be one-and-the-same. But it is a question of the integration of the world, rather than its unification, in the sense of its reduction to one. The world is not one, even if, increasingly, it is without exception or fissure. The world is not all the same, any more than the ocean or the atmosphere is all the same, even there are no places where one can make out divisions in them, or cut them at the joints. Continuity does not entail consistency. Rather than making the world uniform, human habitation has made the world more massively, subtly continuous with itself. The point is not the number of worlds we can participate in, the number of cultural and philosophical *pieds-à-terre* we can maintain, but our capacity for implicated worldliness, the degree to which we are going to be able to live in-the-world, to acknowledge our implication in the world, and the implications of all our worldly acts. This remains true even despite the fact that we currently seem to be required to find a way to acknowledge, as a form of *Dasein* or *in-der-Welt-sein*, conditions and practices that seem so obviously to take us out of this world, temporally and spatially. What is the *Dasein* of Second Life? What would it mean to be worldly, when the world itself has become extraterrestrial, when we have become so exorbitant?

The pinching irony is that, at a time when our implicatedness, not only in the things of the world but in the world itself, has never been more pressing and unneglectable, we seem so capable of living out of this world, or of regarding 'the world' as well lost. Like St. Augustine, who prayed "Lord, make me chaste, but not yet," we seem, just at the point where the world and 'the world' have become so inextricably involved or convolved in each other, and probably for that reason, to want to hold off the gathering of the world. A little like the modern souls spoken of in Eliot's *Dry Salvages*, we have the reality but would do anything to miss the meaning.

In the past, the world was finitude, the condition of always having to have one's being in a particular here and now, rather than in the world as such. The defining condition of being in the world was, in fact, that you could never inhabit the whole of the world that, as Michel Serres is fond of saying, you could never sleep on both ears at once (Serres, *The Troubadour of Knowledge* 16). But now the extraordinary augmentation of human desire and power has reached the point where it seems about to be able to overcome all these forms of finitude, and thus to be able to apprehend, inhabit and even begin to legislate the world as such. And this has become part of our own finitude. It is as if, having progressively domesticated the world, drawing the outside of nature into the inside of human culture, that condition has suddenly flipped, so that our control over the world has become an external necessity, separated from us, and thus a new paradoxical condition of finitude. We are stuck with being *Pantope*, the human who can inhabit all space, *Panchrome*, the participant in all times, *Pangloss*, speaker of many languages, and *Panurge*, unprogrammed in his actions (see Serres, *L'Incadescent* 216–43), as previously we were stuck with mortality, impotence, location, distance, facticity. Our power has become our audacious frailty.

When Goodmanian constructionism attempts to substitute multiple made worlds for the given world, it ignores the fact that the given world has also been under construction for some considerable time, at least since human beings started to change their environment in the Neolithic era. Bruno Latour is right: the world is to be made rather than simply being given. But if he is right about the sense, he is wrong about the tense. For, whether or not we allow it, a world, that cannot but be the world, is in the making. The question may be, not how many worlds we can multiply, but whether we can find a way to live in the world at all, a world that, most hair-raisingly of all, is in large part up, or down, to us. The one choice it seems we do not have is the choice not to make a choice. For so it goes in the world.

References

Bion, Wilfred R. "Attacks on Linking." *Second Thoughts: Selected Papers on Psycho-Analysis.* 1967. London: Maresfield Reprints, 1984. 43–64.

Chardin, Pierre Teilhard de. *The Phenomenon of Man.* Trans. Bernard Wall. London: Collins, 1959.

Dickinson, Emily. *The Complete Poems.* Ed. Thomas H. Johnson. London: Faber and Faber, 1970.

Hegel, Georg Wilhelm Friedrich. *The Philosophy of History.* Trans. J. Sibree. New York: Dover, 1956.

Heidegger, Martin. *Being and Time.* Trans. John Macquarrie and Edward Robinson. Oxford: Basil Blackwell, 1962.

Klein, Melanie. "Some Conclusions Regarding the Emotional Life of the Infant." *Envy and Gratitude, and Other Works 1946–1963.* 1952. London: Vintage, 1997. 61–93.

Latour, Bruno. *We Have Never Been Modern.* Trans. Catherine Porter. New York: Harvester Wheatsheaf, 1993.

—. "From Realpolitik to Dingpolitik or How to Make Things Public." *Making Things Public: Atmospheres of Democracy.* Eds. Bruno Latour and Peter Weibel. Karlsruhe: ZKM Center for Art and Media, Cambridge: MIT Press, 2005. 4–31.

—."A Plea for Earthly Sciences." 2007. 25 Feb 2010. <http://www.bruno-latour.fr/articles/article /102-BSA-GB.pdf>.

Latour, Bruno, and Peter Weibel, eds. *Making Things Public: Atmospheres of Democracy.* Karlsruhe: ZKM Center for Art and Media, Cambridge: MIT Press, 2005.

Lovelock, James. *The Revenge of Gaia.* London: Penguin, 2006.

Milton, John. *Paradise lost.* Repr. of the 1667 ed. Menston: The Scolar Press, 1973.

Pinter, Harold. *Plays: One.* London: Faber and Faber, 1991.

Schelling, Friedrich Wilhelm Joseph. *Von der Weltseele: Eine Hypothese der höheren Physik zur Erklärung des allgemeinen Organismus.* Ed. Jörg Jantzen. Stuttgart: Frommann-Holzboog, 2000.

Serres, Michel. *Atlas.* Paris: Editions Julliard, 1994.

—. *The Natural Contract.* Trans. Elizabeth MacArthur and William Paulson. 1990. Ann Arbor: U of Michigan P, 1995.

—. *The Troubadour of Knowledge*. Trans. Sheila Faria Glaser and William Paulson. Ann Arbor: U of Michigan P, 1997.
—. *Hominescence*. Paris: Le Pommier, 2001.
—. *L'Incandescent*. Paris: Le Pommier, 2003.
Serres, Michel, and Bruno Latour. *Conversations on Science, Culture, and Time*. Trans. Roxanne Lapidus. Ann Arbor: U of Michigan P, 1995.
Sloterdijk, Peter. *Plurale Sphärologie*. Vol. 3. *Schäume: Sphären*. Frankfurt a.M.: Suhrkamp, 2004.
Soubeyran, Olivier, and Jacques Lolive, eds. *L'émergence des cosmopolitiques*. Paris: Broché, 2005.
Stengers, Isabelle. *Cosmopolitiques*. 2 vols. Paris: La Découverte, 2003.
—."The Cosmopolitical Proposal." Trans. Liz Carey-Libbrecht. *Making Things Public: Atmospheres of Democracy*. Eds. Bruno Latour, and Peter Weibel. Karlsruhe: ZKM Center for Art and Media, Cambridge: MIT Press, 2005. 994–1003.
Suess, Eduard. *Die Entstehung der Alpen*. Vienna: W. Braunmüller, 1875.
Tyndale, William. *The Parable of the Wicked Mammon*. Marlborowe [i.e. Antwerp]: J. J. Hoochstraten, 1528.
Uexküll, Jakob von. *Umwelt und Innenwelt der Tiere*. Berlin: Springer, 1909.
Vernadsky, Vladimir I. "Some Words About The Noösphere." 1945. Trans. Rachel Douglas. *21st Century*, 2005. 16–21. 17 Feb 2010 <http://www.21stcentury sciencetech.com/Articles%202005/The_Noosphere.pdf>.

Three Theories of Literary Worldmaking: Phenomenological (Roman Ingarden), Constructivist (Nelson Goodman), Cognitive Psychologist (Schank and Abelson)

Herbert Grabes

'Literary Worldmaking' has become a current term in recent times, yet there are few theories of it that have been worked out in detail. As reception theory has taught us, the worlds that are imagined in the act of reading are the result of an interaction between text and reader, or rather of a special kind of processing of a given literary text. Consequently, there are two domains of preconditions for literary worldmaking, one being that of a text we call 'literary' on account of its special features, impact, or function, the other being the mind of a reader that is already filled with notions of what a 'world' consists of, what its elements are like, how they are assembled into larger wholes, and what kind of relations between them we can expect. In addition, there is the process of interaction between these two domains, a process in which the items of information sequentially taken from the text during reading, and evaluated on the background of what is already known, are complemented if deemed necessary and finally integrated in a way that in the reader's imagination a complex formation is created in analogy to what has been experienced and is known as a 'world.'

One of the first theorists who systematically investigated not only the domain of the textually given but also the process of interaction between the text and the reader was Roman Ingarden. As a student of the early Edmund Husserl, Ingarden became and remained interested above all in a kind of phenomenological ontology, a combination of a primary interest in the ontological structure of an object of philosophical investigation, and the acuteness of observation typical of the method of phenomenology. This approach first became full-fledged in *Das literarische Kunstwerk: Eine Untersuchung aus dem Grenzgebiet der Ontologie, Logik und Literaturwissenschaft* from 1931 (published as an English translation as *The Literary Work of Art* 1973), a work that for various reasons had a great indirect impact on the further development of literary theory. Its conception of the literary work of art as an organic unity still reminds us of nineteenth-century ideas, but the subdivision of this whole into different strata already signals a turn towards a structuralist view that was taken over and popularised by René Wellek and Austin Warren in their extremely influential *Theory of Literature* (1948). As will soon become evident, its influence was even stronger on reception theory, especially regarding Wolfgang Iser's concept of 'blanks' in a literary text that was directly derived from what Ingarden had called "spots of indeterminacy" (*The Literary Work of Art* 249). And with his phenomenological concept of 'schematic aspects' and his view that the literary work is merely "a schematic formation in which, moreover, various elements persevere in a characteristic potentiality" (372) Ingarden also anticipated a central idea of later cognitive psychologist views by half a century. The insight that the mode of presentation in a literary work is merely schematic led Ingarden to the view that "the literary work of art constitutes an aesthetic object only when it is expressed in a concretization" (372) and consequently strengthened the role of the reader in the creation of this kind of artwork.

The same holds true for the worldmaking motivated and guided by a literary text, because it also takes concrete shape only in the act of reading. Worlds are made up of objects in the widest sense, and while giving due attention to the other strata of a literary work of art (such as 'linguistic sound formations,' 'meaning units,' or 'schematised aspects'), Ingarden is fully aware of the fact that the "objects represented in a literary work [...] appear to be the best known of all the strata" and that the reader "not only in a simple reading of the work stops with them and their vicissitudes" (217).

Yet for all its importance, any represented object is "only a schematic formation with spots of indeterminacy of various kinds," and "this schematic structure of represented objects cannot be removed in any finite literary work, even though in the course of the work new spots of indeterminacy may be filled out" (251). The question therefore arises why it is that "while reading a work we are not conscious of any 'gaps,' of any 'spots of indeterminacy,' in the represented objects." And Ingarden's presentation of the reasons for this again shows how far ahead of his time he was. First he points out that the "represented objects are visible to us only from that aspect which is positively determined by the units of meaning," secondly, "some of the spots of indeterminacy are concealed by aspects held in readiness which are predetermined by the units of meaning and are actualized by the reader as he reads," and a third factor working in this direction is the fact that, during his reading and his aesthetic apprehension of the work, the reader usually goes beyond what is simply presented by the text (or projected by it) and in various respects completes the represented objectivities, so that at least some of the spots of indeterminacy are removed" (*The Literary Work of Art* 252).

As to this latter habit of completing, which was to be investigated even more closely later under the influence of cognitive psychology, Ingarden makes a subtle distinction well worth quoting in full because it is rarely observed even today:

> Among the spots of indeterminacy one must distinguish between those which can be removed purely on the basis of textual supplementation and those for which this does not occur in the same sense. In the former, the representing states of affairs designate a strictly circumscribed manifold of possible completions of the spots of indeterminacy, from which we may choose some in the course of reading if we wish to effect this completion in accordance with the already established determinations of the represented objects. In the latter, on the other hand, the textually established states of affairs are not sufficient for designating a strictly circumscribed manifold of possible completions. In that case, each 'completion' or approximate completion actually effected in this way is fully dependent on the reader's (or in a stage play—the director's) discretion. But in the former, too, the reader is not forced to choose a particular one of the possibilities predetermined by the representing states of affairs. The literary work does not necessarily have to be 'consistent' or to be contained within the bounds of what is possible in the actually known world. [...] In principle, there can be literary works which do not trouble themselves at all with staying within the bounds of a particular type of object; but precisely because of this, they can make a particular aesthetic impression by representing a world that is actually impossible or one that is full of contradictions. (253)

The objects presented in a literary work as constituents of a world are, of course, not just 'there,' but appear under a certain perspective and are therefore only discernable in one or the other of their aspects. These aspects are important because "through them it is that represented objects can be made to appear in a manner predetermined by the work itself. "If aspects were totally lacking in a work, represented objects would have to be blankly intended in the reading" (277). The predetermining function works, although not only the objects themselves but also their aspects are—as Ingarden is able to demonstrate—not fully determined themselves, but only schematically given—and not simply given but only held in readiness for readers to let them become concrete in their imagination.

What readers, according to Ingarden, also have to deal with is that "since the (schematized) aspects of a literary work are held in readiness by incompletely determined objects or by non-continuous manifolds of exhibiting states of affairs, they are units separated from each other by jumps" (269). And although some of this stiffness can be reduced in the "unfolding operation of reading, [...] the jumpiness of the succession of aspects can never be entirely removed" (ibid.). Such a "succession of aspects" will be experienced whenever we read a literary text, that is, in what Ingarden calls a "concretization" (372). The temporality inherent in the successiveness of the act of reading has its ontological base in the "order of sequence" of the elements of a literary work of art, a "one-sidedness of conditioning in the constitution" not only of that work as a whole, but also of the worldmaking it motivates and to a considerable degree controls: "every phase of a literary work (except for the first) shows moments of a different, 'earlier' phase. [...] Finally, it contains moments that constitute the basis of foundation of determinate moments of a different, 'subsequent' phase" (310). What is objectified in a literary text is, one could say, a dynamic structure of schematised aspects arranged in a one-directional sequence of presentation.

The "structure of the sequence of parts in a work" and the "temporal perspective in the concretization of the literary work of art" are minutely investigated in Ingarden's complement to *The Literary Work of Art*, which was originally published in Polish in 1937, revised and published in German in 1968 as *Vom Erkennen des literarischen Kunstwerks,* and 1973 in an English translation from the German as *The Cognition of the Literary Work of Art*. It is again amazing to see that most of the later 'innovations' of reception theory were already quite clearly and minutely presented by Ingarden much earlier, for instance when we read that in the act of reading the

> part of the work we are now reading is thus constantly surrounded in concretization by a double horizon (if we may use Husserl's expression here): a) of the parts already read, which sink into the 'past' of the work; and b) of those parts which have not yet been read and which are unknown up to the present moment. This double horizon is constantly present as horizon, but it is always being filled by different parts of the work. (*The Cognition of the Literary Work of Art* 103–4)

And what is most important about this complexity is the fact that

> as we slowly progress from beginning to the end of the work in reading, we apprehend the concretized work from a constantly new temporal point of view but always under a temporal aspect which corresponds both to the standpoint and attitude assumed by the reader and to the part of the work we are presently reading. (144)

For this reason "the first reading has the advantage over all following readings that it decides in large measure whether one will succeed in a correct apprehension of the work at all" (145). The 'correctness' referred to has above all to do with what I have called the particular kind of worldmaking motivated by a literary work of art, a process that should be largely controlled by the dynamic structure of the particular text we read:

> It is important for the constitution of a faithful aesthetic concretization of the work that the order of succession of its parts be preserved. Any alteration of this order, for example by a transposition of its parts, affects the characteristic traits of its composition, often produces completely different dynamic effects, and alters the appearance of specific phenomena of temporal perspective both within the framework of the events in the portrayed world and in the sequence of the parts in the work as a whole. (*The Cognition of the Literary Work of Art* 164)

I would even go as far as saying that as soon as we do not stick to the sequence determined by the formatting of the text we read, we begin to create a different kind of temporal perspective that belongs to a different work, and thus change the particular kind of worldmaking.

Quite different from Ingarden's detailed analysis of the worldmaking to be found in literary works of art and in the process of reading such works, Nelson Goodman in his brief study *Ways of Worldmaking* (1978) operates on a much wider scale and attempts to find answers to more general questions such as "In what sense are there many worlds? What distinguishes genuine from spurious worlds? What are worlds made of? How are they made? What role do symbols play in the making? And how is worldmaking related to knowing?" (Goodman 1). The constructionist assumption that we "can have words without a world but no world without words or symbols" together with the view that "the search for a universal or necessary beginning is best left to theology" leads Goodman to his first and most basic tenet: "Worldmaking as we know it always starts from worlds already at hand; the making is remaking" (6–7). And though he admits that he is "concerned more with certain relationships among worlds than with how or whether particular worlds are made from others" (7–8), he elaborates on the basic process by which the "remaking" of worlds is achieved: a) composition and decomposition, b) weighting, c) ordering, d) deletion and supplementation, and e) deformation. If these are quite generally the "ways that worlds are made," we can assume that they also apply to literary worldmaking, and it will be interesting to see whether Goodman sees any distinctive features of this particular kind and what they can possibly be.

As he devotes a whole chapter to "Style and Structure," one would hope to find some information on such distinctive features there—but in saying "a feature of style may be a feature of what is said, of what is exemplified, or of what is expressed" (32), and in defining style as something that consists of "those features of the symbolic functioning of the work that are characteristic of author, period, place, or school" (35), he stays on such a high level of abstraction that the contribution of style to literary worldmaking remains very vague indeed. The most valuable comment—especially regarding modernist and postmodern literature and art—comes at the very ending of this chapter:

> The less accessible a style is to our approach and the more adjustment we are forced to make, the more insight we gain and the more our powers of discovery are developed. The discernment of style is an integral aspect of the understanding or works of art and the world they present. (40)

As 'worlds' (or what more traditionally has been called 'world views' or 'world pictures') according to Goodman are made from already existing other 'worlds,' quotations play an important role in worldmaking. Because much work had already been done on verbal quotation, he became, however, interested above all in nonverbal quotation. Nevertheless, he first seeks to define verbal quotation and comes to the following conclusion: Necessary conditions for such quotation, direct or indirect, are:

> a) containment of what is quoted or of some other replica or paraphrase of it, and
> b) reference to—by naming or predication— what is quoted. [...]
> c) replacement of the denoted and contained expression by any other of the language results in an expression that denotes the replacing expression. (46)

Direct or indirect quotations are, however, no specific feature of worldmaking in the domains of literature or art. They seem to play an even more important role in some kinds of scientific prose than in other kinds of discourse because they are held to give weight to an argument, to signal that one is well aware of work that has already been done and of how the new findings presented are linked to what counts as 'state of the art.'

Though it is wonderful to learn that "the arts must be taken no less seriously than the sciences as modes of discovery, creation, and enlargement of knowledge in the broad sense of advancement of understanding" (102), Goodman does not convincingly demonstrate why this should be so. A statement like "Fiction operates in actual worlds in much the same way as nonfiction" (104), which is made in this context, may in some areas be justified—but at least when our health is examined by a doctor (to give but one example) we very much hope that this will not be so, and one can test any time whether it makes a difference (outside a dream) to board an airplane or a 'flying carpet' when attempting to get to a distant place with both body and mind. What is neglected in Goodman's description of worldmaking is the overall fictional status, the reduced ontological and epistemological claim to validity of whatever is presented in literature, or—in the words of Derrida—the fact that "there is no literature without a *suspended* relation to meaning and reference" (Derrida 48), that literature is

> this institution of fiction which gives *in principle* the power to say everything, to break free of the rules, to displace them, and thereby to institute, to invent and even to suspect the traditional difference between nature and institution, nature and conventional law, nature and history. (37)

The attempt to demonstrate that the worldmaking in literature and art is also valuable in the sense that it enhances knowledge and understanding must not make us forget that the extraordinary licence it is granted (at least in Western culture) has a price: it depends on the validational modesty with which everything in it is presented, the *"suspended"* relation to meaning and reference" in comparison with scientific discourse and other nonfictional discourses.

Goodman minimises the difference between the various "ways of worldmaking" by stressing the fictional elements in the latter kinds of discourses and by replacing the question of 'truth' by the one of 'fit':

> Briefly, then, truth of statements and rightness of descriptions, representations, exemplifications, expressions—of design, drawing, diction, rhythm—is primarily a matter of fit: fit to what is referred to in one way or another, or to other renderings, or to modes and manners of organization. (138)

This reminds one of Foucault's distinction between having found the truth and being 'in the truth': in order to become acknowledged by the cultural powers that be, one has to make sure to stay 'within the truth,' to take care that what one presents will fit into the field of received 'truths.' Yet for some centuries now, a "strange institution called literature" (Derrida) has been fostered in Western culture whose worldmaking does not have to fit or is even expected *not* to fit—as a cultural safety valve, a strengthening of our culture's ability to change and thereby to enhance its chance of survival.

An unusual approach to literary worldmaking was included in *Scripts, Plans, Goals and Understanding: An Inquiry into Human Knowledge Structures* (1977) by Roger C. Schank and Robert P. Abelson. Located at the "intersection of psychology and artificial intelligence," the rather new 'cognitive science' came to operate on the basis of the assumption that "the best way to approach the problem of building an intelligent machine is to emulate the human conceptual mechanisms that deal with language" (Schank and Abelson 1), and the ensuing analysis of these mechanisms led to very valuable insights into textual worldmaking, including the one motivated and guided by literary texts.

The insight that the vast amount of knowledge about the world readers possess must be structured was, of course, not new, but Schank and Abelson became convinced that "there is no single set of rules and relations for all potential knowledge bases at will" and they therefore believe that "the form of knowledge representation should not be separated too far from its content" (3). Admitting that David E. Rumelhart was right in stressing that schemas are essential in the process of understanding (Rumelhart, passim), they point out, however, that it "does not take one very far to say that schemas are important: one must know the content of the schemas," and "a knowledge structure theory must make a commitment to particular content schemas" (10).

In order to describe any particular "content schema" that is applied in the process of understanding, Schank and Abelson use the categories of the 'Conceptual Dependence Theory' (CDT) presented by Schank in 1972, categories developed because for the programming of understanding, "[a]ny information in a sentence that is implicit must be made explicit in the representation of the meaning of that sentence" (11). Because it is the objective of this article to point out the value of some quite different 'older' theories of worldmaking for an understanding of literary worldmaking, the attempt will not be made, however, to render the artificial kind of notation developed for CDT and used throughout *Scripts, Plans, Goals and Understanding* in order to arrive at a description formalised enough to be turned into a computer programme. This is not to say that the major categories of CDT are not helpful when one aims at an abstract sorting of the activities found in worldmaking, and it should at least become evident what they are like: ATRANS (transfer of an abstract relationship), PTRANS (transfer of the physical location), PROPEL (application of a physical force to an object), MOVE (movement of a body part of an animal by that animal), GRASP (the grasping of an object), INGEST (the taking in of an object), EXPEL (the expulsion of an object), MTRANS (the transfer of mental information), MBUILD (the construction of new information), SPEAK (actions of producing sounds), and ATTEND (attending or focusing a sense organ towards a stimulus) (see 13–14).

A further precondition of Schank and Abelson's theory of human understanding besides CDT is their conviction of the essential importance of human memory organisation, especially of what they term 'episodic memory,' a form of memory "organized around propositions linked together by their occurrence in the same event or time span" (18). This is held to be so because "some episodes are reminiscent of others. As an economy measure in the storage of episodes, when enough of them are alike they are remembered in terms of a standardized generalized episode we will call a script" (19).

Such scripts make it possible that someone who "decides to tell a story that references a script, [...] recognizes that he need not [...] mention every detail of his story" (38), because due to the largely collective nature of scripts, readers will have no problem filling in what seems to be lacking. The central importance of scripts for both worldmaking in general and literary worldmaking in particular lies in their function of mediating between the potential infinity of details and the necessity to structure knowledge in everyday life as well as in storytelling:

> A script is a structure that describes appropriate sequences of events in a particular context. A script is made up of slots and requirements about what can fill those slots. The structure is an interconnected whole, and what is in one slot affects what can be in another. [...] Thus, a script is a predetermined, stereotyped sequence of actions that defines a well-known situation. (41)

Accordingly, scripts not only imply a number of roles but are also written from the point of view of one particular role because this is the way in which they are remembered.

When a script is called up by a concept (for instance, a 'restaurant script' by a mentioning of 'restaurant'—to use Schank and Abelson's favourite example), readers will assume that it proceeds normally as long as no other information is given. As, however, storytellers do not want to bore their listeners or readers with what they are well-acquainted with, "most real stories that deal with scripts relate events that are unusual with respect to standard script. The problem in script application then, besides deciding how much of a script to infer, is to know how to tie together events that are not directly in the script" (45). And the authors mention two kinds of events interrupting scripts: interferences (obstacles or errors) and distractions. Interruptions are also bound to occur when more than one script will be active at once and there is competition regarding incoming items of information.

Schank and Abelson draw attention to the fact that besides the situational scripts to which 'restaurant' belongs there are also 'personal scripts' and 'instrumental scripts.' A personal script exists only in the mind of an actor and consists of a "sequence of possible actions that lead to a desired goal" (62). Though being personal, such scripts can well be common to many individuals, and the scripts of flatterers, jealous spouses, good Samaritans, pickpockets, or spies that are given as examples show that they make up what we tend to call 'knowing the world.' Instrumental scripts, however, are structurally identical with situational scripts, yet "the order of events is very rigid, and every one of the events in the script must be done." In addition, "instrumental scripts take multiple actors, while instrumental scripts have only one participant" (65), and any number of examples can be found, for instance, in a cook book or repair manual.

Helpful as scripts are, people in real life situations and readers of stories will also have to cope with situations they have never encountered before, and they can do so by using 'plans':

> Plans describe the set of choices that a person has when he sets out to accomplish a goal. In listening to discourse, people use plans to make sense of seemingly disconnected sentences. By finding a plan, an understander can make guesses about the intentions of an action in an unfolding story and use these guesses to make sense of the story. (70)

In addition to scripts, there are then sets of possible actions (called 'planboxes' by the authors) that help us to understand and make predictions; and just as "understanding is predictive in its nature" (76), so is worldmaking: "sometimes all plan-based, sometimes all script-based, and sometimes a mix" (78). There are also routine sequences of scripts and plans that the authors call 'Named Plans,' well-known sequences that considerably enhance our worldmaking capability both in terms of creating and of understanding literary worlds. Plans are chosen or developed to accomplish goals, and

> in stories with a lot of contextual information about the main character, and in well developed belief systems about the world, there are many expectations about likely events. These expectations are based on detailed knowledge of the genesis and nature of particular goals. Since such expectations are crucial to understanding, we must know what kinds of goals there are and how they interact with each other in order to formulate expectations. (102)

Goals can be of varying specificity and can form hierarchies of many levels, and Schank and Abelson even attempt a modest taxonomy of goals that has seven forms of 'standard goals' (satisfaction goals; enjoyment goals; achievement goals; preservation goals; crisis goals; instrumental goals; delta goals), "a number of precedence rules governing priorities among goal forms when more than one form is simultaneously activated" (117), and "expectancy rules" based on "a set of beliefs about what an individual is likely to want in a given circumstance" (119). According to the very beginning of Jane Austen's *Pride and Prejudice*, for instance, "[i]t is a truth universally acknowledged that a single man in possession of a good fortune must be in search of a wife" (1).

Then Schank and Abelson, by asking questions like "Where do goals come from? That is, when do we expect certain goals?", are led to look for 'themes,' because themes, we are informed, "contain the background information upon which we base our predictions that an individual will have a certain goal" (132). They divide the domain of themes into three categories: role, interpersonal, and life themes, and then describe what makes up the particular 'bundles of knowledge' of each of these groups of themes. Not unexpectedly, it shows that the interpersonal themes deserve most attention because all social relationships are themes, and mentioned are, for instance, 'Lovers,' 'Husband/Wife,' 'Father/Son,' or 'Boss/Employee.'

What must not be forgotten for all the detailed analyses in *Scripts, Plans, Goals and Understanding* are, however, the reservations finally made by the authors about their system. They stress that it is "oriented towards handling actions by goal-oriented humans. Problems in representing inner affective life, or description of scenes as well as other non-human events, are issues still to be dealt with as well. We are not ready to handle novels, in other words (167–8). Nevertheless, the insights into both everyday and textual worldmaking they gained are considerable—they are in some way more valuable because more specific than many of the more recent categories presented by theorists working in the contact zone between mind science and cognitive psychology. Unfortunately, the formal notation system developed to create a base for the computer programming of 'artificial intelligence' will have deterred and will deter many critics. It must therefore be stressed that there are too many valuable ideas in this study to do without it when investigating worldmaking. It has to be said, though, that, as in the case of Goodman's *Ways of Worldmaking*, the difference between the worldmaking in fictional and referential discourses almost totally disappears and thereby one of the significant features of literary worldmaking does not receive due attention.

For readers who have come this far and may have noticed that it makes sense to include older works in the present discussion I would like to draw attention to a further study that will prove pertinent. What I mean is Hans Vaihinger's *Philosophie des Als Ob: System der theoretischen, praktischen und religiösen Fiktionen der Menschheit* from 1911 that first appeared in English translation in 1924 and again in 1968 under the title *The Philosophy of As If.* The particular reason why this monumental study of 804 pages should come in here is that I read with considerable amazement on the first page of the introduction to Ruth Ronen's more recent *Possible Worlds in Literary*

Theory that "[u]ntil the mid seventies fictionality was an object of separate disciplinary pursuits: it was interpreted as a property of texts by literary theorists and either excluded as logical abnormality or entirely ignored by philosophers" (1). Who is actually guilty of some ignoring becomes obvious when Vaihinger is never even mentioned anywhere in the whole book. And it should be added that it were instances like this one that motivated me to bring Ingarden, Goodman, and Schank and Abelson into the present discussion and to demonstrate thereby that, in contrast to the sciences, research in the humanities is based on an epistemology of complementation rather than on one of substitution. The more recent sequence of trendy 'turns' may have pushed this basic assumption somewhat into the background, and the fact that some traditional publishers in the field of the humanities are being managed now 'American style,' and scholarly books are remaindered after a few years time, has also contributed to cultural amnesia and the ensuing illusion that the wheel has not yet been invented. A sober reflection will, however, reveal that in the humanities there is no straight line of progression but rather a continuous encircling of problem zones by ever new approaches that only very rarely invalidate older ones but rather add further insights. For that reason, the history of literary theory and criticism remains an integral part of systematic research in the field.

References

Austen, Jane. *Pride and Prejudice*. 1813. London: Dent, 1963.
Derrida, Jacques. "'This Strange Institution Called Literature': An Interview with Jacques Derrida." *Jacques Derrida: Acts of Literature*. Ed. Derek Attridge. New York: Routledge, 1992. 33–75.
Goodman, Nelson. *Ways of Worldmaking*. Indianapolis: Hackett, 1978.
Ingarden, Roman. *The Literary Work of Art: An Investigation on the Borderlines of Ontology, Logic, and Theory of Literature*. Trans. George G. Grabowicz. Evanston: Northwestern UP, 1973. Trans. of *Das literarische Kunstwerk: Eine Untersuchung aus dem Grenzgebiet von Ontologie, Logik und Literaturwissenschaft*. Halle: Max Niemeyer, 1931.
—. *The Cognition of the Literary Work of Art*. Trans. Ruth Ann Crowley and Kenneth R Olson. Evanston: Northwestern UP, 1973. Trans. of *Vom Erkennen des literarischen Kunstwerks*. Tübingen: Max Niemeyer, 1968. Trans. of *O poznawaniu dzieła literackiego*. Lvóv: Ossolineum, 1937.
Ronen, Ruth. *Possible Worlds in Literary Theory*. Cambridge: Cambridge UP, 1994.
Rumelhart, David E. "Understanding and Summarizing Brief Stories." *Basic Processes in Reading: Perception and Comprehension*. Eds. Davide LaBerge, and S. Jay Samuels. Hillsdale: Lawrence Erlbaum Associates, 1976. 265–304.
Schank, Roger C. "Conceptual Dependency: A Theory of Natural Language Understanding." *Cognitive Psychology* 3.4 (1972): 552–631.

Schank, Roger C., and Robert P. Abelson. *Scripts, Plans, Goals and Understanding*. Hillsdale: Lawrence Erlbaum Associates, 1977.

Vaihinger, Hans. *The Philosophy of 'As If': A System of the Theoretical, Practical and Religious Fictions of Mankind*. Trans. C.K. Ogden. London: Kegan Paul; New York: Barnes and Noble, 1968. Trans. of *Die Philosophie des Als Ob: System der theoretischen, praktischen und religiösen Fiktionen der Menschheit auf Grund eines idealistischen Positivismus*. 1911. Leipzig: Felix Meiner, 1924.

Wellek, René, and Austin Warren. *Theory of Literature*. New York: Harcourt, Brace & World, 1948.

Worldmaking as Fate

BEN DAWSON

1. The Genesis of Idealism

With the Flood in the time of Noah, nature "abandoned the equipoise of her elements, [...] and poured savage devastation of everything." The state of nature was shattered. And as the human race set about rebuilding and reintegrating the "distracted world" (*zerrissene Welt*), it strove to return "from barbarism [...] to the unity which had been broken." In Genesis, dim traces of this early history are preserved. Humanity, utterly torn apart, sought "to hold out against the outbursts of a nature," formerly friendly and tranquil, "now hostile." For this, "nature had to be mastered" (all Hegel, "Spirit" 182). So began Hegel's philosophical project of reconciliation in "The Spirit of Christianity and Its Fate" (1798–99), not with Creation but the Flood—loss or alienation of humanity's natural state.

This essay will argue that Hegel's early work remains of use in reading and responding to those pluralist and constructivist epistemologies, which, in their rejections of naïve realism, set the discursively or thought-produced worlds of experience and knowledge against 'nature' or 'reality,' barring access to this other. Such theories follow Kant's exemplary distinction between knowledge and things in themselves. As will become clear, it is precisely the emergence of this foundational distinction that Hegel narrates in his strange biblical exegesis. In truth, these constructivist theories themselves sustain a correspondence model of knowledge (which are believed to have transcended, avoided, or dissolved) by maintaining the distinction between experience or knowledge on the one hand, and an unknowable 'reality' on the other. For better or for worse, they hold this distinction open through the block, which they observe, on all access to a world in itself. Spectrally, this keeps the possibility of pure immediacy open where Hegelian thought, acknowledging the culturally shared and historically bound preconditions of those very categories and concepts through which the world is constituted in experience, strips these preconditions of their incomprehensibility and names them 'actual.' In Hegel's eyes, this historical actuality is the rational itself—which is nevertheless far from saying that everything is just as it should be.

In this light, Nelson Goodman's powerful argument for "multiple actual worlds" (2), enhanced by his rich descriptions of various "ways of worldmaking," articulates the tattered and distracted condition of the world. Kant's transcendental epistemology acts in some essential respects as guarantor of this pluralistic and constructivist discourse, and as such, Hegel's phenomenological critique of Kantianism remains of use in understanding it—understanding it, in the sense of locating 'worldmaking' in, and reading it to perceive, the world in which it is true. If Goodman's pluralism exemplifies a certain philosophical repression of the whole, it nonetheless unconsciously sustains hope of its restoration. Hegel's text helps render explicit the possibility and course a recovery of vital unity would have to follow. The worlds and ways of worldmaking described by Goodman have a singular, and historically specific, common actual world—more basic than the poles of subjectivity and objectivity—as their precondition.

Thus, concisely put, the contention of this essay is (1) that to speak of 'ways of worldmaking' is inevitably to repeat the transcendental maxim that we know appearances only, not things in themselves, (2) that the world in which this is true is itself an appearance and as such historically specific (one in which instrumental rationality appears to have triumphed), (3) that pluralistic constructivism no less than transcendental idealism is, within this world, the philosophical cipher and the symptom of societal processes of alienation, instrumentalisation, and domination, and (4) that in sensing what ought to have been given but is not, the working of fate commences; reconciliation and the return to a different (socially mediated) unity, a recovery of ethical life, is promised. This complex body of claims can be found in embryonic form in Hegel's early genealogical exegesis, "The Spirit of Christianity and Its Fate." The fourth element of the argument (hope, or the possibility of reconciliation) will become clear in relation to Hegel's conception of fate.

Hegel's philosophy starts neither with YHWH nor Adam but with Noah and Abraham. In a sense, it thereby avoids a certain naïvety at the outset since the Given, that which was "[i]n the Beginning," begins already in the process of its loss. What's more, far from denying or obfuscating the importance of narrative, Hegel's project decidedly highlights it—but not in the sense of blithely affirming the discursivity and constructedness of 'worlds.' In this strange early mixture of exegesis, genealogy, and critique, Hegel narrates the emergence of the God of Genesis (of the noumenal) as a historical and cultural phenomenon. 'God,' here, is symptomatic of, in its most elementary form, the alienation from and subsequent domination of nature by an instrumentalised and instrumentalising intellect. Noah divided "the whole" into idea and reality, giving "being" to and deifying his own "thought-produced ideal" and then setting "everything else over against it, so that in this opposition everything was reduced to a thought, i.e., to something mastered" (Hegel, "Spirit" 184; modified translation). Hegel reads this ideal Being as essentially an attempt to master a nature deemed indifferent, alien, and even hostile to humanity, a vicarious mastery which at once presupposes, responds to, and reproduces—indeed drastically enhances—humanity's alienation from (its) nature.

With a central ambiguity, implied from the start, 'nature' here signifies both the natural world and human nature. Following the Flood, distraction or division characterises not simply humanity's relation to external nature but also its relation to its own.[1] Relatedly, in the opening pages of Hegel's text, the distraction and division of the whole is twofold—first, in the emergence of nature as force, felt not merely as indifference but devastating hostility, and again (and apparently more fundamentally) in Noah's response. Just as today, technology is turned to for protection against ecology, "[a]gainst the hostile power Noah saved himself by subjecting both it and himself to something more powerful" (Hegel, "Spirit" 184). By contrast, after a flood in their time, the "beautiful" Greek pair, Deucalion and Pyrrha, "invited men once again to friendship with the world, to nature, ... [and] made a peace of *love*" (Hegel, "Spirit" 185).

To this beauty and love, Hegel contrasts Noah's "peace of *necessity*" which, in place of true reconciliation, rather "perpetuated the hostility" (ibid.). Although 'need' has an ambiguous status throughout the text, in the description of Noah's *contractual* resolution here, there flickers the antilegalism that will run through Hegel's entire exegesis. Beneath it, and at moments explicitly, he first begins to formulate his critique of modern philosophy and, more specifically, Kantian idealism.

The concept of law, here, is taken and criticised in a very wide sense. By the time of Moses, legalism characterises the total inner and outer life of this society, which is therefore understood as thoroughly positive, which is to say, non-living. It is only with the appearance of Jesus, in Hegel's text, that a differentiation between "the various kinds of Jewish laws" emerges via his "reaction to them" (Hegel, "Spirit" 206). But at each moment of this work, Hegel attempts to remain within or follow the understanding he perceives and ascribes to his object: for "the Jewish peo-

---

1 Hegel's early thought can easily be assigned neither to the Kantian nor the Herderian pole of philosophical anthropology. Here, he employs the language of the human race and species (*Menschengeschlecht*) alongside that of spirit and people (*Volk*).

ple" and therefore for the text here, "religious, moral, and civil laws were all equally positive" (ibid.). Clearly, practical rather than theoretical reason is primary for Hegel in this work. Yet, to this undifferentiated positivity of religious, moral, and civil law may also be added the (Kantian) 'laws' of the understanding—*a priori* forms 'commanding,' 'dictating,' and 'subjugating' the appearances of nature. In place of "eternal truths" (characterising Greek life and thought), "the Jews" have "laws": "what we find as truth among the Jews did not appear to them under the form of truths and matters of faith" (Hegel, "Spirit" 196). Hegel distinguishes the vitality and beauty of truths from the positivity of commands: "Truth is something free which we neither master nor are mastered by; hence the existence of God appears to the Jews not as a truth but as a command [*Befehl*]. On God the Jews are dependent throughout, and that on which a man depends cannot have the form of truth" (Hegel, "Spirit" 196).

As transcendental formalism and abstract morality, Kantianism may be glimpsed as early as Noah's gesture of setting a "thought-produced ideal," God or the Law, over and against nature (inclinations and desires).[2] As Bernstein explains: "Hegel interprets biblical Judaism as the coming-to-be of transcendental idealism as a form of life, or, what is the same, he interprets Judaism as the genealogical origin of Western reason in its fundamental Platonic and Kantian dispensation" (Bernstein, "Love and Law" 397). Bernstein's summary aptly points to the ambiguous identity of allegorical critique and genealogical narrative that is crucial to the "Spirit" essay's insight and originality.[3] Hegel's narration of the process through which humanity alienated itself, drawing a curtain between itself and the world, allegorically reconstructs the transcendental epistemology in which humanity's intimate and immediate relationship with nature is broken. Yet, at important moments in the essay, the affinity between 'Moses' and 'Kant' and the relationship more generally between the vehicles and tenors of the allegory become unstable. There are moments—not least when Kant emerges, so to speak, *in person* from behind his biblical alter-egos—when the elective affinity between the biblical story and Kantian moral philosophy seems itself the means of telling a more universal history of Western culture. While there are other moments at which the allegorical

---

2 It is important to Hegel's purpose that Kantianism is rather caricaturised here, and certainly stripped of Kant's own consistent interests in the "embodiment of reason" (for an account of which, see Shell, *The Embodiment of Reason: Kant on Spirit, Generation and Community*). Hegel, as it were, fulfils this latter strain in Kant's thought through critiquing the former, i.e., the high moralist and transcendentalist commanding disinterestedness and reverence.

3 While Hegel's presentation of transcendentalism/intellectualism may be as applicable to Plato as it is to Kant, Greek life and culture, of a more Homeric sort, are consistently contrasted to Judaic/Kantian 'legalism.'

and genealogical levels appear as vehicles for deep and focused psychoanalyses of human guilt and the vital need for security. When Noah subjugates nature and himself to his 'thought-product' in order to protect himself from its apparent hostility, Hegel represents Idealism as Fear.

Early on, Hegel gives an indication of his exegetical method which suggests something of his novel (and novelistic) approach. Having rehearsed part of the story of Jacob, he adds: "Here, as in what has preceded, we must grasp this adventure of Israelite liberation not with our intellect, but rather as it was present in the phantasy and recollecting life of the Jews, in accordance with which their spirit acted" (Hegel, *Werke* 281; my translation). This reads as an early and condensed version of what will come to be Hegel's phenomenological approach. The 'mechanical' and subsumptive understanding is suspended or held in check to allow space for the imaginative intuition of the internal dynamics of a certain form of subjectivity. It is by finding, in biblical Judaism, a people and 'spirit' that appear to correspond to Kantian idealism and morality that Hegel is first able to grasp and read philosophy as a structure of feeling or experience.

The manner and form in which the critique of Kant is first constructed here, namely via this narration and rehearsal of the biblical story, gradually becomes essential to the content of Hegel's immanent and historicist sublation of transcendental idealism. In these early exegetical and genealogical writings, Hegel's approach to, and reproach of, transcendentalism emerges as an elaboration of Kant's method and morality, not as a philosophical system, but as a form of life. This strategy essentially involves depriving philosophy of a certain metaphysics by embedding and entangling reason in history. More specifically, it involved, here, staging epistemologies as concrete and historical forms of relation between subjects and their worlds. It is this strategy that would subsequently become essential to the dialectical progression of phenomenological experience towards the standpoint of philosophical science.

Following Foucault, this movement from 'Kantian' to 'Hegelian' idealism can be seen to have characterised one course followed by philosophy following the fracture of "the Classical mathesis" (the rationality and formal unity ordering things and representations throughout the Age of Reason). For those striving to restore such universality, while one philosophical path began with Fichte's undertaking "to deduce genetically the totality of the transcendental domain from the pure, universal, and empty laws of thought" (Foucault 269), another appeared with Hegelian phenomenology. Within the latter, Foucault explains, "the totality of the empirical domain was taken back into the interior of consciousness revealing itself to itself as spirit, in other words, as an empirical and transcendental field simultaneously" (ibid.).

The *Geist* (of Judaism and, then, of Christianity), whose fate is elaborated in Hegel's early text, does not squarely coincide with the spirit which, characterised here by Foucault, forms the (social) substance of Hegel's *Phenomenology*. But familiar aspects of the latter do begin here. In particular, it is of the utmost importance for an understanding of Hegel to recognise the beginnings of his unique form of anti-abstractionist idealism in this early, and in many respects wholly traditional, anti-legalism/anti-Semitism. Hegel's logic in the "Spirit" essay continues that "campaign of critique, or 'antirrhetics,' against the law, doubled by a campaign of putting the Jews into the position of a site of permanent disposal of matters legal" which constitutes, quite simply, the "history of Christianity"[4] (Schütz 129) since Paul's Epistles. Hegel, then, fares no better than Nietzsche in this; at a certain level, both fail to withdraw from "Christian-post-Christian antinomianism" (ibid.). Yet Hegel's critique of the positivity of commands and laws (in a very wide sense) pushes him to look beyond them to the concrete human sources of such alienating abstraction. Representing transcendental ideas and thought-products as definitive of historical situations, actions, and human responses, Hegel reconstructs the foundational act of the Jewish people establishing their opposition to nature, to each other, and 'the whole.' But the true novelty of his thought begins in the conception of 'fate,' which, as will become clear, this act, this diremption of the whole, is viewed as opening. Foucault observed:

> It is probably impossible to give empirical contents transcendental value, or to displace them in the direction of a constituent subjectivity, without giving rise, at least silently to an anthropology—that is, to a mode of thought in which the rightful limitations of acquired knowledge (and consequently all empirical knowledge) are at the same time the concrete forms of existence, precisely as they are given in that same empirical knowledge. (Foucault 270)

As a consequence, he explained, "every dialectical undertaking" threatens to "topple over willy-nilly into an anthropology" (ibid.). A similar danger threatens in Hegel's earliest work, but from, as it were, the opposite direction. For here, "empirical contents" are not so much displaced in the direction of a constituent subjectivity; it is more accurate to see transcendental subjectivity (the paradigm for conceptions of the mind as opposed to everything outside it) situated empirically, anthropologically:

---

4   Schütz is writing of Nietzsche, but on this point the two are very close.

> The whole world Abraham regarded as simply his opposite [...]. Mastery was the only possible relationship in which Abraham could stand to the infinite world opposed to him; but he was unable himself to make this mastery actual, and it therefore remained ceded to his Ideal. (Hegel, "Spirit" 189)

The form of proto-philosophical writing, which Hegel was to subtitle the "Science of the Experience of Consciousness," is first caught sight of as he expounds and critiques Kant's transcendental philosophy through a 'historical' narrative—the story of Noah, Abraham, Moses, and Christ. In the opening pages, Hegel repeatedly alludes to the early books of the Hebrew Bible as 'history.' Thus, as Noah is busy separating the ideal from the real, Hegel's text implicitly works in the opposite direction, presenting the origin of transcendental alienation from the world as a historical process, a fate. Crucially, by narrating idealism as a cultural condition, the diremption of the whole into idea and reality already implicitly contains their reintegration. When the division of empirical/historical reality from thought (categories, concepts, and ideas) is represented as itself historical, the division has already ceased to be absolute. Thus, the speculated reconciliation here—hope itself—is contained in the complex form of Hegel's text.

The famous Hegelian entanglement of reason and history, which Foucault's excavations unearthed as itself a transition in the historical *a priori* conditions of knowledge and experience, emerged in its first form in and as a particular mixing of genres. Spirit, and the dialectic as a medium of thought, are evident only in embryonic form in the young Hegel's approach to Kant through Judaism, but the *Phenomenology*, as it were, begins here, in this tangle of mythology, allegory, genealogy, exegesis, and critique. It is through these forms or styles of philosophical writing, combined with a form of romantic depth psychology, that Hegel begins to transform the transcendental structure of Kant's idealism (which he presents as both more legalistic and more subjectivist than in fact it was) into something immanent, 'objective' or 'communal,' and historical. Most importantly, in "The Spirit of Christianity and Its Fate," it is by narrating or narrativising it that Hegel brings the logical trajectory of Kant's epistemology and moral philosophy phenomenologically to life. As Hyppolite related, immersing oneself in these pages, one has the feeling of assisting at the birth of the dialectic (see Hyppolite 78n20). Readers become imaginative midwives here because the dialectic emerges as a (literary) form of thinking that requires something other than logical understanding. In this way, the work anticipates the programme of phenomenological experience, "Spirit"'s immanent self-criticism of knowledge, and natural consciousness's self-perficient 'way of despair.' Ironically, perhaps paradoxically but not self-defeatingly, it is through the allegorical and genealogical narration of 'Kantianism' that the seemingly ineluctable blindness, if not vacuity, of the world without our conceptual and discursive ways of viewing it is first overcome.[5] It is so because, through such narration, Hegel is able to characterise the oppositions established by modern epistemologies such as Goodman's not as law but as fate.

2. Law and Fate

Noah's 'history' is in truth a prehistory—perhaps because, at least apparently, it begins with nature's active hostility rather than human self-alienation (although that is a somewhat paradoxical distinction). With Abraham, "the true progenitor of the Jews," the history of this people begins. The "first act" is Abraham's, "a disseverance which snaps the bonds of communal life and love." Abraham tore himself free from his family "in order to be a wholly self-subsistent, independent man, to be an overlord himself" (Hegel, "Spirit" 185). He did this, "without having been injured or disowned," solely out of a desire for independence. He acts, and in these circumstances such a deed must always appear as a disseverance of the bonds of community and of natural, given relationships.[6] The will to freedom takes a perverse form, however, as Abraham chooses to tear himself free explicitly by opposing himself to everything: "The whole world Abraham regarded as simply his opposite" (ibid.).

Anticipating Nietzsche, Hegel locates a "slavelike demeanor" in a moral life subordinated to a "melancholy, unfelt unity" ("Spirit" 194), and he laments the transformation of nature into a "mere sign" (of obedience or disobedience to God): "through God alone [...] Abraham came into a mediate relation with the world, the only kind of link with the world possible for him" (187). If original immediacy was broken by nature, it might have been retrieved through love. But "Abraham wanted *not* to love, wanted to be free by not loving" (185).

Hegel imagines Kantian morality as likewise premised on a form of autonomy that is, in truth, "an obedience without joy, without pleasure or love" (206); such morality he presents as self-incurred inhumanity and servitude. When he writes of Jesus's opposition to Judaic law, Hegel's stress falls on the primacy of need and the power to choose to satisfy a

---

5   Blindness and vacuity will be discussed in the third and final section of this essay.
6   The *Phenomenology*, however, reveals that, at any time, the immediate objective context of relationships (habits and customs, etc.) only *seems* given and not made. It is one of the purposes of that work to demonstrate, systematically, that both the communal world and self-consciousness are a historical achievement. For the systematic reading of this text, see Harris, *Hegel's Ladder*.

need, which, in Kant's terms, sets pathological interests and the agency of *Willkür* over the moral law and the autonomous *Wille*. Jesus profanes Mosaic Law by, in his various actions, foregoing "not even the satisfaction of a whim [*eine Willkür*], of a very ordinary need" (208). However, from the caprice with which Jesus, for instance, "desecrates the Sabbath," Hegel interprets not a readiness to profane Jewish sanctities in moments of need (Jesus's stated reason), but rather a much more general renunciation and withdrawal "from the whole life of his people" (207).

In *Religion Within the Boundaries of Mere Reason* (1793), the text to which Hegel's "Spirit" essay most immediately responds, Kant had himself complicated the relations between freedom, law, and the power of choice. He had done so by making the latter (*Willkür*) responsible for deciding the "subjective first ground" of the human species' moral character. It was only the "first act" of this free power of choice, Kant considered, which could have made evil radical and radically imputable: "Nothing is [...] morally (i.e. imputably) evil but that which is our own deed" (Kant, *Religion* 6:31). The radical propensity to evil is therefore a "deed," an act or *factum*; it is the foundational choice not (and therefore never) to adopt the law as the supreme maxim of the will. In this, Kant can be understood to have addressed the criticism (notably Reinhold's) that if the moral law is the law of freedom, evil cannot strictly be considered free or morally imputable. How could evil actions be free if freedom, practical reason, and morality are fundamentally reciprocal (as they appear to be in the *Groundwork* and in the second *Critique*)?[7] In *Religion*, Kant acknowledges that evil actions are not actions in which the will has, by making the moral law the supreme determination of its maxim, transcended the empirical world of causal necessity and acted on the basis of its reason alone. In this light, evil appears to belong to the sphere of 'nature,' not 'morality,' but here Kant added a supplementary moment in which, through an act albeit inscrutable to our understanding, the evil human being freely chose an innate incapacity to accept the moral law as the sole determination of maxims. That is, the "*natural* propensity to evil" of the human species is always already "*morally* evil":

> [The] natural propensity to evil [...] is morally evil, since it must ultimately be sought in a free power of choice, and hence is imputable. This evil is *radical*, since it corrupts the ground of all maxims; as a natural propensity, it is also not to be

---

7   In his *Critique of Practical Reason*, Kant explains that "freedom and unconditional practical law reciprocally refer to each other" (Kant, *Critique* 5:29): "[O]ne would never have considered the daring deed of introducing freedom into science had not the moral law, and with it practical reason, come in and thrust this concept upon us" (5:30).

> *extirpated* through human forces [...]. Yet it must equally be possible to *overcome* this evil, for it is found in the human being as acting freely. (Kant, *Religion* 6:37)

Evil is therefore imputable on the basis that although a particular transgression cannot be an act of freedom (*qua* moral self-legislation), the act through which the criminal originally and intelligibly *chose* to be unfree, to be a slave to the particular—"impulses, inclinations, pathological love, sensuous experience, or whatever else it is called" (Hegel, "Spirit" 211)—*was* free and is therefore imputable. Whatever my nature is, I have chosen it. In a sense, the "intelligible deed" is Kant's *amor fati* (whatever I do, no matter how coerced or incapable of doing otherwise I may appear, it will have been willed by me), albeit without any of the euphoria of Nietzsche's affirmationism.

If in *Religion* he did not exactly invent a faculty in *Willkür*—the free power of choice was an important counterpart to the free will as early as the first *Critique*—, Kant certainly gave it a new and radical function. He asserted that humans have, through an "intelligible deed," freely chosen their incapacity for freedom, which he called "radical innate evil." Original or "innate guilt" is the guilt for having made oneself unfree and therefore, in a certain sense, outside morality insofar as the first choice "renders any imputability entirely uncertain" (Kant, *Religion* 6:38). Convinced, however, of the ineradicable imputability of human actions—that is, committed to the possibility of morality—but appreciating that "the world lieth in evil," Kant posited a "first act" (6:25) in which an incapacity to be free or morally good was freely, yet wholly arbitrarily or whimsically, chosen as the subjective first ground of the will. Hence, beneath the stringency of Kant's practical philosophy, in which freedom and morality rationally and reciprocally refer to one another, an inscrutable arbitrariness appeared. It is upon this that Hegel will capitalise.

Within Kant's moral philosophy, the moral law enables the will to abstract itself from and to transcend the empirical world. At the same time, it functions as the law of freedom, enabling voluntary causality to have effects in that phenomenal realm. As the law of freedom, the moral law connects the transcendentally free will it makes possible to the empirical (Newtonian) world of mechanical causes and effects. As Allison puts it: "As a 'kind of causality' the will must, in some sense, be law-governed"—"a lawless will is an absurdity" (Allison 398). In order for freedom to have any effect (even psychologically), there must be a law that connects it as pure, uncaused cause *to* such an effect. Since this law must be valid for every rational being, it cannot require any empirical experience; it must therefore be without content; it must be the mere form of universal legislation given to consciousness as a "fact of reason" (Kant, *The Critique of*

Practical Reason 5:19ff.). As Pippin elucidates, by "fact of reason," Kant meant "a practical notion, the 'exposition' of which already demonstrated its practical validity, that it was 'in actuality' binding" (Pippin 184). With the introduction or acknowledgement of radical evil, however, the moral law, the simple and empirically empty form of lawfulness itself, can no longer be understood as given to consciousness in this way. Yet the first act of the free power of choice—this capricious faculty responsible for "the foul stain on our species" (Kant, *Religion* 6:38)—*was* fundamentally lawless. It is thus indeed an "absurdity."

The freedom to choose not to make the moral law the supreme incentive determining all maxims cannot be that of the self-legislating/autonomous will, since self-legislation can occur only *through* the moral law, the law of freedom—with what else other than the mere form of universal legislation could the self intelligibly legislate for itself?[8] Through which law, then, can the first choice, the intelligible deed have any effect? With this question, an arbitrariness begins to appear at the root of moral freedom. The kind of freedom at stake in the power to choose our "subjective first ground" or "innate propensity" (Kant, *Religion* 6:42) is not the self-legislating kind reciprocally bound to the moral law. And if it is not self-legislating, then there is a cause (an act or choice) that has effects without any law governing those effects. Neither empirically nor rationally determined, the intelligible deed comes from nowhere. But, moreover, in the absence of any even thinkable law governing it, this freedom's relation to its effects is also arbitrary. It so happens that, as a species, we have chosen hell, but it also just so happens that this choice has any effect.[9]

It is this logic that informs a statement, late in the *Religion* book, which must have been quite painful for Kant:

> Freedom itself, though not containing anything supernatural in its concept, remains just as incomprehensible to us according to its possibility as the supernatural [something, i.e. grace] we might want to assume as surrogate for the independent yet deficient determination of freedom. (Kant, *Religion* 6:191)

---

[8] "Since the matter of a practical law, i.e., the object of a maxim, can never be given except empirically, but a free will—as independent of empirical conditions (i.e., conditions belonging to the world of sense)—must nonetheless be determinable, a free will must, independently of the *matter* of the law, nonetheless find a determining basis in the law. But the law, apart from its matter, contains nothing more than the legislative form. Therefore solely the legislative form, insofar as it is contained in the maxim, can amount to a determining basis of the will" (Kant, *Critique* 5:29).

[9] Because the transcendental choice of our subjective first ground is not empirical, it is not particular. Thus, it is for Kant, apparently quite literally, the imputable choice made by the individual as and for the species.

Thus, Kant followed the implications of radical evil, of humanity's original though not in any sense inherited sin, "*innate* guilt" (Kant, *Religion* 6:38) or "first indebtedness" (6:31), in the direction of a supernatural supplementation: grace.[10]

In "The Spirit of Christianity and Its Fate," Hegel picked up the thread of *Religion Within the Boundaries of Mere Reason*. And he used it further to unravel Kantian morality. Jesus's actions had already, in Hegel's reading, revealed the primacy of whim, and the slightest human need, over command. Where freedom and self-legislation (through the moral law) had begun to separate in Kant's *Religion*, Hegel found in the Sermon on the Mount "a spirit raised above morality [...] directly attacking laws" (Hegel, "Spirit" 212). While Kant had opposed enlightened self-legislation to positive religions involving dogmatic obedience to external authorities (from Siberian Voguls to the Puritans), Hegel writes:

> Between the Shaman of the Tungus, the European prelate who rules over church and state, the Voguls, and the Puritans, on the one hand, and the man who listens to his own command of duty on the other, the difference is not that the former make themselves slaves, while the latter is free, but that the former have the lord outside themselves, while the latter carries his lord in himself, yet at the same time is his own slave. For the particular—impulses, inclinations, pathological love, sensuous experience, or whatever else it is called—the universal is necessarily and always something alien and objective. ("Spirit" 211)

Rather as Marx would see the French Revolution as an incomplete and merely political emancipation, Hegel sees the liberation from dogma Kant achieved as only partial; the opposition between law and inclination, universal and particular, is unresolved.

> There remains a residuum of indestructible positivity which finally shocks us because the content which the universal command of duty acquires, a specific duty, contains the contradiction of being universal and particular at the same time and makes the most stubborn claims for its one-sidedness, i.e., on the strength of containing universality of form. (Ibid.)

True freedom cannot mean obedience to any form of law, and its paradigm cannot be Abraham's total "disseverance" (Hegel, "Spirit" 185) from nature and others, his spurning of all dependence, all empirical determination, snapping "the bonds of communal life and love" (ibid). This line of thought casts a shadow back over Kant's entire critical edifice, and for-

---

10 For an insightful discussion of this issue, see Dews, *The Idea of Evil*.

ward over any philosophy or form of life founded on a division between universal and particular, transcendental and sensible.[11]

Hegel's religious essay is among the first to suggest that the notion of a noumenal sphere, of things in themselves of which nothing can be known, is the cipher (both symptom and cause) of a *culture* drastically alienated from nature. The opposition of freedom and spontaneity to any kind of empirical determination makes them reliant on a law which engenders a feeling only of respect—a feeling in the absence of feeling, an empty feeling of humiliated subservience. This situation is understood to characterise an utterly atomised community in which no one is free because each is his or her own slave. The paradoxical sovereign subject marks the 'coming-to-be' of Kantian idealism.

As his exegesis of Christ's Sermon demonstrates, for Hegel, true freedom is not a self-legislation which suppresses nature—pathological determinations, contingent desires, biological needs, fleeting self-interests. Rather, it is the absolute correspondence of inclination and reason in love, which is raised above their opposition.

> The Sermon [on the Mount] does not teach reverence for the laws; on the contrary, it exhibits that which fulfils the law but annuls it as law and so is something higher than obedience to law and makes law superfluous. Since the commands of duty presuppose a cleavage [between reason and inclination] and since the domination of the concept declares itself in a 'thou shalt,' that which is raised above this cleavage is by contrast an 'is,' a modification of life [...]. (Hegel, "Spirit" 212)

The sublation of law in love (the total correspondence of duty and desire) completes the matter of the law by stripping it of its legal form. Love is raised above the opposition between universal and particular, becoming an immediate modification of life. In contrast to the dutiful freedom commanded and enabled by the moral law, which remains in the antinomical realm of ought, this loving, living, or aesthetic freedom is.

---

11 "*Political* emancipation [...] is not, indeed, the final form of human emancipation, but it is the final form of human emancipation *within* the framework of the prevailing social order. It goes without saying here that we are speaking of real, practical emancipation" (Marx 15). See Marx's criticism of Article 6 of the 1793 *Declaration of the Rights of Man and of the Citizen*: "La liberté est le pouvoir qui appartient à l'homme de faire tout ce qui ne nuit pas aux droits d'autrui" ["Liberty is the power which man has to do everything which does not harm the rights of others"]. To which Marx responds: "This individual liberty, and its application [i.e. the right of property], form the basis of civil society. It leads every man to see in other men, not the *realization*, but rather the *limitation* of his own liberty" (Marx 25). The continuities between Jesus's profanation/sublation of Mosaic Law, Hegel's critique of Kantian morality, and Marx's critique of the bourgeois concept of freedom as limited rather than constituted by others, enshrined in the *Rights of Man*, appear profound.

Beyond all its Schillerian and Romantic features, Hegel's thought here is perfectly in line with a long Christian anti-Jewish/anti-legalist tradition of annulling and fulfilling the dictates of law with an ethics of love and life. At which point then, if any, does Hegelian thought cease to perpetuate and acclaim this "reign of anti-dogmatic dogmatics," to borrow Legendre (147)? One way of approaching this question has been opened by Agamben's suggestion, which picks up Schmitt's famous claim regarding modern political concepts, that "all of [Hegelian thought's] determining concepts," beginning with the relation between *Aufhebung* and *katargein* ('deactivation'), are "more or less conscious interpretations and secularizations of messianic themes" (Agamben 100). In *The Time that Remains*, Agamben uncovers in Paul's messianism an aporetic critique of the law that is irreducible to the antinomial tradition with which his name is associated.[12] If Agamben, who does not have Hegel's early so-called theological writings in mind here, points to the sedimented messianic contents of the dialectical philosophy as a whole, this essay, by contrast, hopes to bring out the relevance of the form Hegel's writing began to take as the dialectic emerged as the medium of his thought.

It was by formulating his critique of Kant in the allegorical-genealogical form of the "Spirit" essay that Hegel achieved his peculiar mode of philosophical historicisation. This is not the contextualisation of philosophical ideas (not a sociology of knowledge), but the interpretative rewriting of an epistemology and moral philosophy as a historical story. Instead of pinpointing logical mistakes or challenging basic presuppositions or using an alternative theory to formulate objections, Hegel in a sense takes Kantian epistemology and morality *literally*. That is, he picks it up along with its impasses, in particular the reciprocal antinomies between noumenal and phenomenal realms and between freedom and law, and, guided (so to speak) by the *aporia* reached in *Religion Within the Boundaries of Mere Reason*, he reads this philosophy as if it were cultural history. Hegel's reading of Kant develops and comes to life as he begins to rewrite the logical trajectory of Kant's moral philosophy as a phenomenology of the individual act of trespass. Specifically, Hegel can be seen here rehearsing, 'anthropologically,' the twists and turns of *Religion*, culminating in the loss of freedom's ultimate comprehensibility and the subsequent need for (or fall to) supernatural grace. Hegel's representation of trespass in many respects resembles what, in his *Religion*, Kant had formulated as the "intelligible deed." For Hegel, however, and this is crucial, the first act, the

---

12 "The messianic law is the law of faith and not just the negation of law. This, however, does not mean substituting the old *miswoth* [legal precepts (Hebrew)] with new precepts; rather, it means setting a non-normative figure of the law against the normative figure of the law" (Agamben 95).

arbitrary crime of the power of choice, does not take place noumenally. On the contrary, it occurs entirely "within the orbit of life" (Hegel, "Spirit" 230), as he says. It is thus that the possibility of reconciliation is possible for a world that lieth in evil—in the terms Kant took from John's Gospel—without the supplementation of moral effort by grace. Instead of grace, and beyond any punishment inflicted on the body of the criminal by penal justice, Hegel points to fate, or, more precisely, to the perspective of fate. That Hegel repeatedly refers to fate as a perspective indicates it is a way of representing what happens. But this representation of events (paradigmatically in trespass and punishment) reveals a deeper actuality of life beyond or beneath distinctions of subjectivity from objectivity, nature from the social. Fate is the representation, then, of what "outranks" (ibid.) all representation, namely, action and the modifications of life. From the vital and wholly immanent perspective of fate, substance is function all the way down.[13]

Fate comes on the scene whenever an individual or a people break what Hegel calls "united life" (229)—the fundamental connection between humanity and nature, encompassing the sense of self found communally in and through each other with whom the individual lives in beautiful union. Such fundamental immanence functions here, in place of the absolute, as the speculative possibility enabling Hegel's narrative critique to get underway:

> Only through a departure from united life which is neither regulated by law nor at variance with law, only through the killing of life, is something alien produced. Destruction of life is not the nullification of life but its diremption; and this destruction consists in its transformation into an enemy. [...] The trespasser intended to have [done] with another's life, but he has only destroyed his own, for life is not different from life, since life dwells in the single Godhead. In his arrogance he has destroyed indeed, but only the friendliness of life; he has perverted life into an enemy. (Ibid.)

The action in which an individual denies another their rights, or life, or freedom, in itself severs freedom and chooses lifeless servitude. Every trespass has something of Abraham's "first act" to it, "a disseverance which snaps the bonds of communal life and love" (185), at the same time that it resembles Kant's "intelligible deed," the ground-constituting "first act" of the power of choice. The trespasser splits his or her will from that

---

13 Much of the complexity of this idea is condensed in Hegel's use of 'as,' of which the exemplary instance is "punishment *as* fate" ("Spirit" 230). The philosophical implications of this 'as' are, obliquely, the subject of the present inquiry. For some indications as to how Hegel's usage might be approached more directly, for instance in relation to the Kantian "as if," see Agamben's discussion of the Pauline "*as not*" (Agamben 23ff.).

of the community and thereby destroys community and the living freedom it allows for him/herself. It is with this logic that Hegel begins his elaboration of the concept of fate—the retroactivity of the individual act of trespass, the return of that nature or life which self-legislative independence represses. And it is here, above all, that his genealogical reading becomes a dialectical and phenomenalising restaging of Kant.

"Trespass," Hegel writes, "is a destruction of nature, and since nature is one, there is as much destruction in what destroys as in what is destroyed" (225). This unity signals the ultimate or 'absolute' indistinction between the particular and the universal, the sensible and the rational, nature and freedom. The diremption of nature, or united life, is not given but accomplished. It was perpetrated by Noah, for instance, in setting his thought-product, an unknowable, intangible and unsayable abstraction, over and against everything natural and sensible; and it is repeated in every individual act of moral trespass. For Hegel, the free choice of unfreedom is not a radical rejection of the law, but rather its constitution. Every trespass is the action of asserting a claim to mastery which thereby enslaves the master. The act of self-legislation does not constitute living freedom; it destroys it. The moral law, and the empty feeling of respect, are ciphers of its loss. Hegel sees the construction of a transcendent and alien authority (a moral law) as an empirical act of enslavement to something abstract.

Transgression of united life is the diremption of the Common into particular and universal. It is this act which places the trespasser under the law in the act of transgressing it. Here Kantian moral law begins to mutate into penal law, and two separate perspectives, or representations of punishment, emerge. From one perspective, that of law, the trespasser has offended and broken it. The trespass has broken the law in the sense of separating its form from its content. But in cancelling its specific content, the form of the law (universality) remains, and it is as this abstract statement of universality (the mere form of universality) that the law, linking itself to a particular minister of justice or executioner, pursues the criminal and "clings to his trespass" (Hegel, "Spirit" 226). From this perspective, however, reconciliation (of the form and content of the law, and of universal and particular in life) is impossible. After punishment, the "law withdraws to a threatening attitude; it has not lost its shape [i.e. a universal opposed to the individual] or been made friendly" (227). On the individual's side, a familiar condition has emerged. For his "bad conscience," punishment alters nothing: "the trespasser always sees himself as a trespasser; over his action as a reality he has no power [i.e., he cannot undo the trespass], and this his reality is in contradiction with his consciousness of the law" (ibid.). All that remains, Hegel writes, is an unbearable disquiet (*Angst*): radical evil together with a still categorical yet now unsatisfiable moral imperative. And "from the terrifying reality of evil and the immutability of the law he can fly to grace alone" (ibid.).

However, as suggested, there is another perspective from which this punishment can be represented. This perspective Hegel describes as fate, and "fate, so far as reconcilability is concerned, has this advantage of [or over] the penal law, that it occurs within the orbit of life" (230). In this light, the trespasser cannot ultimately be understood to have posed his will against the universality of any existing law because, prior to the trespass, there was no law, prior to the trespass, the universal was the communal bonds of love and life. In the "trespass of the man regarded as the toils of fate," there was, prior to his act, "no cleavage, no opposition, much less mastery" (229). Hence, "[o]nly through a departure from united life which is neither regulated by law nor at variance with law, only through the killing of life, is something alien [i.e. the law] *produced*" (229). Represented as fate, "[i]t is the deed itself which has created a law whose domination now comes on the scene" (229–30). And with this recognition of the "hostile power as the power of life made hostile" (231), the possibility of reconciliation and a return to unity and freedom reopens.

From the Kantian/Judaic perspective of law, the trespasser is a particular opposed to the universal and since the act of trespass contradicts the universality of the law, the law must annul that contradiction, "the bungling achievement of the trespass," by dominating, punishing and subsuming the individual. From the perspective of fate, on the other hand, it was the deed itself that created law, created that opposing universality:

> In the case of punishment as fate [...] the law is later than life and is outranked by it. There, the law is only the lack of life, defective life appearing as a power. And life can heal its wounds again; the severed, hostile life can return into itself again and annul the bungling achievement of a trespass, can annul the law and punishment. (Hegel, "Spirit" 230)

Fate belongs, and its representation refers, to a dimension at which universal and the particular are inseparable; its hostility to the trespasser is not felt as an authority wholly alien to him as a particular. Both are, in a sense, individuals—the trespasser and his fate—and fate is therefore just "the enemy," which the trespasser meets, on equal footing, as "a power fighting against it" (231). From this perspective, the diremption of life is not absolute, and the choice of unfreedom is therefore neither timeless nor in need of redemption by supernatural grace. As such, neither immortality nor a divine intervention giving humanity back freedom and the natural capacity to satisfy the moral law are required. Rather, from the perspective of fate, a dissolution of the concept of law itself appears to become possible. It is this dissolution that reconstitutes a living freedom raised above individualist self-determination or abstract self-legislation:

> The fate in which man senses what has been lost creates a longing for the lost life. This longing, if we are to speak of bettering and being bettered [i.e., Kant's concepts of an infinite progression towards the good supplemented by divine grace], may in itself be called a bettering, because, since it is a sense of the loss of life, it recognises what has been lost as life, as what was once its friend, and this recognition is already an enjoyment of life. (Ibid.)

Thus, through his commitment to life's fundamental unity, Hegel is able to posit, beyond or beneath penal justice, "punishment as fate." For Hegel, the trespasser is capable of recognising that in breaking from united life and injuring another, denying another their rights and freedom, he has injured himself, forfeited his own. The trespasser has perverted the community of life into an enemy, which now appears hostile to him. But the law, or empty universality "clothed with might" (226), is at the deepest level an enemy he himself has armed. In Hegel's narration, the structure of Kant's radical evil recurs, save that here, in the absence of any noumenal deed, everything remains immanent to the act of trespass. And for this reason, in "punishment as fate," the perversion of life and freedom can be recognised by the trespasser as an evil which, in a fully immanent and sensible manner, he himself has perpetrated. From the perspective of fate, alienation can be recognised as self-alienation, servitude recognised as chosen. This kind of guilt or bad conscience is already a sensing and, Hegel writes, already an enjoyment of life:

> When the trespasser feels the disruption of his own life (suffers punishment) or knows himself (in his bad conscience) as disrupted, then the working of his fate commences, and this feeling of a life disrupted must become a longing for what has been lost. The deficiency is recognized as a part of himself, as what was to have been in him and is not. This lack is not a not-being but is life known and felt as not-being. (231)

In Kantian terms, Hegel finds hope in the finite being's recognition of the transcendental deed through which he or she freely chose bondage. Here, however, everything is internal to life; the transcendental deed is a self-alienation in which life is split into universal and particular, setting the individual at odds with the infinite universality that is the now hostile form of life. Yet, in fate, "the hostile power is the power of life made hostile; hence fear of fate is not fear of an alien being" (ibid.). It is not straightforward slavery, but freedom known and felt as unfreedom, the unfreedom that one knows and feels has been freely chosen. In this, because it is sensible, there is no absolute disjunction between the freedom that is lost and the chosen unfreedom that remains.

Such, then, is the structure of fate as it emerges from Hegel's narration or narrativisation of transcendental idealism as a form of life. There remains the task of making more explicit its relevance to an understanding of the pluralist and constructivist theory condensed in the phrase 'ways of worldmaking.' The final section of this essay addresses this issue by attempting to consider the experience (and potentially the contradictions in that experience) of the consciousness for which there are many and merely ways of worldmaking.

3. The World of Worldmaking

The world in which there is no such thing as a given world is not given but historically specific and, in a certain manner, made. The "speciousness of 'the given'" (Goodman 1) may be taken as the index and context of a particular shape or form of life, a certain configuration of world-inhabitation. The constructivist and pluralist theory of worldmaking cannot stop short of acknowledging the specific world within which its "ways of worldmaking" appear real or true—the world of *its* making, which is not the world in itself.[14] Such reflection is not without consequence. Already, in this folding or redoubling of construction upon itself, the structure of the 'made,' of 'appearances only,' begins to transform. Through this reflection on itself—the construction of construction, the belonging of appearances to an appearance, which is not simply negation of negation—the spectre of actual unity reappears. And, what is more, its loss may be sensed and acknowledged, as thought draws closer to something that would not be merely or lazily given. When the speciousness of the given is felt as loss, the primacy of conception can appear both correct and untrue.

To suggest a utopian retrieval of unity here does not entail nostalgia for a world given in the Beginning. In one sense, the given world, or pure immediacy, can only ever have existed as it persists: speciously, spectrally, lost. Yet, even in this sense, the given is not simply nothing. On the contrary, it is precisely, minimally, and indissolubly something; the presence and persistence of the lost thing. Such a lost world, together with its presence, has been the theme of this essay, discussed and rehearsed through an early work of Hegel's.

---

14 Goodman seems alive to this in his acknowledgement: "[U]niverses of worlds as well as worlds themselves may be built in many ways" (Goodman 5).

In a section of the *Negative Dialectics* entitled "Idealism as Rage," Adorno writes of the affinity between systematic idealism and economic rationalisation: "What proved idle in theory was ironically borne out in practice" (Adorno, *Negative Dialectics* 23). That is, German idealism's attempt at the systematic rationalisation of everything failed but was "ironically" achieved via the universal fungibility of things in capitalist society, which has practically succeeded in rooting out and evaporating sensuous particularity or non-identity. In an extraordinary, albeit still preliminary manner, something anticipating this thought (the triumph of discursivity "in practice") was first articulated by Hegel in his early writings. Indeed, the utopian strain of Hegel's early allegorical writing anticipates a dialectics as "the ontology of the wrong state of things" (Adorno, *Negative Dialectics* 11).[15] Reflecting upon the transcendental idealism which, in light of Hegel's early work and of Adorno's, can be seen perversely to have realised itself as capitalism, Goodman's 'ways of worldmaking' may be recognised as true of a world that is false.

To highlight briefly this Kantianism gone wrong, it suffices to consider how the constructivist and pluralist theory of worldmaking consciously eliminates the objectivity of the "*canon* of reason" (*Critique of Pure Reason* 205) Kant's critical method sought to prepare—"a sum-total of the *a priori* principles of the *correct employment* of the faculties of knowledge," as Rose has summarised (Rose 42). Exchanging the objective validity and absolute necessity of the Kantian categories and pure concepts for "words and other symbols," Goodman acknowledges the "theme of multiplicity of worlds" is "non-Kantian" (Goodman 6).[16] Yet he sees this multiplicity as "closely akin to the Kantian theme of the *vacuity* of the notion of pure content" (ibid., emphasis added). For Kant, however, and this is crucial, it was conception without content that is vacuous; "pure content" is not "empty" but "*blind.*"[17] This mix-up results when the objectivity of transcendental idealism is missed or erased. Goodman's philosophy (but not, as he writes, Kant's as well) risks "leav[ing] us uncontrolled, spinning out our own inconsequent fantasies" (Goodman 6). Indeed, the critical philosophy seems directed precisely toward securing science against such risks. With his canon, Kant effectively disguised objectivity as subjectiv-

---

15 For some suggestive connections between Adorno's thought and the "Spirit" essay, see Bernstein, "Negative Dialectics as Fate."

16 Significantly, Goodman omits any article in this sentence: he speaks neither of '*a* multiplicity' nor of '*the* multiplicity' but simply (neither definitely nor indefinitely) of "multiplicity of worlds."

17 "Thoughts without content are empty; intuitions without concepts are blind" (Kant, *Critique* A51/B75, 107).

ity.[18] But he disguised it rather too well perhaps. Such constructivist philosophies as Goodman's neglect or discard the canon in pursuit of a pluralised and relativised organon theory of knowledge. Rose distinguishes between canon and organon, noting that, in contrast to a canon, "[a]n organon of reason does not confine itself to judging and justifying the proper use of the principles of the understanding by reference to possible experience. It produces and extends knowledge with reference to its objective content" (Rose 42).[19] Again, a constructivist pluralism might discount or downplay the necessity and universality accompanying such content, the objectivity of made worlds, and it might hesitate to consider reason in this pure sense. But Goodman nonetheless understands our conceptual instruments to be actually creative of worlds, and not merely to be the necessary conditions for their perception and judgment.

Despite his claims for the understanding's creativity, however, Goodman seems sceptical regarding creation in the strong (biblical) sense. His worldmakers are more akin to the Platonic demiurge than YHWH, more architect (or interior designer) than Creator: "Worldmaking as we know it always starts from worlds already on hand; the making is a remaking" (Goodman 6). In this, Goodman gives his worldmakers contexts, he makes their independence to create dependent on the instruments and materials presently at hand (and 'worlds,' with a suggestive if problematic ambiguity, is used to cover both). At first sight, this might seem to approximate, in its elementary form, the transition from Kantian to Hegelian idealism, and the recognition of the objective preconditions (social and historical) for any critique of pure reason. Except that, with Goodman's pluralism, there exists no common or communal (social and historical) whole from and within which we collage together our worlds. Goodman opens the possibility of such a whole, only to cancel it, in a comment on the "equivocal title" of William James's *A Pluralistic Universe*: "If there is but one world, it embraces a multiplicity of contrasting aspects; if there are many worlds, the collection of them all is one" (Goodman 2). He dismisses this equivocation between plurality and unity, however, by claiming simply that it "evaporate[s] under analysis" (ibid.). This is a telling statement, for it is precisely by not merely evaporating such equivocations or contradictions (by analysing without evaporating, by retaining the de-

---

18 For an extended reading along these objectivist lines, see Adorno's lectures on the first *Critique*: in Kant, "the innermost core of subjectivity, its secret, is revealed as something objective, as the power of objectivity itself" (Adorno, *Kant's Critique* 127).

19 As Habermas explains, "Hegel directed himself against the organon theory of knowledge" (Habermas 10). And see Foucault's distinction between the projects of Fichte and Hegel above.

terminacy of a self-cancellation, by allowing itself to be *guided* by aporias), that Hegel's dialectical thought preserves both identity and difference.[20]

Although Goodman hesitates to endorse the suggestion that individuals spin worlds purely out of themselves (out of their forms alone), he does not allow the worlds with which they remake their worlds, the worlds worked upon by words and symbols, any determinacy. All determination belongs to the worldmaking subject: "content vanishes without form" (Goodman 6). As a result of this vanishing, "with substance dissolved into function, and with the given acknowledged as taken," Goodman claims "we face the questions how worlds are made, tested, and known" (ibid.). Yet, might 'we' not rather decide to attend to the vanishing of content, attend precisely to that which vanishes? For 'something' has vanished here, and this vanished something, even if known only in its vanishing, is still less than absolutely indeterminate.

In the sense that it begins with the content absent from any epistemology, absent because epistemology or method is concerned with the instruments of knowledge-production or reception and has therefore suspended the thing itself, or actuality, from the start, Hegel's *Phenomenology* opens with content as vanished, with "pure direction or blank space" (Hegel, *Phenomenology* §73). Present-day, ideologically configured, and perhaps practically "borne out" Kantianism constitutes a "natural assumption" (ibid.). Hegel's project is, in the first instance, directed against those who hold that, before considering particular things themselves, "one must first of all come to an understanding about cognition, which is regarded either as an instrument to get hold of the Absolute, or as the medium through which one discovers it" (ibid.). The criticism might be directed at Goodman save that Goodman's attention is directed not to the conceptual instruments of cognition but to "the processes that go into worldmaking" (Goodman 7), understood more empirically than in the classical epistemologies Hegel has in mind. The constraints on these processes, on individual worldmaking or re-creative practices, are imposed not transcendentally through our categories but by the worlds already made and on hand at a given moment. Goodman does not, however, endow this "moment" with the status of a background or set of common objective preconditions. In the absence of any such whole, he posits "multiple actual worlds" (Goodman 2).

To have spoken, then, of *the* world in which there is no such thing as a given world, to conceive the world of Goodman's worldmakers singularly, seems to violate this "actual" plurality and Goodman's presupposition that "the world" has actually been "displaced by worlds" (Goodman 7). Yet,

---

20 See chapter 2 of the *Phenomenology*, "Perception" (Hegel, *Phenomenology*).

does not the tense of Goodman's sentence imply a transition? And, if so, who could constitute the historical subjects of this development or displacement? "With false hope of a firm foundation gone" (7), 'we' seek to understand the ways in which we have/make our worlds in a different manner to the subjects of an earlier moment in which such "false hope" allegedly prevailed. A difference opens up—a difference in which a 'we,' and therefore a fate, is inescapably constituted. And, in a footnote, Goodman shows he is alive to the implication of this difference: "We might take construction of a history of successive developments of worlds to involve application of something like a Kantian regulative principle" (Goodman 7n8). Yet Goodman notes this in order rather to discredit "the search for a first world"—which, "as misguided as the search for a first moment of time," is "best left to theology" (Goodman 7)—than to acknowledge the genuine investigative necessity of rationally presupposing a whole, not as a determinate concept but as a regulative idea.

Once a whole is admitted, even if only regulatively, differences may emerge between the story a particular worldmaking practice tells itself regarding its world, and the totality, the whole inclusive of this rationality. This is not to say, to use Goodman's terms, that the variety and plurality of worlds become versions of one real world, but rather that "multiplicity of worlds"—each made or remade through its own discursive practice and symbolic instruments—here make up *a* world: indefinite yet singular.

Now, the notion of admitting a whole (in the sense of admitting entry), but only regulatively, can be compared to the postulation of the 'Absolute' at the commencement of the phenomenological 'way of despair.' "The Spirit of Christianity and Its Fate" provides, and this accounts for its ongoing primacy, the ethical and affective basis upon which the absolute (*qua* united life) may be presupposed by phenomenological experience. The absolute as *telos*, in this sense, is first of all or originally lost: not so much given as specious, not so much present as vanished, and yet capable of being sensed as lost, specious, vanished. Such is the only given shared by all, from which 'we' start. Goodman claims that the problem of how we arrived here, and where we came from, is "best left to theology" (7). Perhaps this warrants a return then to Hegel's (editorially entitled) *Early Theological Writings*, through the lens of which transcendental idealism, neo-Kantian constructivism, and modern 'ways of worldmaking' appear as historical forms of life and the world.

In "The Spirit of Christianity and Its Fate," Hegel narrated the process of an originary mythical departure from "united life" (229)—nature or the world prior to abstract independence (and, in a sense, prior to self-consciousness). The transcendental and self-legislating subject, for whom "perception without conception" is "totally inoperative" (as Goodman glosses Kant, 6), emerges in the first instance as a diremption of life. And beneath its self-legislating will lies inscrutable caprice, a radically arbitrary foundation. Nevertheless, represented as fate, the atomistic de-donation of the world into multiple heteronymous worlds composed of words and other symbols includes a longing for the common world lost.

It seems at first unfortunate that it is impossible, as Stephen Dedalus demands, to "open [our] eyes" to a world before and beyond the "coloured signs" (Joyce 3.1–4) that appear. The incautious affirmation of immediacy rings with a desperate hollowness. For us, it is necessary rather "to 'cross the frozen waste of abstraction'" (Adorno, *Negative Dialectics* xix) to salvage and consolidate something which is not only always already given but also, and in any case, indissoluble. Allegory, which is perhaps the least problematic genre within which to place Hegel's philosophical story of diremption and reconciliation, the loss of unity coupled with the impossibility of its complete loss, may be a means of traversing that frozen waste. Hegel allows us to recognise the truth of pluralism together with its untruth. For his presentation of the biblical story can function as a genealogy of the process through which we arrived in a world that appears merely of our making, in which the indissoluble has (and yet cannot, finally, have) melted into air.

Most importantly, perhaps, Hegel's early work includes the promise that if it is 'we' who have, in some fundamental sense, chosen a world with which we are at odds (within which there is no 'we'), we are, minimally, capable of recognising this, of acknowledging what ought to have been *our* world but is not. The hope persists that in this recognition there is a longing that is already a sensing and the beginnings of a retrieval of what is lost. The wholeness of life that is lost, in the romantic terms of the young Hegel, does not become mere "not-being" but "life known and felt as not-being" (Hegel, "Spirit" 231). And here, in the feeling of alienation itself, in the very speciousness of the given, the working of our fate commences, and reconciliation, a return to another nature, community, and unity of life, is promised.

References

Adorno, Theodor W. *Negative Dialectics*. 1966. Trans. E. B. Ashton. New York: Continuum, 1973.
—. *Kant's Critique of Pure Reason*. 1995. Stanford: Stanford UP, 2001.
Agamben, Giorgio. *The Time that Remains: A Commentary on the Letter to the Romans*. 2000. Trans. Patricia Dailey. Stanford: Stanford UP, 2005.
Allison, Henry. "Morality and Freedom: Kant's Reciprocity Thesis." *The Philosophical Review* 95.3 (1986): 393–425.

Bernstein, J. M. "Love and Law: Hegel's Critique of Morality." *Social Research* 70.2 (2003): 393–432.
—. "Negative Dialectic as Fate." *The Cambridge Companion to Adorno*. Ed. Tom Huhn. Cambridge: Cambridge UP, 2004. 19–50.
Dews, Peter. *The Idea of Evil*. Oxford: Blackwell, 2007.
Foucault, Michel. *The Order of Things: An Archaeology of the Human Sciences*. 1966. Trans. Unspecified. London: Routledge, 2002.
Goodman, Nelson. *Ways of Worldmaking*. 1978. Indianapolis: Hackett, 1992.
Habermas, Jürgen. *Knowledge and Human Interests*. 1968. Trans. Jeremy J. Shapiro. London: Heineman, 1972.
Harris, H. S. *Hegel's Ladder*. 2 Vols. Indianapolis: Hackett, 1997.
Hegel, G. W. F. "The Spirit of Christianity and its Fate." *Early Theological Writings*. Trans. T. M. Knox. Philadelphia: U of Pennsylvania P, 1975. 182–301. Trans. of Herman Nohl, ed. *Hegels Theologische Jugendschriften*. Tübingen: J. C. B. Mohr, 1907.
—. *The Phenomenology of Spirit*. Trans. A. V. Miller. Oxford: Oxford UP, 1977. Trans. of *Werke*. Frankfurt a.M.: Suhrkamp Verlag, 1969.
—. *Werke*. Bd.1. *Frühe Schriften*. Frankfurt a.M.: Suhrkamp Verlag, 1971.
Hyppolite, Jean. *Introduction to Hegel's Philosophy of History*. Trans. Bond Harris and Jacqueline Bouchard Spurlock. Bainesville: UP of Florida, 1996.
Joyce, James. *Ulysses*. 1918. New ed. Oxford: Oxford UP, 2008.
Kant, Immanuel. *The Critique of Pure Reason: Unified Edition*. Trans. Werner S. Pluhar. Indianapolis: Hackett, 1996. Trans of *Kant's gesammelte Schriften. Herausgegeben von der Königlich Preußischen Akademie der Wissenschaften. Band III und IV*. Berlin: Georg Reimer, 1911.
—. *The Critique of Practical Reason*. Trans. Werner S. Pluhar. Indianapolis: Hackett, 2002. Trans. of *Kant's gesammelte Schriften. Herausgegeben von der Königlich Preußischen Akademie der Wissenschaften. Band V*. Berlin: Georg Reimer, 1911.
—. *Religion Within the Boundaries of Mere Reason*. Trans. Allen Wood and George di Giovanni. Cambridge: Cambridge UP, 1998. Trans. of *Kant's gesammelte Schriften. Herausgegeben von der Königlich Preußischen Akademie der Wissenschaften. Band VI*. Berlin: Georg Reimer, 1911.
Legendre, Pierre. *De la Société comme Texte*. 2001. Trans. Anton Schütz. *Law, Text, Terror: Essays for Pierre Legendre*. Ed. Peter Goodrich, Lior Barshack, and Anton Schütz. Abingdon: Glass House Press, 2006. 147–54.
Marx, Karl. "On the Jewish Question." *Early Writings*. Trans. and Ed. T. B. Bottomore. London: McGraw-Hill, 1963. 211–42.
Pippin, Robert. "Hegel's Practical Philosophy: The Realization of Freedom." *The Cambridge Companion to German Idealism*. Ed. Karl Ameriks. Cambridge: Cambridge UP, 2000. 180–99.
Rose, Gillian. *Hegel Contra Sociology*. London: Athlone, 1981.
Schütz, Anton. "Nietzsche between Jews and Jurists." *Nietzsche and Legal Theory: Half-Written Laws*. Ed. Peter Goodrich and Mariana Valverde. Abingdon: Routledge, 2005.
Shell, Susan Meld. *The Embodiment of Reason: Kant on Spirit, Generation, and Community*. Chicago: U of Chicago P, 1996.

The Politics of Symbolic Forms

Frederik Tygstrup

In *A Tale of Love and Darkness*, his memoir from 2003, Amos Oz gives an account of the death of his grandmother. When she arrived in Israel in 1933, her first words were "'the Levant is full of germs'" (32). Accordingly, she inaugurated a lifelong ritual practice of cleanness: washing, boiling, disinfecting, and scrubbing everything, including her own body. Eventually one day, in one of her three daily and exceedingly hot baths, she fell dead from a major heart attack. So why did the grandmother die, Oz reflects? The fact is that she died of a heart attack, but the truth is that she died of an exaggerated preoccupation with hygiene. And, Oz continues philosophically, "[f]acts have a tendency to obscure the truth" (ibid.).

1. Facts and Truths

This insight summarises the problem I would like to address, the politics of symbolic forms. Facts are brute, they need narratives that can contextualise and interpret them. A simple, stated fact rarely makes sense by itself. Its meaning depends on how it is adapted to the various representations and narratives at hand to accommodate it. Such representations are what Ernst Cassirer baptised 'symbolic forms'—the images, narratives, and theories through which we make sense of facts. Symbolic forms are interpretive schemes that can turn whatever we apprehend and whatever happens to us into useful experience. This construction and reproduction of symbolic forms, in turn, is a privileged mechanism of worldmaking, as it transforms heterogeneous data and contingent events into—precisely—a world, a universe in which human agency and self-fashioning appear as meaningful and as significant parts of a communal environment (see Goodman; Cassirer).[1]

We should not, then, according to Amos Oz, let ourselves be blinded by the obvious magnificence of a fact. This would deprive us of the possi-

---

[1] The notion of 'worldmaking,' famously developed by Nelson Goodman, draws explicitly on Cassirer's cultural philosophy of symbolic forms.

bility of actually experiencing that fact, of gauging the reasons and motifs underpinning the grandmother's heart attack, her ideas of the body and the world, the West and the East, the spiritual and the sensual, and much more, which eventually come to prescribe how she will die. To Amos Oz, the novelist's—or the narrator's—task is to translate facts into truths, and thus to prevent one tendency in our culture to let the facts—and we have still more facts at hand—dim our sense of truth.

On the other hand, though, it would be equally erroneous to take the side of the truth against the overwhelming mass of facts in an overly rigid manner. Just as facts might blind us to the truth behind them, truth can also turn out to be a nickname for habit, allowing us to see and assess only what we already expect to find. Salman Rushdie, for instance, in *The Satanic Verses*, explicitly aims at representing the tensions, improbable encounters, juxtaposed endeavours and unruly constellations of facts that make up the modern metropolises in which we live, in order to show us, as he puts it, the "visible but unseen reality" (241) of the city. He wants to set up all the facts, all the incompatible but neighbouring and intersecting realities, for which we have no common concept and no all-embracing idea, and by this gesture to defy our sense of truth.

With Oz and Rushdie, then, we have two different poetics which both juxtapose facts and truth. To Oz, we should not rely too much on facts, but try and unfold the not immediately comprehensive layer of truths underpinning them. To Rushdie, on the other hand, it is more important to retrieve the facts that can actually be found out there, to the disadvantage of the expectations we might hold in advance pertaining to what should be considered truthful. These two poetics, admittedly quite stylised, promoting respectively truth over facts and facts over truths, are not necessarily at odds, however. What they share, rather, is an insight in the precarious relationship of facts and truths.

Every society relies on a system of acknowledged truths reproduced through the everyday life-world of individuals: their different professional, private and public practices, the way they consider the time, space, and environment they inhabit, their shared ideas of belonging and becoming, the collective universes of imagination inhabiting their minds, and so on. From this centre of everyday life practices, the system of truths ranges on the one hand towards the more distinguished sphere of beliefs and acknowledged values (mostly referred to in moments of solemn contemplation or manipulation), and, on the other, towards the intimate universes of sensation, sensibility, and self-fashioning.

Such a system of truths in turn relies on facts. What it does, basically, is to make sense of facts by ordering them, sorting them, categorising them, establishing relations among them, and prescribing procedures for how to handle them and how to think about them. Or, in other words: how to make a world out of contingent facts. Systems of truth are the software for this processing of facts. But on a more profound level, it would be incorrect to consider systems of truth only as such a means of processing facts; by setting up categories, possible relations, procedures, and so on, they not only process facts: they also produce facts. Systems of truth work not only through the inclusion of facts in their interpretive grids, but also through tailoring them to fit these grids, and through exclusion of inconvenient facts that cannot be conceived of, thought, handled, or recognised. When a system of thought cannot process a fact, it will have to dismiss it as irrelevant, obscene, and heretical.

This is why the relationship of facts and truths is a precarious one. On the one hand, facts are a threat to truth, because the evidential quality of a fact might lead us off the path towards something true, but also because an insistent fact might challenge the default explanations available within the confines of the system of truths. And, on the other hand, the rule of a given truth system will usually have the power to arbitrate the very facticity of a fact through its mechanisms of inclusion and exclusion. Both of these aspects resound in Michel Foucault's famous remark on Mendel's theory of heredity: "What Mendel said was true, but he wasn't 'within the truth' of the biological discourse of his time" (*Discours* 37).

What Amos Oz and Salman Rushdie both point at, then, is a process of confrontation and negotiation at play in all cultures between the rule of truth and the evidence of facts. This interplay quintessentially captures what is at stake in social processes of worldmaking: the ability to turn facts into socially significant truths and thus to include them in a shared world of certainties, as well as the ability to acknowledge new facts and changing configurations of facts as novel elements in a dynamic world-view flexible enough to embrace the changing environment for social worldmaking.

This negotiation is also a political one. At stake is the power of the system of truth to contain and include the ever-changing constellations of facts it has to deal with, and, conversely, the power of facts to disrupt or deform and reform the rule of truth they confront. Quite a few common political issues could certainly be stated in such terms of juxtaposed truths and facts: One could ask, for instance, if neo-liberalism is a successful attempt to co-opt the fact of growing contestations of authority in the industrialised societies throughout the last third of the twentieth century? And if the policy of perestroika in Eastern Europe was a failed attempt at the same? Or if global warming is a fact that will disrupt the acknowledged truth that growth is the key to welfare? Or if contemporary radical fundamentalism is a fact that challenges the belief in liberal democracy as the cornerstone of Western societies?

Whether or not artists voice their views on such questions generally acknowledged as 'political,' they nonetheless participate in the same kind of negotiation of truths and facts—Oz by his attempt to make the life and death of his grandmother comprehensible, Rushdie by confronting our idea of living together in an urban community. Both novelists perform a political practice in staging such negotiations, by confronting significant facts, and elaborating the language of truth with new narratives, new forms, and new visions.

Before trying to give a bit more substance to these home-grown speculations on truth and facts by taking a look at Ernst Cassirer's philosophy of symbolic forms and at some recent writings by Jacques Rancière, I would like to briefly comment on another work of art where the political nature of the negotiation of facts and truths is quite apparent.

W.G. Sebald's last novel, *Austerlitz* (2001), is a narrative of the quest of protagonist Jacques Austerlitz to explore and come to terms with his own past. At age five, in the late 1930s, he was put on a transport of children from Prague to England by his Jewish parents and subsequently adopted by a British family. He had grown up in England and become an art historian based in London when by the middle of his life he set out to investigate his erased background in Prague and the destinies of his deported parents. This quest, however, by nature an excellent plot of detection and biography, does not have a straightforward narrative thread, but rather consists mainly of a large number of dense descriptions. Being an architectural historian, Austerlitz sets out on his quest equipped with a camera and a notepad. Thus, the novel—told by a first person narrator based on his conversations with Austerlitz, whom he meets accidentally (strikingly so) on a number of occasions over some fifteen years—becomes a series of detailed renditions of an entire array of items such as imperial architecture of European capitals, fortresses and bastions, landscapes and interiors, concentration camps and cemeteries, animals and stones, libraries and collections, and much more. In this respect, the novel is in part a long series of minute descriptions of facts, such as one might find in Proust or Perec, and in part an equally thorough and patient unfolding of the innumerable histories embedded in these facts. It is an encyclopaedic tour de force giving back, as it were, the forgotten history to all these facts. What is performed here is not primarily the art of unfolding a plot in time, but rather the art of reading the sedimentations of time in space.

As these few remarks already indicate, the novel proposes a full orchestration of the negotiation between facts and truths. On the one hand, it performs an almost uncanny exposition of brute and neglected facts surrounding us in buildings, cities, landscapes, and collections, by isolating and scrutinising them as something unfamiliar, far away from our preoccupation with the petty certainties governing our lives. And, on the other hand, it endows these facts with new narratives and glossing, reintegrating them, as it were, in the larger, horrible truth about our world to which they tacitly bear witness.

In this respect, the novel can be read as something like an archaeological encounter with Europe's buried recent history: not a dramatic text, but a contribution, in the words of another Sebald title, to 'the natural history of destruction.' However, the political significance of the novel's thorough reshuffling of facts and truths does not consist only of this tableau of the mute European space given voice; it also relates to the private quest of Austerlitz to encounter and adapt to his own individual history in that space. At stake is not only the resurrection of a forgotten or ignored past, but also the fundamental problem of grounding and unfolding an individual existence in an historical sphere of symbolic forms, of prevailing truths, and a corollary universe of acknowledged facts. It is a matter of, in other words, subjectivisation of historical possibilities and constraints. Here, Austerlitz is again a quite awkward hero as he has refrained from building any of the usual characteristics of an individual life. A bit like a Beckettian protagonist, he resides in an empty house where all surfaces are painted grey and practically lives out of a rucksack; he seems not to have entertained any affective relationship to the people he grew up with, nor anyone since. A singularly neutral and impersonal character, in other words, reminiscent of Everyman, with whom he shares certain allegorical characteristics, such as his lack of individual destiny, and almost conflates his individual history into the grand European history from which it issues and which he incessantly studies. In this way, neutrality almost reverts into quintessentiality—this modern Everyman being the European par excellence, the generic offspring of the history of destruction. His task, on this basis—again one that is politically freighted—is then to *confect* a subjective, truly individual character out of this material. Herein may lie the novel's true suspense: whether or not Austerlitz will succeed in making the neutral Everyman into a somebody through his quest; that is, whether a viable subject can be imagined to arise from the history that Austerlitz retrieves from the European ground on which he, and we, stand.

Before returning to how Sebald organises this effort of reading the European space differently and of imagining what kind of subjectivity matches the space, I will briefly sketch a more elaborated theoretical foundation of my initial remarks on truth and facts.

2. Worldmaking and Contestation

Ernst Cassirer's *The Philosophy of Symbolic Forms,* published between 1923 and 1929, from which I have partially borrowed my title, and indeed his entire production, can be seen as an attempt at historicising the notion of truth, without giving in to a lax relativism in which it no longer makes sense at all to think seriously of truth claims, be they historical, scientific, or philosophical.

Cassirer is usually considered to be a neo-Kantian philosopher, and the critical Kantian philosophy is incontestably the starting point of his thinking. What is really interesting in this context, and what distinguishes him from other neo-Kantians, however, is the strong influence of the romantic philosophy of history, mainly through Vico and Hegel.

Given the Kantian orientation, the point of departure is the critique of knowledge as an understanding of the logic of human cognition: how the intuition of objects is correlated to the concepts and categories of understanding through which we process it in order to properly experience the objects. Thus, the pivotal point in Cassirer's thinking is the introduction of a third term as a kind of transmission point between the notions of truth and facts: the term representation. In keeping with Kant's double critique of the rationalist tradition that made unconditional claims on truth, and of the empiricist tradition hypostasising the fact, Cassirer argues that it is the task of the philosopher to understand neither a general order of truth nor the nature of factual evidence, but rather how facts can be represented truthfully.

In a certain sense, then, the middle term or auxiliary term 'representation,' which was simply introduced as a kind of intermediary between truth and facts, now seems to expand and absorb what was considered to be the content of the two initial realms. On the one hand, we are left without any substantial knowledge about the facts—now to be relegated as distant and unapproachable 'things in themselves'—apart from what perception and intuition has made of them, and, on the other, what is left of truth is merely the proper application of the rules of understanding.

The object of study is no longer the order of truth or the nature of facts, but what goes on within the cognitive machinery, how the content of intuition meets the concepts of understanding to form coherent representations. According to Kant, this is where we find the schemata and symbols, a kind of formal blueprint, accessible both from the side of understanding and from the side of intuition. Kant himself did not bother much to elaborate these concepts; he just assumed that they were there to perform the work of translation.

To Cassirer, however, these mediating formal grids are by contrast the most interesting features of the Kantian critique of knowledge. It is, after all, up to them to assure the cohesion between sense and reason, facts and truth. And it is at this precise point that Cassirer breaks off from the path of neo-Kantianism by introducing a radical historicising of the cognitive machinery. These mediators, schemata, and symbols, he states, are not simple logical and universal functions: they vary in different historical contexts. This is, of course, where Vico and Hegel come into play and with them the romantic idea of the relativity of historical knowledge. Different historical contexts produce and promote different symbolic forms, and these, in turn, tend to organise the spontaneity of intuition and the receptivity of understanding in different and quite distinct forms and patterns. Thereby, the object of study is further specified: not only to study the cognitive machinery, but also to study it in the forms and appearances it takes throughout history.

This way, Cassirer's thinking is not only a distinctive contribution to the theory and history of science and knowledge, which we usually associate with neo-Kantianism, but it also displays a remarkable affinity to the German tradition of *Geistesgeschichte*. It shares with it the claim that a given culture should be understood, not 'from the outside' based on general principles for description of its beliefs, values, and practices, but 'from the inside,' based on the significance of its world-view—the structure of its insights, the order of its practices, and the modes of feeling it entails and supports.

Furthermore, Cassirer adds something extremely valuable to this line of thought, namely a quite crude materialism. Whereas *Geistesgeschichte* can quite obviously often be very spiritual in its understanding of the meaning and significance of a specific historical world view as an immanently cohesive spiritual universe, Cassirer insists that the representations to be studied are not some generalised ideas and intuitions—understood as *Vorstellungen*—but the actually historically produced linguistic and pictorial utterances—understood as *Darstellungen*. There is a certain 'textualism' in Cassirer, in contrast to spiritualism, i.e. an idea that a culture should be assessed on the basis of its explicit performative linguistic practice. What Cassirer thus unfolds, to quote from a French review of one of his books—"is an interwoven field of discourse and thought, of concepts and of words, which he analyzes in their own specific configuration" (Foucault, *Histoire* 574).

To Cassirer, then, the study of cultural history is a study of actual representations and the ways in which they privilege certain systems or axioms of truth and assess—and produce—certain kinds of facts. What might, on the other hand, be missing from this quite admirable programme of cultural studies, is a sense of conflict, an eye for the struggle between truths and facts played out in the sphere of representation. As in *Geistesgeschichte*, Cassirer has a tendency to present the historical tableau as something harmonious, a rounded, homogenous totality. As if a privileged sample of representations were also representative of the social reality in question.

So the question arises of how symbolic forms are also forms of power. How can dominant symbolic forms be considered as forms of domination? How are other possible ways of worldmaking kept in check and excluded?

The Italian Marxist philosopher Antonio Gramsci has addressed this set of problems. On the one hand, he shared the romantic cultural philosophy we also find in Cassirer, but, on the other hand, he very directly introduced the notion of power to this line of reasoning by considering dominant symbolic forms, not as harmonic and homogenous assessments of reality, but as hegemonic assessments, serving—as he would put it—particular class interests. In this view, politics—in a major key, the confrontation of different historical sets of interests and the struggle for social power—is basically a negotiation of symbolic forms: an agonistic confrontation of different forms of worldmaking, reflecting different needs, interests, and visions of a better future.

The politics of symbolic forms should not, however, be restricted to this agonistic sphere of grand politics. Once it is realised that there is an intimate link between an historical regime of symbolic forms—representations of reality forming the backbone of a shared certainty as to the nature of reality—and a corollary architecture of power enforcing specific ways of seeing, thinking, acting, and feeling and prohibiting others precisely by way of such representations, then politics is present everywhere, as the exercising and contestation of power.

This idea of politics in a minor key that does not entail an agonistic confrontation of more or less well-identified collective interests, but more generally and perhaps modestly focuses on practices of subversion, deformation, and deviational modification of effective representations has been theorised by the French philosopher Jacques Rancière. A seminal and recurring notion in his recent work is 'the distribution of the sensible,' defined at one point as "the system of *a priori* forms determining what presents itself to sense experience." In addition:

> It is a delimitation of spaces and times, of the visible and the invisible, of speech and noise, that simultaneously determines the place and the stakes of politics as a form of experience. Politics revolves around who has the ability to see and the talent to speak, around the properties of spaces and the possibilities of time. (Rancière 13)

Having already looked a bit into Cassirer's philosophy of symbolic forms, these remarks on the distribution of the sensible do indeed seem familiar, not only because of the reference to Kant ('the system of *a priori* forms determining what presents itself to sense experience'), but also due to the fact that such a distribution of the sensible—the production of a certain range of facts and nature of factuality—appears to be strictly parallel to the historicist notion of symbolic forms. What should be highlighted in Rancière's reassessment of this theoretical framework (probably influenced by Althusser and Foucault) is, however, the explicit elaboration of an immediate political significance of the distribution of the sensible, allowing the political to be thought not only in its major key, but also in relation to the everyday practices intervening in the socially dominant order of symbolic forms, performing the ongoing negotiation between truths and facts.

3. Representation and Deviation

A second feature to be highlighted in Rancière's notion of politics is the role allotted to aesthetic practices. Art, he says at one point, "is a way of doing and making that intervenes in the general distribution of ways of doing and making as well as in the relationships they maintain to modes of being and forms of visibility" (Rancière 13). To elaborate, art is an innovative practice of representation where the techniques and forms of representation are worked out in order to see and experience reality differently, and thus it is a practice that intervenes in the social fabric of dominant and generally acknowledged symbolic forms.

An important move here is that the political significance of art practices is considered neither in terms of a specifically propagated 'political position' (in the major key) nor any possible political effect. The political, here, is thematised in the form of a proposition, a possible (re-)distribution of the sensible presented in a publicly accessible form in guise of a hypothesis, a heuristic model of worldmaking. This could, of course, be dismissed as insufficient or even inadequate for those who expect immediate political action through art. If, however, we accept the political significance of this kind of heuristic worldmaking through construction of new forms of representation, it is obvious that art practices command a particular interest, precisely because art-making resides in the construction of formal devices aimed at seeing, thinking, and experiencing reality differently. Throughout the twentieth century art theory affirmed, in a number of different ways, that the core of art is not a specific repertoire of forms, nor a specific set of objects, but a moulding of forms that deviate from the habitual forms of intuition, defamiliarise perception, and suspend our beliefs concerning the order of things.

If we should consider art (among other things) as a politics of symbolic forms, it is not least due to this quality of deviation: deformation of the symbolic forms through which we normally orient ourselves in the world. In art, we do not encounter some altogether different, aesthetically enchanted world; we encounter a formal construct through which we have the opportunity to construe the world a bit differently. It might show us aspects and regions of the world we did not know, or that we did not know that we only almost knew, and it might show us how knowing something about the world comes about in the first place—through a specific distribution of the sensible and a specific organisation of symbolic forms.

I will conclude with a word on some of Sebald's techniques of deviation and defamiliarisation, mentioning three that can be conveniently summarised under the headings narratives, archives, and media.

Quite a lot could be said about Sebald's narrative technique and style, but I will limit myself to one observation. The text of the novel is experienced quite materially as a huge, massive and monotonous block, it has no chapters and no paragraphs, only an occasional slash and a handful of asterisks (literally: 5) to break up the text. This sense of monotony is reaffirmed at the level of style; the prose is elegant, a bit archaic, with long, quite elaborated and beautifully articulated sentences, both Mann and Musil come to the mind. There is no stylistic differentiation between the (anonymous) first-person narrator, Austerlitz, and the numerous other people who are quoted. This is formally explained by the fact that the narrator takes down his conversations with Austerlitz in shorthand after their encounters, but still it leaves a peculiar impression of indistinction among the different voices. At the same time this construction is constantly highlighted in voluntarily clumsy constructions like "Gerald found," "explained Alphonso," "said Austerlitz" (Sebald 131)—and we could add, "the narrator reported," "the author wrote." It is like a Chinese box where the voices, all in the same tone, converge and blend—just as the text blends German, French, English, Dutch, Czech—into a kind of collective murmur, recalling the Everyman-motive, and producing something like a generic European voice, echoing "des gémissements poussés par le monde de cadavres au milieu duquel je gisais" (Balzac 31), quoting Balzac's *Colonel Chabert*, several times in the text.

The archive is a very prominent and somewhat puzzling figure in the novel. For one thing, there is an almost obsessive presence of archives in Austerlitz' universe; first of all, at the thematic core of the text, the archives related to his suspended past: of Prague's pre-war inhabitants, deported Jews, their expropriated belongings, documents on concentration camps, and so on. But also other archives or archival constructs like libraries, museums, collections—in particular countless fascinating collections of natural history exhibits: moths, flies, petrifications, stones, plants, and much more. Thus, the archive is a supreme object of fascination, and Austerlitz invariably delves into detailed accounts of the classifications and ordering principles of the different archives and the lessons that can be drawn from the organisation of the collections. Furthermore, of course, the archive is really some sort of an image of the novel itself: a huge collection of tableaux, commented facts, still lives taken from contemporary European history. Only this final archive does not have the neatly designed and rational order that might be seen as the never-attained final object of Austerlitz' quest. The novel itself has the appearance of a haunted archive, with its protagonist suffering from what Derrida famously baptised 'le mal d'archive.' At one point, during his visit to Theresienstadt, Austerlitz halts in front of a curiosity shop with innumerable objects juxtaposed in the display windows, and afterwards reflects:

> Even these still lifes obviously composed entirely at random, which appeared to have grown quite naturally into the black branches of the lime trees standing around the square and reflected in the glass of the windows, exerted such a power on me that it was a long time before I could tear myself away from staring at the hundreds of different objects, as if one of them or their relationship with each other must provide an unequivocal answer to the many questions I found it impossible to ask in my mind. (Sebald 274)

Thus, on the one hand, the novel itself seems to converge towards the archive—in a certain sense the radical opposite of the narrative account of a temporal sequence—an archive of the natural history of destruction, with Austerlitz himself as the failing natural historian unable to give the archive an appropriate order—a denaturalisation of the novel, in other words. But, on the other hand, it is also an intriguing reorientation of our understanding of the archive. We usually think of the archive as an established order that organises a continually expanding and developing collection. Here, it almost takes the opposite shape, a fixed and quite huge collection whose order is slowly emerging or at least developing through Austerlitz' reflections. A way of thinking the archive, in other words, as a living thing, almost an organism, an organism whose gradual development might even deserve to be presented through the plot of a novel.

Austerlitz is, like most of Sebald's books, a work of mixed media: the text is supplemented with images, mostly photographs. They are not illustrations, as one might expect of images accompanying a text, and they do not have any captions, which are arguably the most important paratextual device for identifying images in a text as illustrations. On the other hand, their appearance is quite concordant with the text, displaying an object or a person described or discussed (even the protagonist, whose alleged picture even decorates the cover of the novel), and often photographs are mentioned that obviously are the images we actually see. The presence of the images in the book reverberates in a number of different ways with an entire array of themes, motifs and forms in the novel, but in this connection I will only mention one, namely the thematisation of fictionality they entail. Hardly any reader, I gather, can help wondering about the provenance of these photographs: has the author picked up a collection of photos somewhere and decided to build a novel upon and around them? Or has he researched and chosen them in order to fit them into the story? Such fantasising of course emerges as a response to the initial shock of the improbable encounter of a fiction—and the photographic documentation of its content. (Unless, of course, they are taken from a subsequent film version; my copy of *Colonel Chabert* has Gérard Depardieu on the dust jacket.) Photographs are carriers of indexical proof of what has been in front of the lens at some moment, and consequently they unravel the tacit contract of fictionality on which we rely. This unravelling might not be very subtle, but the very brutality of it is an extraordinarily convincing way of insisting upon the seriousness of the archaeology the novel performs: it makes the photographs say (in Roland Barthes' words): this-has-been (96).

Neutralised representation of personal voices; redistribution of individual and collective positions; intermingling of archival and narrative forms; intersecting media and an ensuing challenge to our sense of reality and fiction—these are some of the devices that underpin Sebald's attempt to show us something we did not know or were not aware of. They work as a technology of seeing and understanding that can disclose facts not available within the habitual range of our attention. And the representations they make possible give us the opportunity to unfold heuristic versions of truth by performing (re-)distributions of the sensible—performing a politics of symbolic forms.

References

Balzac, Honoré de. *Le Colonel Chabert*. 1832. Ed. Wolfgang Orlich. Stuttgart: Reclam, 2006.

Barthes, Roland. *Camera Lucida: Reflections on Photography*. 1980. Trans. Richard Howard. New York: Hill and Wang, 1981.

Cassirer, Ernst. *Philosophie der symbolischen Formen*. Darmstadt: Wissenschaftliche Buchgesellschaft, 1973–75.

Foucault, Michel. *L'Ordre du discours*. Paris: Gallimard, 1971.
—. "Une histoire restée muette." *Dits et écrits*. Vol. 1. Paris: Gallimard, 1994. 545–49.
Goodman, Nelson. "Words, Works, Worlds." *Ways of Worldmaking*. Indianapolis: Hackett Publishing Company, 1978. 1–21.
Oz, Amos. *A Tale of Love and Darkness*. Trans. Nicholas de Lange. London: Vintage Books, 2005.
Ranciére, Jacques. *The Politics of Aethetics: The Distribution of the Sensible*. 2000. Trans. Gabriel Rockhill. New York: Continuum, 2004.
Rushdie, Salman. *The Satanic Verses*. New York: Viking Press, 1988.
Sebald, Winfried G. *Austerlitz*. Trans. Anthea Bell. London: Penguin, 2001.

II. Media as Ways of Worldmaking

Media as Ways of Worldmaking:
Media-specific Structures and Intermedial Dynamics

BIRGIT NEUMANN and MARTIN ZIEROLD

1.

If worlds are intrinsically social, then the formation of a world does rely, fundamentally, on means of sharing and exchanging knowledge. Worldmaking cannot do without symbols that represent or embody knowledge of the past, present, and future and have the capacity to circulate in social groups. In other words, the production and circulation of cultural as well as individual knowledge, i.e. the making of worlds in the broadest sense, is to a large extent dependent on media use and medial externalisation. Cultural worldmaking is constituted by a host of different media, all of which operate within specific symbolic systems: literary texts, TV documentaries, historical painting, newspaper articles, and monuments, for example. Worldmaking cannot do without media that represent or embody cultural knowledge and are capable of circulating in a social group. Furthermore, it is thanks to processes of active media usage that we are socialised and learn how to evaluate social actions and discourses emotionally and rationally, i.e. to construct our realities in a socially viable way, in short: to 'make worlds.'

2.

For any analysis of culture and 'the media,' it is important to note that 'the media,' just like culture, is a rather ambiguous term. Scholars coming from different research traditions have quite different phenomena in mind when they speak of 'the media.' In his comprehensive monograph "Der Sinn und die Sinne" ("Sense and the Senses"), German media scholar Jochen Hörisch offers his view on media history ranging from the 'consecrated wafer' to the internet (see Hörisch), thus proclaiming a very wide-ranging understanding of the term 'media' not everybody will agree with.

However, there are various models and theories about 'the media' available, each stressing certain aspects of 'mediality'—e.g. technological aspects, the content of certain media, its impact on users or the freedom of the recipients to develop creative uses—and at the same time, neglecting other aspects.

Siegfried J. Schmidt has developed an integrative model of modern mass media which tries not to isolate single aspects of media systems on the one hand, but which, on the other, still makes heuristic distinctions (see Schmidt *Kalte Faszination* 93ff., "Medienkompaktbegriff" 144ff.; see also Zierold 161ff.). Schmidt lists four aspects of media systems for his model, which can be separated on an analytical level but should always be considered as interrelated:

1. Semiotic Material/Communication Instruments ('Kommunikationsinstrumente')
   The term 'Communication Instruments' refers to any kind of semiotic sign such as language, but also visual images or musical sounds. In mass media, this semiotic material is usually mediated by the means of

2. Media Technologies ('Technisches Dispositiv')
   Schmidt already considers script, or even cave paintings, as media technologies, because a certain (yet in these cases rather simple) apparatus is needed to bring semiotic material into an at least temporarily durable form. 'Media history,' as it is often understood, is generally told as the history of media technologies, starting with oral and scriptural cultures, and going forward to the complex electronic and digital media technologies of today.

3. Social Contextualisation/Institutionalisation ('Sozialsystemische Institutionalisierung')
   However, the history of mass media is not only a history of technology, but also of the development of complex social institutions on the levels of production and distribution of media products on the one hand, and reception on the other. Publishing houses, editorial offices, the social role of 'journalists,' but also advertising agencies or film studios—each are specific social institutionalisations which have co-evolved with the modern system of mass media technologies. Obviously, while certain media technologies open up specific creative possibilities and delimit others (TV needs images to work, whereas papers traditionally rely more on language and the written word), 'the medium' (and its technology) is certainly not on its own 'the message,' as Marshall McLuhan has put it. As the debates about public vs. commercial forms of broadcasting, or the difference between professional journalists and amateur bloggers illustrate, the social contexts of the production of media have an enormous influence on a media system's output. Thus, the different kinds of social institutionalisations of the production, distribution and reception (and uses) of the media always have to be included in any analysis of media products.

4. Media offers / Media products ('Medienangebote')
   Schmidt refers to the actual material products of media systems as 'media offers,' indicating that the existence of any text or other material media is no more than

an offer to potential recipients, who need to actually make use of the media product in order to give it social or cultural relevance. This process of reception cannot be determined by the media product, but again is embedded in the dimension of social institutions or contexts and can thus differ enormously with different people in different contexts, times, or spaces. The 'media offer' can be considered as an effect of, and at the same time, an influence on aspects 1–3, i.e. the communication instruments, media technologies and social contexts. The product is, on the one hand, a result of people in social contexts making use of communication instruments with media technologies, thus creating a media product. On the other hand, the process of producing and using media offers is always pre-shaped by schemata which are based on the social experiences with previous media products, and every new product serves as a way to constantly support or redefine the cultural schemata of a society.

This multi-level yet integrated model calls for a complex analysis of media systems which should always try to include as many of the aforementioned aspects as possible. 'Media effects' for example, are very often only debated from either a technological perspective (e.g. McLuhan, Kittler etc.), or a hermeneutic perspective analysing the specific content of isolated media products trying to measure their effect (e.g. advertising research, content analysis etc.). Schmidt's model allows scholars to differentiate different kinds of media effects, which again are interrelated: There certainly are effects of specific media products such as advertising campaigns, television news, or novels—which are usually very hard to measure empirically—, Schmidt refers to these as 'semantic effects.' However, on the technological level there are also 'structural effects' in the sense that the mere availability of a technology has a social and cultural effect (e.g. in the sense that the cultural meaning or significance of a letter sent by traditional mail changes with the development of fax and e-mail).

Regarding the 'worldmaking'-potential of media, the same principle holds true: Media products can be used to create semantic knowledge or models of the world (or possible alternative worlds); at the same time media technologies structurally create and shape the social and cultural worlds we live in, even if we do not personally make use of them. If the technology of mobile phones is available, a non-user also makes a statement (willingly or not) and shapes his or her world (as a non-conformist or individualistic person etc.). On the level of social life, roles, and institutions, media are made use of to create worlds in another way: for media producers, for instance journalists, script-writers, advertising consultants, or film-stars, 'the media' create their worlds in a very practical sense as they spend a large amount of their lifetime producing media products, distributing them etc. But media users also creatively use media to create worlds beyond the semantic uses they may make of news, novels, or films.

Putting on your favourite record to relax, switching on the TV without actually watching in order to have some background noise, listening to the radio in the car out of pure routine, gathering around a DVD with friends each Friday night—all of these practices are media-based ways of creating personal worlds and social spaces, where the actual media content might play a secondary role.

3.

Given the importance of media to ways of worldmaking, it is not surprising that there should be widespread interest in media studies among cultural scholars. For our context, it is helpful to introduce the distinction between "primary intermediality" and "secondary intermediality" coined by German media theorist Rainer Leschke (see 33ff., 299–300). Leschke distinguishes the discourse about "primary intermediality," which deals with technological differences and the consequences of different media technologies (e.g. printing press vs. radio), from phenomena of "secondary intermediality." The latter refer to the interrelation of aesthetic forms, topics or motives between different media offers and different media systems. Debates on primary intermediality usually occur in times of the introduction of 'new' media, and they usually remain on a rather abstract level comparing the cultural implications of established and 'new' media technologies. Research on secondary intermediality has proven to be particularly productive in the different academic fields of the (media) philologies, analysing particular media products and their interrelations, thus demonstrating how particular aspects of knowledge, ideas, motives, stereotypes etc. are interrelatedly (re-)mediated within different media offers and media technologies.

Both perspectives on intermediality in fact deal with the question of how media become relevant as ways of worldmaking: specific technologies act as a 'dispositif,' i.e. they allow us to mediate the world and construct reality in specific ways. Accordingly, these aspects of primary intermediality refer to structural media effects. At the same time, sets of specific media products can play a major role in establishing forms of cultural knowledge, norms, and values by constantly re-narrating, re-mediating and re-constructing them.

In the following, we will concentrate on the latter aspects of media as a way of worldmaking, touching upon forms of structural effects and media as ways of worldmaking at the end of our contribution.

4.

Although there is a vast body of research on intermediality, including investigations into the role of media in processes of worldmaking, the focus has thus far mainly been on individual media such as literary texts and films.[1] Accordingly, existing research has mainly investigated the ways in which these media are used to make worlds through the way they pay attention to certain things rather than others, structure information in certain ways and use specific narrative forms and aesthetic means to create and disseminate cultural knowledge. One especially fruitful line of inquiry, which is particularly prominent in literary studies, has addressed the role played by genre- and media-specific structures in the construction of cultural knowledge. Hence, these approaches stress that different genres and media, such as travelogues, poems, dramas, or satirical prints, deploy genre- or medium-specific devices to create powerful, aesthetically condensed worlds, worlds that are bound up with cultural norms, predispositions, and values. Whenever worlds are made, the choice of semiotic material and media technologies has an effect on the kind of world that is created. Literary texts, for instance, will use different aesthetic devices to represent a war than documentary films, devices which will ultimately affect the interpretation of the war in question itself. To the extent that these devices are semanticised, they implicitly convey specific values, thus reinforcing or reshaping specific constructions of the world. Media-specific structures are thus best understood as constitutive elements of worldmaking.

Yet it is important to note that this cultural power of media offers is located not so much in the offers themselves, but also in their social institutionalisation, as we have argued above. To a large extent, the social institutionalisation of media offers is constituted by other media offers, i.e. by inter- and transmedial adaptations (see Erll; Rigney). Thus, constant processes of translation, appropriation, renarration, and remediation turn media offers into culturally potent media, i.e. media which create and mould cultural knowledge. The production and dissemination of culturally influential knowledge, hence, in a broader sense 'worldmaking,' is an ongoing process in which the same messages, contents, values, or concepts are represented again and again, often over decades and centuries, in diverse genres and media. Rather than focusing on individual media offers and their particular way of worldmaking, it seems more promising to turn attention to the cultural dynamics and intermedial processes in which

---

1   Several passages of section IV and V are part of an article that has been published in *The European Journal of English Studies* (Neumann, "Cultural and Historical Imagology").

these products are caught up and in which they acquire their cultural significance (see Neumann, "Cultural and Historical Imagology"). Behind this shift lies, among other things, the idea that the process which Nelson Goodman refers to as 'worldmaking' is part of the cultural circulation of meanings, values, and norms, and the idea that worldmaking as such is never fixed once and for all but is something that has to be processed and circulated time and again in different media and concomitant processes of inter- and transmedial translation: Adaptation, translation, reception, appropriation and remediation "have thus become key words" (Rigney 349), with the cultural power of a specific medium "being located in the cultural activities it gives rise to, rather than in what it is in itself" (ibid.). Hence, to understand fully the role of media in cultural world- or knowledge-making, it is necessary to go beyond the analysis of individual media to the study of the complex and manifold interactions with other acts of worldmaking in a variety of media and genres. When locating individual media within broader dynamics, the various roles played by them in the construction and dissemination of knowledge come to the fore.

Cultural knowledge in the broadest sense, i.e. cultural stereotypes, concepts of gender, identity, and alterity, as well as prevalent cultural premises, norms, and values, are transmedial phenomena because their representation is not tied to a single medium but manifests itself in a broad spectrum of different textual, visual and performative media. The very transformation of specific epistemic constellations into potent figures of knowledge relies on transmedial procedures, i.e. on continuous recursive representations in a variety of genres and media (without necessarily referring consciously to a specific text). While 'knowledge' might refer to single utterances, cultural knowledge and concomitant processes of worldmaking always work on the basis of transmediality. Media typically build on or recycle earlier forms of worldmaking and in this way they can end up becoming collective points of reference. Revisions or remakes of earlier ways of worldmaking and the remediation of knowledge in new media also represent an important means of keeping earlier worlds 'up to date,' i.e. relevant according to the norms and values of new social constellations (see Rigney 351).

It is important to note that remediation is not restricted to specific contents but can also choose forms and aesthetic strategies as its objects. In fact, cultural knowledge not only consists of systems of ideals, beliefs, presuppositions and convictions which provide agreed-upon codes for understanding the world (see Erll). Rather it is also a formal and even aesthetic construct. Individual media can make use of a whole range of structural features to create suggestive epistemic constellations and bolster their claim to cultural authority. Thus, the making of worlds is also about giving a symbolic form to what is constructed as a world, i.e. of narratively (or visually) structuring these representations and adding aesthetic value to them.

By means of intermedial procedures the epistemic configurations are related to each other in such a way that their meaning is co-constituted in a successive back and forth of appreciative interpretations, commentaries, or critical parodies (see Jäger). The intermedial dynamics of specific media offers are constituted by all the appreciative commentaries, parodies, translations, adaptations and imitations that a particular offer has given rise to. Typically, culturally formative media offers are embedded in a tight network of intermedial references which recall, reaffirm or revise a text's or film's interpretations of cultural knowledge, endowing them with cultural authority and marking them out as significant patterns of signification. Thus, a tight network of other medial representations and commentaries structures the reception process and endows specific media offers and their figures of knowledge with their cultural power (see Rigney).

The trans- and intermedial dynamics of cultural worldmaking contribute to the stabilisation and solidification of specific figures of knowledge, as well as to their symbolic forms of narrative (or iconic) structuring. Arguably, all figures of knowledge derive their potential to organise the cultural knowledge about, for instance, gender or national self and other, from repeated processes of representation in a variety of texts, genres, and media. Recursive processes of inter- and transmedial representation endow specific figures with an aura of authenticity, thus producing powerful reality effects. Hence, rather than referring to what one might cautiously call 'historical reality,' cultural knowledge relates to earlier medial representations, be it in fiction, documentary texts, TV, films, or songs (see Erll 392). By thus linking specific epistemic constellations to preceding medial representations, an indexical relation between representation and reality is suggested which endows media offers with their peculiar sense of authenticity and cultural power.

5.

Even the patient reader will by now be longing for some flesh to be put to this conceptual skeleton. Using the foregoing theoretical underpinnings as our point of departure, we will explore the inter- and transmedial dynamics of worldmaking in eighteenth-century British media (see Neumann, *Rhetorik der Nation*). In order to illustrate the dynamic functioning of worldmaking we will focus on one cultural phenomenon in particular, namely on national stereotyping, i.e. images of self and other: In the eighteenth century, "[t]he habit of pitting unfavourable and unflattering images of foreigners against the outstanding qualities of the 'true-born' of 'freeborn Englishman' became especially prominent" (Nünning 73). The eighteenth century witnessed unprecedented increases in cultural contact with national others, contacts which clearly spurred the struggle for political and cultural hegemony. Representations of national others helped interpret the striking experience of cultural difference and satisfied the need for national self-assurance.

In the eighteenth century, the discourse related to national characters formed a lively and culturally controversial issue (see Hayman). Certainly, cultural stereotyping is not an invention of this century but dates back as far as written records reach and seems to be present in all human societies. What is new, however, in the eighteenth century is the increasing nationalisation of tribal and ethnic stereotypes (see Leerssen 272). As Michael Meehan has observed, the broad movement that can be discerned in England (later Great Britain) through the eighteenth century "is one of a nationalisation of ideas that had their origins in party propaganda, but which lost the tang of factional dispute employment against collective foes, against radicals at home and enemies abroad, in the name of all that was truly English" (20).

In eighteenth-century Britain, national stereotyping manifests itself in a broad spectrum of genres and media, ranging from pamphlets, journals, newspapers, hack histories, and poems to travelogues, novels, and drama. In the following, we will present a brief outline of the transmedial scope of national stereotyping to illustrate the dynamic mechanism of worldmaking. Regarding the premises of media studies we are particularly interested in three questions: first, which media-specific features are used to construct persuasive national images? Second, how are specific images relayed across media and genres, i.e. how are they stabilised by inter- and transmedial strategies? And third, how are specific images distributed by social institutions on the levels of production and reception? Publishing houses, reviews, advertisements—each is a specific social institutionalisation which contributes to solidifying certain images of self and other. In order to illustrate the dynamic functioning of worldmaking we will focus on one stereotype in particular, namely the image of the freeborn, commonsensical and prosperous Briton and its counterpart, the oppressed, "vain, proud, poor and slothful" French (Smollett 51).

As far as genres central to the negotiation of national stereotypes are concerned, eighteenth-century travel writing provides a particularly important arena. Because most Britons lacked first-hand experience of foreign countries, seemingly authentic evidence played a major role in imagining cultural otherness, i.e. in the making of foreign worlds. Travelogues are apt to respond to this need since this genre is typically assumed to provide knowledge which is rooted in direct experience. Tobias Smollett's *Travels Through France and Italy* (1979 [1766]) is one of many travelogues in which the construction of the French other functions powerfully to define a consensual formulation of British national character. Going abroad provides Smollett's persona with ever new occasions for fashioning his own British identity against the background of what he constructs as typically foreign. In particular, the nature and effects of French tyranny, in relation to British liberty and prosperity, are a persistent theme of the *Travels*.

Besides numerous explicit references to national characteristics in dialogues and descriptions, national stereotyping manifests itself in at least three distinct features. First, Smollett's narrator uses the semanticisation of space to construct an ideologically charged nationscape that reflects differences between France and Britain in a seemingly natural way. The minute descriptions of French cities and landscapes appear to provide an accurate, objective and authentic impression of reality, thus achieving a naturalisation of the storyworld and its values. In the *Travels*, the hierarchies between the dominant British and deficient French cultures take shape in the binary polarity between North and South. The further Smollett travels to the South of France, the dirtier the country appears to become: "They have not even the implements of cleanliness in this country" (Smollett 33). As a seemingly transparent reflection of the French character, space serves as a naturalised sign for the equally corrupted nature of its inhabitants: "If there is no cleanliness among these people, much less shall we find delicacy, which is the cleanliness of the mind. Indeed they are utter strangers to what we call common decency" (ibid.). Having thus paved the path for a promulgation of a sense of the real, the narrator exploits the presentation of the setting to construct a spatial opposition between 'here' and 'there,' which he then ties to semantic oppositions (between prosperity and poverty, rationality and irrationality, political liberty and oppression).

Second, the constellation of characters serves to insistently dramatise cultural difference. The travelogue features the odd foreigner who metonymically represents the national other, thus throwing into high relief the peculiarities of the British character. Time and again, Smollett's narrator derides the French as "a people" among which "there are undoubtedly many circumstances truly ridiculous" (Smollett 48). In particular, the French love of fashion and their levity spur his xenophobia: "I will be bold to affirm, that France is the general reservoir from which all the absurdities of false taste, luxury, and extravagance have overflowed the different kingdoms and states of Europe" (52). In the *Travels*, the body of the French, their manners and styles of dressing constitute the base to define a particular kind of social and moral order. This metonymy, which takes the individual body as representative of the social entity, is a master-trope upon which cultural categories are inscribed. He criticises French aristocrats for allowing fashion to dominate their lives, thus succumbing to a form of cultural dependency and ultimately effeminising themselves (see Smollett 56–57). The formation of feminised men has larger consequences since it leads to the feminisation of the body politic, which for the narrator is a weak and inactive body. His own assertion of remaining unadorned and free plays on eighteenth-century middle-class concepts of citizenship, common sense, and patriotism, thus bolstering claims to moral and political virtue.

Third, the melodramatic plot is another element of worldmaking in the *Travels*, helping to give closure to the events and endowing the constructed images of national self and other with an intelligible pattern. The melodramatic plot is useful to worldmaking precisely because it reduces a potentially threatening cultural complexity "to the simplicities of the essential romance terminology: heroes and villains" (Hulme 211), and thus effectively normalises, fixes and codifies the nationalist ideology. Thus, the melodramatic pattern helps make the national characterisations meaningful and memorable by figuring the images in a structured way: in the *Travels*, the plot is structured by the protagonist's quest for identity—on an individual and collective level—through a symbolic descent into the figurative underworld of France and a corresponding ascent to self-recognition and wish-fulfilment, i.e. his return to England and the recognition of the true, now empirically confirmed, superiority. Smollett's persona can return home feeling optimistic about his nation because in educating his British audience about the dangers of French aristocratic cosmopolitanism, he has created the basis of an ideal polity committed to a new set of civic virtues—virtues that he himself embodies (see Bowers 13). Hence, the melodramatic plot is used to ratify the norms of a specific group, i.e. of the middling sort of Britons who valued liberty, common-sense, and independence as central to British nationhood.

As indicated above, the worlds that are constructed in Smollett's *Travels* are not significant in themselves, but derive their cultural significance from intermedial and transmedial dynamics. The intermedial dynamics of worldmaking are constituted by all the appreciative commentaries, parodies, translations, adaptations, and imitations that a particular text has given rise to. Smollett's *Travels Through France and Italy* is embedded in a tight network of intermedial references which recall, reaffirm or revise the text's interpretations of cultural otherness, endowing them with cultural authority and marking them out as significant patterns of signification. Smollett's travelogue was greeted by contemporary critics as a work which "may be of infinite service to our country, by giving some check to the follies of our Apes, male and female, of French fashions and politeness, with whom we are over run" (qtd. in Kelly 184). Other critics praised it as a work of a "man of sense, divested of partiality, reasoning with freedom" (*Critical Review* 406). For readers of the *St. James's Chronicle*, as well as for many who formulated their judgment independently, Smollett's *Travels* were congenial in presenting a domestic and manly patriotism, offering a 'just' representation of the French character:

> In this Paris-loving Age, we will venture to say, they will not be without their Merit also, in keeping others at home; as after the contemptible, but just Character given in them, of the French, no one who is not through Necessity driven there, will wish to spend his Money among them. (*St. James's Chronicle*, 8 May 1766)

Moreover, other travelogues which responded to Smollett function as consolidating factors for the national stereotypes constructed in the *Travels*. For Philip Thicknesse's *Observations on the Customs and Manners of the French Nation, in a Series of Letters, in which the Nation is vindicated from the Misrepresentations of some Late Writers* (1766) as well as for Laurence Sterne's *A Sentimental Journey through France and Italy* (1768), the *Travels* are a privileged point of reference, if only as a punch bag, in their discussion of the peculiarities of the French and English character. All of these commentaries and renarrations illustrate that worldmaking is not produced in a single medium, but through the interplay of diverse media. These reviews and renarrations are therefore both a means of reinforcing constructed stereotypes, and a testimony to their cultural power and social relevance.

Besides the intermedial dynamics, the transmediality of worldmaking contributes to the cultural power of the definitions of self and other created in the *Travels*. The *Travels* are located at the interface of a wide range of other texts and media which take up, translate, renarrate or remediate the images of the manly, commonsensical and freeborn Briton and the effeminate, vain and oppressed French (without necessarily referring consciously to Smollett's travelogue). Thus, the stereotypes that are constructed in and disseminated by the *Travels* have to be read against a whole range of culturally circulating texts and other media, each of which employs genre- or media-specific devices to deal with these images. Here a few examples will have to suffice to illustrate the transmedial dynamics that turn some national images into culturally powerful knowledge and establish them as socially relevant patterns of signification.

Eighteenth-century comedies are certainly among those media which were central in constructing and disseminating the stereotype of the freeborn, commonsensical and manly Englishman, pitting him against his counterpart, the image of the oppressed, vain and effeminate French. Susanna Centlivre's *A Bold Stroke for a Wife* (1718), Samuel Foote's *The Englishman in Paris* (1753) and *The Englishman Return'd from Paris* (1756), and Hannah Cowley's *The Belle's Stratagem* (1780) are just four comedies which centre on these stereotypes. In comedies, the rhetoric of national character manifests itself on manifold structural levels: prologues, epilogues and dialogues are often used to explicitly explore and indeed construct national differences. Moreover, the constellation of the characters and the perspective structure of many of the plays are typically organised in terms of a rhetoric of 'us' and 'them' (see Nünning 79), thus highlighting national peculiarities. Frequently, these binary oppositions are supported by the presentation of the setting, i.e. an imaginative geography, drawing a boundary between an idealised 'here' and a seemingly derogated 'there.' Last but not least, comedies often exploit the romance plot in order to translate the conflict between a loving couple and the blocking characters into an antagonism between national self and others, thus illustrating the successive installation of national ideals and rendering patriotism unambiguously attractive. Of course, the performative quality of drama gives an added value to the national stereotypes: dramatic performances derive their media-specific power from the embodied enactment of national stereotypes. They translate verbally mediated images into full-blown *imagines agentes*, which communicate national values to the British audience as part of their embodied practices.

National stereotyping also structurally controls eighteenth-century poems, many of which are quite "self-conscious, motivated exercises in the production of the images of the nation" (Kaul 19). Poets who evoke the image of the freeborn Englishman and his abhorrence of French tyranny include, among others, Alexander Pope, Richard Blackmore, Mark Akenside, James Thomson, Edward Young, Samuel Johnson, Richard Glover, and John Dyer. The logic of apostrophe and personification, the use of imagery and tropes, the compression of the subject-matter and the often highly condensed language render poems highly potent—and in the eighteenth century indeed recommended—vehicles for producing weighty images of national character. Because poems are usually extremely selective, bringing into focus only certain aspects, occluding many others, and because repetition is very much their principle of organisation, they are extremely conducive to national stereotyping. Frequently, poems such as Samuel Johnson's "London" (1738) invoke a weighty world-picture, "particularly one appropriate to a Britain proving itself [...] great at home and abroad" (Kaul 5), and do so in verses that are populist in their ballad-like ease.

In order to fully appreciate the transmedial dynamics of worldmaking in the eighteenth century it is also necessary to acknowledge the role played by British historiography, novels, newspapers, magazines, songs, and leaflets (see Neumann, *Rhetorik der Nation* "Cultural and Historical Imagology"). Finally, one might at least mention in passing that the dynamics of worldmaking were by no means confined to texts. In particular, satirical prints played a central role in constructing, disseminating and transmitting images of the Englishman and the foreigner. By deploying an 'iconography of national character,' satirical prints, as for instance Richard Hogarth's famous *The Roast Beef of Old England* (1749), accentuated the difference between the freeborn Englishman and the enslaved and impoverished Frenchman. Satirical prints abound with what Duffy has aptly called "gastronomic chauvinism" (34) and thus exploit the popular patriotic contrast between a well-fed Englishman, with roast beef and frothing ale by his side, and his meagre French counterpart who has to feed upon such awful edibles as frogs, snails, and the proverbial *soupe-maigre* (see also Spiering 53). The iconic nationalisation of popular motives, a ubiquitous strategy in times of crisis, allows direct visual comparisons between French despotism and English prosperity, comparisons which could appeal to almost all classes (also to illiterate members of the lower classes) and mobilise active cooperation in order to repel the threat of a French invasion.

Thus, it is clear from the above that the process of worldmaking is a complex and dynamic one, which can only be assessed by going beyond the analysis of individual works to the study of inter- and transmedial interplay with other genres and media. It is important to note that the relationship between different media is not only a formal issue but also an issue of the forms that sociability takes, the kinds of institutions, values and knowledge formed by a media culture. By focussing on the inter- and transmedial dynamics it becomes possible to rethink worldmaking as a plural, open and necessarily contested process. This process is also a political one. At stake is the power of media to transform heterogeneous data and events into a world, a universe in which human agency appears as a meaningful and significant part of a shared environment. From this perspective, politics is essentially a negotiation of different forms of worldmaking, reflecting different social needs, values, and interests.[2] Yet, as has been shown, an account of the power of worldmaking or of the medium in which these worlds are created is not to be had simply by reading it as a representation of power relations that influenced its production. One must pay attention to the specificity of effects and to the kinds of

---

2   See the contribution of Frederik Tygstrup in this volume.

media-specific structures employed by a medium at a particular historical juncture (see Mitchell 3).

6.

After this exemplary analysis of the intermedial dynamics of processes of worldmaking on the level of specific cultural knowledge and evaluation, let us get back to the idea that media do not only mould forms of social knowledge, norms, and values by intermedially representing and debating stereotypes, narratives, images etc.. Rather the mere social availability and use of specific media technologies can also be seen as an agent of worldmaking (see Gell). Media are not just artifacts or products, but also agents.

Within media studies and media history, the notion that media technologies are never 'neutral' but play an active role in the construction of reality has axiomatic status. This idea can be traced back as far as Plato's *Phaidros*. In the early twentieth century, Canadian media theorist Harold A. Innis introduced the distinction between time-binding and space-binding media and argued that the dominating media technologies of a time play a seminal role in defining whether a culture will be oriented rather towards a stabilisation and expansion in time or in space (see Innis). Many scholars such as Marshall McLuhan, Vilém Flusser, and Friedrich Kittler have developed and elaborated the idea of media technologies shaping our ways of worldmaking, and have pushed this line of argument in different directions.

Today, the term 'mediatisation' has become a new keyword in the debate on the ways in which media shape our experience of the world and social and cultural life, i.e. in the ways which media play an active part in processes of worldmaking (see Lundby). Sonia Livingstone has self-critically and perhaps somewhat ironically titled her ICA presidential address 2008 "On the Mediation of Everything" (see Livingstone). Here she analyses the various terms which are currently being debated including 'mediation,' 'mediatisation,' 'medialisation,' or 'mediasation.' Vast and vague as the discussion may currently seem, social scientists increasingly argue that the media are no longer one field of social action among others (political, economical, educational systems etc.), but that they play a more fundamental role for every social system or field:

> It seems that we have moved from a social analysis in which the mass media comprise one among many influential but independent institutions whose relations with the media can be usefully analyzed to a social analysis in which everything is mediated, the consequence being that all influential institutions in society

have themselves been transformed, reconstituted, by contemporary processes of mediation. (Livingstone 2)

Even though it is debatable which terminologies, theories, and models may best describe the relation of media to our social and cultural realities, it seems safe to say that the key role that media play in our individual, social and cultural ways of worldmaking can hardly be overestimated.

References

Bowers, Terence. "Reconstituting the National Body in Smollett's *Travels Through France and Italy*." *Eighteenth-Century Life* 21.1 (1997): 1–25.
Centlivre, Susanna. *A Bold Stroke for a Wife*. 1718. Ed. Thalia Stathas. London: William Clowes, 1969.
Cowley, Hannah. *The Belle's Stratagem*. 1780. *Eighteenth-Century Women Dramatists*. Ed. Melinda C. Finberg. Oxford: Oxford UP, 2001.
The Critical Review: Or, Annals of Literature 21 (June 1766): 401–6.
Defoe, Daniel. *The True-Born Englishman: A Satyr*. London: n.p., 1701.
Duffy, Michael. *The Englishman and the Foreigner: The English Satirical Print 1600–1832*. Cambridge: Chadwyck-Healey, 1986.
Erll, Astrid. "Literature, Film, and the Mediality of Cultural Memory." *Cultural Memory Studies: An International and Interdisciplinary Handbook*. Eds. Astrid Erll, and Ansgar Nünning. Berlin/New York: de Gruyter, 2008. 389–98.
Foote, Samuel. *The Englishman in Paris*. 1753. Dublin: Richard James, 1773.
—. *The Englishman Return'd From Paris*. Dublin: Richard James, 1756.
Frye, Northrop. *Anatomy of Criticism*. Princeton, NJ: Princeton UP, 1986.
Gell, Alfred. *Art and Agency: An Anthropological Theory*. Oxford: Oxford UP, 1998.
Hayman, John G. "Notions on National Characters in the Eighteenth Century." *Huntington Library Quarterly* 35 (1971/72): 1–17.
Hörisch, Jochen. *Der Sinn und die Sinne: Eine Geschichte der Medien*. Frankfurt a.M.: Eichborn, 2001.
Hulme, Peter. *Colonial Encounters: Europe and the Native Caribbean, 1492–1797*. London: Routledge, 1986.
Innis, Harold A. *The Bias of Communication*. 1951. Toronto et al.: U of Toronto P, 2006.
Jäger, Ludwig. "Gedächtnis als Verfahren: Zur transkriptiven Logik der Erinnerung." *Mythosaktualisierungen: Tradierungs- und Generierungspotentiale einer alten Erinnerungsform*. Eds. Stephanie Wodianka, and Dietmar Rieger. Berlin/New York: de Gruyter, 2006. 57–80.
Johnson, Samuel. *London: A Poem*. London: R. Dodsley, 1738.
Kaul, Suvir. *Poems of Nation, Anthems of Empire: English Verse in the Long Eighteenth Century*. Charlottesville, VA: UP of Virginia, 2000.
Kelly, Lionel, ed. *Tobias Smollett: The Critical Heritage*. New York: Routledge, 1987.
Leerssen, Joep. "The Rhetoric of National Character: A Programmatic Survey." *Poetics Today* 21 (2000): 267–92.
Leschke, Rainer. *Einführung in die Medientheorie*. München: Wilhelm Fink, 2003.

Livingstone, Sonia. "On the Mediation of Everything: ICA Presidential Address 2008." *Journal of Communication* 59 (2009): 1–18.
Lundby, Knut, ed. *Mediatization: Concept, Changes, Consequences*. New York et al.: Peter Lang, 2009.
Meehan, Michael. *Liberty and Poetics in Eighteenth-Century England*. London: Croom Helm, 1986.
Mitchell, W.J.T. "Introduction." *Landscape and Power*. Ed. W.J.T. Mitchell. Chicago: Chicago UP, 2002. 1–4.
Neumann, Birgit. *Die Rhetorik der Nation in britischer Literatur und anderen Medien des 18. Jahrhunderts*. Trier: WVT, 2009.
—. "Towards a Cultural and Historical Imagology: The Rhetoric of National Character in 18th-Century Literature and other Media." *EJES* 13.3 (2009): 275–91.
Nünning, Ansgar. "Historicizing British Cultural Studies: Patriotic Xenophobia and the Rhetoric of National Character in Eighteenth-Century British Literature." *Journal for the Study of British Culture* 1 (2002): 69–94.
Rigney, Ann. "The Dynamics of Remembrance: Texts between Monumentality and Morphing." *Cultural Memory Studies: An International and Interdisciplinary Handbook*. Eds. Astrid Erll, and Ansgar Nünning. Berlin/New York: de Gruyter, 2008. 345–56.
Schmidt, Siegfried J. "Der Medienkompaktbegriff." *Was ist ein Medium?* Eds. Stefan Münker, and Alexander Roesler. Frankfurt a.M.: Suhrkamp, 2008: 144–57.
—. *Kalte Faszination: Medien, Kultur, Wissenschaft in der Mediengesellschaft*. Weilerswist: Velbrück Wissenschaft, 2000.
Smollett, Tobias. *Travels Through France and Italy*. Ed. Frank Felsenstein. 1766. Oxford: Oxford UP, 1979.
Spiering, Menno. "Food, Phagophobia and English National Identity." *Food, Drink and Identity in Europe*. Ed. Thomas M. Wilson. Amsterdam: Rodopi, 2006. 31–48.
The St. James's Chronicle, or the British Evening-Post. London: n.p, May 1766.
Sterne, Laurence. *A Sentimental Journey and Continuation of the Bramine's Journal*. 1768. Eds. Melvyn New, and Geoffrey Day. Indianapolis: Hackett, 2006.
Thicknesse, Philip. *Observations on the Customs and Manners of the French Nation, in a Series of Letters, in which the Nation is vindicated from the Misrepresentations of some late Writers*. London: Robert Davis, 1766.
Turner, Katherine. *British Travel Writers in Europe 1750–1800: Authorship, Gender, and National Identity*. Aldershot: Ashgate, 2001.
Zierold, Martin. *Gesellschaftliche Erinnerung: Eine medienkulturwissenschaftliche Perspektive*. Berlin/New York: de Gruyter, 2006.

Remarks on the Historicity of the Media Concept

Knut Ove Eliassen

1. Introduction

From the beginning of the modern world, questions of anthropology seem to have been intrinsically linked to those of technology. According to the testimony of Samuel Johnson it is to Benjamin Franklin we owe the famous dictum "Man is a tool-making animal." The phrase was later, and famously, further elaborated by Thomas Carlyle: "Without tools he is nothing, with them he is all" (152). Many of the prominent figures of the philosophy and sociology of the nineteenth and twentieth century have made important contributions to the understanding of how the historicity of mind and body can only be understood by taking into consideration, as Heidegger famously put it, the question of technology. Historically situated life worlds may be inhabited by bodies, but they are built and maintained by technologies; thus without *techné*, no *oikos*, no human dwelling. Life forms and worlds of experience find their conditions of possibility in a technological substratum. The *Bildung* of the five senses, the young Karl Marx wrote, not only in the aesthetic, interior sense, but also in the physiological sense, was the product of the labour of the entire world history—"eine Arbeit der ganzen bisherigen Weltgeschichte" (Marx and Engels 541). *Techné*, our technologically shaped skills, is that by which our worlds are brought to be and given shape; without *techné* there is no life world, no *Lichtung*, no anthropology.

The construction of worlds takes place at the nexus of bodies and technologies. Technology is not external to the body, neither to the world; it is the in-between that mediates, participating in and forming the tool-wielding subject as the basis of the ecology in which it acts. Technology is an inherent part of the history of the human species, as Leroi-Gourhan has shown in *Le Geste et la parole* (1964), and the development of its genotype. Neither world nor body, exist before mediation takes place; mediation is the act by which the two are brought forth and their opposition relation established.

That which we in common parlance refer to as 'the media' is a special case, a particular historical subset of the many interfaces technology has produced between man and world, or rather, the many particular man-world relations technology as the in-between has generated. Media, in the sense of 'communication media,' are mediating technologies of a particular sort, belonging to a particular historical era, that we, to be brief, will call modernity. It is generally recognised that media are among modernity's most influential forces of world production. Media are nexuses where history, body, and technology intersect in what has been called media ecologies; ecologies that spawn life forms and worlds of experience.

While there is no lack of penetrating and analytically productive sociological definitions of the media concept, considerable less energy has gone into elaborating a media concept that takes into account the concept's own historicity. Even in high-quality work with explicit media history perspectives, analyses of the historicity of the semantics of the media concept are often dealt with in superficial ways. Media are treated and applied as an analytical conceptual tool that is not in any way marked by the history that is inherent neither in the concept nor in what it refers to. Bearing in mind the nominalist principle that concepts have no claim to ontological reality prior to their elaborations, an analysis of the historicity of media requires the historical circumscription of the media concept.

It is generally acknowledged that the media are powerful agents of world production—"Ways of Worldmaking" (Goodman)—the lesson of nominalism is that concepts are not less so. Worldmaking should here be understood in a literal sense as bringing forth a world to inhabit. World is here synonymous with milieu or *Umwelt*, that is, that which surrounds us and which creates a middle for us to inhabit, while also allowing for and giving form to our interaction with other entities. What, to once again to recur to young Marx, separates human beings from animals, such as bees, in bringing forth worlds is that, contrary to animals, they make mental representations of what they undertake. Thus world making also entails the symbolic production of worlds, of which media are an eminent example. This also explains the affinities between media theory and phenomenology.

2. Phenomenology and Media

Modern media studies have been heavily marked by Marshall McLuhan's influence and his insistence of analysing media with regard to their consequences for the ways in which we perceive, construct, and inhabit the world. According to McLuhan, the history of the human sensorium, or formulated differently, that of Western subjectivity, cannot be separated from the history of the media. One well-known and striking illustration of this is his division of the history of Western civilisation into two large media regimes, the concrete, auditive-tactile of the oral pre-modern society and the abstract, visual one of the "Gutenberg Galaxy."

Thus at least since McLuhan, a recurrent topic in cultural theory has been how modern media serve as powerful agents of world making. It has become a generally accepted position to claim that not only have modern media technologies had a massive impact on the social and cultural structures of the Western world, but that they have in fact most profoundly influenced and changed our forms of cognition, informing even the larger framework of time and space that grounds the cognitive interfaces through which we regulate our interaction with the world. Modern media are more than mere representational technologies that distribute information; they provide the schemata that format modernity's quotidian world of experience. The dominant media technologies function as what McLuhan famously called "extensions of man" (*Understanding Media*). But they are more than mere prostheses as they in fact take part in the shaping of the procedures of the cognitive mappings that establish and sustain our life worlds. The historicity of the human sensorium is thus deeply marked by the history of media technologies.

According to another popular McLuhanesque notion, the famous formula of "the medium is the message," (*Understanding Media* 7) the fundamental nature of media is to be found in their intransitivity. Put more plainly, this means that the content of a message cannot be separated from the media by which it is transmitted. Such a perspective, it must be added, is adverse to a conception of media as channels of communication, to the idea that logos is, as it were, the inherent *telos* of communication technologies. On the contrary, it follows from this line of reasoning that logos is neither the cause of nor the reason for mediation, but should be rather seen as its product. To oversimplify: Just like the content of a poem cannot be transferred to a novel, the content of the radio cannot be transferred to television; their reality effects are incommensurable. Or to paraphrase Niklas Luhmann's formula: After the book, we think in the format of the book.

Given this premise, the question arises of how the various and different worlds made possible by the multitude of modern media coexist and how their internal differences are negotiated. A common solution to that question is—to rewrite an old Marxist formula—to claim that the dominant thought is that of the dominant media form, and that other media forms emulate this with various degrees of success. Conceptual elaborations like Norbert Bolz's notion of "media clusters" ("Medienverbände,"

Am Ende der Gutenberg-Galaxis 143), or, for that matter, Neil Postman's "media ecologies" ("Reformed English Curriculum" 161), are further developments of this idea, implying that media are organised in technological ensembles with a certain level of compatibility; if not in content, so at least in function. Examples of this would be the various media of the printed word, the analogue media of the nineteenth century or the electronic media of the twentieth, to refer to some of the more commonplace ones.

A term like 'media ecology' neatly sums up how the technologies of information produce a particular life world, providing the forms of experience that make up and give shape to the interiority of the socially constituted individual. If this argument is extended to the concept of media itself, an obvious concern is how and by what terms the circulation and organisation of information in the age before the media might be conceptualised. Such an approach has the bonus of permitting the analysis to escape from the immanentism of media-formatted epistemology, emphasised, for instance, by Norbert Bolz (45), thereby indirectly shedding light on the specificity of the media-informed life world of modernity.

It follows from the assumption that one media cannot be translated into another that media history must be deeply marked by discontinuity. If the function of the medium is not primarily to serve as an amplifier for logos, and its essence resides in its intransitivity, media history cannot be envisaged as the history of technological progress in the service of communication. Given that intermedia relations are characterised by mutual intranslatability, the implication is that the content of older media remains inaccessible to a thought formatted by later media. Or as Charles Baudelaire lamented, according to Walter Benjamin, the communication forms of emerging modernity had made poetry both obsolete and inaccessible for experience. The notion of the heterogeneous nature of media is thus easily combined with the resources of radical historicism and its idea of historical discontinuities, for instance with those found in Foucault's notion of an "archaeology of knowledge." The Foucauldian perspective offers a large number of possibilities. Its historicism can be coupled with the historicism already latent in media theory's emphasis on the non-negotiable differences between oral and literal cultures. And Foucault's stress on the material and technological aspects of power structures can be fused with the study of the technologies, practices, and institutions of media.

However, it remains an open question if the full consequences of the historicity inherent in the Foucauldian impulse have been taken in full. Foucauldian discourse analysis emphasises the shifting historical semantic content of scientific and philosophical concepts and explicitly criticises a notion of the history of ideas that sees concepts as vehicles for the accumulation of tradition and historical continuities. On the contrary: for Foucault concepts derive their content and function from the discursive orders in which they participate and should not be analysed separately from these. What I would like to suggest is that rather to retroactively apply a term that lexically belongs to modernity, or at least to the nineteenth century, as an analytical tool with general validity, the term media itself must be seen as a part of a particular and limited discursive order. It belongs to what one could call 'the archive of modernity.' To be able to get a grip on the historicity of the term, it might be helpful to have a closer look at its semantic history.

3. The Historicity of Media

What today is understood by the term 'media' in the Germanic and Romance languages owes a great deal to Marshall McLuhan. Until the impact of *The Gutenberg Galaxy* (1962) and *Understanding Media* (1964) had reached beyond the narrow circles of academia, what most people associated with the word 'medium' was a person endowed with paranormal psychological powers. However the word has a much longer history, going back to Latin *medium* or 'middle.' And McLuhan was not the inventor of the modern meaning of the term. Its modern semantics can, according to John Durham Peters (*Speaking Into the Air*), be traced back to the years around 1850, to the decade following two of the major events in the history of communication technology: the inventions of telegraphy and photography.

Like any analytical tool, the concept of media thus has a history of its own. Not only are the current semantics and analytical status of the term the result of centuries of conceptual elaborations; the concept also orders, organises and produces the epistemology of the field in which it plays, such an important role (yielding institutions like media departments and research centres, political initiatives, and so forth, as well as retroactively structuring its own prehistory). The term 'media' does not exist or function independently of the techniques, technologies, communication forms, and practices it denotes, nor of the institutions that uphold it and in turn are being upheld by it; the notion is neither arbitrary nor epiphenomenal, but an element in the processes of the epistemological field it circumscribes and may thus serve as a basis for an immanent historical analysis. The question is thus: Is 'media' an adequate term to analyse and describe the technologies that transferred information and formatted worlds in the period before the term receives its present meaning? Particularly if it is correct that its modern signification, to be a "channel of mass communication," did not appear before the late 1840s? (According to the *Oxford English Dictionary* two of the earliest examples are from 1850 and 1851. In the first case, found in the American newspaper *The Princeton Review*, magazines and journals are described as "media of influence." The other, taken from Charles Dickens's journal *Household Words*, refers to the commercials being projected on stage curtains in theatres during pauses.) Thus it might be appropriate to ask whether or not 'media' must be considered an anachronism with regard to any historical analyses of communication forms that antedate the mass media ecologies of the nineteenth century. Or, put differently: maybe media should be considered both a term and a phenomenon belonging to an era and social formation that is often referred to as modernity.

It appears that the term up until the nineteenth century was employed primarily in the singular. For a long time its significations seem to have been organised around two semantic clusters: A medium was either a material means of expression or the milieu in which a communication took place. A quotation from Francis Bacon will illustrate the former: "Cogitations be expressed by the Medium of Words" (138). The latter sense of the term can be exemplified with the scientific notion of *aether*, a substance that in the physics of the seventeenth century allowed for the transmission of light waves, and in the eighteenth century permitted natural forces such as electricity or magnetism to work at a distance. One should note that 'medium' at this time does not connote technology or invention, or even *techné*. Rather, a medium was either a representation (both separating and joining) or a milieu that created contact between separate entities. It appears that the plural form did not become common usage until the nineteenth century, and then significantly in relation to technologies and cultural phenomena that later, in the early twentieth century, were to be referred to as the 'mass media.'

In his study on the history of the visuality of the nineteenth century, *Techniques of the Observer*, Jonathan Crary (1990) showed how the development within physics and the advent of new sciences like biology and psychology entailed a new understanding of the nature of human perception. Contrary to eighteenth-century notions of the sensory apparatus, the physiology of the nineteenth century no longer conceived of the senses as open receivers to a materially given outside world, Crary argues, but as productive faculties, most famously illustrated by the late-eighteenth-century discovery of the visual phenomenon known as the after-image, the sensory impression that is left on the retina when we suddenly close our eyes. Henceforth, perception is essentially defined by its limits or flaws. From now on the human sensorium was a possible source of impure representation, due to noise produced by the sense organs themselves. In addition, one could now demonstrate that human perceptions were essentially marked by the limited 'band width' of the sensory channels; the early-nineteenth-century discovery of 'invisible light,' infrared and ultraviolet, fundamentally undermined the belief in the exactitude of sense perception.

The nineteenth-century stereoscope plays an important role in Crary's narrative, as it challenged the commonly accepted idea of the human subject as a stable centre of perception. It is the shortcoming of human perception that is exploited by stereoscopy. Our eyes show us a three-dimensional and continuous room even though what we in fact are looking at are two flat and separate surfaces. In this perspective the stereoscope becomes an emblem for the relation that modern media theory establishes between the media technologies and the human sensorium: it demonstrates the shortcomings of human abilities and at the same time provides the tool that helps us overcome them. It is, however, more than a perceptual prosthesis; it does not enhance human vision but replaces 'natural' vision with nothing less than a simulacrum. The natural functioning is thus replaced by a technologically produced illusion.

Crary is not alone in highlighting the first half of the nineteenth century as a turning point in the man-media relationship and the history of information technologies. In *The Language of New Media* (2001), Lev Manovich, another widely read media theorist, suggests (although his errand differs somewhat from Crary) that the modern media regime springs from two nineteenth-century inventions: the daguerreotype of Louis Daguerre and the analytical engine of Charles Babbage. As means of reproducing and computing data, respectively, these two inventions are seen by Manovich as technological dispositifs of later information systems. However, there is one element missing in Manovich's account of the grounding technologies of modern media: the technology of distribution, Samuel Morse's electrical telegraph. With this, a modern dispositif for registering, storing, and distributing data was in place.

What the telegraph shares with photography and the analogue computer is not only that the information processes are automated, but also that their mode of operation eludes human perception. This is a central concern for another of today's leading media historians, Friedrich Kittler. In *Optische Medien* (2002) he argues that the removal of the human agent from the communication loop is one of the decisive features of the new communication technologies of the first half of the nineteenth century. In these new information circuits such as the telegraph, photography, or Babbage's analytical engine, the dominant forms of information processing were no longer mediated by eye and hand, passing through the interiority of an individual occupying the middle position in the chain of transmission—as was the case with older communications systems such as painting, text copying, and optical telegraphs. In modern discourse networks human operators are, as Crary argued, sources of noise and error, and thus beyond the control mechanisms of the system.

Following up the leads left by Kittler, Crary, and Manovich, as well as those that can be gathered from the semantic history of the term, a formula like "modern media" has the ring of a pleonasm. Media is an inherent part of modernity; it is one of its constituents. Hence the question if the term should not be considered a "false friend," to borrow a formula from the French "mediologue" Régis Debray:

> In *mediology*, "medio" does not signify media nor medium but *mediations*, that is the dynamic assemblage of procedures and intermediary bodies that insert themselves between a production of signs and a production of events. These inbetweens belong to the "hybrids" (Bruno Latour), mediations that are at the same time technological, cultural, and social. (29, my translation)

Thus the benefit of replacing the media concept with that of mediation is twofold: first, the risk of anachronism and historical projections would be reduced when dealing with subject matter and time periods that pre-cede the emergence of the modern media term; second, a term like mediation downplays the techno-determinism that often accompanies the use of the media concept in historical analyses. Mediation is a concept that to a much larger degree allows for the inclusion of discursive, institutional, and political practices as well as contingencies in the analysis of how media technologies function.

4. Media Before the Media

It has occasionally been noted that neither the seventeenth nor the eighteenth century thematised on its channels of propagation of information in any explicit way, be they oral, written or pictorial (for instance by Joad Raymond). Despite seventeenth-century neologisms like 'propaganda' (from the Counter Reformation institution *Sacra Congregatio de propaganda fide*), or the use of terms like 'communication' and 'transfer,' there is to my knowledge, prior to the nineteenth century, no attempt at establishing overreaching conceptual elaborations aimed at determining the common aspects of such various media technologies as books, pamphlets, newsletters, posters, engravings, coins, and magic lanterns. Thus, if the demarcation between the flaws of the sensory apparatus and the automated signal flows plays such an important role in the establishment of the notion of modern media as the arguments of Crary and Kittler imply, it might be worthwhile to look at the how the idea of information flows is conceived from an eighteenth-century phenomenological point of view. If we accept Crary's Foucault-inspired claim that the eighteenth century did not perceive the human senses as epistemological obstacles in any absolute sense, and that we, furthermore, concede that the technologies, which the parlance of a subsequent era was to refer to as 'media,' were not defined essentially as means of representation and distribution external to the mind or the body (but also of a completely different nature), but rather were conceived along the line of the human sensorium, the possibility of a different configuration of the nature of the flows and processes of information emerges, and, of course, also the contours of a different anthropology.

A recent German Encyclopedia, *Ästhetische Grundbegriffe* ('Aesthetic Basic Terms'), claims that the first instance of a modern use of the word 'medium' in German is to be found in Johann Gottfried Herder's *Vom Erkennen und Empfinden der menschlichen Seele* (*On the Cognition and Sensation of the Human Soul*) from 1778. Schulte-Sasse quotes the following passage:

> Then my mind uses all the acquired skills and finesse of a blind man with his rod, to grope, to feel, to learn about distance, difference, measures; and in the end, without this medium we do not know anything, we must trust it. [...] For a thousand other sensing individuals through a thousand other media, the object may also appear as something quite different, even in itself be a complete abyss, of which I sense or suspect nothing; for me it is only that which my mind and its medium [...] present to me. (Qtd. from Schulte-Sasse 9, my translation)

The author of that particular article, "Medium," Jochen Schulte-Sasse, employs the passage reproduced above to advocate Herder's status as a precursor to later media theory. Rather than reading Herder as a pioneer in the field of media theory I am inclined to emphasise the elements in the quote that situate it within the framework of a "pre-media" reflection upon the nature of communication forms.

5. Molyneux's Problem

Herder's blind man is a recurrent topic in seventeenth- and eighteenth-century philosophy. One of its origins is Descartes's *Dioptrics* (1637). The philosopher suggests that someone deprived of sight could triangulate distances using crossed hand-held rods by sensing hand separation and wrist angles. Thus, a blind person might familiarise himself with his surroundings by tapping the objects around him with a rod. Descartes goes on to argue that perceptual operations of those with normal vision resemble the blind man in the way he with his rod probingly explores and maps the world. The similarities between visual and tactile perception of the world, between the eye and the rod, are also discussed in one of Descartes's earlier works, *Le Monde, ou Traité de la lumière* (1629-1633). The treatise suggests that light rays passing from luminous bodies to human eyes are material entities travelling instantaneously and in straight lines through space. The comparison of light rays and rods is thus not a didactic metaphor. In principle the light rays are analogue to rods. But as the particles that pass in straight and unbroken lines between an outer world and the human eye are so exceedingly small, the physical link that connects to the objects is thinner than all the other rods at our disposal, hence we are also unable to grasp the light rays as easily as the blind man grasps the rod in his hands (see Descartes, *Dioptrics* 181–83; 204; 220).

In the narratives of the history of philosophy, Descartes's mechanical explanation of vision is often introduced as the beginning of "Molyneux's problem." Named after the Irish natural philosopher, this remained for a long time a crucial point and a matter of contention in empiricist and sensualist philosophy. In 1690, it was famously articulated by John Locke in his *Essay Concerning Human Understanding* (but in fact paraphrasing Molyneux):

> Suppose a man born blind, and now adult, and taught by his touch to distinguish between a cube and a sphere of the same metal. Suppose then the cube and sphere were placed on a table, and the blind man made to see: query, whether by his sight, before he touched them, could he distinguish and tell which was the globe and which the cube? (Book 11, Chap. 9, Sect. 8, 84)

Descartes's rod-wielding man and Molyneux's problem converge in a series of questions: what are the functions of the sensory apparatus in the mapping and recognition of the world? How does it mediate between the mute outside of things and the sensitive inside of the body? And what are its relations to the talkative and denominating mind? And, last but not least, how are the shortcomings of the human senses improved upon, but thus also formatted? This set of problems was a recurrent topic in the epistemology of the eighteenth century, discussed by virtually every philosopher who had an opinion on epistemological issues: Leibniz, Berkeley, Voltaire, Diderot, Hume, La Mettrie and Condillac, to name a few. I will chose as my illustration Etienne Bonnot de Condillac's *Traité des Sensations*, originally published in 1754. Both as an analysis of perception and an anthropological essay its central question is: how is the information the mind gathers from the world that surrounds it mediated and organised?

6. Condillac's Statue

The starting point of Condillac's treatise is the fable of a statue in a garden that is brought to life. The statue is unusual in the sense that it has the same mental potential as someone who has never experienced any sense impressions. The statue's awakening is conceived as a parallel to the processes of human cognition, as a psychogenesis. Organised inwardly like any individual, it is however devoid not only of experience, but also of innate ideas or intuitive knowledge. The statue's mind is initially not a consciousness in the sense of a centre of reflexivity or a container of knowledge; hence the statue is at first completely absorbed by its initial sense impression, the pure presence of smell, creating its primary and basic psychological response, attention. From this simple stimuli model, the experience of sensation deepens as experience broadens and diversifies: some smells are pleasant, others less, and others are again unpleasant, even painful. On and off, presence or absence, pleasure or pain, are the basic principles for the statue's knowledge of its environment; and such binary oppositions continue to determine the operations of its mind even as these operations grow in complexity. Complexity follows from memory, the ability to recall sense impressions and to compare new ones with older ones. Recollections permit comparisons and thereby lay the ground for judgment; memories of earlier sense impressions lead the statue to the discovery of its own temporal existence, generating consciousness. By comparisons and judgments aided by memory, series of impressions are established, habits are formed, and general ideas born.

The two most prominent senses according to Condillac are sight and tactition, and these two function in an analogue way even though touch remains the most important one as it is through the hand that we establish a certain relationship and interact with the world that surrounds us: "The way in which the hands judge objects with the aid of a rod, of two rods, or even a larger number, resembles so strongly the way in which the eyes judge, aided by rays, that since Descartes, one usually explains the one problem by the other" (167). The nature of vision is repeatedly defined as tactile. "The eye can be seen as an organ that in a way has an infinite number of hands to grip an infinite number of rods" (Condillac 167).

After having analysed the particular nature of the various senses and the particular character of touch, Condillac's next step is to discuss the combination of sensations. Step by step, he follows the initial hierarchy and, thus, the first mixed sensual experience is that of touch combined with smell. Interestingly, the example chosen is that of flowers: Condillac brings the statue out into a field of flowers. Like many philosophers and natural historians of the eighteenth century, the statue appears to have a natural penchant for botany, not only enjoying the flowers for the olfactory pleasures they provide, but also finding gratification in categorising them by linking tactile form to smell and thus imposing the geometrical order of tactility on the less tangible nature of olfactory impressions. "That a certain odour is, for instance, always in a triangle, another one in a square. [...] It believes sensing a figure in an odour, and touching an odour in a triangle." and "The rose differs from the carnation, because it has this form, this tissue." ["Qu'une certaine odeur soit, par exemple, toujours dans un triangle, une autre dans un carré. [...] Elle croira sentir une figure dans une odeur, et toucher une odeur dans une figure." "La rose diffère de l'œillet, parce qu'elle a telle forme, tel tissu" (Condillac 161ff.).]

The passage quoted is significant for at least two reasons: not only because its naturalises the activities of the botanist, turning him into an anthropological emblem, as the exemplary figure of the activity of mapping the objects of the world and the system of their internal order, but also because it links sensation to representation. What we are witnessing bears a striking resemblance to taxonomy, the organising of the world into representations and tableaux, a central epistemological procedure of the seventeenth and eighteenth centuries, that, according to Foucault's *The Order of Things*, spans from the grammatical treaties of Port-Royal and the mathematical world systems of Leibniz, by way of the geographical maps of the explorers and the tabulations of the new statistical sciences, to the *tableaux économiques* of Quesnay and the botanical systems of Linné. And finally, as Foucault underlines several times: Taxonomy does not preclude communication; it orders the world, thus providing the medium through which the transfer of information, of representations of the world, may take place. These representations are, in Condillac's analogy, neither linguistic nor geometrical in a strict mathematical sense, but are nevertheless of a general character and have the nature of signs. Thus sensations are turned into objects that can be represented, organised, and in the end, transferred and set into circulation.

Information is thus the result of a series of operations beginning with sensation. The first step consists of sensations that are, with regard to the individual form of perception, differentiated, systematised and ordered into series. "Single channel" information is juxtaposed to and compared with information stemming from other channels, thus by the act of reflection producing abstract ideas, mental representations: to abstract is for Condillac to separate one idea from several others that enter with it in a composite whole. Knowledge is the product of repeated abstractions leading to habits and general ideas. The repetition or serial nature of sense impressions is the condition of the possibility of recognising an object, turning perception into cognition. Cognition is thus based on habits, in other words automated cognitive processes: seeing and judging are done simultaneously and are confused.

Condillac's emphasis on the automation of cognition is worth dwelling upon, as he expressly considers it one of philosophy's callings to analyse those notions where a phenomenon experienced tends to be confused with its causes. Philosophy thus runs contrary to the nature of common experience, which Condillac in fact considers a by-product of the way our sensation-based mind works. However there is another facet of this argument that is more interesting in this context. As we have seen, the increasing lucidity of the statue is conceived as the result of a series of binary processes as its memory works by establishing series of categories. This analytical and systematic nature of the statue's mental processes does in fact point towards an obvious analogy: the statue is analogous to an automaton, an android, set into movement by its maker; it is a complex machine for registering, recording and even, in principle, distributing information about the world. What we are confronted with is an entity that is receptive and programmable at the same time; a kind of organic mechanism, controlled by external stimuli and with responses.

7. Automatons and Automation

Condillac's imagined statue finds a remarkable parallel in another recurring figure of the eighteenth century, the android. As Alfred Chapuis and Edmond Droz have taught us, the century of the Enlightenment was also the century of automatons. Among these are not only the famous and brilliant works of engineers and watchmakers like Vaucanson, Jacquart-Droz, Kempelen and others, but also a large number of lesser known automated puppets and figures of various quality. From the courts to the market places, from royal societies to church spires, these mechanised humanoids are found throughout the eighteenth century, providing ample material both for literature and philosophy. The android plays a particularly important role for the era's defenders of the notion of the mechanic nature of living organisms. However, the android's relation to philosophy goes back a century to a remark in the *Discourse on the Method* (1637) where Descartes notes that animals must be considered automatons as the two cannot be distinguished from each other. Descartes elaborates his ideas on *la bête machine* when he stresses that in principle it would be possible that automata might be so cleverly designed that they could not be discriminated from a living organism. Animals are complex organic machines, thus susceptible to mechanistic explanation. From a Cartesian point of view, there is with regard to physical activities no absolute criterion separating the animate subject from the animated object.

The mechanised puppets of the eighteenth century surpassed those of the previous century with skills that were not only astonishing, but in fact quite convincing. The three famous androids made by father and son Droz—the piano player, the draughtsman, and the scribe—were able to play, draw, and write. The scribe, reportedly, even took dictation. Vaucanson's famous flutist combined mechanics and pneumatics with such sophistication that his flute could be exchanged with any other flute and the puppet would still produce the most beautiful music. Well-known is also Vaucanson's duck that not only flapped its wings and quacked, but also ate and defecated. However, the most famous is probably Vargas Kempelen's chess player, which toured the courts of Europe for decades, virtually a counterpart to the modern media event, and, like Vaucanson's and Droz's dolls, an element in the propaganda of the new rationality heralded by the spokesmen of the Enlightenment. The importance of these puppets, at least in this context, lies not in the obvious tensions between the rationalism of the mechanistic world view they illustrated and the elements of trickery or illusionism involved in the successful presentation and staging of the dolls (well-known from Kempelen's chess player and Vaucanson's duck), but rather in the phantasmagorical or even utopian dimension of the android. Vaucanson was reputed for his ambition to build a moving and talking mechanical man. The representatives of what Jonathan Israel has recently called "Radical Enlightenment" subscribed more or less wholly to Spinoza's famous definition of man as a spiritual automaton (*automata spirituale*). And even the more moderate Leibniz states in *The Monadology* (1698), that "the organic body of each living being is a kind of divine machine or natural automaton" (paragraph 64).

Vaucanson—who is one of the inventors of the punch card and who thus helped pave the way for Babbage—was not the only one playing with the idea of making a genuine automated individual. However, there is to a modern observer a remarkable absence of any uncanny dimensions in the eighteenth-century's androids. They are a far cry from Hoffman's or Shelley's Romantic troubling and troubled monsters. "What finesse in the details! What grace does not its mechanism have in all its details!" Denis Diderot exclaims in admiration of Vaucanson's mechanical miracles in the *Encyclopedia* article "Androïde" (1751). And in his novel *Jacques le fataliste et son maître* the idea of the natural automaton is explicitly celebrated and becomes an emblem for the causal relationships that govern organic and psychological life. The narrator and the novel's two central characters are referred to as automatons throughout the text, the former complaining that the reader treats him like an automaton, while both the master and his servant Jacques act as if they are pre-programmed on numerous occasions. Their automated behaviour is in line with the materialistic philosophy of the time as it is formulated, for instance, in Diderot's own *Pensées philosophiques* (1746). "The world is quite simply a machine, with wheels, ropes, blocks and tackles, springs and weights" (17, my translation).

Condillac's humanoid statue is thus very much in accordance with the eighteenth century anthropology. Its kinship to one of the era's most popular myths, Pygmalion, is obvious. Like its more famous mythological predecessor, Condillac's statue is set into movement and its animation is a function of its anima. The crucial moment in Condillac's psychology occurs, as we have seen, when the statue reaches out and gropes for its rod. However, the significance of the gesture is not limited to the fact that the statue in doing so proves to be animated. The gesture also implies another ambition, the desire or need to map the world as the rod is turned into a measuring tool, a piece of technology that allows the statue to discover, analyse and format its surroundings. The measuring rod is a prerequisite for the necessary ordering of the sensual impressions; it mediates between senses and objects, providing a scale that allows for the representation of the world.

8. Mediation or Media

I am, of course, aware that my argument requires considerably more examples and test cases to lay claim to any validity. However, at least for now, allow me to be brief: from the early nineteenth century on the sensorial interface that organises the experimental world was increasingly thought of as formatted by media. Contrary to views commonly held in the eighteenth century, sense impressions were now understood in contrast to the new emerging technologies of reproduction and new insights in the physiology of perception. The new technologies of reproduction were characterised by the fact that they were information channels that by-passed the human sensorium. At the same time their mode of functioning was comparable to that of the senses as they stored, processed, and distributed information in the form of physical effects such as light and sound waves, analogue to the way the senses worked. They established a different, objective standard for reproducing the world. Thereby the technology matched the epistemology of the post-Kantian era. The objective of the camera reproduced the objective world. On the other hand, the human sensorium became characterised by its perceptual shortcomings. Doomed to be subjective, it was not to be trusted. The media thus influence the experimental world in several ways. On the one hand they provide the standards of how the world should be perceived: they reproduce reality truthfully, objectively, without the interference of any interpreting or erring human agent; thereby they help solidify a new regime of epistemological realism—the idea that the world is out there, objectified and objectifiable, divided in discrete entities, always already there awaiting its measuring—as well as proving the flaws of the sensorial apparatus, thus in a double operation both establishing the factual and objective world of things, and the phenomenological and subjective world of experience. On the other hand, media also format the world of experience—not merely as acting as prostheses, but also refiguring and refunctionalising our perceptual schemata.

For the epistemology of the nineteenth-century media regime the world is a given, for the eighteenth century, the world is a product. What Descartes's, Molyneux's, Diderot's and Herder's blind man is an emblem for is that the facticity of the world does not exist before the cognitive and experimental activities of the human agent. It is rather the product of our interference with our surroundings. This might be one reason why it would make sense to replace the notion of medium with that of mediation, or rather, to circumscribe historically the validity of the media concept. Mediation it a more fitting term for describing what takes places in the Cartesian and Lockeian analogy of the blind man as an emblem for how a world is made experimental by measuring. It is furthermore a term that fits well with Foucault's understanding of the seventeenth- and the eighteenth-century key epistemological concept, representation. Of course the term mediation, as conceptualised be Régis Debray, is a much larger concept than what has been hinted at in my discussion of Condillac, not the least because it allows for the inclusion of social and political practices. That however will have to wait for another occasion.

One could argue that replacing one term with another is merely a question of technical nature. However, it is this kind of analytical distinction that is our daily bread as it makes distinctions possible, as well as allowing for generalisations, in other words the play of identity and difference that make up the fabric of our reality. Concepts are propositions about the nature of the world; they are the academic's most developed tool for world making.

References

Bacon, Francis. *The Advancement of Learning*. Ed. Stephen Jay Gould. 1605. New York: Modern Library, 2005.

Benjamin, Walter, and Charles Baudelaire. *Ein Lyriker im Zeitalter der Hochkapitalismus*. 1970. Frankfurt: Suhrkamp, 1990.
Bolz, Norbert. *Am Ende der Gutenberg-Galaxis: Die neuen Kommunikationsverhältnisse*. München: Wilhelm Fink, 1993.
Carlyle, Thomas. *Carlyle Reader*. Ed. G. B. Tennyson. Cambridge: Cambridge UP, 1984.
Chapuis, Alfred, and Edmond Droz. *Automata: A Historical and Technological Study*. Neuchâtel: Editions du Griffon, 1958.
Condillac, Etienne Bonnot de. *Traité des Sensations*. Paris: Houel, 1754.
Crary, Jonathan. *Techniques of the Observer*. Cambridge, MA: MIT Press, 1990.
Debray, Régis. *Manifestes médiologiques*. Paris: Gallimard, 1994.
Descartes, René. *Le Monde, ou Traité de la lumière. Œuvres*. 1629–1633. Paris: Librairie Vrin, 1996.
—. *Dioptrics, I*. In: *Œuvres*. 1637. Paris: Gallimard, 1953.
Diderot, Denis. *Pensées philosophiques*. In: *Œuvres complètes*. Vol. II. 1746. Paris: Hermann, 1975.
—. "Androïde." *Œuvres complètes*. Vol. VI. 1751. Paris: Hermann, 1976.
Foucault, Michel. *Les Mots et les choses*. Paris: Gallimard, 1966.
Goodman, Nelson. *Ways of Worldmaking*. Indianapolis: Hackett, 1978.
Herder, Johann Gottfried. *Vom Erkennen und Empfinden der menschlichen Seele*. Riga: n.p., 1778.
Israel, Jonathan. *Radical Enlightenment: Philosophy and the Making of Modernity 1650–1750*. Oxford: Oxford UP, 2002.
Kittler, Friedrich A. *Aufschreibesysteme 1800/1900*. 1985. München: Wilhelm Fink Verlag, 1995.
—. *Optische Medien: Berliner Vorlesung*. 1999. Berlin: Merve Verlag, 2002.
Leibniz, Gottfried Wilhelm. *Monadology*. Ed. Nicholas Rescher. 1698. London: Routledge, 1992.
Leroi-Gourhan, André. *Le Geste et la parole. Vol. 1. Technique et langage*. Paris: Albin Michel, 1964.
Locke, John. *Essay Concerning Human Understanding*. 1690. Oxford: Oxford UP, 2008.
Luhmann, Niklas. *Die Realität der Massenmedien*. Opladen: Westdeutscher Verlag, 1996.
Manovich, Lev. *The Language of New Media*. Cambridge, MA: MIT Press, 2001.
Marx, Karl and Friedrich Engels, *Werke*, Ergänzungsband, 1. Teil. Berlin (DDR): Dietz Verlag, 1968.
McLuhan, Marshall. *The Gutenberg Galaxy: The Making of Typographic Man*. 1962. London: Routledge, 2002.
—. *Understanding Media: The Extensions of Man*. 1964. London: Routledge, 2001.
Peters, John Durham. *Speaking into the Air: A History of the Idea of Communication*. Chicago: Chicago UP, 1999
Postman, Neil. "The Reformed English Curriculum." *High School 1980: The Shape of the Future in American Secondary Education*. Ed. Alvin Eurich. New York: Pitman, 1970. 160–68.
Raymond, Joad. "Introduction." *News Networks in the Seventeenth Century: Britain and Europe*. Ed. Joad Raymond. London: Routledge, 2006. 1–19.
Schulte-Sasse, Jochen. "Medien/medial." *Ästhetische Grundbegriffe*. Ed. Karlheinz Barck et al. Vol. 4.9. Stuttgart: Metzler, 2001. 1–37.

Do Media Determine Our Situation? Friedrich Kittler's Application of Information Theory to the Humanities

Stephen Sale

A common criticism of the constructivist approach to worldmaking is that it fails to consider the conditions of possibility for its irreducibly plural 'worlds': the conventions that govern their selection (the archive), or the material conditions that shape their articulation (the media). If we are to contemplate the ways in which worlds are made then it is only right that we take into account the materials with which we make them. In its engagement with the topic of worldmaking then, this essay focuses on the constitutive role that communications media play in cultural production. Recent work in this area has led to the introduction of a new set of critical tools into the domain of the humanities including, perhaps surprisingly, information theory. It is through a discussion of these new applications of information theory that this essay explores some of the methodological issues that arise when analysing the medial configurations that support our ways of worldmaking. Guiding the discussion will be a critique of the work of Friedrich Kittler, a media historian and literary theorist who has played a major role in the rejuvenation of German media theory since the 1980s.

What has come to be called 'first-generation' information theory was formulated by Claude Shannon and Warren Weaver in *The Mathematical Theory of Communication* (1963), first published in 1949. Shannon was an engineer at Bell Labs in the United States where he was concerned with optimising the national telephone network. He devised a generic model for communications systems comprising the following five elements:

1. The information source, typically the human brain, that produces a message or a sequence of messages. A message may consist of written or spoken words, or a series of images or sounds.
2. The transmitter, which operates on the message to produce a suitable signal. This could be, for example, the human voice mechanism, a

telephone handset that converts sound into electromagnetic pulses or a digital video camera that captures moving images as mpeg-files.
3. The channel: the actual medium over which the signal is transmitted. This could be air, in the case of sound waves, copper wires, or beams of light in a fibre-optic cable.
4. The receiver. This performs the inverse operation of that done by the transmitter, reconstructing a message from the signal. The ear, for example, or a television set.
5. The destination for the message, typically another human brain.

Shannon was concerned with the efficiencies of such a system. He wanted to work out a method for the quantification of information together with a set of design principles that would allow him to maximise usage of system capacity while minimising communications errors. For Shannon's purposes, the semantic aspects of communication were of little consequence and he instead formulated a definition of information as "the measure of one's freedom of choice when one selects a message. [...] The concept of information applies not to the individual messages (as the concept of meaning would), but rather to the situation as a whole" (Shannon and Weaver 9). For Shannon, what is most important about information is that it relates not to what one actually says but to what one could say. We are dealing here with the selection of data from an archive. A situation is said to be characterised by a greater degree of information when there is a greater pool of options to choose from. And there is still more information when the selection of each option is equally probable. An example: after standing in a queue at the supermarket my conversation with the employee at the check-out typically takes the form of 'Hello, How are you?' 'Fine, thanks. You?' Silence as some barcodes are scanned. 'That'll be x euros, please.' 'There you are.' 'Here's your change.' 'Thank you. Bye.' The situation is one of low information. Of course, it may be that we start fighting, kissing, or debating the neo-Scholastic revival of the nineteenth century, but it is unlikely given that we know little about each other and there is a line of impatient shoppers behind me. The experience of reading a collection of academic essays, on the other hand, offers a high level of information (unless, of course, you know all about information theory and Kittler's media histories in which case you will probably find this very predictable). From this situational redefinition of information, Shannon formulated an equation that expresses information as a statistical measure of uncertainty: information is the inverse sum of the logarithms to the base 2 of the probabilities of each option. Or, $H = -\Sigma p_i \log p_i$.

So far, we have only considered perfect communications systems, but there is no such thing as a perfect system: they always suffer from noise. If noise is introduced, then the received message contains distortions, errors, and extraneous material. Noise adds uncertainty and thereby increases the amount of information, albeit in an undesirable manner. This is combated in most systems by an element of redundancy. For example, the English language is about 50% redundant (that is, given the loss of half of the letters in a sentence it can be reconstructed on the basis of a number of rules: a 'q' is usually followed by a 'u,' the letters 'n' and 'b' are found together much less frequently than 't' and 'h,' and so on). A certain amount of error can be tolerated by a redundant system at a given capacity. Shannon's theory, then, provides equations for calculating the redundancy levels and channel capacity necessary for communications in a noisy channel at different fidelity requirements. It directly relates the characteristics of a code or language to the material conditions of its transmission.

Shannon's theory has been readily applied to engineering problems and he could be claimed as one of the architects of the information revolution of recent decades—his capacity formula has informed the development of storage media such as magnetic tapes and compact disks as well as transmission technologies such as broadband internet access and broadcast high-definition television, but his ideas have also had an influence beyond engineering, most notably in linguistics and the social sciences. In his introductory note to Shannon's work Warren Weaver offers information theory as an explanatory model of all human behaviour. To justify this claim he establishes three levels at which communications problems can be analysed:

Level A. The technical problem of ensuring the accuracy of transmission of the symbols of communication.

Level B. The semantic problem of the correlation of the transmitted symbols with desired meaning.

Level C. The effectiveness problem. That is the effectiveness of the received meaning in affecting conduct in a desired way.

These levels are interrelated and overlap in different ways but Weaver asserts that Level A is far from superficial. Rather, the significance of Shannon's theory of communications at Level A is derived from the claim that levels B and C rely upon the signal accuracies at Level A. Indeed, Weaver goes so far as to assert that "the theory of Level A is, at least to a significant degree, also a theory of levels B and C" (Shannon and Weaver 6). In other words, in order to analyse the ways in which meaning is constructed one must first analyse the conditions that structure communication regardless of meaning or intent. Worldmaking becomes a technical issue.

In its application in the humanities, information theory has supported a shift away from textual analyses and considerations of media ownership towards an examination of 'mediality' itself, perhaps most famously with Marshall McLuhan's proclamation that the 'medium is the message.' For McLuhan the 'message' of a medium or technology is "the change of scale or pace or pattern that it introduces into human affairs" and it is the medium, not the content, of a message "that shapes and controls the scale and form of human association and action" (McLuhan 8–9). He offers the example of a contentless medium that has transformed social activity: the light bulb, without which we would be unable to perform brain surgery or watch night-time baseball games, among other things. Friedrich Kittler, too, adopts Shannon's theory, but he radicalises its technological focus. While McLuhan views media technologies as "extensions of man" externalising the human central nervous system, Kittler is anxious to avoid what he views as a residual humanism: "McLuhan, who was by trade a literary theorist, understood more about perception than about electronics, and for that reason attempted to think about technologies from the perspective of the body and not vice versa" (Kittler, *Optische Medien* 21, my translation). Kittler, also a literary theorist but one who solders circuit boards in his spare time and has taught courses in computer programming, instead suggests that we "forget humans, language and sense and instead turn to details of the five elements and functions of Shannon" (44, my translation).

Kittler and other German poststructuralists saw an affinity between Shannon's theory and Foucault's work from his 'archaeological' period.[1] This school of thought emphasised the focus of discourse analysis on the fact that particular statements were made rather than not and excluded any hermeneutic questions of meaning. They were concerned with the discursive regularities which determine the selection of a particular statement and the effect that this has on contiguous statements. But in Kittler's view Foucault's archaeology had two main shortcomings: it had a limited conception of the archive as synonymous with the library, the repository of written sentences; and it paid insufficient attention to the media that shape the articulation of worlds or, here, discursive regimes. Kittler, then, with the help of information theory, reformulated discourse analysis to take into account the technological media of the twentieth century. Kittler suggests that Foucault "merely describes the *production* of discourses. There are, for example, no descriptions in Foucault's book [*The Order of*

---

1   See Winthrop-Young (394) for a discussion of Foucault's reception in Germany.

Things] of the *source* of these discourses, of the *channels* or the *receivers* of discourse in the form of […] readers or consumers" (Armitage 19). Accordingly, in *Discourse Networks 1800/1900* (1990), Kittler identifies the "source" of discourse circa 1800 as a transformation in pedagogical methods that gives the mother responsibility for a child's acquisition of language. Placing this development into an institutional framework of burgeoning bureaucracy and the production of classical poetry and its attendant readership Kittler reworks Foucault's account to relate the shift from what he terms the "Republic of Scholars" (*Discourse Networks* 4) to the Discourse Network of 1800, which roughly corresponds to the shift from Foucault's Classical to the Modern episteme. In turn, the transition from 'Discourse Network 1800' to 'Discourse Network 1900' is caused by the break-up of the monopoly of writing with the invention of alternative communications media: the gramophone, film, and typewriter. This is akin to Foucault's 'return of language' at the end of the nineteenth century. Kittler's medial approach allows him to extend and, to a certain extent, empirically ground Foucault by linking changes in social configurations to the introduction of new storage and communication technologies.

In Kittler's view literature must be redefined as an information system that processes, stores, and transmits data, thus rendering many of the previous tools of literary criticism obsolete: "[m]eaning as the fundamental concept of hermeneutics […] bypass[es] writing as a channel of information and those institutions, whether schools or universities, that connect books with people" (Kittler, *Discourse Networks* 370). Kittler shifts attention away from individual authors as world-makers to the discursive rules and technologies of mediation that construct them as senders and readers as recipients. In effect, he argues for a reclassification of literary criticism as a sub-branch of media studies[2] with Shannon's theory as the privileged tool of analysis. Kittler then recruits Shannon to his assault on what he terms as the prevailing Lockeian model of communications, a model based on the rendering into speech of perceived ideas and the linking of isolated individuals through the bonds of language.[3] He argues that it is only with Shannon that we are liberated from the 'unfathomable confusion' of the Lockeian model which fails to enquire, how, without language, people came up with ideas in the first place (see Kittler, *History of Communications Media*).

---

2   See David E. Wellbery's foreword to the English translation for a discussion of what he terms as "post-hermeneutic criticism" (Wellbery xiii).
3   It could be argued that Weaver's application of Shannon's model to human communication retains many of the assumptions of the Lockeian model, such as the original or subjective intention of a message and the desire for a neutral and clear medium. See Day (38–59).

Kittler's positivist call for us to "learn from an information theory that has formalised the current state of technical knowledge" (*Discourse Networks* 369) can be seen as an intervention in a long-standing argument in German thought. The 'substantive' view of technology, or the ascription of agency to technological objects, is often associated with conservatism in Germany and, in particular, the 'reactionary modernists'[4] of the Weimar period such as Carl Schmitt, Ernst Jünger, and Martin Heidegger. (Kittler has himself described *Discourse Networks 1800/1900* as 'black in every sense of the word,' referring to the traditional colour of German conservatism.) In their various ways, these Weimar thinkers urged us to think of technology 'mediately,' as constitutive of the relationship between human and world. Jünger, for example, believed that industrial modernity was a call for mankind to be 'mobilised' through technology in an existential transformation, a formulation that strongly influenced Heidegger's thinking on technology. In the aftermath of the Second World War, however, the technocracy proposed by elements of the Weimar Right became one of the principle targets of Adorno and Horkheimer's diagnosis of the ills of the twentieth century in *Dialectic of Enlightenment* (1997). Adorno and Horkheimer identified the development of an 'instrumental reason' marked with an excessive concern with 'means,' the deployment of which suspends debate about the legitimacy of any given end, so that it can devote itself more fully to the perfection of its means. For Adorno and Horkheimer, instrumental reason is "the organ of calculation, of planning; it is neutral in regard to ends; its element is coordination" (88). Modern science is its apogee and 'techno-logy is the essence of this knowledge.'[5] In opposition to Jünger's glorification of technological transformation, they argued that industrial capitalism and a technological rationality were extending means-ends rationality to the conduct of life. But, at its heart, instrumental reason is a subjugating force that adjusts the world for the ends of self-preservation. Means merely expedite a passage determined by some other agency such as the market or the rating polls. To the founders of the Frankfurt School, the conservative thinkers' theoretical investment in questions of means/media all-too-often deflected attention from pressing matters of social reform, i.e. communist revolution. Even Walter Ben-

---

4   A term coined in Herf, *Reactionary Modernism*.

5   The relationship between what I have crudely described as two opposing schools of thought is by no means straight-forward. For example, Adorno and Horkheimer's critique of the prevailing positivism in the human sciences parallels many of Husserl's arguments in *The Crisis of European Sciences and Transcendental Phenomenology*. Husserl, whose influence on Heidegger is well known, wrote that modern science operates "like a machine, reliable in accomplishing obviously very useful things, a machine everyone can learn to operate correctly without in the least understanding the inner possibility and necessity of this sort of accomplishment" (Husserl 52).

jamin attracted the ire of Adorno for his focus on mediality. Arguments for "technology's right of determination" (Benjamin, "Theories of German Fascism" 312) led to his being criticised for a 'vulgar Marxism' and for being 'insufficiently dialectical.' Later, Frederic Jameson went further, suggesting that Benjamin's stress on invention and technique as the primary cause of historical change was an attempt to ground his work materially while neglecting the economic factors of class and social organisation (Jameson 74). However, while they draw attention to some of the political problems associated with thinking mediately, Adorno and Horkheimer failed to offer their own analysis of means; their critique merely focused on illegitimate ends.

If we now return to information theory we can see a similar argument being played out. In the words of Katherine Hayles:

> Shannon's distinction between signal and noise has a conservative bias that privileges stasis over change. Noise interferes with the message's exact replication, which is presumed to be the desired result. The structure of the theory implied that change was deviation and that deviation should be corrected. (63)

This criticism was the starting point for the British cyberneticist Donald MacKay who saw that Shannon's model presupposed a pool of statements from which 'messages' could be selected, but offered no explanation for the context in which a message was received. MacKay believed that Weaver's universalising claims for the theory were unfounded: information is intrinsically connected with meaning and Shannon's theory would require supplementation in order to function as a theory of human communication. MacKay introduced the idea of 'structural information' which indicates how a selective piece of information is to be understood. An example: if I tell a joke and it falls flat, I may resort to telling my interlocutor 'That was a joke' in a vain attempt to achieve my aim of getting a laugh. This is a message about how the first message should be interpreted. But to establish the effectiveness of this structural information an observer is required. MacKay's theory, in effect, reasserts the importance of Weaver's 'Level C' by reclaiming the autonomy of the non-technical context: it needs to register the differences in the state of the receiver's mind before and after the message arrived. This 'second-generation' information theory is a major inspiration for Niklas Luhmann's observer-based systems theory, which is often set alongside Kittler's work.[6] But despite its sophisticated account of communicative dynamics this systems theory remains within the instrumentalist account of technology of Adorno and Horkheimer. Communications technologies are dealt with in

---

6   For a very useful comparison of Kittler and Luhmann see Winthrop-Young.

terms of functional simplification; it is only when communications fail at 'Level C' that the underlying media come to our attention. This is to fall into the trap that Heidegger describes with his maxim "technology itself prevents any experience of its essence" (qtd. in Kittler, *Gramophone* xl). Technology only becomes an issue when, as Heidegger tells us, it is no longer ready-to-hand.

Kittler's own solution to the 'effectiveness problem' is to historicise Shannon's model so as to eliminate the 'human' as a stable category. We have already seen how Kittler described the two varying historical configurations of Shannon's model that he identified in *Discourse Networks 1800/1900*. He offers a more detailed explanation of his methodology in *The History of Communication Media* (1996) where he suggests that it has only become possible for us to describe a formal model of communication with its implementation as an independent system that is with the development of computer networks that can control the processing of commands. This is the latest stage in a gradual decoupling of information networks from human networks. To support this account, Kittler retells the transition from oral to written culture to technical media in terms of the gradual autonomy of technology: literate cultures break with face-to-face interaction to institute communication at a distance; the invention of technical media give rise to dedicated communication networks such as the telegraphy and telephony systems (and, with the ability of computers to mediate communications, today's internet). Kittler then argues for a reformulation of our concepts to make them universally applicable and free from a Romantic anthropocentrism: people become addresses, messages become commands, and goods represent data in an order of exchange. In Kittler's schema Levels B and C are restricted to the level of programmed responses to commands issued by a digital medium that is emerging as autonomous and all-powerful. Semantic 'worldmaking' is, therefore, reduced to mere contingency in the discourse network of today. Kittler tells us that we should forget about 'emotional dispositions' and instead focus our efforts on an exposition of the underlying technical conditions. In this post-human vision, Kittler's elevation of mediality refuses the redemptions variously offered by the aforementioned thinkers of media, whether it be Benjamin's revolutionary rewiring of the proletariat, Jünger's heroic rapture of the technologised soldier-worker or Heidegger's ontological remedy in the form of a 'saving power.' Kittler's response to the Frankfurt School's criticisms is to discard ends altogether. He marks his departure from Heidegger with "in lieu of philosophical inquiries into essence, simple knowledge will do" (Kittler, *Gramophone* xl). There is no play in this system. The ends are the end.

So, where do we go from here? I would argue that this hard-line approach from Kittler is chiefly a polemical position against the Frankfurt School's continued refusal to budge on the issue of mediality,[7] and that there is room for manoeuvre. Kittler's work, for all its rhetorical excesses, has shown us that media do matter and that any account of worldmaking must take into account its material conditions. The humanities will need to adopt new methodological tools, and information theory, while problematic, can be a productive way to analyse the medial configurations that structure our ways of worldmaking, as Kittler has demonstrated. A number of other thinkers have made ethical claims for information theory, chiefly through a rethinking of notions of community. Rather than thinking of noise as an intrusion that disturbs the statistical distribution of a system it can be thought as a logically necessary component of the system. Michel Serres takes this position and follows the French biologist Henri Atlan in arguing that noise prompts a system to reorganise in a more complex form that incorporates the disturbance. Noise simultaneously breaches the boundary of a system while marking a set of relations as a system. Serres describes this in terms of the parasite, which in French can mean one of three things: a biological parasite, a social parasite (both these correspond to English meanings) and noise, static in a system or interference in a channel. In each case, the parasite interferes in, and ultimately upsets, some existing set of relations and pattern of movement. It compels us either to expel it, or to readjust our internal workings so that we can accommodate the needs of the parasite. Noise, in other words, is to communication what a virus is to an organism, or a scapegoat is to a community. It is not simply an obstacle, but rather a productive force around the exclusion of which the system is organised. In contrast to Shannon and Weaver's positivist assumption of a self-contained intentionality, this alternative approach suggests that the existence of the communication system itself depends upon noise as a logical exteriority rather than as an empirical fact. In opposition to an information theory that assumes a stable and predictable language (a pool of alternatives), this revised view offers an alternative model of language as calling and response reminiscent of that described by Benjamin in "The Task of the Translator."

In Serres' schema, 'guest,' 'host' and 'parasite' are not substantial entities. They are positions or functions through which any entity—informational, social, or biological—must pass. In other words, each point in the system assumes in turn the roles of host, guest, and parasite. The

---

7   While some notion of mediality entered Frankfurt thought with Marcuse (a student of Heidegger's), Habermas rejected Marcuse's view of modern science and technology as inherently ideological claiming that this was characteristic of a residual Romanticism. See e.g. Habermas.

parasite then is in neither the position of the subject or the object. It is a device or operator by means of which one is able to turn into the subject or object. Furthermore, it is relational: the guest and host functions are always coupled together in a working relationship. To work, they must cooperate in excluding a 'third man' and neutralising the milieu in which their exchange takes place (Serres 80). Whatever occupies the third 'parasitic' position, however, always works toward the inclusion of the middle.

This in turn can help us understand some of the later and more explicitly political work of Giorgio Agamben that draws upon some of the thinkers mentioned earlier. In *State of Exception* (2005), Agamben describes the political as a 'pure medium' that relates law and life, but, like the parasite, must be excluded from the social and juridical order before any normalcy can be achieved. Agamben arrives at his theory of the exception through a somewhat unorthodox reading of Carl Schmitt who he reads with and against Walter Benjamin. Coming from opposed political positions, Benjamin and Schmitt nonetheless recognise that sovereignty is not based on the positive content of law, so much as its relation to its outside, or its medium. Schmitt tries to incorporate the exception and explain it as a necessary part of the juridical apparatus. In this way, he 'normalises' the exceptional powers of fascism. Walter Benjamin, however, insists on its radical otherness, and sees the exception as the basis of a more wide-ranging critique of the legal order whose legitimacy rests on the doctrine of the end justifies the means. Like Serres (and Kittler), Benjamin sees the medium as an insurmountable force of deposition. It is precisely because it lacks any specific programme and is useless for the purposes of rule that he appeals to it as a basic resource for any anti-statist and anti-juridical revolutionary activity.

To conclude then, both Serres and Agamben draw upon biological principles that Kittler would probably reject. This would amount to a technological fall from grace from Kittler's point of view since it places undue emphasis on notions of life and mortality. However, I think we can view his position as a corrective to the dominant view of technology in the German academy: that of the Frankfurt School. By bracketing off semantic questions Kittler has succeeded in offering some ways of thinking beyond subject/object agency by drawing our attention to the networks (both institutional and technological) that underpin our ways of worldmaking. However, his polemical account of the post-human autonomy of technology is an all-too-absolute vacation of the subject that has now made its point and requires some modification. The assertion of a biological subject could allow us to think mediately, retaining a determinism that would still support a line of Nietzsche's that Kittler is fond of quoting: "our writing tools are working on our thoughts" (Nietzsche 97).

His very fruitful accounts of the technological configuration of different epochs would still remain intact. It would also, however, open up a space for potential lacking in his doom-laden teleology.

References

Agamben, Giorgio. *State of Exception*. 2003. Trans. Kevin Attell. London, Chicago: U of Chicago P, 2005.

Adorno, Theodor W. and Max Horkheimer. *Dialectic of Enlightenment*. 1972. Trans. John Cumming. London/New York: Verso, 1997.

Armitage, John. "From Discourse Networks to Cultural Mathematics: An Interview with Friedrich A. Kittler." *Theory, Culture & Society* 23.7–8 (2006): 17–38.

Benjamin, Walter. "The Task of the Translator: An Introduction to the Translation of Baudelaire's Tableaux Parisiens." *Illuminations*. Ed. Hannah Arendt. Trans Harry Zohn. New York: Schocken, 1968. 69–82.

—. "Theories of German Fascism." *Walter Benjamin: Selected Writings, Volume 2, 1927–34*. Eds. Michael W. Jennings, Howard Eiland and Gary Smith. Cambridge, MA/London: The Belknap Press of Harvard UP, 1999. 312–21.

Day, Ronald E. *The Modern Invention of Information: Discourse, History, and Power*. Carbondale and Edwardsville, Illinois: Southern IL UP, 2001.

Foucault, Michel. The *Order of Things: An Archaeology of Human Sciences*. 1966. New York: Random House, 1970.

Habermas, Jürgen. "Technology and Science as 'Ideology.'" *Towards a Rational Society*. Ed. Jürgen Habermas. Trans. Jeremy J. Shapiro. London: Heinemann, 1970.

Hayles, N. Katherine. *How We Became Posthuman: Virtual Bodies in Cybernetics, Literature and Informatics*. Chicago: U of Chicago P, 1999.

Heidegger, Martin. *Holzwege*. Frankfurt a.M.: Klostermann, 1951.

Herf, Jeffery. *Reactionary Modernism: Technology, Culture and Politics in Weimar and the Third Reich*. Cambridge: Cambridge UP, 1984.

Husserl, Edmund. *The Crisis of the European Sciences and Transcendental Phenomenology: An Introduction to Phenomenological Philosophy*. Trans. David Carr. Evanston, IL: Northwestern UP, 1970.

Jameson, Frederic. *Marxism and Form: Twentieth-Century Dialectical Theories of Literature*. Princeton, NJ: Princeton UP, 1971.

Kittler, Friedrich. *Discourse Networks 1800/1900*. Trans. Michael Metter and Chris Cullens. Stanford: Stanford UP, 1990.

—. *History of Communications Media*, 1996. 21 Jan 2010. <www.ctheory.net/articles.aspx?id=45>.

—. *Gramophone, Film, Typewriter*. Trans. Geoffrey Winthrop-Young and Michael Wutz. Stanford: Stanford UP, 1999.

—. *Optische Medien*. Berlin: Merve, 2002.

McLuhan, Marshall. *Understanding Media: The Extensions of Man*. 1964. London/New York: Routledge, 2001.

MacKay, Donald *Information, Mechanism, and Meaning*. Cambridge: MIT Press, 1969.

Nietzsche, Friedrich. "Genoa, gegen Ende Februar 1882." *Friedrich Nietzsches Gesammelte Briefe IV*. Ed. Peter Gast. Berlin, 1902–1909. 97.

Serres, Michel. *The Parasite*. Trans. Lawrence R. Schehr. Minneapolis/London: U of Minnesota P, 2007.

Schmitt, Carl. *Political Theology: Four Chapters on the Concepts of Sovereignty*. Trans. George Schwab. Chicago: U of Chicago P, 2005.

Shannon, Claude and Warren Weaver. *The Mathematical Theory of Communications*. 1949. Urbana/Chicago: U of Illinois P, 1963.

Wellbery, David E. "Foreword." *Discourse Networks 1800/1900*. Ed. Friedrich A. Kittler. Trans. Michael Metter, and Chris Cullens. Stanford: Stanford UP, 1990. vii–xxxiii.

Winthrop-Young, Geoffrey. "Silicon Sociology, or, Two Kings on Hegel's Throne? Kittler, Luhmann and the Posthuman Merger of German Media Theory." *The Yale Journal of Criticism* 13.2 (2000): 391–420.

Irreducible Vagueness: Augmented Worldmaking in Diller & Scofidio's *Blur Building*

ULRIK EKMAN

1. Of the End of the World I: Augmentation and the Embeddedness of Pervasive Computing

> ...we are not intending to make a volume of space covered with fog. We intend to make a building of fog with integrated media. (Diller and Scofidio, *Blur* 39)

American artist-architects Diller & Scofidio and their co-operators passed through years of projective planning and invention when working towards their impressive building which made an intriguing, soft impact on its visitor-inhabitants—not least via the complexity and dynamics of its vast, artifactual mist-cloud.[1] Then came all the obstacles involved in the actual construction and installation of this contribution to the Swiss Expo. In between inventive projection and actualisation quite a few creative initiatives were abandoned. Unfortunately, then, the final building did not comprise a LED text forest of vertical panels with scrolling text (whether from Internet feeds or from artist Jenny Holzer), nor a Hole in the Water restaurant made of submerged twin glass cylinders with an aquarium layer in between, in which diners would sit at eye level with the lake and eat sushi. Nor did we get an open air Angel Bar in the top part of the mist-cloud of the building (to be served: an infinite variety of water beverages, from glacial tappings to municipal waters from around the world) (Diller and Scofidio, *Blur* 100ff., 146ff., 163, 324). Nevertheless, the opening of the *Blur Building* in 2002 was provocative and transformative enough in its innovative endeavors to present us with 'the end of the world,' to put it

---

1   This article does not include visual representation or graphic illustration of Diller & Scofidio's project. I refer the reader to: Kiser, "Diller & Scofidio. Blur Building"; Designboom, "Diller & Scofidio: The Blur Building"; Leerberg, "Blur by Diller & Scofidio"; Milara, "Diller + Scofidio: How They Obtained the Blur Effect"; Rubin "Diller + Scofidio: The Blur Building, National Expo 2002, Yverdon-Les-Bains, Switzerland."

pointedly. How is it that one will have had to approach *Blur Building* as a question of 'the end of the world'?[2]

Blur Building is of 'the end of the world' because it presents an exemplary artistic-architectural project whose innovations involve new media and information technology in various ways and so extensively as to begin to problematise any strict distinction between any given sense of 'the world' and what one might call contemporary ecotechnics. Ecotechnics here designates the almost sovereign capacity of current information technology to perform calculative operations by quantifiable means which pervade the exchanges in globalised culture, cosmopolitan democratic values, a socio-cultural sense of community, and embodied attempts to delineate 'the world' as an already meaningful environment.[3] For any one visitor-inhabitant of the *Blur Building*, then, it is the body as the spacing or sharing out of sense which emerges as the place of that originary relation of technicity which is at work both in the presencing of bodies and the way we disclose a world. In numerous ways it is the relation of bodily sense to ecotechnical apparatus that informs the way the world of Blur may come to seem meaningful to us. It is a pervasive and originary technicity, the manner you are connected or plugged in all around which sketches out your mode of existence and your experience or constitution of world-hood. If Blur affirms this originary technicity at stake in the world-hood of the world, it is without positing technology as a substantial fixed origin or as a projected finality. Rather, it is a matter of worlding in radical finitude, that is, the event of the emergence of the world in the absence of solid ground or determinable end.[4] As Jean-Luc Nancy formulates it, "[e]cotechnics [...] substitutes projections of linear history and of

---

2   In my treatment of the sense of the world I draw in particular on Nancy, *The Sense of the World*.

3   The term 'ecotechnics' is coined by Jean-Luc Nancy, and I endorse both his careful delineation of the ways in which technology tends to conceal our inability to grapple with the infinite finitude of our existence, and his insistence that we speak of technologies in the singular plural so as to avoid the assumption that, both generally and now specifically in the case of pervasive computing, we are dealing with an omnipresent techno-conspiracy qua an absolute nexus of a vast machinic or combinatorial apparatus embracing all particular technologies. One does better by staying with the difficult task of deconstructing globalised ecotechnics so as to meet again the finitude of sense, taking note along the way of the multiple ways in which technologies both shatter the notion of such a nexus and disseminate potential relations for a human culture and world to come—even when transforming and partly destroying nature, even when approaching a technicisation of existence itself so as to exhaust human life and seemingly withdraw or efface the sense of the world. Nancy, *Being Singular Plural* 185; Hutchens and Nancy, "Interview: The Future of Philosophy" 161ff., esp.165.

4   Ian James offers an interesting exposition of Nancy's thought of ecotechnics in James (143ff.).

final goals with local differences and multiple bifurcations. Ecotechnics deconstructs the system of ends, it renders them nonsystematisable and nonorganic" (Nancy, *Corpus* 78). In Blur as an event of worlding we depend upon that sharing out of embodied sense which takes place as a technical-mechanical relation between material bodies, *partes extra partes*, or as a delineation of material bodies in a contact-separation, touching-letting go, of sense and matter. When inhabiting Blur one would have to concede, with Nancy, that our world is of the ecotechnical that marks out our bodies, lets them proliferate, and plugs us in—in a multitude of directions:

> Our world is the world of 'technical,' the world whose cosmos, nature, gods, whose system, complete in its intimate jointure, are exposed as 'technical': the world of an *ecotechnics*. Ecotechnics functions with technical apparatus, with which it connects us in all directions. But what it *makes* is our bodies, which it puts into the world and connects to its system, our bodies, which in this way it creates as more visible, more proliferating, more polymorphous, more pressed together, more in 'masses' and 'zones' than they have ever been. (Nancy, *Corpus* 78)

Diller & Scofidio's building project, its pursuit of ecotechnics, and its polymorphous zoning of bodies partake of an epoch when the third main wave of computing is emerging, a movement partly sidestepping and going beyond the earlier developments of mainframes, desktops, laptops, and their stable networked infrastructure. Their work does not so much reflect what is currently happening on the large infrastructural scale (where the speed and data-capacity of GRID computing promises to enhance and gradually replace the Internet),[5] nor on the scale of supercomputing (where quantum computing is still under development),[6] nor on the microscale of biomedia and nanotechnology.[7] Rather, *Blur Building* inserts itself into the middle, into a context marked by the research into and actual installation of pervasive or ubiquitous computing, whose deployment of multitudes of relatively inexpensive, mobile, wireless, and relatively intelligent machines is flexible, complex, and massive enough to warrant speaking of a technicity whose sensors and actants not only pervade the human life world, but become almost indistinguishable from the environment or the world as such (*Umwelt*).[8] Whether in terms of spacing or temporal unfolding, Diller & Scofidio's project presents an mutual

---

5   For a more detailed account, see Foster and Kesselman.
6   For a short introduction to recent advances in quantum computing, see Daley, Cirac, and Zoller 62ff.
7   See also Hayles and Foushee; Thacker *Biomedia* and *The Global Genome*.
8   Michael Beigl presents a thought-provoking introduction to the status of ubiquitous computing (Beigl 52ff.). For more detailed book-length studies see Cook and Das; Robinson, Vogt, and Wagealla; Loke; Steventon and Wright.

overlaying of the world and technics arising from a transductive relation, that is, both the world and technics appear in their co-implication on the basis of their more primary individuating relation.⁹

Hence *Blur Building* is of the end of the world to the extent that here 'the world' does not have nor display a pre-given sense. Rather, the sense of the world may be emergent as undergoing a vague and uncertain transformation, via the movement of this project—where the overlaying of pervasive computing and existential worlding paves the way for an augmented reality.¹⁰ In other words, Diller & Scofidio raise the question of our existence with augmented worlding today, where augmented or mixed reality emerges as our problematic of temporalisation and spacing in the here and now of the first decade of a young millennium. Here pervasive computing would pose as the concrete technical way to approach a decidedly augmented reality where virtuality and actuality are combined and mixed in such modes and to such a degree that one is not readily separable or distinguishable from the other. One would like to point out, then, that upon encountering *Blur Building* we are not least sensing a complex set of relations between a real physical world and the potential generated via virtualisations, something that has us wonder whether their mutual overlays or interlacing interfaces constitute and transform our experiential reality. The world of the *Blur Building* does not display a given sense— because it comes into presence as an 'augmented worlding' where actuality and virtuality (of *phusis* and *téchné* both) are overlaid or superposed upon each other. If Blur is of an augmented worlding in which physical and

---

9   I am referring to the notion of transduction as thought by Gilbert Simondon, see Simondon, *Du Mode D'existence des Objets Techniques* and *L'Individuation Psychique Et Collective*.

10 Augmented reality displays close links with ubiquitous computing and wearable computing. For instance, Mark Weiser used 'embodied virtuality' as a key term before coining 'ubiquitous computing,' with the intention to express the opposite of abstract conceptualisations of VR. AR and ubiquitous computing differ most markedly in that the latter usually maintains the notion of explicit, conscious, and intentional interaction which often blurs in AR. In AR, then, individuals are inextricably intertwined with the feedback loops of one or many computational processes which typically do not require conscious thought or effort. Ronald Azuma's influential definition of AR addresses a strict subset of AR's original goal, but it has come to be understood as representative: 'Augmented reality' is an environment that includes both virtual reality and real-world elements, and an augmented reality system is one that combines real and virtual, is interactive in real time, and is registered in 3D (see Azuma 355–85). Typical examples, in a concrete technical sense, would comprise what Lev Manovich describes generally as the new but already broadly distributed technologies of augmented space such as surveillance technologies (translating physical space and its inhabitants to data), cellspace technologies (continuously presenting data in and as mobile inhabitants' changing surroundings or milieu), and not least dynamic electronic planes (surfaces and interfaces, typically in the form of displays or screens). See Manovich, "The poetics of Augmented Space" 219–40. See also Bimber and Raskar; Haller, Billinghurst, and Thomas.

virtual reality not only overlap but has the latter deeply embedded in the former, we are situated in a complex environment or an entire milieu where the two cannot immediately be distinguished or even be made an object of awareness, and thus we must consider the question of an invisible, vague, unnoticeable, and typically pre-conscious *combinatoire* of interminglings in real time and in a 3D-world space.

Notably, this overlaying of world and pervasive computing, actuality and virtuality, perhaps constitutes the enigma of Diller & Scofidio's project, insofar as the latter is largely embedded, before awareness and to the point of invisibility, one main characteristic of pervasive or ubiquitous computing being its efforts to proceed towards pure immanence or strict embeddedness in the world. Approached from that angle, one might say that the vagueness, disappearing act, enigma, or secrecy of Blur as augmented worlding increases, along with the inhabitants' problems concerning becoming aware, to the degree that it pursues the ideal goal of embeddedness that Mark Weiser and others at PARC set up for 'calm computing':

> We wanted to put computing back in its place, to reposition it into the environmental background, to concentrate on human-to-human interfaces and less on human-to-computer ones[…] In the end, ubi-comp created a new field of computer science, one that speculated on a physical world richly and invisibly interwoven with sensors, actuators, displays, and computational elements, embedded seamlessly in the everyday objects of our lives and connected through a continuous network […]. [We] have begun to speak of calm computing as the goal, describing the desired state of mind of the user, as opposed to the hardware configuration of the computer. Just as a good, well-balanced hammer 'disappears' in the hands of a carpenter and allows him or her to concentrate on the big picture, we hope that computers can participate in a similar magic disappearing act. (Weiser, Gold and Brown)

Blur Building, as an augmentation of the world involving 'calm' ubiquitous computing, performs an entire series of such more or less complete disappearing acts, a whole flock of moves towards a more or less pure immanence which our modes of embodiment and sense meet as so many variants of a vagueness that comes to seem irreducible.[11]

---

11   I refer, indirectly, to 'the body' and 'embodiment' with a view to the distinction between these which Katherine Hayles deploys. That is, 'the body' would refer to an abstract, generalising, and normative concept which grasps the body as a cultural construct, while 'embodiment' would indicate an individual's unique experiences of embodiment as an experience lived from the inside—including the entire span from one's own sensations and affects to 'textures of life' on different biological and physical planes. See Hayles, "Flesh and Metal" 297–320. I remain interested in the investigation of distinctions today among (1) our experience (*Erfahrung*) of a generalising and normatively trendsetting design of the

2. Of the End of the World II: Blurring the Given Worldview

> The complete critique is perhaps not one that aims at totality (as does *le regard surplombant*) nor that which aims at intimacy (as does identifying intuition); it is the look that knows how to demand, in their turn, distance and intimacy, knowing in advance that the truth lies not in one or the other attempt, but in the movement that passes indefatigably from one to the other. One must desire that double excess where the look is always near to losing all its powers. (Starobinski 52)
>
> Diller and Scofidio have concentrated on the undefined. It is almost as if they are reacting against their own desire to control and produce recognizable images, places, and objects by creating works in which one is never quite certain what one is seeing. (Betsky, "Display Engineers" 35)

Of the several immanentising moves at stake in the augmented worlding of Blur Building, perhaps the one most easily noticed is the disturbance, blurring, or bringing down of world-vision. The mist-cloud, the biogenetic pumping system at the Expo site lakeshore, and the smart weather system embedded in the building are the most obvious generators of a new immanentism because disrupting the obvious: they impinge on and disturb our cultural and bodily habits of privileging the obvious, notably our continuous foregrounding of vision and its allegedly true clarity of sense. Extremely aware that their project found itself inserted in the context of a World Fair, or a world expo in the epoch of globalisation, information technology, and cosmopolitanism, Diller & Scofidio went very far to let their building become a counter-strategy to the predominant access to the world via visual appropriation and an assured world view. One might say that in its immanentising problematisation of an assured, meaningful *Weltbild Blur Building* partakes of a wider exploration of the phenomenology of the senses, an exploration that circumvents what Hans Jonas has called "the nobility of sight."

Hence what is at stake here is not so much yet another hailing of vision as the most excellent sense, nor the pursuit of *theoria* as the noblest activity of the mind—traditionally described primarily in metaphors taken from the visual domain. Rather, it involves a certain experimentation with the supports or supplements of vision, i.e., with the other senses, sensation in general, as well as "the more vulgar modes of commerce with the importunity of things" (Jonas 136). To that extent, augmented worlding cannot but blur the three main characteristics of the image-performance unique to sight. *Blur Building* resists having its presentation of a sensate

---

body, (2) our lived experiences (*Erlebnis*) of embodiment, and (3) singularly living embodiment and its contingently possible interlacing with (in)human complexity and otherness, specifically respecting implications and ramifications making themselves felt along with Diller & Scofidio's project towards a worlding of mixed or augmented realities.

manifold yield to simultaneity, the causality of sense-affection insists on its non-neutrality, and it will remain difficult, if not impossible, to achieve a proper, objectifying distance in the spatial and cognitive mental senses. In other words, Diller & Scofidio's counter-strategy very much brings vision to a different sort of attention, in the process making felt the otherwise forgotten or suppressed, but all the more originary, need for complementation from the other senses and from the motility of our bodies in the practical sphere of interaction (Jonas 152). Thus, blurring here implies a movement towards embodied performativity and the forces at play within differentiated and distributed sensation.[12]

More specifically, *Blur Building* was of 'the end of the world' on any general, grand scale of viewing, since it went far with its transimmanent resistance to becoming part of tourism as dominated by spectacular sights and attractions, an official set of scenic views, image expectations qua 'good' photo opportunities, and by a certain scopic control granted to the 'sightseer' (Diller and Scofidio, "Suitcase Studies" 42ff.). This artifactual architectural installation refused being primarily a visual culture object for consumption in the experience economy of today, just as it problematised in quite ironic ways any God's-or eagle-eye view of the world from above. As the architects themselves had it in an interview:

> We knew right away that we wanted to use the touristic setting as a foil. We realized we could use the lake water to problematize vision, to get in the way of the lake view. We also wanted to produce an anti-heroic architecture in the form of a special effect, an atmosphere. It was a reaction to the new orthodoxy of high-definition and simulation technologies. We wanted to create a low-definition space, a blur. (Betsky 147)

If there is any view of the world involved in this lo-fi world-spacing, partaking of a clear vision of the sense of the world, this is minimised placewise and remains a delayed and deferred epiphenomenon; namely, what takes place on 'the Angel Deck' hovering quite uncertainly above the more primary, extensive, and chaotically dynamic mist-clouds down here, which all inhabitants of this fuzzy augmented world must traverse first and last. Diller & Scofidio's alternative engagement with the commodification of vision by globalised tourism might well lead one to suspect that *Blur Building* concretised a strong version of that "profound suspicion of vision and its hegemonic role in the modern era" (Jay 14) which Martin Jay has

---

12 Note Edward Dimendberg's characterisation of Diller & Scofidio, stressing as key in their installations their status as embodied conceptual art "[...] in which visitors 'perform' the installation through their bodily negotiation of its space and their varying intellectual and emotional responses to it" (Dimendberg 67–80, esp. 71).

traced, with a certain disapproval, in recent French thought, only to counter such anti-ocularcentrism with an unrepentant resuscitation of enlightened clarification.[13] On that approach, *Blur Building* would be of 'the end of the world' to the extent that it simply and strictly refused any certain, stable, and visual domestication of world space as both inherently meaningful and clarifiable to the point of having light or enlightenment eradicate all remnants of obscure metaphorical texture. However, identifying in this project only a pure "denigration of vision" remains too reductive, as does an inverse movement towards an altogether live metaphor of the sun, i.e., what Jacques Derrida retraces as the circle of the heliotrope whose pervasive, dazzling light (whether ideal or a question of *lumen naturale*) allegedly illuminates everything (Derrida, "White Mythology" 266–67). Here the blurring of *Weltbild* and vision is neither a matter of a fall into strict blindness, nor of an unwarranted celebration of an accidental obscurity that is to be removed by the return of or to radiant enlightenment. Rather, Diller & Scofidio's project pursues what moves differently *within* vision and its illuminating image-performance: what has presencing disappear in its own radiance, or the indefinite self-erasure of light that permits it to come as light. Blur is after another self-erasure or withdrawal of the visible, one whose different and deferred textures of light touch its world-inhabitants in practice.[14] Perhaps in that way it approximates an archi-texture within an architectural project, drawing on supplementary haptic practices so as to transform a visible building into inhabitants' unfolding of 'critical' debate of and interactive engagement

---

13   I am thinking here not least of Jay's statement: "[…] I remain unrepentantly beholden to the ideal of illumination that suggests an Enlightenment faith in clarifying indistinct ideas […] I will employ a method that unapologetically embraces one of the anti-ocularcentric discourse's other major targets, a synoptic survey of an intellectual field at some remove from it" (Jay 17).

14   See Derrida, "White Mythology" 207–72. Responding to Jay's reading on this score, one would want to emphasise that Derrida traces *two* courses open to a heliotrope constructing its destruction. One course would remain close to Jay's call for enlightenment, never ceasing to follow a line of resistance to the dissemination of the metaphorical in syntactics and meaning. The other, however, while resembling the first to the point of being taken for it, will traverse and double it as its supplementation without limit, thus disrupting the oppositions of the semantic and the syntactic, the metaphoric and the proper—along with the traditional privileging of the latter above the former. In this context, Blur remains with vision and illumination, but is perhaps more enticing in its affirmation of the haptic textures of light that move as immanent, sensate supplements to clear sight and *Weltbild*. I am alluding also to the attractions of Cathryn Vasseleu's reading of Luce Irigaray's thought of erotic light as texture. Here texture would be both the language and material of visual practices, an invisible interweaving of differences which form the fabric of the visible. One interesting aspect of the texture of light is that it "implicates touch in vision in ways that challenge the traditional differentiation of these senses within the sensible/intelligible binarism of photology" (Vasseleu 12).

with vision. Diller & Scofidio's is thus a gentle, and affirmative 'critique' of tourism from within.[15] It makes itself felt as an ongoing questioning of the very fabrication of the aura and authenticity of tourist sites, the gaze, and meaningful imaging of memorial or memorable places in the world of today (Zavatta 12ff.).

3. Before Announced or Desired World-Construction: Practicing Haptic World-Vision

> The media event is integrated with the enveloping fog. Our objective is to weave together architecture and electronic technologies, yet exchange the properties of each for the other. Thus, architecture would dematerialize and electronic media, normally ephemeral, would become palpable in space. Both would require sophisticated technologies that would be entirely invisible, leaving only their effects. (Diller and Scofidio, *Blur* 44)

Blur Building achieves something on the order of interrogating all built and controlled environment, including the climate, along with that predominantly visual, cognitively mapped, and perceptually oriented culture that surrounds us. Doubtlessly, this achievement is intimately related to Diller & Scofidio being among the first architects to embrace the potential for alternate productions of presence found in twenty-first-century information technology and new forms of electronic mediation. Notably, in opening a blurred augmented world in the epoch of globalisation, they both affirm and move forward Frederic Jameson's diagnosis of postmodernism as predominantly synchronic and spatial, stating that it is in the realm of architecture qua living space that modifications of cultural and aesthetic production make themselves felt most dramatically—not least in terms of a problematisation of modernist distinctions between high and low culture along with a more populist shaping and sharing out of the multiplicitous surfaces of our milieu or world.[16] Blur Building, as an open-ended becoming of augmented or mixed reality, not only takes on "the new machine" (Jameson, Hardt, and Weeks 225) (the networked computer) of a hyperspatial postmodernism of surfaces, along with the imperative from new architecture "to grow new organs, to expand our sensorium and our body to some new, as yet unimaginable, perhaps ultimately impossible, dimensions" (219). Blur also leaps ahead to overtake more recent developments

---

15 See Diller & Scofidio's statement that they operate "[...] with an understanding that the target and the weapon can be the same: a 'gentle' critique of tourism from within, for the installation accepts its own role as tourist attraction" (Diller and Scofidio, "Suitcase Studies" 32–107, esp. 50).

16 See Jameson 189, 200.

in architecture as well as IT and new media. This installation project takes up presencing, *qua* new modes of technological and mediatory production of our life form, as an informative principle of work which leads to a certain displacement of at least two architectural trends: first, the more traditional view of digital technology and electronic mediation as inherently foreign to any architecture of durability, utility, and beauty; secondly, the tendency over the last 10 years for a contemporary generation of architects, who do embrace virtual architecture, to remain stuck with fascinatingly innovative, but very abstract computer models that only seldomly become actual buildings.[17] The 'blobs' of Greg Lynn and others, Marcus Novak's 'liquid architectures,' the work of NOX and Lars Spruybroek, Neil Leach's 'swarm tectonics,' Asymptote's New York trading floor, and the late Peter Eisenman's rethinking of his notion of the 'interiority of architecture' via the 'diagram' would perhaps serve as a first set of indices of the development of virtual hypersurface architecture.[18] Although Diller & Scofidio undertake a different move towards actualisation, there is no little echo here—in their obsession with the fluid flock, the cloud, and the movement in time of water—of the virtual architects' efforts to embrace the computer as an instrument for viewing form as generated in time, so as to stop modelling from the outside, and so as to undertake a shift, as Lars Spuybroek has it, "from Euclidian geometry to topology, from tectonics to textile, from object to process, from crystalline space to the undulating field or medium" (Spuybroek 20). *Blur Building* embraces a virtual and computational architecture for ubiquity and goes on seeking its actualisations, so that architecture, along with life itself, moves on in a mediatory negotiation of habitable spaces, each unfolding as very provisional 'solutions' to the problem of how to inhabit space bodily with others. Diller & Scofidio's architecture inclines towards further experimental negotiation of the problem of spatialisation that life poses to bodies, a negotiation that opens itself to the movements of time and becoming (see Grosz 148). Hence *Blur Building* inserts itself experimentally and virtuactually at the current edge of research and artistic productions involving IT and new media. That is, after the strong interest in virtuality in the 1990s, and after the exploration of more radically actual modes of tele-presence since the mid-90s. Diller & Scofidio's work bespeaks a slow re-

---

17 The general theoretical and computer scientific context for virtual architecture has been treated by Daniela Bertol and David Foell, see Bertol and Foell. A rich set of exchanges among practicing architects, cultural critics, and theoreticians appeared shortly after the millennial turn, see Leach, Turnbull, et al.. Around the same time, Malcolm McCoullough provided an in-depth theoretical study of architecture and computation, see McCullough.

18 For two influential and very interesting volumes cutting across the issues of the theory and practice of hypersurface architecture, see Perrella, *Hypersurface Architecture I & II*.

ontologising of these fields, which one might call an immanentising 'physical turn.' It could be described as a turn towards augmented worlding, understood as a dynamic 'ecotechnics' liable to sense, as Jean-Luc Nancy has it. Or a turn towards technologised worlding as a 'virtualisation of the physical,' but one whose actualisation of technics facilitates embodied relations and interaction.

Part of such a turn, *Blur Building* relinquishes the earlier emphasis on first generation virtual reality, Head Mounted Displays, immersion in perfect simulation of 3D-scenery, and a long line of formal, abstract, or metaphysical idealisations, perhaps best known from William Gibson's literary evocation of 'cyberspace' and the engagement with virtuality in the Wachowski brothers' *Matrix* movies. Accordingly, *Blur Building* 'turns physical' to put a different emphasis on corporeality and actualisation of the virtual. This situates its architecture in a context of developments we also meet in the art world today. Broadly speaking, the mutual coupling of artistic cultural production and IT plus new media today leads to the emergence of a multiplicity of large, complex, intermedial, and interactive installations, sometimes spanning the planet networkwise. This has made the installation something like a paradigmatic art form—momentarily parenthesising traditional mass-media frames for visual information-culture (images, advertising, mainstream movies, TV). Blur relates to a world of installation art with which we live in museums and art institutions, but also in all the public spaces of globalised culture. Via networks, computers, cell phones, and a host of new types of interfaces, actants, and sensors, such installations find their way across traditional distinctions between bodily intimacy and distance, the private and the public, interiority and exteriority—so as to make them extraordinarily porous. In "The Poetics of Augmented Space," Lev Manovich sketches in historicising fashion precisely such a 'physical turn' and articulates its media-specific and technological tendencies in a compact form:

> The 1990s were about the virtual. We were fascinated by new virtual spaces made possible by computer technologies. The images of an escape into a virtual space that leaves the physical space useless and of cyberspace—a virtual world that exists in parallel to our world—dominated the decade. It started with the media obsession with Virtual Reality (VR)[…]. It is quite possible that this decade of the 2000s will turn out to be about the physical—that is, physical space filled with electronic and visual information[…]. While the technologies imagined by [current] research paradigms accomplish this in a number of different ways, the end result is the same: overlaying layers of data over the physical space. (Manovich, "The Poetics of Augmented Space" 220)

Blur Building is a singular fragment of the installed world which does not have a pre-existing sense. It takes place as an intersection of contemporary architecture, art, and cybernetics. It installs augmented worlding to the extent that it opens not only such an 'augmented space,' with physical and information dimensions overlaid, but also an 'augmented temporality' comprising 'the temporal object' as layered with digital eventualisation of experience. This project towards augmented worlding may not have a sense. But the ingenuity and the innovations involved on artistic, architectural, and cybernetic planes might well lead one to claim that *Blur Building* is all about an already announced or desired construction or creation of the sense of the augmented world, relying on what goes on in practice or in performance. Such a claim would then be in alignment with a number of efforts in more or less radical versions of socio-cultural constructivism and with certain implications of ideas of unfolding parallel worlds (possible and/or actual).[19] On this score, Diller & Scofidio's work and our involvement supposedly demonstrate that contemporary world*making* has the augmented world make sense through cultural and technological inventions mixing virtuality and actuality functionally, given various contextual constraints for us and the architects. Hence Blur would be of interest because it makes a double enactive and constructive effort: not only towards virtualising an otherwise stable architecture to the point of "losing the building" in any traditional (visual) sense,[20] but also an effort towards actualising an otherwise transcendentally inclined technology so as to affect embodiment and inhabitants' relation to sense and the sensible. This will lead away from a transcendent worldview and an image of Blur as having a pre-given sense to be revealed or disclosed. It will likewise distantiate notions of an external, pre-existing, independent world, and attendant ideas of resemblance and representation. It should lead one past thinking that this project is meaningful by way of that adequate resemblance to the world which we as visitor-inhabitants may uncover. Rather, as an augmented world it would become meaningful through a more difficult or complex practice of worldmaking. This through the architects' ingenious creation and construction, or our experiences that surely reconstruct the sense of this world in many ways. It partakes of an adaptive, functional symbolism of the world which we might come to share, through a long, perhaps infinite pragmatic conversation concerned with a worlding blurred in various ways.[21]

---

19 See Goodman; Ryan; Glasersfeld; Glasersfeld, Dörfler, et al.
20 I am alluding to Wolfe.
21 In approaching Blur we are, most often, beyond the strictly epistemological frame of cognitive-symbolic mental worldmaking proper to the work of Goodman or Glaserfeld.

Certainly, constructive worldmaking accounts for much of what is at stake in Blur as inventive augmentation. The relevance of this approach is what makes critics consider the possibility of characterising Diller & Scofidio as "*engineers* of experience,"[22] and it seemingly allows a treatment of their work as part and parcel of constructing a "technological sublime" for an augmented world—one that has landscape, climate, and technology intersect with its inhabitants.[23] On this view, Blur is essentially a manufactured cloud with an embedded viewing deck, 'the Angel Deck,' hovering over Lake Neuchâtel in Switzerland. Emphasis is here on seeing that, architecturally speaking, the entire exterior 'skin' of the building is based on reactualising the 'tensegrity' concept developed by Buckminster Fuller in the 1950s. Hence all the decks and the entire building (100 meters wide, 65 meters deep, and 25 meters in height) can be seen to be composed as a structure that is, in principle, omnidirectional, non-linear, and yet able to distribute all the local loads. This because the combinations of tension and integrity allow for coupling a number of continuous cables (in tension) and discontinuous members (in compression) so as to enclose a volume (Schafer 101). Access is secured by tunnels and bridges across the water, along with walkways and stairs starting and ending low down, at the surface of the lake, so as to allow passages through the *Blur Building* as a made environment.

A constructivist approach would also inform us that the artifactual mist-cloud is generated from the lake through a hidden, complex system

---

Here worldmaking is obviously extended far into practice, aesthetics, technics, and the physical -- into delimitations of the existential -- just as we cannot but encounter the virtual which Goodman (but not Ryan) explicitly brackets by considering only the actual world.

22 See Aaron Betsky's argument that Diller and Scofidio make us aware of the seductions of visual sense-making in contemporary consumer culture by "displaying display," "[...] by heightening, questioning, or frustrating the act of display, and by doing this within display itself" (Betsky 23–6, esp. 23).

23 I am referring to David Nye's coinage of this term, see Nye 1994. When reactualising this term, I am at one with Wolfe (§§4–5) in resisting the temptation to set a tone of Romantic sublimity of the kind sought by Ned Cramer in his article on Blur Building (see Cramer 51ff.). Diller & Scofidio rather approach a notion of the technological sublime that would bespeak a mutually implicatory interlacing of human culture and technology, where technology is sought for its generative potential to be more and other than conventional, productive, and efficient. Here, technology would be approached neither in technophobic, nor in technophilic terms, but for its open-endedness and uncertain or artistically inventive in-operation (see Schafer 93–102, esp. 93–4). Compare Wolfe's remark to the effect that Diller & Scofidio "understand the relationship between art, the subject, and world in resolutely *post* humanist terms[...] the human and the non or anti or a human do not exist in fundamentally discrete ontological registers but—quite the contrary—inhabit the same space in mutual relations of co-implication and instability. This boundary-breakdown tends to be thematised in their work in the interlacing of the human and the technological" (Wolfe §8).

pumping and filtering the water. Visitor-inhabitants meet it primarily at the end-interface, as more than 31.000 small, high-pressure fog nozzles pervading the building—enabled not least by Japanese artist Fujiko Nakaya who invented this for the Pepsi Pavilion at the 1970 World Fair in Osaka. Additional information from the architects, or thorough investigation of the building, would disclose that the pumps are operated via a virtual computerised climate control. This 'smart weather system' reads temperature, humidity, as well as speed and direction of winds, in order to regulate water pressure and continuously adjust to changing climate conditions. The weather system is what keeps the spread of the mist-cloud largely within range (a 300 meter radius from the lakeshore entry), but is also what controls the intensity of the fog, as well as those limit values for chlorine, bacteria, and toxins in water and fog decreed by the Swiss authorities (Diller and Scofidio, *Blur* 363). One might observe that this is the dimension of *Blur Building* that goes furthest in stressing the porosity of the distinction between architecture and the environment, and in commenting, somewhat silently, on the remarkable development today of environmentally sustainable architecture.[24]

However, although the mist-cloud itself as well as the smart weather system controlling it can thus be said to make rather good constructive sense of this world, they are also hinges around which turn all practically constructive strategies for redeeming a clear vision of and insight into this world. For they are at the same time what unceasingly introduces a blurring of any horizon and imprints registers of sensation other than those open to the clear and appropriative sense of sight. In fact, the delimiting exploration in *Blur Building* of visual modalities of sense and sensation might well lead one to rather strong statements regarding epistemological and ontological aspects of the augmented world in play. To be sure, with this project there is very little world in the visual sense of an exterior, transcendent *mundus*, a cosmos as a well-composed, complete order in which one might find a place, a dwelling, and identifiable elements of an orientation. Thus, this is not of a world down here that one could pass through to a *télos* outside this world, just as there is no longer any spirit of

---

[24] I am thinking broadly here of the off-the-grid buildings which now demonstrate complete energetic self-sufficiency, recent 'zero energy buildings' reducing net annual energy consumption while producing excess energy and selling it back to the power company, as well as passive solar building design reducing energy consumption by 70% to 90%. More specifically, I have in mind the statement from the American Institute of Architects that immediate action by the building sector is essential to avoid hazardous man-made climate change, since half of the global warming greenhouse gas emissions today come from buildings—more than transportation or industry. See also the "Architecture 2030" plan for reducing new building energy consumption by 90% over the next two decades, submitted to the Obama administration.

the world, nor a History before whose tribunal one could stand. The blur as 'the vague open' of the building, as the fuzzy sense of an augmented world, suggests that there is no longer any assignable signification of 'world.' Or that the 'world' is withdrawing, bit by bit, from the entire order of clear signification available to us as its living, traversing, desiring inhabitants. Except, perhaps, the non-assured 'cosmic' signification of world as 'universe'—announced or called up as an infinite, misty expansion. An augmented world, *Blur Building* is not a matter of revealed or disclosed, nor announced or desired meaning.

It is no doubt continued consideration of this condition which leads Mark B. Hansen to claim, rather pointedly, that Diller & Scofidio's project takes the consequence of today's "historically unprecedented interpenetration of body and media," namely, following up on the necessity to develop "a post-visual, affective phenomenology": "what is at stake in the *Blur Building* is not simply a 'seeing that can no longer interpret,' but a wholesale short-circuiting of the role of vision, such that the affective body is *literally* compelled to 'space the void'" (Hansen 369–70). What makes itself felt as the strongest affirmation of such a claim for blur qua "a wholesale short-circuiting of the role of vision," whose literal forces operate before or beyond insight, is perhaps found rather deeply embedded within the constructions mentioned above: the system of wearable computing as yet another cluster of computers, an extensive wireless network with tracking capacity, distributed across the building. Visitors meet this system at the lakeshore in a two-fold manner. Partly as a personal-preferences questionnaire to be filled out at the log-in station. This is scanned and sent to a (hidden) central computer which interprets the information supplied into a social profile. These profiles are then downloaded into the wireless devices in waterproof 'braincoats.' That is, as a second component of the wireless system, 'wearable computing' raincoats are handed out to all visitors. Once inside the wet mist-cloud of Blur, the wireless network functions as an embedded surveillance system which is, both as a back-end system and as a front-end multitude of micro-scale device-components, largely on the order of the invisible as far as visitor-inhabitants or wearers of its augmented spacing are concerned.

Nevertheless, one would want, I think, to move at a slower pace here, relinquishing, at least in a first moment, the emphasis on the historically unprecedented, the strictly post-visual, as well as the literally compelling, non-hermeneutic, and extra-significatory force of Blur qua augmented worlding. To begin with, the dematerialisation of architecture takes place alongside and inside a revitalisation of existing, concrete architectural traditions (e.g. Buckminster Fuller). There is, moreover, no shortage of visual presencing when approaching *Blur Building* from a distance, just as a certain modicum of visibility is retained when sight is deployed on the more or less foggy decks, when the numerous LED posts and their coloured displays installed as part of the system of wearables send off their blinking signals, and when the braincoats operate their visual interface in red and green colourisations. Finally, the experiental passage through linguistic or discursive signification towards the literal force of mixing with alterity in augmentation might well be taken to remain complex, to the point of being infinitely extendable. Hence, generally speaking, the 'post-visuality' at stake, if there is any, seems to solicit a different internal working-through of image-performance and the visible—by way of the various immanent modes of blurring vision encountered in this project. Moving carefully on this path, one could begin to approach blurring via both the visible and the auditory spheres of haptics so as to trace how *Blur Building* is perhaps not immediately of a literal force beyond sense, but rather remains 'liable to sense'—insofar as it touches us both via haptic vision and via an auditory ambience or atmosphere (*Stimmung*) before or beyond a worldview qua definite cognitive map (*Leitbild*).

As regards blurred visibility experienced in the mode of haptic vision, one would insist that insofar as it touches us from the outside inside global visual culture and its image-world, Blur is not forcing us outside sense without further ado but remains 'liable to sense' as it exposes us to worlding as (our) infinite finitude, letting us exist on the contours, at the sensate limit of the world of sense. It keeps leading us to this limit. It attracts us toward what draws the contours of the world as sense by integrating a set of originally or surprisingly inventive cultural-technological experiments in interactive practice. It is these experiments which undertake an immanent transformation of visuality, displacing clarity of sight and sense—here towards a haptic vision in the first place. One might say that in terms of lighting the dynamics of the mist-cloud, the multitude of LED displays, and the entire vaguely graded spectrum of red and green emissions from all the braincoats worn have versions of a new Egypt rise up in Diller & Scofidio's project: haptic spaces composed in unique ways, of colour and by colour, juxtapose so many pure tones on flat surfaces.[25] These haptic spaces solicit a properly haptic functioning of the eye capable of dealing with the 'sense' of colours, not primarily in the representational manner relating to depth, contour, or relief in an ideal tactile-optical space, nor in a purely manual space where touch is strictly superordinate to the eye. Rather, the sense of Blur qua haptic space implies an in-between 'seeing,' a non-optical close-up rhythm of viewing whose sense

---

25 My usage of "haptic vision" refers, of course, to Gilles Deleuze's rethinking of this aspect of Alois Riegl's work (see Deleuze, *Francis Bacon* 107ff.).

of sight behaves just like the sense of touch and generates an inventive experience where form and ground are on the same plane.

Thus, Diller & Scofidio's inventive experiments afford links among cultural conventions and contemporary technics so as to facilitate and even necessitate a haptic exploration of ways to transform the sense of the world. This involves haptic vision but also comprises, sometimes alongside and at other times internal to this, several more planes and events in what one would call the multisensory dimension and process of Blur. To the extent that even haptic vision blurs, converting haptic in the direction of manual space, the sense of this augmented world draws increasingly on other modes of sensation, notably the hearing involved in delineating minimal rhythms and refrains, not only within the large scale ambience of the environment as such, but also, and perhaps especially, within the more intimate data space laid out via the auditory sonar pulsing interface integrated into the braincoats (Diller and Scofidio, *Blur* 209–23). This pulse undergoes continuous variation, but never ceases to indicate whether other visitor-inhabitants are far away (decelerated or steady sonar pinging pulse) or close by (accelerated sonar pinging pulse) and so touches one auditorily, providing pressures that are vaguely dispersed but retain a certain regularity that makes possible a drawing up of semi-distinct dot-lines or sensible navigational horizons—in the auditory atmosphere, in the soundscape forming a rather indeterminate ambient socio-cultural environment.[26]

4. Blurred to Blindness:
From Haptic World-Spacing to Originary Tactility

> [...]salut, obscurity! Salut to this erasure of figures and schemas! And salut to the blind whom we become[...] salut to the vision that did not cling to forms and ideas but that let itself be touched by forces. (Nancy, "Salut to You, Salut to the Blind We Become" 313)

Approaches via constructivist paths, even ones of haptic vision and hearing, will surely provide us with a sensible image of the *Blur Building* as an augmented world that mixes virtuality and actuality in several hybrid ways,

---

26 See Diller & Scofidio's strategy of embedding augmentation qua blurring/navigational ambience: "We propose to replace the focused attention of a visual spectacle with the attenuated attention of an immersive acoustic encounter. As disorientation is structured into the Blur experience, navigation is put to the test. [...] However, in this space of disorientation and unregulated movement, a very precisely spatial logic is invisibly mapped: space is acoustically digitised and can only be comprehended through physical movement" (Diller and Scofidio, *Blur* 198).

just as it will facilitate an interpretation of it as a functionalist symbolisation of the world at large. Such approaches may vary considerably, may be open to perturbation, meet constraints, and go on to undertake reconstruction in the face of a complex environment—like this one. Nonetheless, they may be missing the point, precisely by being too sensible, by making too much sense constructively, and by providing too much of a world-image, be it only one of lo-fi ambient tones. All this does not address what remains the most difficult question: how is it that Diller & Scofidio's augmented worlding never ceases to elude enacted vision, the desire for clear sight, and its productive, efficient making and announcement of sense? Address of this question cannot happen if one presumes that we operate primarily, or even just largely, as demiurges, semi-transcendent creators of the sense of the world.[27] Augmented worlding is hardly addressed or approached as what touches us, in a blur radical enough to blind, if one stops short with a notion that we, or Diller & Scofidio, are the creative enactors at the genesis of the sense of the world, if not the world as such. For with this project one feels very rapidly that here the architect is not the traditional manager bringing order to social space by designing and fashioning the world. Perhaps there is here rather a feeling for experiments open to innovation, for an anticipatory everyday architecture that tends towards parenthesising form, style, and signature in favour of the processual opening of a situation, relinquishing control in favour of a lived experience of indefiniteness and chance, and downplaying order and the permanency of inclusion in favour of a more flexible, plastic, and fragmentary potential for transductive individuation. Along such lines, Blur is less a demiurgic, semi-sublime construction of a meaningful world than an opening formation felt through the ongoing arrangements and modular elements it proposes in reciprocal cooperation with its visitor-inhabitant users. It moves as a uniquely mediating ecotechnical assemblage (of landscape, air, water, steel, and a host of actual architectural vectors alongside networks, computers, databases, sensors and actuants, and software code) that proposes to reweave a strong affective bond with and between people, liable in its mixes to unfold towards yet

---

27 This is, in other words, where one would want to consider departing from a number of the implicit shortcomings of versions of social and cultural constructivism that remain on quasi-transcendental planes of active, functional discourse and significant, semantic sense-making. Not only because these will consistently and reductively circle back from any contact with the complex risks pertaining to a transimmanent and existential practice with and as *téchné* (rather than semiotic mediation), but also because their principled ontological silence will reduce questions concerning the *dynamis* and *energeia* of a multiplicitous chaosmos to mere perturbations and irritations by the 'other' of 'our' positively constructive processing of sense.

another territory without its milieu exactly being constructed as one.[28] If one would still wish to say that a kind of collaborative 'appropriation' of the actual arrangements and virtual devicing of a situation is at stake here, this should perhaps be tempered by becoming aware of the degree to which Blur remains variable, presents possibilities for meaning that cannot be foreseen, and offers an architectural spacing of the moment that involves time-effects and installs a movement rather like a developing organism, one juggling with context and the unresolvable tensions pertaining to negotiating a mixed territorialisation for our life form.[29]

Blur is, as Mark Hansen has observed, an installation involving wearable space, understood as our experience of phenomenalising embodiment (our mediatory relation to a now highly technologised life world).[30] But it is perhaps not primarily as an experience of wearable space that it touches us. Blur is also, as Cary Wolfe has argued, a matter of an artful system of social communication that uses a perceptual blur to perturb the

---

28 By betokening here Blur Building as a singularly mediating assemblage involving ecotechnics, I am signaling a certain agreement with a call for a media-specific approach to this artistic-architectural project, as structurally earlier than any (digital) convergence. This would perhaps not belong too easily to any modernist notions of moving towards 'medium-specificity' via technical and material supports or conceptual-situational constellations. It would rather take for granted the problematisation after postmodernism of the work of art and of aesthetic autonomy and would thus be responding to the multiplicitous dissemination of the aesthetic and aesthetic experience throughout the socio-cultural field. This response would, generally speaking, unfold as a pursuit of differential specificity in which the medium as such will have to be reinvented, which is also to say that 'media' must be approached as differential or self-differing (see also Krauss 53ff.). More precisely, the medium-specificity of installation projects of ubicomp and augmented reality, such as this architectural one, would have to become sensitive to both sides of the mixing oscillation between the actual and the virtual, and to the transductive oscillation itself. One would, for instance, wish to cross social constructivist discourses with the kind of somewhat more robust notion of materiality that Katherine Hayles calls for, in order to entwine instantiation and signification from the outset, by conceiving of 'materiality' as the interplay of physical characteristics and signifying strategies. This would open towards media-specific analysis by making materiality an emergent property open to debate and interpretation, while also allowing the consideration of concrete projects as embodied entities to be interpreted (see Hayles 67–90). But one would also, for instance, wish to cross the valuable and materially aware but decidedly technicist analyses of (new) media (e.g., the early Friedrich Kittler), with a different sensitivity to software studies in an age of post-media aesthetics. In a manner of speaking, this is also what is currently taking place, see the developments in Marino; Fuller; Manovich; Wardrip-Fruin. In short, I am moving towards a sensation and affect of the differential media-specificity of a mixed ecotechnics which emerges transductively between phenomenology and materiality, where media-specifics invent displacements and deferrals of our traditional sense of the empirical transcendental divide

29 For a brief delineation of architectural problems in a globalised network economy of flows, see Simonot 10ff.

30 Hansen's text was published in revised form in his more recent book volume. Hansen, "Wearable Space" 321–70.

normativity of mass-mediated global communication (see Wolfe). Diller & Scofidio's project is clearly both, and Hansen and Wolfe respond to important traits; notably, embodiment, wearable computing, and media intimacy in Hansen's case; perception, communication, and artistic perturbation of mass-media constructions of reality in Wolfe's. But they also both proceed a bit too fast to enact semantic sense, via strict foci on embodied experience (although this is open to affective sensation) and social communication (although this is undergoing perturbations of perception). They tend to marginalise or leave out that Blur is not just of a world on meaningful display: it first and last gets to us as a problematisation of making clear, visual, imaged, productive, consumptive sense of the world.

As the subtitle of the artist-architects' book indicates, Blur attests to a certain care for "the making of nothing." They, along with Blur, can problematise making and its sense because the remnants of transcendence in an announced or desired sense, inherent in constructivist making, have already been abandoned. In favour of affirming haptic world-spacing as the transimmanence of the world.[31] In favour of a practico-tactile sense as existence and *téchné* (Nancy, *The Sense of the World* 45). The world is not the sense we make of it, but rather what we transform transimmanently during our approach to it as a presencing liable to sense. *Blur Building* comes into presence not only as a dynamic set of informational affordances liable to sense, but also, and earlier on, as flows of matter and energy affecting us, so as to have us feel anew that architectural mediation qua territorial spacing was always already intimately connected with providing a protected set of food sources, and that it is the flow of energy that creates stabilisations of worlding in the first place.[32] On this approach, we would be towards Blur when touching it as a singular fragment of an energetic history of the present. Touching it as being of an eventual process of augmented worlding that comes before and surprises current versions of

---

31 Architecture affects us in and as a haptic space, it is embodied in felt sensation, and experienced perceptually as a sense of place, location, and orientation in haptic or smooth space. Such a sense of place emerges from haptically embodied signals and affective traces of exterior forces such as light, sounds, smells, tastes, temperatures, resistances, weights, contours, and textures. Architecture may likewise have a certain haptico-affective impact on the senses when a given place momentarily returns a symbolic or semantic weight to perception. On this approach, *Blur Building* presents a haptic medium closely related to kinaesthesia, proprioception, and interoception, and to the fact that human embodiment processes (its own) haptic information as it moves through (sensible) space. Going very fast, I am here interested in the multiple ways in which one exists with a culturally and technically informed sentiment in Blur Building, just as one is moved by the indefinite number of live and machinic intensities at play in its smooth space. See Nancy, *The Sense of the World* passim; Deleuze and Guattari 310–50, 474–500.

32 See De Landa.

experiencing the life world as making common sense every day. It is, then, of an avisual architexture; a matter of tactile relations opening onto a different existential contact, reaching out energetically at the blurred limit of sight and vision, ear and hearing.[33] As Diller & Scofidio have it, Blur is "decidedly low definition: there is nothing to see but our dependence on vision itself" (Diller and Scofidio, *Blur* 81). Blurring world-vision and imaging, beyond, or rather inside-below, haptic vision and *Stimmung*, to the point of contacting what affects and animates us, it is of what remains structurally 'earlier than' or 'ahead of' any commonsensical hermeneutic horizon of meaning, as Husserl's thought of the life world would have it. When the tactile interface of your braincoat, located at the lower and rather intimate bodily regions, are activated at the encounter with another world-inhabitant whose scanned profile matches yours with 100% affinity, its tactile vibrancy is hardly a matter of sensible interpretation of an experience.[34] Rather, this coming to presence of the touch of the other's life form, and of other forces and *energeia*, takes you to the limit of *Erlebnis* qua a sensation of originary tactility. This is because the ongoing specific differentiation of *Blur Building* offers up to us a mixed medium, that is, a dynamic environment for a life in transduction between technology and live culture or, in other words, a mixed medium qua an epiphylogenetic processing of culture, biology, and technics which also lets us live on through means other than life.[35]

---

33 I embrace Pallasmaa's notion of the skin as the primordial architecture (of the senses), including his displacement of the bias towards vision and the suppression of the other senses in favour of approaching the heart of lived experience as moulded by hapticity, and thus by an irreducibly peripheral, unfocused, and blurred vision. I approach all the senses as extensions of the tactile, as specialisations of skin tissue, and all sensations as modalities of touching. If touch is the mode that (dis-)integrates our experience of the world with that of ourselves, *Blur Building* is perhaps best approached as a 'life-(in)formative' architecture addressing all the senses simultaneously to articulate the edge of a lived experience of being in the world while permitting our sense of reality and self. See Pallasmaa 10–11.

34 See "[t]here is also a tactile response. Occasionally, visitors in Blur will have a 100% affinity. To register this rare occurrence, a third response system may be integrated into the coat. A small vibrating pad, modelled after the vibrating motor of a pager [...] would send a vibration through the coat, mimicking the tingle of excitement that comes with physical attraction" (Diller and Scofidio, *Blur* 217).

35 I refer to Hansen's notion of 'medium' as "an environment for life," where the medium is implicated in technical life, naming that transduction between the organism and the environment which constitutes life as essentially technical. 'Medium' concerns the exteriorisation of the living along with the selective actualisation of the (architectural) environment, the demarcation of a world, or the differential delineation of an existential domain (see Hansen 297ff., 299–300). I am also indicating the relevance, for approaching our life form in mixed realities today, of Bernard Stiegler's rethinking of André Leroi-Gourhan and Gilbert Simodon's important work so as to offer contemporary notions of "ephiphylogenesis" and "technics." Our co-evolution with technics in mixed realities can perhaps best be approached in its interlacing hybridisations of lifeforms by drawing on a notion of technics

5. At Our Discretion: Among the Almost Immanent... and Untouchable Embeddedness

> [...] the *there* is nothing other than the Wittgensteinian 'That' of the world, while at the same time being the world's original 'how.' [...] It is not a place of places, or a *sensorium Dei*, or an a priori form. More likely, it would be a priori matter—but here the a priori, in its *act of birth*, would be the sensible entelechy itself: the unity, opened within itself, of the touched/touching[...] the worldliness of the world, qua absolute existential condition, exhausts its finite sense—exhausts it, that is, opens it infinitely. *Mundus patet*. (Nancy, *The sense of the World* 159–60)

As augmented worlding Blur directly engages the way in which information and communication technologies today move towards becoming indiscernible from any ontological exterior inside (nature, the environment, the milieu, embodiment, organs, bodies, the body). Partaking of the emergent movement of pervasive computing, Diller & Scofidio's project pursues the disappearance of the computer and the pervasive embedding of computing, and so places us not least among the invisibly integrated world-spacings of ubi-comp, as described, for example, by Malcolm McCullough when he cites the statements issued by Intel Corporation around 2001:

> Computing, not computers will characterize the next era of the computer age. The critical focus in the very near future will be on ubiquitous access to pervasive and largely invisible computing resources. A continuum of information processing devices ranging from microscopic embedded devices to giant server farms will be woven together with a communication fabric that integrates all of today's networks with networks of the future. Adaptive software will be self-organizing, self-configuring, robust, and renewable. At every level and in every conceivable environment, computing will be fully integrated with our daily lives.[36]

---

qua a third ontic domain of "organized inorganic beings," and on a notion of "epiphylogenesis" qua that co-originarity of the human and technics which lets us evolve specifically via the invention of technics, i.e., via living on through means other than life (see Stiegler 17).

36 See McCullough. See also the more recent statement from the research programme "Future and Emerging Technologies" launched by DG Information Society and Media, the European Commission: "[...] 'the-computer-as-we-know-it' will soon have no role in our future everyday lives and environments. It will be replaced by a new generation of technologies, which will move the computing power off the desktop and ultimately integrate it with real world objects and everyday environments. Computing becomes thus an inseparable part of our everyday activities, while simultaneously *disappearing* into the background. It becomes a *ubiquitous utility* taking on a role similar to electricity—an enabling but invisible and pervasive medium revealing its functionality on request in an unobtrusive way and supporting people in their everyday lives" (Streitz et al. n.pag).

At such a here and now, the Blur world and its events are not what we make sense of. Rather, blurred worlding invisibly overlaid with the pervasively embedded and calm computing of augmented reality (in the widest 'sense') is ecotechnics as how we exist. The world is not what we make or manipulate, but how we exist with a cultural and technological sentiment or affect.[37] The sensible entelechy of Blur, its originary opening of the touching/touched in uniquely vague artifactual dynamics and movements, calls for and allows transformation of the sense of our existence, in an interactive and performative practice at the edge of the world. It attracts and leads us the most when and where it approaches an infinitely finite world delimiting sense, sentiment, and affect. An impersonal, inoperative, disorganised, shattered, and discrete world of tactility prior to rhythmic pulse, image, and clear vision. Structurally earlier than or evading haptic vision, hearing, and manual spacing. Withdrawing even from the distinction between self- and other-reference which it allows. A world of relational existential *tangens* which remains fuzzily vague, because liable to sense at the most, whether originarily or as a world to come. One whose traits are perhaps not just being-in-the-world or being-towards, but just as much being-with, being-between, being-among other existents and things. An irreducibly vague world of ecotechnics, because discretely different. One whose touches are delightful or terrifying, beautiful or technologically sublime, depending on the character of the exposition to becoming other elsewhere, in singularly plural 'contact-among.'

Perhaps the *tangens* of this augmented worlding in a place and an epoch of ubiquitous computing is at its most difficult when its demand is exorbitant: when the embeddedness of the pervasive altogether smoothes out space and time and thus demands an impossible tact. At this level of tactful giving/withdrawal, the augmenting of the augmented world, which may be all, cannot be struck, grasped, stroked, caressed, kissed, licked, or tasted on any one contour. Of necessity, it can only be mourned, with a certain respect for what exceeds the most minute fragment of erotic light or *Eros* qua texture, at the limit where touch cannot remain within the confines of the tactile but is all about learning anew what it feels like to touch without touching. Blur and its blurring goes and comes as it invents the world as an affinity of disjunction and conjunction (do not touch: but touch): as an inventive building of the world, it brings into contiguity, *partes extra partes*, contact and non-contact where all it touches is the other.[38]

---

37 Indicating sense in the greatest semantic generality as sensing, affective directionality, and orientation.

38 I remain inventively indebted to the other places Jacques Derrida will have gone with the untouchable. Hence I will not even thank. See Derrida, "The Untouchable" 66–91.

References

2030: Architecture. "The 2030 Challenge Stimulus Plan." 2008. 21 Jan 2010 <http://www.architecture2030.org/downloads/2030stimulusplan.pdf>.

Azuma, Ronald T. "A Survey of Augmented Reality." *Presence: Teleoperators and Virtual Environments* 6.4 (1997): 355–85.

Beigl, Michael. "Ubiquitous Computing: Computation Embedded in the World." *Disappearing Architecture: From Real to Virtual to Quantum.* Eds. Michael Beigl and Peter Weibel. Berlin: Birkhäuser, 2005. 52–61.

Bertol, Daniela and David Foell. *Designing Digital Space.* New York: Wiley, 1997.

Betsky, Aaron. "Display Engineers." *Scanning: The Aberrant Architectures of Diller + Scofidio.* New York: Whitney Museum of American Art, 2003, 23–36.

—. *Scanning: The Aberrant Architectures of Diller + Scofidio.* New York: Whitney Museum of American Art, 2003.

Bimber, Oliver and Ramesh Raskar. *Spatial Augmented Reality.* Wellesley, MA.: A. K. Peters, 2005.

Cook, Diane and Sajal K. Das. *Smart Environments.* Hoboken, NJ: John Wiley, 2005.

Cramer, Ned. "All Natural." *Architecture* 91.7 (2002): 51–9.

Daley, Andrew, Ignacio Cirac, et al.. "The Development of Quantum Hardware for Quantum Computing." *Disappearing Architecture: From Real to Virtual to Quantum.* Eds. Michael Beigl and Peter Weibel. Berlin: Birkhäuser, 2005. 62–76.

De Landa, Manuel. "Homes: Meshwork or Hierarchy." 1995. 21 Jan 2010 <http://www.mediamatic.nl/Doors/Doors2/DeLanda/DeLanda-Doors2-E3.html>.

Deleuze, Gilles. *Francis Bacon: The Logic of Sensation.* New York: Continuum, 2003.

Deleuze, Gilles and Félix Guattari. *A Thousand Plateaus.* Minneapolis: U of Minnesota P, 1987.

Derrida, Jacques. "White Mythology: Metaphor in the Text of Philosophy." *Margins of Philosophy.* Chicago: U of Chicago P, 1982. 207–72.

—. "§4: The Untouchable, or the Vow of Abstinence." *On Touching, Jean-Luc Nancy.* Stanford: Stanford UP, 2005. 66–91.

Designboom. "Diller & Scofidio. The Blur Building." 2007. 21 Jan 2010. <http://www.design boom.com/eng/funclub/dillerscofidio.html>.

Diller, Elizabeth and Ricardo Scofidio "Suitcase Studies: The Production of a National Past." *Back to the Front: Tourisms of War.* Eds. Elizabeth Diller and Ricardo Scofidio. New York: Princeton Architectural Press, 1994. 32–107.

—. *Visite Aux Armées: Tourismes De Guerre.* New York: Princeton Architectural Press, 1994.

—. *Blur: The Making of Nothing.* New York: Harry N. Abrams, 2002.

Dimendberg, Edward. "Blurring Genres." *Scanning: The Aberrant Architectures of Diller + Scofidio.* Ed. Aaron Betsky. New York: Whitney Museum of American Art, 2003. 67–80.

Foster, Ian and Carl Kesselman. *The Grid.* Amsterdam: Elsevier, 2004.

Fuller, Matthew. *Software Studies: A Lexicon.* Cambridge, MA: MIT Press, 2008.

Gibson, William. *Neuromancer.* New York: Ace Books, 1984.

Glasersfeld, Ernst v. *Radical Constructivism: A Way of Knowing and Learning.* London: Falmer Press, 1995.

Glasersfeld, Ernst v., Willibald Dörfler, et al. *Konstruktivismus Statt Erkenntnistheorie.* Klagenfurt: Drava, 1998.

Goodman, Nelson. *Ways of Worldmaking*. Indianapolis: Hackett Publishing, 1978.
Grosz, Elizabeth A. *Architecture from the Outside: Essays on Virtual and Real Space*. Cambridge, MA: MIT Press, 2001.
Haller, Michael, Mark Billinghurst, et al. *Emerging Technologies of Augmented Reality*. Hershey: Idea Group, 2007.
Hansen, Mark B. N. "Wearable Space." *Configurations* 10.2 (2003): 321–70.
—.*Bodies in Code: Interfaces with Digital Media*. New York: Routledge, 2006.
—."Media Theory." *Theory Culture Society* 23.2–3 (2006): 297–306.
Hayles, N. Katherine. "Flesh and Metal: Reconfiguring the Mindbody in Virtual Environments." *Configurations* 10 (2002): 297–320.
—."Print Is Flat, Code Is Deep: The Importance of Media-Specific Analysis." *Poetics Today* 25.1 (2004): 67–90.
Hayles, N. Katherine and Danielle Foushee, eds. *Nanoculture: Implications of the New Technoscience*. Bristol: Intellect Books, 2004.
Hutchens, Benjamin C. and Jean-Luc Nancy. "Interview: The Future of Philosophy." *Jean-Luc Nancy and the Future of Philosophy*. Ed. B. C. Hutchens. Chesham: Acumen, 2005. 161–66.
James, Ian. *The Fragmentary Demand: An Introduction to the Philosophy of Jean-Luc Nancy*. Stanford: Stanford UP, 2006.
Jameson, Frederic. "Postmodernism, or the Cultural Logic of Late Capitalism." *The Jameson Reader*. Eds. Frederic Jameson, Michael Hardt, et al. Oxford: Blackwell, 2000.
Jameson, Fredric and Michael Hardt, et al. *The Jameson Reader*. Oxford: Blackwell, 2000.
Jay, Martin. *Downcast Eyes*. Berkeley: U of California P, 1993.
Jonas, Hans. "The Nobility of Sight: A Study in the Phenomenology of the Senses." *The Phenomenon of Life: Toward a Philosophical Biology*. Evanston: Northwestern UP, 2001. 135–56.
Kiser, Kirsten. "Diller & Scofidio: Blur Building." Arcspace. 2007. 21 Jan 2010 <http://www.arcspace.com/architects/DillerScofidio/blur_building/index.htm>.
Krauss, Rosalind E. "A Voyage on the North Sea." *Art in the Age of the Post-Medium Condition*. London: Thames & Hudson, 2000.
Leach, N., D. Turnbull, et al. *Digital Tectonics*. Hoboken, NJ: Wiley-Academy, 2004.
Leerberg, Thomas. "Blur by Diller & Scofidio." 2006. 21 Jan 2010 <http://thl.dskd.dk/view.php/page/BLUR>.
Loke, Seng. *Context-Aware Pervasive Systems*. Boca Raton, FL: Auerbach Publications, 2006.
Manovich, Lev. "The Poetics of Augmented Space." *Visual Communication* 5.2 (2006): 219–40.
—. "Software Takes Command." 2008. 21 Jan 2010 <http://lab.softwarestudies.com/ 2008/11/softbook.html>.
Marino, Mark C. "Critical Code Studies." 2006. 21 Jan. 2010 <http://www.electronicbookreview. com/thread/electropoetics/codology>.
McCullough, Malcom. *Digital Ground: Architecture, Pervasive Computing, and Environmental Knowing*. Cambridge, MA: MIT Press, 2004.
Milara, Javier. "Diller + Scofidio: How They Obtained the Blur Effect." *Hipercroquis*. 2006. 21 Jan 2010 <http://hipercroquis.net/2006/10/page/2/>.
Nancy, Jean-Luc. *Corpus*. 1992. Paris: Éditions Métailié, 2006.

—. *The Sense of the World*. Minneapolis: U of Minnesota P, 1997.
—. *Being Singular Plural*. Stanford: Stanford UP, 2000.
—. "Salut to You, Salut to the Blind We Become." *On Touching: Jean-Luc Nancy*. Ed. Jacques Derrida. Stanford: Stanford UP, 2005. 313–4.
Nye, David E. *American Technological Sublime*. Cambridge, MA: MIT Press, 1994.
Pallasmaa, Juhani. *The Eyes of the Skin: Architecture and the Senses*. Hoboken, NJ: John Wiley & Sons, 2005.
Perrella, Stephen, ed. *Hypersurface Architecture*. New York: John Wiley & Sons, 1998.
—. *Hypersurface Architecture II*. New York: John Wiley & Sons, 1999.
Robinson, Philip and Harald Vogt, et al. *Privacy, Security, and Trust within the Context of Pervasive Computing*. New York: Springer, 2005.
Rubin, Ben. "Diller + Scofidio: The Blur Building, National Expo 2002, Yverdon-Les-Bains, Switzerland." 2002. 21 Jan 2010 <http://hammer.prohosting.com/~soa/diller/>.
Ryan, Marie-Laure. *Possible Worlds, Artificial Intelligence, and Narrative Theory*. Bloomington: Indiana UP, 1991.
Schafer, Ashley. "Designing Inefficiencies." *Scanning : The Aberrant Architectures of Diller + Scofidio*. A. Betsky. New York: Whitney Museum of American Art, 2003. 93–102.
Simondon, Gilbert. *Du Mode D'existence Des Objets Techniques*. Paris: Aubier, 1989.
—. *L'individuation Psychique Et Collective*. Paris: Aubier, 1989.
Simonot, Beatrice. "Strategies and Tactics." *Archilab's Future House: Radical Experiments in Living Space*. Eds. Marie-Ange Brayer and Beatrice Simonot. London: Thames & Hudson, 2002. 10–13.
Spuybroek, Lars. "The Motorization of Reality." *Archis* 11 (1998): 18–21.
Starobinski, Jean. *L'oeil Vivant, Essai*. Paris: Gallimard, 1961.
Steventon, Alan and Steve Wright. *Intelligent Spaces*. London: Springer, 2006.
Stiegler, Barbara. *Technics and Time. Vol. 1: The Fault of Epimetheus*. Stanford: Stanford UP, 1998.
Streitz, Norbert A. et al., eds. *The Disappearing Computer*. Berlin: Springer, 2007.
Thacker, Eugene. *Biomedia*. Minneapolis: U of Minnesota P, 2004.
—. *The Global Genome: Biotechnology, Politics, and Culture*. Cambridge, MA: MIT Press, 2005.
Vasseleu, Cathryn. *Textures of Light: Vision and Touch in Irigaray, Levinas, and Merleau-Ponty*. New York: Routledge, 1998.
Wachowski Andy, and Larry Wachowski, dir. *The Matrix*. Prod. Joel Silver. Warner Brothers, 1999.
Wardrip-Fruin, Noah. *Expressive Processing*. Cambridge, MA: MIT Press, 2009.
Weiser, Mark and Rich Gold, et al. "The Origins of Ubiquitous Computing Research at Parc in the Late 1980s." 21 Jan 2010 <http://www.research.ibm.com/journal/sj/384/ weiser.html>.
Wolfe, Cary. "Lose the Building: Systems Theory, Architecture, and Diller + Scofidio's Blur." *Postmodern Culture* 16.3 (2006): 32 paragraphs.
Zavatta, Sylvie. "Preface." *Back to the Front: Tourisms of War*. Ed. Elizabeth Diller and Ricardo Scofidio. New York: Princeton Architectural Press, 1994. 8–17.

Worlds Made of Concrete and Celluloid: The London Council Estate in *Nil By Mouth* and *Wonderland*

MATTHEW TAUNTON

Nelson Goodman's constructivist definition of the process of worldmaking (Goodman 1–22) brings with it some of the traditional problems of relativism. Jerome Bruner has well described Goodman's theory of worldmaking as being underwritten by the thesis that "contrary to common sense there is no unique 'real world' that pre-exists and is independent of human mental activity and human symbolic language; that what we call the world is a product of some mind whose symbolic procedures construct the world" (Bruner 95). Goodman would hold, then, that worldmaking is not just some secondary process that draws on materials in the world, and frames, shapes, and describes them in the terms of a given symbolic system: the point is rather that 'the world' does not exist except as a composite construction of different frames of reference or world-versions (Goodman 4). Any attempt to place these worlds in a hierarchy of importance, or to test their validity by some objective criterion, would itself be merely to propose a new way of construing the world, which—with its own internal logic—will be justifiable in its own limited terms, but devoid of general significance.

There are elements of Goodman's theory that are useful, and can help us to describe some of the processes—he names composition and decomposition, weighting, ordering, deletion and supplementation, and deformation—by which meaning is produced. However, the pluralism that would ask us not only to recognise the validity of alternative world-versions (in their own terms, for there are no others by which to judge them), but also to accept that what we thought was the world is only one world among many, is hugely problematic for a number of reasons. This paper seeks to problematise Goodman's constructivist notion of worldmaking by exploring the construction of the London council estate, first in a literal sense as a development in the history of British social housing and then, metaphorically, in the sense of its cultural construction in cinema.

On one level, I will argue, this is a world that is made through social policy, and the emergence of the council estate—a world made of concrete—can in this sense be understood as a meeting of architectural modernism with the ideals of the British welfare state. This is a form of worldmaking—indeed it is in some senses the definitive form of worldmaking—since it literally entails the construction of a physical environment in which people will live. To suggest that the characteristic architecture of the council estate is simply to blame for the social problems associated with it would be to lapse into architectural determinism, but, on the other hand, it must be conceded that this architecture is by now inextricably associated with social decay. In order to fully understand this phenomenon, it will be necessary to examine cultural constructions of the estate, and therefore to consider another level of worldmaking. By examining two films in which the council estate forms a key part of the *mise en scène*—namely Gary Oldman's *Nil By Mouth* (1997) and Michael Winterbottom's *Wonderland* (1999)—I will seek to show how the films make very different celluloid worlds from similar raw materials.

In doing so it will be necessary to consider the medium-specific ways of worldmaking that pertain to film. Most notably, film is an indexical medium, and as such like photography it relies for its content on the world that is in front of the lens. The art of set design suggests that this world is subject to manipulation—as is the photographic image itself in the era of Computer-Generated Imagery (see Prince 27–37)—but what interests me here is how pre-existing worlds are transformed by the characteristic elements of the medium of cinema, namely narrative, the framing of the *mise en scène*, and montage. Narrative is key in both of the films that will be discussed here, which interpolate their fictional characters into the real spaces of the council estate in order to explore the social problems and possibilities that it presents to its inhabitants. The framing of the *mise en scène* becomes important when we consider the specific ways in which the estate is photographed, which itself can serve to construct a world in which, for example, the estate forms a continuous part of the city. Montage is equally important to the way in which a film constructs a world, but it works through juxtaposition, switching between shots and so making spatial and temporal leaps that invite the audience either to make connections or to dwell on incongruities. This paper will focus on the way film uses these means to engage with the world of the council estate and imagine ways in which this world might be reconstituted. These two films about the council estate should be seen as part of a wider discourse (particularly around class) that is as significant in defining the specific world of the estate as is its distinctive architecture. They also, in their relation to the wider history of the development of social housing within the British welfare state, give us reason to doubt Goodman's clear implication that worlds are not referred ultimately to some underlying reality.

Before turning to the films I will sketch the social, political and architectural background of the council estate. After the World War II, Britain was faced with a chronic housing shortage. Building of new homes had stopped during the war, and at the same time, hundreds of thousands of homes were damaged or destroyed by bombing (Timmins 141). Dwelling patterns were also changing, and with sharp increases in marriage, divorce and birth rates, new households were being formed at an unprecedented rate (Power 186). Labour, who won a landslide victory in the general election of 1945, had promised to build 5 million dwellings "in quick time" if elected (Timmins 141). Nye Bevan was minister for health and housing in Clement Attlee's government, and he was, in Lynsey Hanley's phrase, on a mission to "build equality into the fabric of the national landscape" (Hanley 77). He set high standards for social housing, specifying a minimum of 900 square feet of floor space and the guarantee of a garden: this clearly meant brick-built cottages, and not cheaply constructed flats (79). He was influenced by the Garden City movement, and as well as a general preference for houses over flats, he took from this movement the desire to produce variegated communities where classes intermingled. As he put it, "I believe it is essential for the full life of a citizen […] to see the living tapestry of a mixed community" (Timmins 145).

Bevan's commitment to quality over quantity meant that reconstruction did not proceed as quickly as many had hoped, and fell well short of the target of 5 million dwellings by 1951. Harold Macmillan—who became housing minister in the Conservative government that won the 1951 election—made his name with an election pledge to build 300,000 homes a year. That he managed this in his first year of office is a remarkable achievement, but one that came at a price. As Patrick Dunleavy points out, he oversaw "drastic reductions in the space standards and amenity of public housing" (Dunleavy 35).

This switch of emphasis from quality to quantity in 1951 has in many ways determined the subsequent history of social housing in Britain. For many years, the two main parties were locked in a bidding war over which could build the most units per year, and in a time of housing shortage this proved to be a success with the electorate. Bevan's ideal of the 'mixed community' was abandoned in favour of building cheap, industrially constructed flats, which were essentially intended to house the poor. Labour had at one stage proposed nationalising up to 70 percent of the total housing stock, meaning that much of the middle class would be council tenants. But in 1965, Harold Wilson's Labour government issued a white paper that "recognized owner-occupation as the 'normal' tenure and, by implication, relegated public housing to the position of a residual, short-term expedient" (Burnett 287). This reflected a new cross-party consensus, and the negation of Bevan's idea of the 'mixed community': henceforth, council estates were to be residential zones exclusively for working class and unemployed tenants.

Architectural modernism became the gospel for those who wanted to create a new Britain, and—with the potential it offered for prefabrication and industrialised building techniques—it also meant that it could be done on the cheap. Alison and Peter Smithson imported many modernist ideas into Britain, and continued Le Corbusier's critique of the street, arguing that the task of "[r]e-identifying man with his environment cannot be achieved by using historical forms of house-groupings: streets, squares, greens, etc., as the social reality they represent no longer exists" (Smithson 22). They proposed instead "a multi-level city with residential streets-in-the-air" (Smithson 26). As Dunleavy writes, the Smithsons' 'new Brutalist' manifesto did much to promote the use of "avowedly 'hard' designs using dramatic building forms and a great deal of exposed concrete" (Dunleavy 58). Government—on both the local and national level—embraced the new style through legislation, a notable example being the Housing Subsidy Act of 1956, which incentivised the building of high-rise blocks by offering additional funding to local authorities for every additional storey built above the sixth floor (Hanley 93; Timmins 184).

So when considering the council estate as an example of worldmaking, it is crucial that the process is not simply viewed simply as a consequence of the individual agencies of architects. As Robert Hughes points out, "[t]he most influential architecture of the twentieth century, in many ways, was paper architecture that never got off the drawing board" (Hughes 165), and paper architecture could in itself be considered a form of worldmaking. But I am concerned here with the building of a physical environment in which people can live, and in this case—especially on the kind of scale that became necessary in post-war Britain—it becomes clear that architecture's capacity for worldmaking is heavily circumscribed and directed by planning legislation and funding. The project of building system-built housing estates only began when the state and its agencies threw their weight behind it. Even then, building did not proceed on the architects' terms, and budgetary and other restraints played a key role in the urban landscape that resulted. Architectural worldmaking is very far from being an autonomous process, and it is important to keep in mind, as I turn to an analysis of *Nil By Mouth*, the complex web of social, political and economic factors that are fundamental to the emergence of the council estate.

Nil By Mouth—a grisly tale of unemployment, drug addiction and domestic violence—was shot on location at the Ferrier Estate in South East London, which offers the basic materials for the film's *mise en scène*. The raised walkways, the long corridors bathed in a perpetual neon glare, and the sinister car parks of the estate figure prominently. One of the central arguments of modernism was that these areas between individual dwellings should take on the social function of the street and become a site for interaction between tenants. More than that, for Karel Teige—whose vision of collectivised housing is laid out in his book *The Minimum Dwelling*—the paring back of the size and function of the individual apartment was to be accompanied by a pooling of certain domestic functions elsewhere: communal laundry facilities, and even communal meals, were intended both to socialise and to domesticate the areas outside individual flats (Teige 247).

The way in which Oldman photographs the estate deliberately emphasises the failure of these areas to function as social spaces. Billy—a wandering heroin addict—is frequently photographed isolated against the concrete backdrop of the estate, an unfriendly space which proclaims the death of the street, but offers nothing to replace it. This refusal of the council estate to recreate traditional urban forms—streets, squares and so on—accentuates its dislocation from the ordinary urban fabric. As Lynsey Hanley writes, "from the mid-1960s onwards you could tell council estates from a mile off, giving you the chance to avoid them, to duck out and treat them with the suspicion that their reputations seemed to warrant" (Hanley 65). What *Nil By Mouth* does very well is to emphasise the way in which the peculiar terrain of the council estate has come to symbolise unemployment, crime and addiction, attributes associated with the new kind of lumpen class which the film depicts. Indeed, the film suggests that the world of the council estate exists outside of traditional understandings of class structures.

Oldman's film is at pains to emphasise the discrepancy that exists between the lumpen council estate dweller and the old working class. With the exception of Billy's mother Janet—who we see at work in a factory—the film's characters are unemployed and rely on crime and welfare payments for their survival. Ray—the alcoholic, played by Ray Winstone, who savagely beats his pregnant wife in a scene which is hard to watch—is openly contemptuous of work, and finds other ways of funding his prodigious consumption of alcohol and cocaine. He is involved in illicit dealings of which we never hear the details, but as his long-suffering wife Val attests, "he ain't got no fucking work."[1] In fact, in terms of a traditional Marxist view of class, the characters in *Nil By Mouth* are not working class at all, but lumpenproletariat. Marx saw this as a historically insignificant class with no revolutionary potential, doomed to whither away as the stage is set for a historic confrontation of bourgeoisie and proletariat. As he writes, the lumpenproletariat "the social scum, that passively rotting mass thrown off by the lowest layers of the old society, may, here and there, be swept into the movement by a proletarian revolution; its conditions of life, however, prepare it more for the part of a bribed tool of reactionary intrigue" (Marx and Engels 92). By making addiction, violence and crime the major parameters of class, *Nil By Mouth* suggests that it is culturally constructed rather than merely an economic relationship. And the council estate functions as a kind of echo chamber for these things. It is unthinkable that a revolutionary class consciousness—or indeed a more modest desire for political representation—could emerge in the council estate of *Nil By Mouth*.

If *Nil By Mouth* suggests that the council estate is central to the imagery of the underclass, then the association can also be backed up by sociological analysis. As Chris Hamnett points out in his detailed study of inequality in London:

> London has become polarised into two distinct housing markets: on the one hand, the increasingly expensive market where prices are set at the top end by the demand from highly paid workers in finance, law and related areas, as well as the international wealthy, and on the other, the council and social rented sector which houses most of those who cannot gain access to home ownership or high-cost private renting. The social divide between the tenures has grown rapidly since the 1960s, leading to the increasing social residualisation of council housing and an increased social polarisation between council tenants and homeowners. (Hamnett 129)

Hamnett also demonstrates that this "residualisation" has been increasingly characterised by unemployment and its ruinous effects. By 1991, he notes, the proportion of households letting from local authorities in Inner London without a single member in employment was 57 percent, rising from 27 percent in 1971 (149). The figures from owner-occupying households are much lower. In the world of *Nil By Mouth*, class is culturally and geographically defined, with the limits of the estate forming an impermeable boundary between the new lumpen class and the owner-occupying, petit-bourgeois majority.

---

[1] Quotations from films are transcribed directly from the released version, and not from the script.

Now I have described the making of the concrete world of the London council estate, and how *Nil By Mouth* constructs a celluloid world that emphasises both through its photography and through its narrative the insulation of that world from the city as a whole. Michael Winterbottom's *Wonderland* offers a fundamentally different view of the council estate. As examples of cinematic worldmaking these films present internally coherent and entirely distinct takes on the council estate. But the construction of a cinematic world occurs at a level of remove from the social, political and architectural worldmaking that initially constitutes the council estate. Indeed, rather than simply being two entirely separate celluloid worlds, the two films are ontologically grounded in the reality of the estate through the indexicality of film as a medium, or what Bazin termed the "ontology of the photographic image" (Bazin, "The Ontology of the Photographic Image" 9). Furthermore, as I will show, the films are critically engaged with contemporary housing policy from different sides. On several different levels, then, these celluloid worlds are not simply the capricious inventions of their makers, independent from the given world. This is because they are ultimately referred to the pre-existing underlying world of the council estate, which itself evokes a complex web of intractable real-world problems.

I want to begin my comparison of the two films by looking at two very short scenes that depict the lifts. According to a recent study, problems with lifts were the most common cause of discontent with high-rise life (Warburton 160). In *Nil By Mouth*, the lift forms a part of the unfriendly terrain that I have described, another element of the network of nondescript and vaguely menacing corridors and walkways that link the flats. In one sequence, just after he has been beaten up by Ray in a dispute over drugs, Billy takes the lift down from Val and Ray's flat. The first shot in the sequence, filmed through the scuffed Perspex of a fire door, shows him walking down the corridor outside the flat and into the heavily vandalised hallway outside the lift. Hurried by the first pangs of withdrawal, Billy impatiently hammers the button, and we hear the lift mechanism stirring into life. The whole sequence retains that feeling of an ill-defined space, an inconvenient and perhaps perilous interstitial realm that only exists to be passed through, and has constantly to be negotiated. In the next shot, we see the lift doors on the ground floor from outside. When they open and Billy comes out, into another hallway covered in graffiti, the camera pans around to show the empty corridor, and lingers on this.

Figure 1: *Nil By Mouth*: a deserted corridor in the Ferrier estate.

This short sequence illustrates the disorientating effect of the lift, particularly in the context of multi-storey housing developments. The doors open and one emerges into a space which is indistinguishable from any other floor. This shot (Fig.1) is typical of *Nil By Mouth* in that it is directed inward, reproducing for the viewer the sense of being in a strictly delimited and confined space, from which no escape is offered.

Wonderland is a very different kind of film: where *Nil By Mouth* is depressing, *Wonderland* is merely melancholy, depicting a November weekend in the lives of three sisters and their parents, who are dispersed across a variety of London dwellings, most of which are on council estates. But it is fundamentally more optimistic about the future of the city, and the role the council estate has to play in that city. One of the main protagonists, Nadia, lives in a high-rise block near the Oval cricket ground, and there is a lift scene here that is comparable to the one I have just described. On the one hand, Winterbottom—like Oldman—stresses the loneliness and the anonymity of the journey, and the humdrum spaces Nadia passes through. The camera dwells, again, on her impatience as she presses the button, holding it down for longer than strictly necessary, and waits for the lift to arrive. When in the lift, we see her staring blankly toward the camera. Meanwhile, on the soundtrack, we hear the recorded responses to a lonely hearts ad that Nadia has placed. On a basic level, this juxtaposition serves to place Nadia's loneliness and her search for love in the context of her environment, emphasising her solitariness and the absence of the street as a place of neighbourly interaction. The voices are played over one another, each message fading out as new ones begin, setting up a kind of chorus of lonely hearts. So the sequence to some extent counters the strong sense of loneliness and anomie that it creates by insisting at the same time that this is an experience shared by many. The audience is thus invited to think beyond Nadia's confinement and to consider the realm of possibility—romantic or otherwise—offered by the city.

This outward-looking perspective is reinforced by the way in which the sequence is shot. While *Nil By Mouth* dwelled on the identical, institutional corridors and so emphasised the sense of an inescapable enclosure, in *Wonderland*, the sequence begins with a view over the rainy city, out of the window of the high-rise. After holding this admittedly rather drear prospect for a few seconds, the camera whip pans to Nadia locking the door of her flat, and follows her down the corridor to the lift. This use of the pan from the wider city as a whole to the individual high-rise dweller creates a sense that the estate and its inhabitants are continuous with the city, rather than—as in *Nil By Mouth*—utterly alienated from it. In the words of André Bazin, "[c]lassical editing … separated reality into successive shots which were just a series of either logical or subjective points of view of an event" (Bazin, "An Aesthetic of Reality" 28). Winterbottom's use of a pan instead of a cut here can be read as a kind of refusal to separate reality into separate worlds, or "subjective points of view of an event," and an assertion of the continuity of that reality, or "the world." This is a vital point in terms of the kind of media-specific worldmaking that I have described. While montage can be used to imply discontinuities or suggest differing subjective views of an event, Winterbottom's use of the pan implies a unity of perspective by stressing the continuity of the indexical capture of the real. Both approaches are possible and would produce very different celluloid worlds, but both are ultimately grounded in the concrete world of the *mise en scène*.

Various inventive cinematographic techniques are used in *Wonderland* to stress the continuity of estates with the city—often through the use of familiar London landmarks—to the extent that this is fundamental to the film's style. As Charlotte Brunsdon writes, "[i]t is more common […] for naturalist cinema—which *Wonderland* isn't quite—to mark its authenticity through its eschewal of landmark London. There are no views north in Gary Oldman's *Nil By Mouth* (1997), nor south in Ken Loach's *Riff-Raff* (1991)" (Brunsdon 65–6). In *Wonderland*, the attempt to place the banal uniformity of the council estate into relation with the instantly recognisable landmarks of central London is a deliberate strategy, as when the dome of St. Paul's cathedral appears framed by the balcony of the gallery-access flat in which Debbie lives.

Figure 2: *Wonderland*: the dome of St. Paul's framed by council estate architecture.

The use of depth of focus here is an exaggerated version of the technique which Bazin noted in *Citizen Kane*, where, "[t]hanks to the depth of focus of the lens, Orson Welles restored to reality its visible continuity" (Bazin, "An Aesthetic of Reality" 28). Where *Nil By Mouth* had insisted that the council estate was a hermetically sealed container which effectively contained the new lumpen class and excluded them from urban society, *Wonderland* everywhere seeks to look beyond this barrier, and reconnect the council estate dweller with the city. The visible continuity made possible by the use of depth of field is used to sententiously suggest a kind of social continuity, making an organic whole of a fractured and divided metropolis.

This is also manifested in the use of a variety of locations outside the estates. Teige's view that with the advent of the minimum dwelling various domestic functions could be "aggregated for common use outside the apartment" (Teige 247) is made possible by the highly developed division of labour and the specialised land use associated with urban conditions. *Wonderland* sees hope in this aggregation of various social and domestic functions in dedicated spaces, suggesting that these places play a role in stitching together a fragmented city. Both Nadia and Debbie work in such places, Nadia in a café and Debbie in a hairdresser's. In the London of *Wonderland*, some of the functions of the living room have devolved to the café, and this has proved to be a progressive step. The convivial atmosphere of the café offers some compensation for the isolation which the characters often seem to feel in their flats. It is perhaps telling that the only scene in which we see the three sisters together takes place in the café. This is not a scene of domestic harmony, indeed there is a palpable tension between the tearful Molly and Nadia, who laughs when she hears that her heavily pregnant sister has been deserted by her partner. But it does suggest that although the spaces for this kind of interaction might be missing from the urban home, and, perhaps, from the council estate in particular, they are provided by the city; that functions previously ascribed to the home are pooled in functionally specialised spaces such as the café. The family survives and adapts to the urban context through its use of such facilities.

Now, in *Nil By Mouth*, by contrast, one consequence of the horrors of the meaningless interstitial realm that has in the council estate replaced the street is that the individual flat is re-imagined as a place of refuge. In one scene, when Val is in hospital after Ray beats her up, we witness Ray trying to get his daughter back from Janet (Val's mother), who is inside her flat. He directs a torrent of abuse and homicidal threats at his mother-in-law. The concrete slabs and the iron bars that are fundamental to the architectural grammar of the council estate had seemed to reinforce the usual metaphor of the urban dwelling as prison. But in this scene they serve a defensive purpose, protecting the women—and the family—from the myriad dangers of the exterior. Ray is photographed through a set of iron bars, straining to get in but prevented from doing so. The flat is not a prison, here, but a fortress. Ray picks up some kind of rock or brick and, leaning around the iron grille, throws it through the window of the flat, smashing the window and narrowly missing Janet. There is a real sense that a protective skin has been punctured, and that the evil miasma which hangs in the air of the estate might waft in.

When Val returns from hospital, she and her daughter move in with her mother and her grandmother, Kath. Kath's flat becomes a refuge for these four generations of women, and there is a rare and memorable scene of real domestic warmth when Val—her injuries slowly healing—dances with her. So the flat becomes a sanctuary for the women, who are now able to demonstrate openly their mutual familial love without fear. While there is some limited redemption here, it is essentially a defensive measure, a retreat from the city into the interior which has none of the optimism present in *Wonderland*.

I have described the ways in which *Wonderland* seeks to recuperate the council estate dweller into the fabric of the city. The film's emphasis on the continuity of the internal spaces of the estate with the city as a whole would tend to warn against our applying Goodman's concept of worldmaking to either the estate itself or to the film. Indeed, it suggests that the theory itself is problematic because in its eagerness to define and delimit worlds, it tends to be blind to the ways in which they are inevitably and irretrievably interconnected. It is blind (in other words) to 'the world.' Goodman writes:

> If I ask about the world, you can offer to tell me how it is under one or more frames of reference; but if I insist that you tell me how it is apart from all frames, what can you say? We are confined to ways of describing whatever is described. Our universe, so to speak, consists of these ways rather than of a world or of worlds. (Goodman 2–3)

So it is possible to imagine, in these terms, a reading of the two films that would see them as different ways of framing the council estate, as two subjective accounts among a potentially infinite number. But it is not so simple as to say that the two films represent different worlds, or different "ways of describing whatever is described." For while, as I have argued, *Nil By Mouth* made the estate's isolation from the city a central element of its depiction of it, *Wonderland* did not merely define the estate in different terms, but asserted its continuity with the city and the world.

One issue that can be raised with respect to this aspect of *Wonderland* is that it ignores some of the intractable problems of class which *Nil By Mouth* had explored to good effect. For in Oldman's film, it is social class—reinforced by the boundaries of the estate—which keeps the characters from interacting with the metropolitan culture of London. Is there also a sense, then, that the impulse of Winterbottom's film is to deny class, by imagining an exclusively middle-class city? The modern-day lumpenproletariat that inhabits the Ferrier Estate in *Nil by Mouth* have been replaced here by a family who are not exactly affluent, but who have arguably hoisted themselves into the lower reaches of the middle classes. The council estate is thus effectively re-imagined in a way that ignores its culture, the self-perpetuating cycles of unemployment, addiction, and crime which are associated with the estate.

This is in an important sense true, but I would suggest that the real significance of this discrepancy between the two films can only be understood in light of the history of British social housing, upon which they both reflect. Indeed, both films can be understood as being shaped by Thatcher's Right-To-Buy policy, which allowed council tenants to buy their flats at vastly reduced prices and so to become owner-occupiers. *Wonderland* sees in this policy the possibility that the Bevanite dream of the 'mixed community' might be resurrected, with middle-class owner-occupiers living alongside council tenants and the council estate no longer being a barrier to social mobility. This is not simply wrong: right-to-buy has had some positive effects for better-off tenants, who have in many cases become homeowners, and it can be seen to have contributed to the "*embourgeoisement* of the higher working classes" (Ravetz 161). The world of *Nil By Mouth* may seem to move in a contradictory direction, but it is really the flipside of the same coin, the dark underbelly of the policy. For while in the more desirable estates Right-To-Buy uptake has had beneficial effects, as Hamnett points out, "[i]n areas where the majority of council property is made up of high-rise and high-density blocks RTB [Right-To-Buy] sales have been limited" (Hamnett 145). As the better off members of the working class—those with jobs—cashed in on Right-To-Buy, became fully paid up members of Thatcher's property-owning democracy, and escaped the ghetto of social renting, places like the Ferrier Estate housed those that were left behind.

Worldmaking on one level serves as a useful metaphor for the making of films, but a closer examination of *Nil By Mouth* and *Wonderland* has revealed that they are deeply embedded in something like the "real world" whose existence (as Bruner argues) is precluded by Goodman's theory. Steven Connor has recently written: "[w]hen constructivism attempts to substitute multiple made worlds for the given world, it ignores the fact that the given world has also been for some considerable time under construction, at least since human beings started to change their environment in the Neolithic era" (Connor in this volume).

The force of Connor's argument is that in rejecting the pluralism of Goodman's approach, it does not reject the complexity and the radical disjointedness of the world. In this view, the given world is a dynamic entity, always under construction, and it is manifestly not the "neutral and underlying world" that Goodman is so keen to dismiss (Goodman 20). The council estate is one of humankind's more recent attempts to shape its environment, and as I have explained it would be reductive to view its emergence as an act of architectural worldmaking, and hence to see it as an independent and autonomous world with its own rules and its own logic. Indeed, as Connor suggests, "the frothing paroxysms of worldmaking are perhaps not generative, as we want them to be, but fiercely defensive, conservative, reductive" (Connor, in this volume). Only by approaching the council estate as a constructed part of the given world can we fully understand it, and so begin to understand the underlying social, political and economic problems which it manifests. Similarly, the films I have discussed are best understood not as examples of constructivist worldmaking—which in this context can seem like a frivolous and solipsistic game—but as living critical engagements with the world. The world may not be neutral, but it is real.

References

Bazin, André. "The Ontology of the Photographic Image." *What is Cinema?* Vol. 1. Trans. Hugh Gray. Berkeley: U of California P, 2005. 9–16.
—. "An Aesthetic of Reality: Neorealism." *What is Cinema?* Vol. 1. Trans. Hugh Gray. Berkeley: U of California P, 2005. 16–40.

Bruner, Jerome. *Actual Minds, Possible Worlds*. Cambridge: Harvard UP, 1986.
Brunsdon, Charlotte. "The Poignancy of Place': London and the Cinema." *Visual Culture in Britain* 5.1 (2004): 59–74.
Burnett, John. *A Social History of Housing, 1815–1985*. 2nd ed. London: Methuen, 1986.
Dunleavy, Patrick. *The Politics of Mass Housing in Britain, 1945–1975: A Study of Corporate Power and Professional Influence in the Welfare State*. Oxford: Oxford UP, 1981.
Goodman, Nelson. *Ways of Worldmaking*. Indianapolis: Hackett, 1992.
Hamnett, Chris. *Unequal City: London in the Global Arena*. London: Routledge, 2003.
Hanley, Lynsey. *Estates: An Intimate History*. London: Granta, 2007.
Hughes, Robert. *The Shock of the New*. London: Thames & Hudson, 1991.
Marx, Karl, and Friedrich Engels. *The Communist Manifesto*. Trans. Samuel Moore. London: Penguin, 1985.
Oldman, Gary, dir. *Nil By Mouth*. Twentieth Century Fox, 1997.
Power, Anne. *Hovels to High Rise: State Housing in Europe Since 1850*. London: Routledge, 1993.
Prince, Steven. "True Lies: Perceptual Realism, Digital Images, and Film Theory." *Film Quarterly* 49.3 (1996): 27–37.
Ravetz, Alison. *Council Housing and Culture: The History of a Social Experiment*. London: Routledge, 2001.
Teige, Karel. *The Minimum Dwelling*. Trans. Eric Dluhosch. Cambridge, MA: MIT Press, 2002.
Timmins, Nicholas. *The Five Giants: A Biography of the Welfare State*. London: Harper Collins, 1995.
Smithson, Alison and Peter Smithson. *Urban Structuring: Studies of Alison and Peter Smithson*. Ed. John Lewis. London: Studio Vista, 1967.
Warburton, Nigel. *Ernö Goldfinger: The Life of an Architect*. London: Routledge, 2005.
Winterbottom, Michael, dir. *Wonderland*. USA Films, 1999.

III. Narratives as Ways of Worldmaking

Making Events – Making Stories – Making Worlds: Ways of Worldmaking from a Narratological Point of View

ANSGAR NÜNNING

1. Narrative as a Way of Worldmaking: Questions and Objectives

One might as well begin with the observation that narratives are one of the most powerful ways of worldmaking. The main reason for this is that storytelling not only generates possible worlds, narratives also exert performative power. In her groundbreaking monograph *Shakespeare's Storytellers*, Barbara Hardy pins it down with great precision in talking about "the theatrical power of narrative, its capacity to change events, its control and compounding, its passion and its immediacy" (60). This performative force or even power of narration stems from the reality-constituting, identity-, sense-, and indeed world-making qualities that characterise narration and narratives.

When the philosopher Nelson Goodman coined the felicitous term 'ways of worldmaking,' he was mainly concerned with the claim that the world we know is always already made "from other worlds" (Goodman 6). According to Goodman, there is no such thing as a given world—the only thing we can ever have access to are culturally shaped world models or versions. Goodman managed to shed a great deal of light on the question of how worlds are made, identifying and discussing five basic procedures for constructing worlds, viz. composition and decomposition, weighting (i.e. emphasis or ratings of relevance), ordering (and reordering), deletion and supplementation, and deformation (see Goodman 7–17; for an excellent brief summary, see Herman 77–78). However, Goodman was not particularly concerned with narratives as a way of worldmaking. As Herman has rightly pointed out, "there is nothing distinctively story-like about the worlds over which Goodman's account ranges, though there is nothing about the analysis that excludes storyworlds, either" (ibid. 78). Recent years have seen an increasing interest across a broad range of disciplines in the question of exactly how worlds are made and how the relation between worldmaking and orders of knowledge can be described.

It is only very recently, however, that narratology has begun to concern itself with "Narrative Ways of Worldmaking," to quote the title of an excellent pioneering article by David Herman, who proceeds from the same point of departure: "Narrative worldmaking," Herman argues, "involves specific, identifiable procedures set off against a larger set of background conditions for world-creation—irrespective of the medium in which the narrative practices are being conducted" (Herman 71). Whereas Herman is mainly concerned with "the cognitive processes underlying narrative ways of worldmaking" (ibid.), i.e. with the question of how textual cues encourage the reader or viewer to build up a "mentally configured storyworld" (ibid.) or representations of the worlds evoked by stories, this essay will focus on narrative ways of worldmaking from a classical narratological rather than a cognitive point of view. Though I agree with Herman that "classical, structuralist narratologists failed to come to terms with the referential or world-creating properties of narrative" (ibid.), I will argue that the analytical toolkit developed by classical, structuralist narratology can shed quite a bit of light on the actual procedures that go into and shape world-construction in narrative contexts. Since narratology has provided a range of useful concepts for exploring this question, the focus of this essay is on the questions of how events, stories or histories, and storyworlds are made, and how narratological categories can serve to illuminate the worldmaking power of narratives and of storytelling.

Though most people would probably agree that narratives are of fundamental importance for the ways in which we make sense of our experiences and of the world at large, the worldmaking capacity of stories and of storytelling has not received the degree of attention that it arguably deserves. In his pioneering account of the creation of an autobiographical self, felicitously entitled *How our Lives Become Stories: Making Selves*, Paul John Eakin has shown that narratives are at work in processes such as identity formation, ordering experiences, remembering, and negotiating values. In a similar vein, I will argue that stories, and storytelling, are not only the most important means of making autobiographical selves, but an equally important means of worldmaking. The essay is particularly concerned with the building-blocks of narrative worldmaking, i.e. with the so-called 'event' as the elementary unit of narratives, with the notion of emplotment, and with the role of point of view and storytelling in worldmaking. It does not pretend to offer a comprehensive, let alone exhaustive, account of narrative ways of worldmaking at large, but is rather intended to complement other recent attempts to come to terms with narrative as an important way of worldmaking (see Herman; Sommer; Vera Nünning's essay in this volume).

This essay takes as its point of departure the somewhat astounding observation that whilst the terms 'event' and 'media event' are indeed omnipresent in both historiography and the media, they are used "without ever systematically following up on the question of what events actually are, and how occurrences and incidents become events" (Rathmann 4, my translation). What Nelson Goodman said about the modes of organisation and worldmaking that he was particularly interested in applies equally well to the notions of the event and narrative: "they are not 'found in the world' but built into a world" (Goodman 14).

By drawing on concepts from the theory of history and from narratology (including, among others, event, configuration, emplotment, cultural plots, and perspectives), the aim of this article is, on the one hand, to illuminate the processes and discourse strategies by which a mere historical happening becomes an event, an established story and part of 'history' in the first place. On the other hand, it tries to illustrate, and comment on, some of the processes that go into narrative worldmaking. Without aiming to cast doubt on historical facts, the goal is to show that what we call historical or media events—such as the Crimean War, the so-called Indian Mutiny (see Erll), 9/11 or the War in Iraq—are not only the result of selection, abstraction, ordering, and prioritisation, but are also perspective-dependent, culturally specific and historically variable contingent constructs which are produced by discourses, narratives, and media. Lots of things happen every day but only very few of them become events, let alone what posterity will regard as 'great historical events.' At this point, we still know very little about how a mere happening becomes a historical or media event at all, despite the fact that pioneering works by, for instance, Daniel Dayan and Elihu Katz, and Jay David Bolter and Richard Grusin respectively, have served to develop sophisticated models of media events and the role of pre- and remediation respectively. Though it is generally agreed that the constitution of a media event as such is a product of the modes of media representation and mediation, as well as of social communication, this hypothesis does not really provide much in the way of enlightenment about how events are constructed and how stories, histories, and storyworlds are made in the first place. Therefore it might be worthwhile to examine some narrative ways of worldmaking and the performative power of narrative in greater detail.

2. The Performative Power of Narrative

Let us first of all look at two random examples in order to illustrate what is meant by 'narrative ways of worldmaking' and by the 'performative power of narrative.' Since narrative is ubiquitous in the contemporary world, any newspaper could serve as an example. Since the mechanisms of worldmaking are of particular interest for literary and cultural historians, as well as for media experts, we might as well begin with Shakespeare and then go on to George W. Bush, two strange bedfellows, indeed, but very powerful worldmakers.

For anyone interested in the role of narrative as a way of worldmaking, Shakespeare's plays provide a veritable goldmine. His tragedy *Othello* provides a case in point in that the action mainly revolves around the power of storytelling as a means of worldmaking. By reporting how narrating his life story helped him win Desdemona's grace and love, and by emphasising that this is the only form of witchcraft he used, Othello, in the third scene of the first act, simultaneously points to the remarkable power storytelling has in a number of Shakespeare's plays. How Othello himself falls victim to this seductive and dangerous power as the action unfolds is not just an example of the dramatic irony which, as is widely known, abounds in this tragedy. More to the point, the fact that Iago maliciously alludes via insinuations and fragments of narrative, or rather narrative kernels, to Desdemona's alleged unfaithfulness, which becomes a fully fledged story only in Othello's imagination, exemplifies the performative power of narration that stems from its reality-constituting potential: by means of storytelling, potential worlds emerge, even though their respective correspondence to reality, or to the actual textual storyworld, is oftentimes dubitable in Shakespeare's plays. The play *Othello* in particular shows that narrations which do not correspond to (fictional) reality still frequently have the capacity to change that very reality or storyworld. This reality-changing potential largely depends on their correspondence to the culturally available schemata and plots of the respective time and whether they appear sufficiently plausible to the characters in the play. As the example from *Othello* also serves to show, narratives and storytelling in Shakespeare's plays frequently not only significantly influence the progress of the action with far-reaching consequences for the characters' destiny; additionally, they also determine what is 'really' the case in the fictional world (see Nünning and Sommer for a detailed account).

On a larger, and politically much more important scale, many of the stories generated and disseminated by the Bush administration since 9/11, especially those about the alleged production of weapons of mass destruction in Iraq, underline the fact that narratives are a very powerful, and potentially dangerous, way of worldmaking. Though we now know that these narratives failed to correspond to either reality or truth, they nonetheless had the capacity to construct events and to change the course of history. The reality-changing potential of these stories also depended on their correspondence to the culturally available schemata, metaphors, and plots that contemporary American society lives by, i.e. whether they appear sufficiently plausible to the majority of people. This example also serves to show that powerful narratives can themselves be weapons of mass destruction. The same holds true for other stories generated by the Bush administration, the War against Terror being the most destructive case in point. When a story or a metaphor comes to be regarded as a political argument, what an irresistible argument it always seems!

What do these random examples tell us about ways of narrative worldmaking and the performative power of narratives, then? Perceiving imaginary infidelities or weapons of mass destruction seems to consist in producing not only weapons in the mind but also stories that can change reality, having far-reaching consequences for a potentially great number of people. Recognising a crisis in Iraq, or any other country for that matter, can be very much a matter of inventing it: once the diagnosis that there 'is' a crisis comes to be regarded as a political or economic reality, culturally available crises-plots are activated, assigning not only roles to the participants involved, but also a particular meaning to the event thus designated (see Nünning, "Narratologie der Krise" and "Steps Towards"). In short, the activity of narrative worldmaking, including the choice of a particular kind of metaphor and story, is not so much a matter of recognising crises or historical changes 'out there,' but of imposing order and meaning on a mere sequence of happenings. All of this should give anyone interested in narrative as a way of worldmaking reason to pause and to take a fresh look at the ways in which events are created and stories are made through the complex processes involved in narrative worldmaking.

3. Creating Events, Making Stories: The Construction of Events, Stories and Media Events from a Narratological Point of View

Using these random examples from literature and recent history as a point of departure, let us now turn our attention to the processes that go into narrative ways of worldmaking. How can narratology—that is, the theory of narration—contribute to illuminating the process which has as its beginning a mere sequence of happenings, and which has at its end an event, a story, a plot, or a so-called 'media event'? The question already implies that from the point of view of literary and cultural theory, an event, a story, or a media event is not understood as something given or natural, but rather as something made or constructed. What Brian McHale said about literary-historical objects is equally true of events, stories, and histories: "If literary-historical 'objects' [...] are constructed, not given or found, then the issue of how such objects are constructed, in particular the genre of discourse in which they are constructed, becomes crucial" (McHale 3).

Thus, the interest is shifted away from the completed product called the event, a particular story or storyworld, or history or the world at large towards the construction process, to the question of how events, stories, or histories, and (story)worlds are produced, in particular the genres of discourse in which, and the procedures through which, they are constructed. In order to gain a better understanding of what has been called 'narrative ways of worldmaking,' let us explore the processes of selection, configuration, and textual representation which go into it. Though the following description of these processes is merely a sketch and neither will nor could make any claim to completeness, it may nonetheless serve the purpose of pointing out that the terminological and analytical instruments of narratology provide a number of useful approaches and categories for developing a descriptive model for coming to terms with narrative worldmaking. The latter arguably consists of at least five procedures or processes which can be found across different genres, media, and communicative contexts (see Herman 75; Sommer). Let us call these procedures or processes narrative worldmaking acts I, II, III, IV, and V.

3.1 Narrative Worldmaking, Act I: Events as the Result of Selection, Abstraction and Prioritisation

In order to come to terms with the question of how narratives evoke, generate or make worlds in general and storyworlds in particular, the concept of the event seems to be as good a place to start as any, since events are generally agreed to be among the constitutive properties that make up both stories and storyworlds. At first sight, the meaning of the key term 'event' seems to be self-evident. Intuitively, probably everybody knows what an event is. At the same time, however, there are few concepts which are more pre-conditioned than that of the event, a term which is anything but self-explanatory or indeed well-defined. Since events are the stuff that narratives, stories, and histories are made of, outlining some criteria for the definition of the terms 'event' and 'happening,' as well as for the gradation of 'eventfulness,' can throw light on the ways in which narratives make worlds.

In the light of the importance of events for military and political history, it is, at first glance, astonishing that the central term 'event' has hardly ever been the subject of definitions or of theoretical reflections. Definitions of the key term 'event' itself are rare, and this fundamental concept cannot even be found in most of the salient historical reference works. Paul Ricœur once laconically noted that "most historians have a poor concept of 'event'" (Ricœur, "Narrative Time" 171). However, in *Time and Narrative* he himself had comparatively little to say about the event, which supposedly constitutes the smallest unit of narratives and the fundamental constituents of the story. In his useful *Dictionary of Narratology*, Gerald Price defines 'event' as a "change of state manifested in discourse by a process statement in the mode of Do or Happen" (Prince 28). While any change of state can be regarded as an event in general, only particular kinds of happenings will qualify as an event in more emphatic sense or will ever be turned into a media event.

That is to say that from a narratological perspective, events are neither givens nor anything natural, but should rather be conceived of as the result of particular ways of worldmaking, including selection, deletion, abstraction, and prioritisation or 'weighting' (in the sense of Goodman 10–12). Narratology provides a number of useful criteria to define the term 'event' by setting it off from the term 'happening,' and to distinguish different degrees of 'eventfulness' (see Hühn; Schmid). Tying in with the everyday meaning of 'event' as a 'significant incident' or a 'significant occurrence,' narrative theory first of all makes a distinction between the chaotic and contingent things that happen—i.e. the totality of all occurrences—, and the event as an especially relevant and significant part of it. Just as narratology takes an emphatic stance in defining an 'event,' so media event research is concerned not with everyday incidents but with occurrences which are accredited with a high degree of relevance as well as great importance. Therefore, the constitution of an event is based upon its being singled out from the continuous flow of occurrences and thereby being qualified as something special or surprising: thus, it is based on selection and distinction by an observer. In the last chapter of his important book *La Pensée sauvage* (1962), i.e. *The Savage Mind* (1966), Claude Lévi-Strauss clearly describes the way that there is always a high degree of abstraction involved in determining a historical fact:

> For, *ex hypothesi*, a historical fact is what really took place, but where did anything take place? Each episode in a revolution or a war resolves itself into a multitude of individual psychic movements. [...] Consequently, historical facts are no more *given* than any other. It is the historian, or the agent of history, who constitutes them by abstraction and as though under the threat of an infinite regress. (Lévi-Strauss 257)

Consequently, the construction of events, and narrative worldmaking at large, is not only based on selection, which, of course, inevitably involves deletion (see Goodman 14–16), but on a high degree of abstraction as well. Every historical event itself consists of a multitude of actions, condition changes and movements which are then subsumed under a generalising generic term. The designation of historical events and most media events provides cases in point, with terms like 'the Crimean War,' 'the Indian Mutiny,' or indeed the abbreviated mega-event '9/11' being typical examples in that all of these abstractions actually refer to a heterogeneous multitude of political decisions, military sieges, battles, attacks, and any number of other, allegedly minor, events.

Hence, the constitution of an event is an act of worldmaking in and of itself in that it is the result of a complex set of procedures involving selection, deletion, and, even more so, the kind of privileging Goodman called "weighting" (Goodman 10–12), which implies "ratings of relevance, importance, utility, value" (12) through which what is regarded as substantial is highlighted while the irrelevant elements are disregarded. All of these procedures reflect, but arguably also yield or even generate, cultural hierarchies of norms and values (see Erll, Grabes, and Nünning). The fact that these distinctions and hierarchies are neither given nor found, but are rather a matter of attribution, valuation, and assigning meaning becomes even clearer in the case of historical key events and transnational media events which are considered as 'big' or 'epoch-making.' This was already stressed by Nietzsche at the beginning of the fourth *Unmodern Observations* of 1875:

> In itself no event is great; even if whole constellations disappear, nations collapse, powerful states are founded, and incredibly violent and destructive wars are waged, the breath of history may scatter them like down. [...] History seldom remembers such nonevents. (Nietzsche 253)

Thus other criteria are needed by means of which we can agree on when happenings or mere occurrences are perceived as an event or as a 'great historical event.' An important condition for qualifying a certain historical happening as an event is, at first, that the happening transgresses the norms and routine of everyday experience. There must be a certain degree of surprise for something that happens to qualify as a 'great event.' In his insightful essay on "The Narrative Construction of Reality," the psychologist Jerome Bruner already drew attention to some of the key dimensions of eventfulness, especially to the important role of deviation and of norms as a point of reference. He uses the felicitous concepts of "canonicity and breach" (Bruner 11–13) to describe how an event usually results from a deviation from the canonical, i.e. from what is regarded as normal, pointing out that any break with expectations always involves norms (see ibid. 15–16). Decisions about what constitutes an important event thus always partake in the culture's ways of worldmaking, including its hierarchies of norms and values.

Narratology presents further indicators for defining the term 'event' and for distinguishing varying degrees of eventfulness. Working within a structuralist narratological framework, Wolf Schmid defines the event as "a change of condition which meets with certain requirements" (Schmid 20, our translation). To my knowledge, Schmid was the first narratologist to compile a systematic list of criteria or fundamental requirements which a change of condition must fulfil in order to be recognised and distinguished as an 'event.' According to Schmid, events are to be defined as changes of state or condition which initially need to meet two stipulations, namely 'facticity' (or reality) and 'resultivity.' The criterion of facticity distinguishes events from mere subjective desires, dreams, or imaginations, i.e. from what Marie-Laure Ryan and other representatives of the Possible-Worlds Theory call 'possible worlds.' Resultivity means that events are not only begun in the narrative world but are brought to a close as well.

These basic criteria are supplemented by five properties that a change of state must display in order to qualify as an event and to be attributed a high degree of eventfulness. According to this model, changes can be "more or less eventful depending on the extent to which these five properties are present" (Hühn 89). The approximate degree of eventfulness can thus be measured by means of the following five characteristics (see Schmid 22–26):

1. Relevance (or significance) of the change of state: Eventfulness increases at the rate at which the change of condition in the respective narrative world that is represented is felt.
2. Unpredictability (or unexpectedness, unpredictability) of the change: Eventfulness increases at the rate of the deviation from the narrative 'doxa,' i.e. from what is generally expected in the respective world. An event can also consist in the break with an expectation (see Bruner).
3. Effect (or consecutivity) of the change: The eventfulness of a change of condition increases at the rate at which a change, in the frame of the narrated world, has consequences for the thinking and the acting of the affected subjects.
4. Irreversibility (or irrevocability) of the consequences of the change: The eventfulness increases through the improbability of revoking the achieved state.
5. Non-iterativity (or non-repeatability), i.e. the singularity of the change: Changes which are repeated only constitute a remote degree of eventfulness at most, even if they are relevant and unpredictable.

When transferring these narratological characteristics for eventfulness to the domain of narrative worldmaking in the real world, it is important, however, to remember that they were developed for the analysis of novels and other kinds of fictional narratives, not for the examination of the making of real or historical events. Nonetheless, they offer useful starting points for the questions at hand: first, they provide precise criteria for the selection and qualification of especially 'eventful' occurrences. Secondly, they raise the awareness of the preconditions that have to be fulfilled in order for things that happen ever to become a historical event or a big media event at all. The first criterion as well as the criteria numbered three to five can be transferred to real historical or media events without a problem when using historical reality as the point of reference instead of the represented fictional storyworld. The second criterion must, however, be modified to the effect that the essential point of reference is not the variation from the narrative 'doxa,' i.e. the general expectance of the respective world, but the respective collective horizon of expectation shared by the majority of historical participants. Only by considering the historically and culturally mutable preconditions and horizons of expectation, which the German historian Reinhart Koselleck has designated 'space of expectations' (*Erwartungsraum*) and 'horizon of expectations' (*Erwartungshorizont*, see Koselleck 330), as a relevant category can the narratological term 'event' be made fruitful for the reconstruction of the creation of historical events and media events. In contrast to fictional worlds in which it can actually make sense to identify an event and its degree of eventfulness in relation to individual subjects or main characters, as Schmid does when he speaks of consequences for the thinking and the acting of the affected subject, real events and media events always also have a social, collective and communicative dimension.

When comparing these narratological criteria for eventfulness with those which have been formulated in recent discussions of the term 'event' in social history, one can identify not only analogies but some significant modifications as well. Andreas Suter and Manfred Hettling proposed three criteria in order to mark certain sequences of action as events and to distinguish them from mere happenings (see Suter and Hettling 24–25): according to the first criterion, i.e. the incidence of surprise or the unusual, events tend to unsettle the experience, expectations, and the imagination of the contemporaries. The second criterion, collectivity, stipulates that the measures by which shocking or surprising events are distinguished from normal everyday experience should be of a collective nature. Third, in contrast to mere happenings, events generally have consequences which alter structural features in such a way that the contemporaries notice these changes.

Just like the above parameters for distinguishing degrees of eventfulness, these criteria also shed light on what is involved in ways of worldmaking: while the first criterion corresponds approximately to that of relevance in Schmid's catalogue, and the third to effect or consecutivity, the indication of a collective dimension, which seems to be important for the definition of eventfulness in the real world and of media events in particular, is new and important. On the other hand, Rathmann's criticism of the catalogue of criteria established by Suter and Hettling rightly points out that at least the incidence of surprise is not a necessary criterion. This evaluation is confirmed by the history of the most recent war in Iraq which, admittedly, did not come as a surprise after the long diplomatic prehistory but which nonetheless quickly advanced to a first rank media event, a number one news story regularly updated by television and other media. Altogether, the criteria mentioned above emphasise the hypothesis that events are not something that is objectively given but rather the result of selection, abstraction, prioritisation, and weighting, and are made into such by means of hierarchies of values which are collectively valid and intersubjectively traceable.

3.2 Narrative Worldmaking, Act II: Transforming Happenings into Events, Stories and Textual Representations of Narratives

The above-mentioned distinction between a mere happening and an event provides the basis for further illustrating the processes of transformation that are involved in narrative worldmaking. For this purpose, one can resort to the terminological triad "happenings, story, and textual representation of the story or narrative," which goes back to a seminal article by Karlheinz Stierle, and which Wolf Schmid developed into a four-stage model (see Stierle 49–55; Schmid 232–77, our translation). These models can be profitably adapted in order to answer the question of how narratives turn historical happenings into events, stories, and media events. Stierle and Schmid understand by the term 'happening' the totality of all situations, occurrences, and actions. A happening is spatially and temporally unlimited, it is a continuum without beginning or end and without meaning.

For an event to become a story a certain temporal section must be singled out and—not least through such ways of worldmaking as selection, ordering, and weighting—be given meaning, and it is thereby already interpreted in a certain way. Accordingly, the respective story told is the result of a selection of certain moments and qualities from the happening, whose amorphous endlessness is thereby transferred into a limited, structured form which is enriched with meaning. The story contains the selected moments of action in their chronological order, however, without already transferring them into a plot. The latter does not happen until the story is transformed into a particular narrative, or plot, which is the result of shaping and arrangement.

Whereas the levels of story and narrative can, in the sense of Stierle, be considered as deep structures which can only be identified through abstraction, the level of the text of the story or plot, i.e. the textual representation of the narrative, is the only level which can be observed directly. In the case of narrative texts, verbalisation and narrativisation are the constitutive methods used on this level. In the case of pictures it is the iconisation or pictoral composition. When examining media events we always look at, and analyse, medial (re-)presentation of events, stories, and narratives, never the brute happenings that actually occur in the real world which are inaccessible unless they are represented in some form or other. Thus, as a narrative media event or news story, any war does not present itself as a sequence of decisions, actions, or battles, but rather as an ensemble of discursive representations and media products.

The immediate relevance of these narratological considerations for the question of narrative worldmaking is based on the fact that the chaotic events of a war, for example, can only be made accessible and communicated in society after having been transferred into comprehensible stories and pictures. This, again, requires narrative and rhetorical strategies (see Rigney) which are by no means inherent in the events as such, but are imposed on the actual events by the narrative discourse which functions as a shaping pattern. As Ulrich Keller has argued in his perspicacious analysis of the Crimean War as the first fully-fledged media war, "military and other history needs to be told/pictured reasonably, otherwise it cannot be relevant for society and found social identity—and this is not possible without making use of rhetoric, narrative and interpreting structures" (Keller 25).

There is yet another enlightening consequence for the analysis of narrative worldmaking which results from the distinction between happening, story, narrative, and the textual representation of history: as every story is not only "the result of a selection from the happenings" (ibid. 24), but also the result of a multitude of methods of narrative arrangement, ordering and (linguistic, narrative, literary etc.) composition of the selected moments of what happened, there is, as a result, a plurality of stories, narratives, texts and other media products that can be generated about any event. Moreover, since different meanings can be assigned to the 'same event' by different observers, the choice of a point of view also has to be taken into consideration in any account of narrative ways of worldmaking.

Stories and narratives are characterised by the methods of configuration and perspectivisation, which are described below as acts III and IV.

3.3 Narrative Worldmaking, Act III: Configuration, Emplotment and the "Ideology of Form" as Modes of Organisation and Construction of Meaning

As far as the processes that go into narrative worldmaking are concerned, it is not just the selection of certain things that happen and the deletion of others which is important for the analysis of how events, stories, and worlds are constructed or made, but the narrative arrangement of the selected material into certain narratives plays an equally important role. The significance of what Goodman calls "ordering" (12), i.e. the structuring of events through narrative procedures, lies in the fact that processes of configuration must first establish a relationship between the selected elements to turn them into an orderly, meaningful whole: "First, the configurational arrangement transforms the succession of events into one meaningful whole [...]. Second, the configuration of the plot imposes the 'sense of an ending' [...] on the indefinite succession of incidents" (Ricœur, *Time and Narrative* 65). The configuration of the selected events, persons, and situations consists in establishing connections, interrelations, and patterns between them, turning them into a particular kind of story and generating a storyworld.

The works of the metahistorian Hayden White have provided us with manifold insights into the constitutive meaning of narrativity and emplotment for the representation of events and for narrative worldmaking at large. By coining the term 'emplotment,' White called attention to the way that historical facts and events are always embedded in a superordinate context. Adopting particular frames of reference, emplotment-strategies serve the purpose of overcoming the contingency of historical occurrences, narratively structuring the selected events and shaping them into a certain story: "Emplotment is the way by which a sequence of events fashioned into a story is gradually revealed to be a story of a particular kind" (White, *Metahistory* 7). The contextual meaning is not inherent in the historical occurrence or the event as such, but is primarily created through the choice of a certain genre pattern. Through processes of narrativisation, an event is given not only a certain structural and narrative pattern, but also a meaning and a sense as well.

White's theses on the significance of emplotment sheds additional light on the questions of how mere occurrences become a historical or media event, and of which procedures are involved in narrative ways of worldmaking. His metahistorical works have raised the awareness of the fact that the narrative structures of historiography are always already semanticised, viz. that they are loaded with ideological and political implications. He furthermore showed that the narrative discourse is not a transparent medium by means of which historic events and processes can be presented neutrally (see White, *The Content of the Form*). In fact, White continues, it is the narrative discourse which initially integrates the occurrences into a narrative context and framework by means of emplotment strategies. Thus the form of the linguistic and narrative mode of representation inevitably endows 'facts' and events with meaning. Like White, Helms emphasises that "narrative techniques are not neutral and transparent forms to be filled with content, and that dialogic relations in narrative structures are ideologically informed" (Helms 7). Any account of narrative ways of worldmaking would be simplistic if it did not take into consideration what Fredric Jameson felicitously called the "ideology of the form" (141), which implies that "form is immanently and intrinsically an ideology in its own right":

> What must now be stressed is that at this level 'form' is apprehended as content. The study of the ideology of form is no doubt grounded on a technical and formalistic analysis in the narrower sense, even though, unlike much traditional formal analysis, it seeks to reveal the active presence within the text of a number of discontinuous and heterogeneous formal processes. But at the level of analysis in question here, a dialectical reversal has taken place in which it has become possible to grasp such formal processes as sedimented content in their own right, as carrying ideological messages of their own, distinct from the ostensible or manifest content of the works. (Jameson 99)

The concepts of emplotment and the ideology of form are crucial for coming to terms with the complex procedures of narrative ways of worldmaking in that they allow us to understand how a mere sequence of events is fashioned into a story, and storyworld, of a particular kind and how formal processes and narrative structures are always imbued with content, meaning, and even ideology. Based on the insight that the narrative configuration is always a mode of sense- and worldmaking, Andrea Gutenberg elaborated several dimensions of the constitution of meaning through the methods of emplotment in her book *Possible Worlds* (*Mögliche Welten*, 2000). Firstly, the selection and emphasis of the chosen plot elements leads to a "hierarchisation of meanings" (see Gutenberg 108, our translation) on the paradigmatic axis, representing one of the procedures of "weighting" (Goodman 10). Secondly, the methods of plot configuration on the syntagmatic axis, i.e. the arrangement, combination, and causal and logical interconnections, are crucial for the processes of narrative meaning- and worldmaking. Depending on the selected principles of the interrelatedness of plot elements and the favoured macrostructural types of configuration, an occurrence can be transformed into a variety of different stories and narratives. Thirdly, the discursive axis plays a pivotal role in narrative worldmaking because the explicit and implicit constitution of meaning also greatly depends on narrative mediation and perspectivisation. Perspective or point of view deserves special attention as yet another act or procedure of narrative worldmaking in its own right because it influences all of the processes involved in the making of events, plots, and storyworlds discussed above.

3.4 Narrative Worldmaking, Act IV: Events, Stories, and Narrated Worlds as Perspective-dependent Attributions of Meaning and Significance

In addition to the making of events, stories, and emplotment, narrative worldmaking also involves another important aspect which has, however, faded into the background, and undeservedly so: the extensive importance of perspectivity or point of view, which is arguably at least as important as emplotment. Different dimensions of perspective or point of view, viz. perceptional, spatial, temporal and ideological perspective, impinge on all the processes that are involved in the transformation of mere happenings or occurrences into stories, narratives of a particular kind, and textual representations of narratives (for a detailed account see Schmid 241–72, especially the model on page 267). Not only does the observer's spatial and temporal perspective of perception already play a decisive role in the choice of certain elements of the event, but his or her ideological perspective, i.e. his or her values and norms, is important as well. The same is true for the processes of composition through which a story becomes a narrative of a particular kind, as well as for the verbalisation which creates the text or the representation of the story.

Narratology has developed a sophisticated toolbox for the analysis of forms and kinds of point of view and the use of single point of view or multiple perspectives (see Neumann and Nünning; Herman, Jahn, and Ryan), which can also be of some use for the examination of narrative worldmaking and the analysis of representations of media events. Key narratological concepts such as focalisation, unreliable narration, and narrative perspective have proved very fine descriptive and analytical tools, but they have only rarely been deployed in order to come to grips with the procedures of worldmaking. Narrative theory emphasises that choice of point of view and methods of perspectivisation always play a crucial role in narrative worldmaking. Whether or not a given event or story is attributed a high degree of significance, and what kind of meaning is assigned to it, largely depends on the point of view from which a narrative is focalised or told.

Narrative representations of wars offer a case in point that serves to illustrate that the events, stories, and worlds largely depend on the point of view from which the story is presented. In the case of news coverage of war, the extensive importance which the chosen perspective has for the narrative representation or staging of media events is immediately evident. The various dimensions of perspectivity, i.e. the spatial, temporal, perceptional and ideological dimensions, each colour the narratives and stories that are disseminated. As Goodman observes, "some changes are reshapings or deformations that may according to point of view be considered either corrections or distortions" (16). Narrative representations of wars are always coloured by perspective and point of view, regardless of whether they are manifested in literary, historiographic, journalistic or photographic representations. However, not only do the perspectives of alleged witnesses, authors of press reportage, or photographers need to be considered. In addition, both the cultural frames of reference and culturally available plots, and the genre-specific and media-specific conventions of representation, genres and media used, need to be taken into account as well.

3.5 Narrative Worldmaking, Act V: Events, Stories, and Storyworlds as Discursively Created, Medially Represented, Culturally Specific and Historically Mutable Constructs

One does not need to be a constructivist, discourse or media theorist in order to want to add further characteristics to the criteria of eventfulness and the procedures of narrative worldmaking which have been formulated so far: what immediately comes to mind is the constructivity, performativity, discursivity, and mediality of events, stories and news stories, and media events. A happening only becomes an event through being reflected, or rather (re-)constructed, in discourses and stories and by being represented or staged by media productions (see the articles in section II of this volume). The constructedness of events and their mediality are based on the fact that events are never simply given or found 'out there,' but are made by the people and media giving accounts of them in narrative or visual form: the event only constitutes itself as such as media event, it displays itself only in the media event, as Isekenmeier ("Medienereignis" 469), following Derrida and others, argues. As analyses of the representations of great historical events like the so-called 'Indian Mutiny' (see Erll), the war in Iraq (see Isekenmeier, *The Medium is the Witness*), or '9/11' have amply demonstrated, the narratives and images disseminated by the media have a performative function insofar as medial representations "make the event as opposed to merely displaying it" (Derrida 22).

Two further characteristics derive from the constructivity, mediality and discursivity of events: namely, their cultural specificity and variability, and their historic mutability. As a result of their being the results of construction processes, events, stories and plots, and media events are always dependent on the system of concepts, conventions, discourses and media technology available in the respective epoch. One cannot define, once and for all, what is considered as particularly eventful since it depends on the respective criteria of relevance, the cultural hierarchies of norms and values, and the collective patterns of interpretation and weighting; and all of these parameters and procedures are subject to historical change. At the same time this means that whatever is considered as a 'big' event in history from today's point of view may not always have been perceived as such from the perspective of the members of the contemporary society who participated in that very history. Conversely, a not insignificant number of media events of the past have largely sunk into oblivion today, and many of today's news stories and media events are very likely to do as well.

From the point of view of a culturally sensitive narrative theory, narrative ways of worldmaking thus inevitably partake in a culture's ways of knowing, judging, and valuing. Lotman already formulated the groundbreaking insight that "the qualification of a fact as an event is dependent on the conceptual system" of the respective period, and that it always happens "in accordance with the general conception of the world" (Lotman 334) as well as with the respective world pictures prevalent at a given time and in a given culture. It is therefore desirable to supplement Goodman's analytical system of general procedures of worldmaking with a number of complementary disciplinary perspectives, approaches, and concepts (see the introduction to this volume), including concepts drawn from the study of culture and from narrative theory.

If one agrees that the character of the event should be conceived of as "a culturally specific and historically variable phenomenon of narrative representations" (Schmid 27), narrative ways of worldmaking are unlikely to be universals. Rather, as proponents of contextual, cultural and historical approaches to narratives have argued (for an overview see Nünning, "Surveying"), one can assume that there are always certain culturally available plots as well as cross-cultural variations between the locally specific ways in which narratives represent events, tell stories, and make worlds. In one of the best narrative or narrativist theories of culture to date, Wolfgang Müller-Funk has argued that cultures differ not only with regard to the subjects and themes they are particularly interested in, but also with regard to their favoured modes of storytelling, their forms of constructing narratives (see Müller-Funk 53). From this point of view, cultures are not so much 'imagined communities' *sensu* Anderson but 'narrative communities,' i.e. communities forged and held together by the stories the members tell about themselves and their culture, as well as by conventionalised forms of storytelling and cultural plots. Müller-Funk has therefore made the valuable suggestion to conceptualise cultures as 'narrative and memorial communities':

> Without any doubt it is narratives that form the basis of collective, national memories and that constitute politics of identity and difference. Cultures should always also be conceived of as narrative communities which are distinguished from each other by their reservoir of narratives. (Müller-Funk 14, my translation)

Narrative ways of worldmaking arguably not only reflect but also partake in and shape the narrative communities and the hierarchies of norms and values that distinguish cultures from one another. Conceptualising narrative fictions as both cognitive forces in their own right and as cultural ways of worldmaking, a yet to be fully developed cultural narratology should explore the ways in which the formal procedures of narrative worldmaking outlined above reflect and influence the unspoken mental assumptions and cultural issues of a given period. Cultural narratology recognises that since "ideology is located in narrative structures themselves" (Helms 14), analyses of the semanticisation of narrative forms can shed light on unspoken assumptions, attitudes, and ideologies, as well as on values and norms prevalent in any given text, genre, and period. Once narrative forms are understood as socially constructed cognitive forces, narratives become valuable sources for cultural history and cultural studies because analyses of "their narrative forms provide information about ideological concepts and world views" (ibid.). Such an approach promises to shed new light on the performative power of narratives to make worlds and to disseminate worldviews, two key aspects of narratives about which we know only too little and which narrative theory has largely ignored up to now.

4. Epilogue on Processes of Compression: Iconisation, Topicalisation, Pre-mediation and Re-mediation as Ways of Narrative Worldmaking

If we want to come to terms with the "world-creating properties of narrative" (Herman 71), we would be well-advised to pay more attention to the various acts or procedures of narrative worldmaking outlined above. One of the conclusions which can be drawn from this account of narratives as ways of worldmaking is that historical events, media events, and media wars do not emerge 'naturally' but should rather be understood as the result of a series of complex procedures and processes of selection, abstraction, ordering, compression, emplotment, and perspectivisation that go into narrative worldmaking. By telling a story, narrative texts as well as other media, are constructing events at the same time, shaping them in a certain way and endowing them with meaning. In doing so, the respective cultural plots function as the "organising principle of meaning" (Gutenberg 71, my translation).

This rough narratological sketch of narrative ways of worldmaking does not, however, pretend to have offered a comprehensive or exhaustive account of all the complex dimensions, mechanisms, and processes that are involved in cultural worldmaking. Aside from the procedures of narrative worldmaking already discussed in terms of narrative transformation and the perspective-dependent attribution of meaning, at least two further methods or ways of worldmaking which function as kinds of compression need to be mentioned. Knut Hickethier terms them 'iconisation' and 'topicalisation.' The term 'iconisation' draws attention to the central role which images and pictures play in the representation and production of media events. 'Topicalisation' refers to the close relationship between media events and certain places or sites. It also refers to the tendency of news coverage to develop recurring linguistic formulae and phrases.

In addition, Paul Ricœur's three-stage model of a processual mimesis is very useful for the analysis of narrative worldmaking. First, Ricœur's model reminds us that all such representations are related to and preformed by an antecedent, extra-literary reality which Ricœur (*Time and Narrative*) designates as 'prefiguration' (Mimesis I): Narrative worldmaking always occurs in the context of cultures in the symbolic system of which certain stories and culturally prevalent plots (objectified, for example, in literary traditions and media of other symbolic systems) are already available. Secondly, schemata and plots such as these are combined into certain stories in a narrative by means of 'configuration' (Mimesis II). Thirdly, representations can retroact into the extra-literary reality in a process of 'refiguration' (Mimesis III).

Drawing on Ricœur's concepts, Astrid Erll developed this model in a productive way for use in a wide-ranging cultural and historical examination of representations of the so-called 'Indian Mutiny' as a media event. She supplements Ricœur's categories with the fruitful concepts of 'pre-mediation' and 're-mediation' (see Bolter and Grusin; Grusin; Erll). These concepts transcend and productively supplement the narratological categories introduced thus far because they make allowances for the diachronic dimension of worldmaking, the processual character, and the evident significance of intermedial references, as well as the dynamics of pre- and remediation, that are involved in the representation of media events and in narrative worldmaking at large. The terms 'pre-mediation' and 're-mediation' describe the ways in which narratives and media refer back to, but also anticipate, other media and medial representations. The concepts of premediation and remediation raise our awareness of a certain dynamic which plays an especially important role in the representation of media events: the processual, diachronic and dynamic dimension of medial representation which connects media products with past and future media cultures.

Much more work, therefore, needs to be done before we can hope to come to terms with the complex question of how narratives and media interact as ways of cultural worldmaking. On the one hand, we need more systematic analyses of the genre- and media-specific formats of the representation, staging and perspectivisation of events and media events. On the other hand, studies on the cultural and historical variability of 'event models,' i.e. on what a given culture regards as a key event, are needed which, at the same time, consider the culturally available plots, schemata and frames that are dominant in a given society. Furthermore, the question of the extent to which the respective dominant media and institutional practices provide certain formats and media genres for media events arises. Recently, this has become apparent in the form of the specific television genres which have been developed for what has been termed the "Live Broadcasting of History" (Dayan and Katz). As Ulrich Keller, however, has impressively shown, many of the fictions of authenticity which are connected with this can be traced back to the methods of representation which were developed during the Crimean War (see Keller).

The approach outlined in this essay could, and should, be further developed in the framework of what has been called a "transmedial narratology" (see Ryan), the more so since narrative ways of worldmaking are arguably among the key issues of *Narratology in the Age of Cross-Disciplinary Narrative Research*, to quote the title of a stimulating collection of articles recently edited by Sandra Heinen and Roy Sommer. Combining the insights of transmedial narratology and cognitive narratology, David Herman even goes so far as to argue that "explorations of the protocols for making, unmaking, and remaking storyworlds is one of the exciting new frontiers of narratology in the age of interdisciplinary narrative research" (86).

Though the present essay is but an attempt to make a very modest contribution to such an ambitious project, what I hope to have shown is how pre-conditioned the notions of events, stories, and media events are, and how complex the processes of narrative worldmaking are through which mere happenings, occurrences, or incidents are gradually transformed into events, stories of a particular kind, and fully-fledged worlds or storyworlds. These procedures and processes which go into narrative worldmaking include selection, deletion, abstraction, weighting and ratings of relevance, configuration, ordering and emplotment, and last but not least, the choice of point of view and the arrangement of perspectives. The range of procedures of narrative worldmaking suggests that Goodman's discussion of ways of worldmaking needs to be supplemented with additional categories if we want to come to grips with the complex dynamics of cultural worldmaking and with the ways in which the dynamics of narrative form (see Pier) partake in these processes. The narratological approaches and concepts discussed above are not only useful for the analysis of the different procedures and the complex dynamics of narrative worldmaking, but they can also shed light on the cultural functions that narratives fulfil as a performative, powerful, and world-creating text type. Now that many practitioners of such new contextualist and cultural approaches to narrative as feminist narratology, intercultural narratology, and postcolonial narratology have begun putting the analytic toolkits of narratology "to the service of other concerns considered more vital for cultural studies," as Bal put it in an article tellingly entitled "The Point of Narratology," it seems to be high time that we started to examine more closely the world-creating procedures of narratives as particular ways of worldmaking. I should like to leave the last word to Nelson Goodman, however, who strikes the right sort of balance between, on the one hand, recognising the usefulness of surveying and systematising the processes of worldmaking and, on the other hand, acknowledging the incompleteness and provisional nature that any attempt at systematising the variety of ways of worldmaking necessarily entails: "All I have tried to do is to suggest something of the variety of processes in constant use. While a tighter systematization could surely be developed, none can be ultimate" (Goodman 17).

References

Anderson, Benedict. *Imagined Communities: Reflections on the Origins and Spread of Nationalism*. London: Verso, 1983.
Bachmann-Medick, Doris, ed. *Cultural Turns*. Reinbek bei Hamburg: Rowohlt, 2006.
Bal, Mieke. "The Point of Narratology." *Poetics Today* 11.4 (1990): 727–53.
Beuthner, Michael et al., eds. *Bilder des Terrors – Terror der Bilder? Krisenberichterstattung am und nach dem 11. September*. Köln: Halem, 2003.
Bolter, Jay David, and Richard Grusin. "Remediation." *Configurations: A Journal of Literature, Science, and Technology* 4.3 (1996): 311–58.
Brown, Theodore L. *Making Truth: Metaphor in Science*. Urbana/Chicago: U of Illinois P, 2003.
Bruner, Jerome. "The Narrative Construction of Reality." *Critical Inquiry* 18 (1991): 1–21.
Dayan, Daniel, and Elihu Katz. *Media Events: The Live Broadcasting of History*. Cambridge, MA/London: Harvard UP, 1994.
Derrida, Jacques. *Eine gewisse unmögliche Möglichkeit, vom Ereignis zu sprechen*. Berlin: Merve, 2003.
Eakin, Paul John. *How Our Lives Become Stories: Making Selves*. Ithaca/London: Cornell UP, 1999.
Erll, Astrid. *Prämediation – Remediation: Repräsentationen des indischen Aufstands in imperialen und post-kolonialen Medienkulturen (von 1857 bis zur Gegenwart)*. ELCH 23. Trier: WVT, 2007.
Erll, Astrid, Herbert Grabes, and Ansgar Nünning, eds. *Ethics in Culture: The Dissemination of Values through Literature and other Media*. Berlin/New York: de Gruyter, 2008.
Goodman, Nelson. *Ways of Worldmaking*. 1978. Indianapolis: Hackett Publishing, 1992.
Grabes, Herbert, Ansgar Nünning, and Sibylle Baumbach, eds. *Metaphors: Shaping Culture and Theory*. REAL - Yearbook of Research in English and American Literature 25. Tübingen: Narr, 2009.
Grunwald, Henning, and Manfred Pfister, eds. *Krisis! Krisenszenarien, Diagnosen und Diskursstrategien*. München: Fink, 2007.
Grusin, Richard. "Premediation." *Criticism* 46.1 (2004): 17–39.
Gutenberg, Andrea. *Mögliche Welten: Plot und Sinnstiftung im englischen Frauenroman*. Heidelberg: Winter, 2000.
Hardy, Barbara: *Shakespeare's Storytellers: Dramatic Narration*. London/Chester Springs, PA: Peter Owen, 1997.
Heinen, Sandra, and Roy Sommer, eds. *Narratology in the Age of Cross-Disciplinary Narrative Research*. Narratologia 20. Berlin/New York: de Gruyter, 2009.
Helms, Gabriele. *Challenging Canada: Dialogism and Narrative Technique in Canadian Novels*. Montreal/Kingston/London/Ithaca: McGill-Queen's UP, 2003.
Herman, David. "Narrative Ways of Worldmaking." *Narratology in the Age of Cross-Disciplinary Narrative Research*. Eds. Sandra Heinen, and Roy Sommer. Berlin/New York: de Gruyter, 2009. 71–87.
Herman, David, Manfred Jahn, and Marie-Laure Ryan, eds. *Routledge Encyclopedia of Narrative Theory*. London/New York: Routledge, 2005.
Hickethier, Knut. "Wie aus der Katastrophe eine Nachrichtengeschichte wurde: Ulrich Wickert und der '11. September.'" *Bilder des Terrors – Terror der Bilder? Kri-*

senberichterstattung am und nach dem 11. September. Eds. Michael Beuthner et al. Köln: Halem, 2003. 103–12.

Holzer, Anton, ed. *Mit der Kamera bewaffnet: Krieg und Fotografie*. Marburg: Jonas, 2003.

Hühn, Peter. "Event and Eventfulness." *Handbook to Narratology*. Eds. Peter Hühn, John Pier, Wolf Schmid, and Jörg Schönert. New York: de Gruyter, 2009. 80–97.

Isekenmeier, Guido. "Medienereignis." *Metzler Lexikon Literatur- und Kulturtheorie: Ansätze – Personen – Grundbegriffe*. 1998. Ed. Ansgar Nünning. 4th updated and enlarged ed. Stuttgart/Weimar: Metzler, 2008. 469–70.

—. *'The Medium is the Witness.' Zur Ereignis-Darstellung in Medientexten: Entwurf einer Theorie des Medienereignisses und Analyse der Fernsehnachrichten vom Irakkrieg*. Trier: WVT, 2008.

Jahn, Manfred. "Frames, Preferences, and the Reading of Third-Person Narrative: Towards a Cognitive Narratology." *Poetics Today* 18 (1997): 441–68.

Jameson, Fredric. *The Political Unconscious: Narrative as a Socially Symbolic Act*. 1981. London: Methuen, 1983.

Keller, Ulrich, "Authentizität und Schaustellung: Der Krimkrieg als erster Medienkrieg." *Mit der Kamera bewaffnet: Krieg und Fotografie*. Ed. Anton Holzer. Marburg: Jonas, 2003. 21–38.

Koselleck, Reinhart. *Zeitschichten: Studien zur Historik*. Frankfurt a.M.: Suhrkamp, 2000.

Lévi-Strauss, Claude. *The Savage Mind*. 1966. Eds. Julian Pitt-Rivers, and Ernest Gellner. London: Weidenfeld and Nicholson, 1972.

Lotman, Jurij M. "Das Problem des Sujets." *Die Struktur literarischer Texte*. 1972. München: Fink, 1993. 329–40.

McHale, Brian. *Constructing Postmodernism*. London: Routledge, 1992.

Meitser, Jan Christoph, ed. *Narratology Beyond Literary Criticism: Mediality, Disciplinarity*. Berlin/New York: de Gruyter, 2005.

Müller-Funk, Wolfgang. *Die Kultur und ihre Narrative: Eine Einführung*. 2002. Wien/New York: Springer, 2008.

Neumann, Birgit, and Ansgar Nünning. *An Introduction to the Study of Narrative Fiction*. Stuttgart: Klett, 2008.

Nietzsche, Friedrich. *Unmodern Observations*. Ed. William Arrowsmith. New Haven/London: Yale UP, 1990. Trans. of *Unzeitgemäße Betrachtungen*. 1875. Ed. Karl Schlechta. München: Hanser, 1954.

Nünning, Ansgar. "Narratologie der Krise: Wie aus einer Situation ein Plot und eine Krise (konstruiert) werden." *Krisis! Krisenszenarien, Diagnosen und Diskursstrategien*. Eds. Henning Grunwald, and Manfred Pfister. München: Fink, 2007. 48–71.

—. "Steps Towards a Metaphorology (and Narratology) of Crises: On The Functions of Metaphors as Figurative Knowledge and Mininarrations." *Metaphors: Shaping Culture and Theory*. REAL – Yearbook of Research in English and American Literature 25. Eds. Herbert Grabes, Ansgar Nünning, and Sibylle Baumbach. Tübingen: Narr, 2009. 229–62.

—. "Surveying Contextualist and Cultural Narratologies: Towards an Outline of Approaches, Concepts and Potentials." *Narratology in the Age of Cross-Disciplinary Narrative Research*. Narratologia 20. Eds. Sandra Heinen, and Roy Sommer. Berlin/New York: de Gruyter, 2009. 48–70.

Nünning, Ansgar, ed. *Metzler Lexikon Literatur- und Kulturtheorie: Ansätze – Personen – Grundbegriffe*. 1998. 4th updated and enlarged ed. Stuttgart/Weimar: Metzler, 2008.

Nünning, Ansgar, and Roy Sommer. "The Performative Power of Narrative in Drama: On the Forms and Functions of Dramatic Storytelling in Shakespeare's Plays." *Current Trends in Narratology.* Ed. Greta Olson. Berlin/New York: de Gruyter, 2010 (under review).

Olson, Greta, ed. *Current Trends in Narratology.* Berlin/New York: de Gruyter, 2010 (under review).

Pier, John, ed. *The Dynamics of Narrative Form: Studies in Anglo-American Narratology,* Narratologia Bd. 4. Berlin/New York: de Gruyter, 2005.

Prince, Gerald. *A Dictionary of Narratology.* Lincoln/London: U of Nebraska P, 1987.

Rathmann, Thomas. "Ereignisse Konstrukte Geschichten." *Ereignis: Konzeptionen eines Begriffs in Geschichte, Kunst und Literatur.* Ed. Thomas Rathmann. Köln/Weimar/Wien: Böhlau, 2003. 1–19.

Ricœur, Paul. "Narrative Time." *Critical Inquiry* 7 (1980): 169–90.

—. *Time and Narrative,* Vol. 1, Chicago/London: U of Chicago P, 1984. Trans. of *Temps et récit,* Paris: Seuil, 1983.

Rigney, Ann. *The Rhetoric of Historical Representation: Three Narrative Histories of the French Revolution,* Cambridge: Cambridge UP, 1990.

Ryan, Marie-Laure. "On the Theoretical Foundations of Transmedial Narratology." *Narratology Beyond Literary Criticism: Mediality, Disciplinarity.* Ed. Jan Christoph Meister. Berlin/New York: de Gruyter, 2005.

Schmid, Wolf. *Elemente der Narratologie.* Berlin/New York: de Gruyter, 2005.

Sommer, Roy. "Making Narrative Worlds: A Cross-Disciplinary Approach to Literary Storytelling." *Narratology in the Age of Cross-Disciplinary Narrative Research.* Eds. Sandra Heinen, and Roy Sommer. Berlin/New York: de Gruyter, 2009. 88–108.

Stierle, Karlheinz. "Geschehen, Geschichte, Text der Geschichte." *Text als Handlung.* München: Fink, 1975. 49–55.

Suter, Andreas, and Manfred Hettling, eds. *Struktur und Ereignis.* Special Issue 19 of *Geschichte und Gesellschaft.* Göttingen: Vandenhoeck & Ruprecht, 2001.

White, Hayden. *Metahistory: The Historical Imagination in Nineteenth Century Europe.* Baltimore/London: Johns Hopkins UP, 1973.

—. "The Value of Narrativity in the Representation of Reality." *Critical Inquiry* 7.1 (1980): 5–27.

—. *The Content of the Form: Narrative Discourse and Historical Representation.* Baltimore/London: Johns Hopkins UP, 1987.

The Making of Fictional Worlds:
Processes, Features, and Functions

Vera Nünning

1. Introduction

In his seminal work *Ways of Worldmaking* (1978), Nelson Goodman not only raised our awareness of the processes which are involved in the construction of worlds that we tend to think of as 'natural' or 'true'; he also stressed that, although different worlds are built on diverging premises, there is no reason to try to reduce them to a single base, since "many different world-versions are of independent interest and importance" (Goodman 4). In this view, the worlds constructed by science are not inherently 'better' or more adequate for an understanding of life than other worlds; instead,

> [t]he pluralists' acceptance of [world versions] other than physics implies no relaxation of rigor but a recognition that standards different from yet no less exacting than those applied in science are appropriate for appraising what is conveyed in perceptual or pictorial or literary versions. (5)

The making of fictional worlds—in the narrow sense of a work of literature that is created by the use of narrative—seems to be a rather specific aspect of Goodman's wide-ranging enquiry. Why limit oneself to such a field, to literary texts like novels, short stories, or other forms of fictional prose, while leaving out plays and poetry? Or, if one wants to stress the importance of narrative, why not consider story worlds, without regard to their fictional character, as has David Herman in his recent article, "Narrative Ways of Worldmaking"? After all, a growing number of 'narrative' psychologists in the wake of Jerome Bruner and others as well as academics involved in the various fields of the cognitive sciences stress the importance of narration as a "tool for thinking."[1] Narratives, as has been

---

[1] This quote is part of the title of one of David Herman's recent publications on the topic (see Herman "Stories as a Tool for Thinking"). I think that many of the observations

shown in many recent publications, are not just neutral vessels into which experiences are put in retrospect in order to remember them and communicate them to others; they rather shape and inform our thoughts and actions on many different levels, for instance as far as the encoding and remembering of events is concerned. However, the concentration on fictional narratives does not result in as drastic a limitation as might be expected. After all, fictional worldmaking shares all the important features of narrative worldmaking; moreover, the additional quality of literary fictions, which are both situated in a specific communicative situation and divorced from it, makes it possible to allude to some interesting aspects and functions of worldmaking which would have to be neglected otherwise.

Unfortunately, Goodman did not concern himself with the specific processes that result in the construction of narrative and fictional worlds. However, he distinguished five general processes which are inherent in the construction of worlds. In the following, I will first explore to what extent these five processes of composition and decomposition, weighting, ordering, deletion and supplementation as well as deformation and reshaping are involved in the making of fictional worlds. Though these processes indeed inform fiction, they are not the only principles that should be stressed if one wants to understand the specificity of fictional worlds. In the main part of this paper, I will therefore discuss eight additional features which might be relevant for fictional worldmaking; I will conclude my essay with a very brief sketch of some of the functions fictional worlds might fulfil.

2. Fictional Worldmaking in the Light of Goodman's Principles

Goodman's assumption that worlds are always constructed out of existing worlds is of particular relevance to fictional narratives. As Paul Ricœur has shown in his seminal work *Time and Narrative*, there is a 'circle of mimesis' which involves literary texts as well as other discourses. Ricœur's terms 'pre-figuration,' 're-figuration,' and 'con-figuration' refer to the fact that fictional narratives always make use of material that is 'pre-figured' by both literature and other discourses. Elements present in and shaped by

---

which I will put forth in this paper might be pertinent for an understanding of the worldmaking that is involved in films as well; but since I am no expert in this field I will leave the application of the following to this medium to more sagacious readers. For the importance of narratives both as a mode of thinking and for our understanding of ourselves and establishing our identity see also Bruner ("Narrative Construction"; "Self-making and Worldmaking"); Eakin; Conway; McAdams ("Identity"; "Narrative Coherence"); Nelson.

the conventions of literary and other discourses are 'con-figured' in the literary work in a specific manner which Nelson Goodman would term the fictional way of worldmaking. After the publication, the literary work becomes itself part of the circle, as it provides material which is 're-figured' in other texts (see Ricœur, esp. 52ff.).

Ricœur's thesis already highlights the importance of intertextuality and intermediality in fictional narratives. Fictional narratives make use of motifs, ways of characterisation, scenes, themes, and ways of writing that have been used in other texts before, thus establishing relations between the work in question and various 'pre-texts' which have already employed and shaped this particular element before. The same holds true with regard to relations to other media, to painting, film, or music, which are referred to in literary narratives. In this respect, there are no differences between the arts and other discourses, between what we think we know about the world and what has been imagined by others. Works of fiction are made out of material belonging to both literary works and non-fictional texts.

The five processes of worldmaking that Goodman differentiates also inform the construction of fictional narratives; but the making of fictional worlds seems to be a messy affair, and in many of the processes I refer to, more than one principle is at work at the same time—indeed, Goodman himself conceded that many factors involved in the making of worlds can be subsumed under more than one heading (see Goodman 17). In order to illustrate at once the common ground between fictional and other worlds and some specificities of fictional worlds, I will briefly consider how these processes work in particular literary texts. Probably all of them are pertinent to the world of any work of art—but I have tried to refer to principles of construction which are dominant, even though others may be at play simultaneously. I will, moreover, shift Goodman's order of discussing the principles and end up with 'ordering,' which is arguably most important to fictional worldmaking.

1. Composition and decomposition (Goodman 7–10). These processes are closely related to Goodman's premise that worlds are always made out of something else. A new world is composed out of the elements of several others, whereas one former world may be subdivided and function as the kernel of a new world. The process of 'composition' is dominant in Jürgen Link's (1988) concept of literature as an 'interdiscourse,' which joins elements and 'rules of speaking' of several other discourses. Novels in particular are prone to function as part of an 'interdiscourse,' since their depiction of characters in love or people dealing with money provide an encompassing view, integrating what has been couched in the discourses of religion, law, medicine, the economy, and so

on. In order to illustrate the importance of 'decomposition,' one might point to the differentiation of genres and the creation of new sub-genres. In the nineteenth century, for instance, the novel was subdivided into social novels, sensation novels, detective novels, and so on; even sub-genres like the bildungsroman or historical fiction are prone to be differentiated into several kinds, each of which featuring different, though closely related, genre conventions.

2. Deletion and supplementation (Goodman 14–16). While the first process relates to larger entities, the second is mainly concerned with the treatment of smaller units that are taken over from existing worlds. We should bear in mind, moreover, that the deletion of elements is governed by the frame established in the particular work of art. We tend to neglect "what cannot be fitted into the architecture of the world we are building" (15). With regard to the construction of fictional narratives, we can differentiate between their references to fictional and non-fictional 'sources.' Texts referring to our 'cultural knowledge' which was taken to be true at a given time, have, of course, to be selective—even if they encompass several hundred pages. Usually, such novels do not take one specific body of texts as their reference point, which is then 'weeded out' and enlarged upon according to narrative conventions—though this was important to Disraeli's novel *Sybil: Or Two Nations* (1845), which made extensive use of parliamentary reports (so called 'blue-books'). They rather use the knowledge comprised from many texts as subject matter. In a very inspiring essay, Catherine Elgin has proposed that literature should be conceptualised as a 'thought experiment.' As such, it is characterised by the deletion of non-salient features, which is an important precondition for the process of understanding: "To achieve a cognitive grasp of p, we need to ignore much available information about p and organize the rest" (Elgin, "Laboratory of the Mind" 44). Literature, and, I will argue, narrative fiction in particular, provides this kind of representation, which is based on the selection of salient facts.

With regard to literary texts, at least two levels of abstraction have to be considered when we want to become aware of the importance of deletion and supplementation. The first level involves the development of genres; that is, the relation between a particular text and the existing works which belong to the same class of text. A case in point would be, for instance, the first British 'vampire novels,' which took over nearly all of the elements developed in Gothic fiction up to the early nineteenth century, but deleted the various kinds of evil magical agents (like the devil, or evil spirits) and added the character of the vampire with its own manner of causing harm and inspiring fear. The second level pertains to the relation between a given work and a single 'pre-text.' Samuel Richardson's well-known novel about the 'maiden in distress,' *Pamela, Or: Virtue Rewarded* (1740), has given way to several parodies, for instance, the most famous of which is Henry Fielding's *Shamela* (1741), in which all of the characters and the plotline of the former work are retained; only the protagonist is substituted by Shamela, a shameless and self-serving young woman who surely does not deserve the marriage with which she is rewarded in the end.

3. Deformation (Goodman 16). This feature involves the reshaping of already existing elements and is, as far as fictional worlds are concerned, mostly found in combination with deletion and supplementation. In many works which 're-write' existing texts, we are confronted not just with the leaving out of some characters or attributes and the substitution of others, but also with a 'deformation' which modifies existing elements in such a way as to give them a new meaning. William Shakespeare's love poem "My mistress' eyes are nothing like the sun," for instance, used the poetical conventions of the sonnet form and provided a description of the appearance of his alleged mistress which formally adhered to the lists of attributes conventionalised in many poems making use of the Renaissance ideal of beauty. However, Shakespeare used those attributes only with a view to deconstructing them and substituting others, which seem to be rather unattractive at first sight: the eyes of the adored women do not resemble the sun, and there are no roses in her cheeks. Though this text closely adheres to the forms and the content of love sonnets, there is a kind of reshaping involved as well, for in the last couplet Shakespeare undercuts his former denigration of his mistress by stating that his love is even more true than that described in the other poems, which set up "false compare." What we find is therefore a 'deformation,' a modification of the forms of praising one's mistress by partly reverting to old traditions, partly introducing new ones. More obvious cases of deforming and re-interpreting works which have achieved canonical status and embody the dominant thought patterns and hierarchy of values at their time are, of course, post-colonial re-writings of classics like Shakespeare's *The Tempest* (1623) or Charlotte Brontë's *Jane Eyre* (1847).

4. Weighting (Goodman 10–12). The process of remaking worlds by shifting the emphasis and thereby changing the meaning of an existing world can perhaps best be exemplified with regard to the development of the novel in the early twentieth century. While modernist writers did not differ from the Victorians in their attempt to describe characters and actions, they shifted their concern from the events to the perception of those events, from the characters' agency in the fictional world to their consciousness—with the result that the form of the novel was changed drastically. A more intricate shift in emphasis is involved in the difference

between two ways of writing held to be typical of postmodernism: pastiche and parody. While pastiche closely imitates specific styles without adding another layer of meaning of its own—apart from the implicit statement that all possible modes of writing have been used already and are, to use John Barth's famous phrase, 'exhausted'—in parodies this imitation serves to expose the original to ridicule. The shift of emphasis between the two modes may be slight; one can, for instance, argue that the style of John Fowles' famous novel *The French Lieutenant's Woman* (1969) is a pastiche of Victorian realism. If one takes into account the metafictional elements which are also prominent in the text and which have no equivalent in Victorian realist conventions, however, one is led to the conclusion that it is a parody rather than a pastiche.

5. Ordering (Goodman 12–14). Ways of worldmaking are also distinguished by their modes of ordering experience, for instance by establishing and adhering to categories for measuring space and time to provide some kind of order within the constructed world. This is probably the most fruitful principle as far as fictional texts are concerned, and a detailed analysis would have to take into account the differences of ordering on the level of the story and on the level of the narration, which I shall refer to in more detail later. Since both levels are closely interlinked and since the mode of narration shapes our understanding of the story, I shall deal with them together and only refer to important differences in passing.

In a rather basic, but very important manner, narratives order our ongoing stream of consciousness by providing what Herman in "Stories as a Tool for Thinking" calls "chunks" (172–73), and therefore presenting "cognizable, and thus usable structures" (173), by offering classifiable, recognisable and memorisable units. This process is so ubiquitous that it usually goes unnoticed, but it is vital to our way of life. Narrative ordering concerns first of all the establishment of basic units like a "delimited set of participants, states, actions, and events and structures" (174) which can be transformed into a coherent whole. The most obvious unit is achieved by the differentiation into several characters, which we are able to recognise over a larger stretch of time (and narrative), although they may have considerably changed in between, both as far as outward appearance, mode of dress, characteristics and ways of acting are concerned. In order to accomplish this, we need, of course, an implicit personality theory, but we also need narrative—which is an important basis for distinguishing ways of characterisation, for instance, or for establishing the nexus between a stable set of characteristics and the motives and actions which might be expected from such a person.

Another only seemingly simple means of narrative ordering is the construction of a chronology: the choice of a beginning, a middle and an end. These are all of overall importance as far as our understanding of the respective event or development is concerned; but for brevity's sake I will confine myself to a few remarks on the construction of a beginning. In Western societies, we tend to see narrative beginnings also as origins, as the 'root' of what happened later, as the non-analysable event that somehow led to all the other happenings that follow from it. As Niels Buch Leander points out in a remarkable essay, "there can be no beginning independent of the particular narrative we bring to it" (19). This also implies the impossibility of setting a 'true' beginning: even the birth of the hero is only an arbitrary start, which neglects both the internal perspective of the character (who does not remember this event; see also ibid. 24–25) and the possibility of other determining factors, such as the genes of father and mother and their social situation, both of which go back far beyond the hero's birth. Setting a beginning therefore always shapes our understanding of the story, as Watzlawick's example of the simple tale of a wife who complains and a husband who withdraws illustrates: the choice of a beginning has an enormous impact on our interpretation of this story. We need beginnings in order to make sense of our experience; but we construct a particular event by our choice of the narrative point of departure. Since we are so used to narratives, however, we are not prone to question this selection, which also pertains to our understanding of historical events.

Apart from setting a beginning, the ordering of time and sequence is central to stories, and Bruner therefore holds "diachronicity" ("Narrative Construction" 6) to be a defining feature of the narrative construction of reality. This mode is central to both our understanding of a story world and to the sequence that is provided by the narrator, which may diverge quite radically from the 'natural' chronology. Flashbacks and flashforwards, for instance, are common characteristics of tales that are mainly ordered in a chronological manner, whereas some kinds of detective fiction begin with the end—the murder—and then go back in time in order to establish the sequence that led to this event. The establishing of beginnings is thus even more complex, since a novel may offer us several beginnings, depending on the narrator(s). Moreover, simultaneity is translated into linearity, and since the beginning of the twentieth century, fictional worldmaking has also involved the difference between an abstract 'clock time' and the sense of time of the characters who may partly 'live in the past' and experience seconds as an eternity.

In addition to the individual sense of time (and thus of ordering experience) that the different characters have, the narrative as a whole provides several means of structuring the text. One overall pattern is, for instance, provided by the genre, such as the Bildungsroman, which sets the events against an overall development which implies the growth of the protagonist. A different pattern would be provided by the structure of tragedies or the omnipresent way of ordering according to the organic metaphor of 'growth and decline.' This larger structure is often subdivided into scenes or episodes, which again can be differentiated into smaller narrative units. An important feature of narratives in the emphatic sense are 'turning points' (see Bruner, "Narrative Construction" 73–74; "Self-making and World-making" 11–12), in which the expectations raised by canonical story forms are breached. We do not believe in smooth developments from the cradle to the grave anymore, and thus we even have expectations about the breaching of such forms, "those episodes in which [...] the narrator attributes a crucial change or stance in the protagonist's story to a belief, a conviction, a thought" (Bruner, "Self-making and World-making" 73). The narrative mode of presenting sequences therefore raises expectations in readers, who often have to re-arrange their view of the data collected so far in order to re-interpret them in the light of what happens later. In contrast to specific scientific worlds, which are usually developed in a logical way, and in which every new information is based on or differentiates and develops further the facts which have been provided so far, the information provided in narratives often asks for a re-assessment of what has been told before (see also Nünning, "Literatur als Lebenswissen" 156–61; 166). Characters appear in a new light; their actions may be evaluated in a completely different way once a crucial piece of knowledge has been provided. Even a popular genre like crime fiction is based on these reversals, which provide a kind of rather reductive tension which only relates to the questions of who the culprit was, or of what happens next.

The arrangement of time sequences and the development of the plot are not the only ways in which narratives provide their worlds with coherence. Themes which are taken up with regard to different scenes and characters are a case in point, and even life stories which are told orally may be given coherence by having recourse to the same metaphoric theme (see Bruner, "Self-making and World-making" 70). Fictional worlds are, moreover, given internal coherence by the repetition or slight variation of images, which may also acquire the status of symbols. As far as the establishment of connections between characters or events that belong to different 'subplots' or strands of the story are concerned, I would also like to mention commonalities with regard to intertextual references, for instance quotes and preferences for the same literary works or the connection to the same semantic fields (for instance with regard to animals or flowers).

3. Additional Features of Fictional Narrative Worlds

Goodman's processes of worldmaking are thus a good starting point to understand the construction of fictional worlds. In order to provide a more thorough discussion of fictional worldmaking, I will now introduce eight additional features. These are based on the path-breaking essay by Jerome Bruner, and it will be seen that some of his ten features of "the narrative construction of reality" are incorporated into the following. My proposal here is slightly different, however, since I will be concerned mainly with fictional worlds, and since my approach is guided not only by insights from psychology, but also from narratology.

1. Situatedness. First of all one should bear in mind that narratives are a means of communication; they are addressed by a human being at a specific point in time with a particular cultural background to someone else (see also Herman, "Narrative Ways of Worldmaking" 74; McAdams, "Narrative Coherence" 111). This does not presuppose that every narrative must be told to someone who is able to listen to the teller; indeed, stories are often used to make sense of situations by telling them to oneself. In Western cultures, moreover, there seems to be a tendency to tell stories to imagined personalities, who may be invented by the narrator or who may be personas of human beings like relatives, friends, or media personalities (see Hermans 41). In any case, narratives are told to addressees who are ascribed certain characteristics, which in turn influences the make-up of the story. This implies that narratives are also placed in specific contexts, in cultures with shared values, beliefs, canons, and stories, and in particular spatio-temporal settings. This situatedness in a cultural context informs the narrative world on many different levels: it influences the depiction of characters and actions, which have to be understandable with some sort of reference to the shared knowledge of the world, it influences the ways of telling the story (which will be enlarged upon later on), and it provides the overall context of interpretation as well as our expectations with regard to why the teller engages in this act of narration.[2]

2. Structure: story vs. discourse. Secondly, narrative worlds contain at least two layers or, in narratological terms, two levels of existence. In every narration we distinguish between the story world, i.e. the world of the characters, and the level of discourse, i.e. the narrative mediation of the world of the characters, which is ascribed to a particular narrator. Both levels are important for the kind of meaning narratives generate. Readers

---

2   The last point is already present in Bruner's account ("Narrative Construction" 16–17); it is his ninth characteristic of the narrative construction of reality, called context sensitivity, and discussed together with the concept of negotiability.

usually try to extract some basic facts about the story world, for instance about agents, space, and chronology, though the narrative mediation of these 'fictional facts' may be quite difficult to detect (see Herman, "Narrative Ways of Worldmaking"; McAdams, "Narrative Coherence" 111–12). It is important to bear in mind, however, that the way of telling the events influences our understanding of them: the same events appear differently in a comedy or in a tragedy, and the choice of metaphors or 'focalisers' (which will be discussed later on) can present the same story in a completely different light.³

3. Narrative as mode of thinking and understanding. More important than this rather basic differentiation between the levels of the story world, the level of narrative transmission (or 'discourse') and the acts and intentions of the human beings involved in this kind of communication, may be another feature of narrative worlds, which are governed by rules and assumptions that differ from those worlds constructed by science. The thesis that narratives do not adhere to the same logic as other construc-

---

3   This differentiation within the narrative world has to be distinguished from the everyday life and the actions of the teller. This is of particular importance with regard to literary narratives—Cervantes is not the same person as Don Quixote, and Nabokov did not make love to the thirteen-year-old Lolita—but it may also pertain to the stories that are told in face-to-face situations or in genres like autobiographies. The teller of his or her own life is part of the discourse which constructs the narrative world; there is a textual 'self' that is given shape by the words, the assumptions and the genre conventions the 'real' teller of the tale employs in order to tell his story. This narrating textual 'I' is situated on a different level from the experiencing textual self both in terms of place and time, and it addresses an implied listener or 'addressee' who is situated at the level of narrative transmission. If the narrating 'I' tells his or her own story, he or she is still quite different from her former self, not least because the narrator knows how the story ended, a knowledge that is denied to the character who is part of the events. If a work of fiction employs the device of a 'heterodiegetic' or 'omniscient' narrator, of a seemingly neutral instance that knows everything about the story and the characters and is located at a different ontological (textual) level, the use of this convention implies that we are to trust this kind of narrator implicitly. It does not imply, however, that the author of the text claims to know and believe everything that the narrator tells—otherwise we would have to have serious doubts about the psychological make-up of the writers of fantasy stories or science fiction, for instance. This illustrates that, with regard to fictional worlds, it is important to differentiate between different levels of communication. The author Daniel Defoe is not the young Robinson Crusoe who is stranded upon an island, and this young protagonist has to be distinguished from the old and mature Robinson, who, according to the fictional facts, tells his own story. The same holds true with regard to the differences between the implied addressee on the level of the story: the character Robinson talks to Friday; but the old narrator talks to an implied addressee who is not present in the story world. And Defoe, of course, writes the novel with a view to the eighteenth-century reading public and the hope of making money. In face-to-face situations, the 'real' listener to the story may sometimes prefer to distance himself from the addressee that the narrating self addresses in his account: by justifying one's actions to an unusual extent, for instance, the narrator implicitly ascribes harsh standards of judgements to the 'implied' listener of the story—standards which might not be shared by the actual listener, who may think of him- or herself as open-minded.

tions of the world can be approached from two angles: as far as individuals creating narratives are concerned they use narratives as a mode of thinking, whereas listeners or readers need a specific mode of understanding, which some philosophers and literary theorists have called 'hermeneutic understanding.' As a mode of, or, in David Herman's terms a "tool for thinking" ("Stories as a Tool for Thinking") and a "cognitive structure or way of making sense of experience" ("Narrative Ways of Worldmaking" 73), narratives differ from abstract propositional or scientific modes of thought. While we are aware of our acquisition of typologies and formula which govern our assessment of natural phenomena, we are usually not aware of the fact that "we organize our experience and our memory of human happenings mainly in the form of narrative—stories, excuses, myths, reasons for doing and not doing, and so on" (Bruner, "Narrative Construction" 4). Narrative is so ubiquitous, and we acquire mastery of it so early in our development, that we often do not recognise the crucial ways in which it shapes our construction of reality. The most important ways of organising experience have been sketched above; in addition, it bears emphasising that narratives do not posit causal relations. The narrative construction of reality—the 'chunking' of experience, the establishment of a beginning, turning points and an end, for instance—often induce us to draw inferences and to understand an event in a particular way. However, this should be distinguished from causal relations; instead, what we are supplied with is material for the interpretation of events. This process of understanding is concerned with the 'reasons' for things happening, the intentions of characters, their choice of actions, and the (intended or unintended) results. As Bruner stresses, there is only a "loose link between intentional states and subsequent action" ("Narrative Construction" 7). Roland Barthes (94) already drew our attention to the persuasiveness of narratives, which sanctions the application of the fallacy post hoc, propter hoc—what happens later must be the reason for that which happened first. We tend to believe that what we are told first in a story with a limited amount of events and characters must be causally related to that which is told later on. Narrative leads us to construct a relation between two events (or any other items of stories), to believe that they together are part of an overarching development. David Herman has given a very short and basic, but also telling example for this kind of thinking:

> Most speakers of English would agree that the string (S) Tom bought a security system and had his house burgled differs from the string (S1) Tom had his house burgled and bought a security system. Yet there is nothing in the connective 'and' to mark a particular temporal ordering of (or causal relation between) the two conjuncts. ("Stories as a Tool for Thinking" 176)

When dealing with narratives, readers tend to construct these temporal and causal relations, which supply both coherence and meaning. Our understanding of events and characters is therefore not based on a logical analysis of the causes and effects. Indeed, it would be next to impossible to arrive at an understanding of 'human time,' of intentions and their relation to actions as well as results, personal development, empathy, and social interaction without having recourse to the narrative construction of reality. By placing characters and events in a particular story world as well as by situating them in a narrative discourse we give them meaning and invite readers to understand them in a particular way.

Interpreting narratives is, however, anything but simple. In particular, there are two aspects to be considered. On the one hand, the interpretation of narratives involves relating the parts of the story to the whole. Elements are understandable only with regard to the whole story—the narrative discourse as well as the overall values of the text. It is not possible to grasp 'the meaning' of an episode without having recourse to the whole; neither can we understand the whole narrative without being able to place the episodes in a meaningful way and to determine the functions which they fulfil; we are caught in what has been called a 'hermeneutic circle.'[4] This may be illustrated with regard to autobiographical stories, in which the experiences of the child only make sense as part of the development that 'leads up to' the identity of the narrator; obviously, the earlier episodes become a means of establishing and illustrating this process of 'growth' (see Bruner, "Self-making and World-making" 69–70). The visit of a child to a relative imprisoned in a jail, for instance, will take on quite a different meaning if it is part of the life story of a judge, a criminal, or a reformer—it may even be given contradictory meanings at different points in the same story if, for instance, a criminal experiences a decisive 'turning point,' mends his ways, and revisits the episode in the prison later on in his narrative.

There is, in addition, an even more wide-ranging effect of the hermeneutic process of interpretation, for particular parts of a narrative as well as narratives as a whole can acquire a 'double meaning.' On the one hand, we can try to deduct the 'literal' meaning of narratives, which is common to both oral accounts and narratives which are used as ways of providing excuses in private life or justifications in a court of law. This mode of interpretation is, however, only one particular way of assigning meaning to narratives, a way that is common with regard to the understanding of realistic stories. Even in such stories, however, we are sometimes led to

---

4 For a very good elucidation of the hermeneutic mode of interpreting texts see Berensmeyer, "Hermeneutische und neohermeneutische Methoden der Textinterpretation."

interpret the events on a different level, when we assume that the characters and incidents stand for something else. This mode of understanding would be adequate to allegorical accounts, and famous fables and allegories provide the readers with any number of clues. The shepherds and maidens in pastorals often 'stand in' for political agents, who could not safely be criticised by authors who wanted to avoid drastic punishments in former times, and Orwell's *Animal Farm* (1945) is just one famous example in modern literature. The allegorical mode of interpretation, however, might be more important than these examples suggest, since many realist stories can acquire a second layer of meaning as well. In this vein, *Robinson Crusoe* (1719) could be understood as a representative 'conversion story' of the truant son finally arriving at the true faith, and the developments of characters in realist stories can be understood as symbolising aspects of the human psyche, the (fruitless but never ceasing) revolt of man against fate or the heroic fight against social injustice. In this manner, we might even read the account of a witness in a law court as an attempt to project the persona of a reliable citizen rather than an account of past events. If narrative psychologists, who have stressed that listeners tend to evaluate positively those life stories which not only provide coherence and a conventional sequence of actions, but which also allow them to 'draw lessons' from the tale, are right, and if we assume that there are several quite different ways of 'drawing lessons,' this mode of interpretation might be more important than is usually assumed.[5]

4. Referentiality and self-reflexivity. The absence of causal relations and the complexities involved in the interpretation of stories are closely linked to another feature of narratives: they do not provide us with a possible means of verification of the narrative 'facts'—we can only judge them with regard to the concept of verisimilitude (see Bruner, "Narrative Construction" 13–14). This is particularly obvious with regard to fictional texts which do not refer to agents or events in the real world. The characters are products of the author's imaginations, and it would be in vain to check them against people whom they seem to resemble. Even the setting of realist novels should not be equated with the places they purportedly signify: Oliver Twist's London is as removed from the 'real' capital of Great Britain as the 'real' Dublin is from the place which Stephen and Bloom inhabit in Joyce's *Ulysses* (1922). In this text, the title—and the many intertextual references to Homer's epic—indicates that the space that is part of the story world (and thus has to be situated within the

---

[5] See McAdams ("Narrative Coherence" 117). McAdams also refers to the findings by Blagov and Singer. These psychologists, however, rather think of drawing direct lessons from particular incidents; they are not concerned with an allegorical understanding of stories.

whole story of Joyce's text and, because of the pronounced intertextuality, to the places of Homer's narrative) carries different meanings than the well-known city in Ireland. In an essay dealing with autobiography, Jerome Bruner stresses that the 'stages' of development of a person can only be checked against the memory of that person—certainly a very hazy and unreliable referent ("Self-making and World-making" 70), especially if we take into account that the encoding of memories is already governed by the form of narrative (see Conway 492, 508; Nelson 13, 16). Even a comparison with the memories of another family member could not lead to any kind of verification, since this would be pitting narratively-informed memory against the memory of someone else, which is constructed according to the same principles, albeit a different point of view.[6] A common way of trying to assure oneself of the 'truth' of one's own memory is the comparison with other narratives, in order to see whether they fit the culturally accepted forms of the representation of one's experiences, for instance with regard to canonical accounts of adolescence or culturally prevalent models of childhood. This is dubious even as far as the process of falsification is concerned (even what is highly unusual and improbable is not necessarily non-existent) and might lead to a de-individualisation or conventionalisation of the representation of one's own life as one's memories of the events fade. Indeed, missing links or gaps in memory are sometimes filled with reference to existing genre conventions, often without one's being aware that this part of one's life story cannot be traced back to one's own experiences.

The problem of establishing a referent is even more pronounced with regard to fictional narratives. This is not only due to the difficulty of relating imagined events to actual happenings, but also because of a feature that narratologists call 'self-reflexivity' and that Roman Jakobson has called the 'poetic function' of literature. Rather than being directly related to the factual world of the reader or viewer, fictional worlds are marked by their references to themselves. Fictional narratives usually feature several kinds of coherence, with the words in the text referring to other words. The hermeneutic mode of interpretation therefore stresses the necessity of relating the parts to each other and to the overarching whole, in the light of which the particular events are constituted. Fictional narratives are marked by a self-reflexivity that is assumed to go beyond that of less complex, everyday accounts. In fictional worlds, the elements (be they words that are connected by semantic fields or isotopies or larger units

---

6   Moreover, psychologists emphasise that remembering is a social process, which is always judged and shaped by the members of one's group (see, for instance, Nelson; McAdams, "Identity" 191–92).

like events or patterns of perception) are not only connected in many ways; works of fiction also reflect upon the manner of their composition; they not only use genre conventions, but they also handle them in ways that make readers aware that these are conventions; they parody features and use them to establish new features at the same time.

5. Polyvalence and suspension of disbelief. While many of the points I have raised with regard to the narrative mode of thinking seem to be just as relevant to fictional as to non-fictional narratives, I would like to mention one aspect that is specific to the creation and reception of fictional worlds. Such worlds are, of course, connected to the culture in which they are produced and to the intentions of the author. Even in utopias we are presented with a world which is completely different from, but closely related to the society which is implicitly criticised by this representation of an ideal world in which human relations and social problems are handled in a different way. However, since the eighteenth century an understanding of literature has gained ground in Western societies which stresses the 'autonomy' of works of art, which are mainly characterised by their self-references. Although Coleridge's dictum of the 'suspension of disbelief' has been criticised in so far as readers need their knowledge not only of the physical world and human relations, but also of genre conventions in order to understand texts, the idea still makes sense when it is related to the divorce of the reader from the pragmatic context which usually characterises speech acts. Grice's conversational maxims do not apply to the production and reception of literary works, and modern readers are aware of the 'aesthetic convention' as well as the 'polyvalence convention' (see Schmidt 110–43). This implies that works of art are approached in a different manner, that the interpretation of literary narratives may diverge from the interpretation of other tales. While we usually assume that the stories we are told in real life are either true or false, that they are relevant in a given pragmatic context (in which Grice's maxims should be heeded), and that the narrator has specific intentions which are closely connected to this context, these presuppositions do not govern the understanding of literary narratives. We do not expect that the characters and incidents directly represent persons and events that we know; we do not think that the incidents in the narrative have an immediate bearing on our everyday life; and we are prone to 'suspend disbelief,' and, for instance, accept for the time being that the fictional world is populated by ghosts, or vampires, or people with very strange character traits. More sophisticated readers will also be aware of the fact that fictional narratives are polyvalent, that the attempt to tease out several convincing interpretations and layers of meaning forms part of the pleasure of reading literature. Fictional narra-

tives invite readers to follow a mode of thought that is not only shaped by its narrativity, but also by its fictionality.

6. Embedded values. Narratives create a world with an inherent set of values and beliefs. Stories that are 'tellable' in Bruner's sense—that is stories that are interesting in that they do not simply repeat well-known schemata—construct their own morality; they establish text-internal norms which supply the reference to which the behaviour of the characters and/or narrators is to be judged. In *Robinson Crusoe*, for instance, the values of piety and hard work are foregrounded; usually, readers do not notice the complete lack of care for the environment or the absence of an appreciation of beauty in the novel: the narrative produces its own set of values. A more complex case in point is H.G. Wells's novel *The War of the Worlds* (1898)—which Orson Welles later on turned into a radio play that had such a degree of 'narrative necessity' that a host of Americans panicked and behaved in a most irrational manner. Wells's utopia establishes the values of empathy and sympathy with the human victims of the cruel behaviour of the 'Martians'; it also highlights the similarities between the behaviour of the 'Martians' and their treatment of human beings on the one hand, and the British behaviour with regard to the indigenous population in many colonies on the other. The values constructed in this novel are therefore not only used to denigrate the Martians, but they also provide a norm for a criticism of British imperialism. A mere list of the characteristics of the protagonists or even the events of the novel would not evoke such a set of values—instead, we might come up with a different view of 'powerful and successful Martians' and 'incompetent, cowardly humans.' The values embodied in the story derive from the way of narration; they are not inherent in the 'fictional facts.'

In fictional narratives it is important to differentiate these values from those embodied by the characters or even the opinions held by the narrator, let alone the author of a story. It is often impossible to rely on the interpretation of the beliefs and rules of behaviour of characters alone, since there is usually (at least) one protagonist and one antagonist with opposite values and models for explaining and evaluating the fictional world. Neither can we rely on the simple rule of 'poetic justice,' because, unfortunately, the governess in Oscar Wilde's play *The Importance of Being Earnest* is quite wrong when she opines: "The good ended happily, and the bad unhappily. That is what Fiction means" (Wilde 275). In tragedies, the good ones end up badly—genre conventions can counteract principles like 'poetic justice.' To construct the overall scheme of values of a fictional narrative is therefore a complex endeavour which cannot be solved by just pointing to the successful character or 'hero' and look at the values he or she embodies.

In order to arrive at a sophisticated reading of a story, it is also not advisable to rely on the words of the narrator. This may work with tales like *Robinson Crusoe*, in which there is no indication that the values that are put forth in the many comments and evaluations by the mature narrator diverge from those of the younger Crusoe. It does not work, however, with regard to stories like Robert Browning's "My Last Duchess" (1842) or Vladimir Nabokov's *Lolita* (1955). In Browning's dramatic monologue, the duke tells the story of his 'last duchess,' his late wife, who is presented in a beautiful portrait in the picture gallery, to an implied narratee, allegedly someone who is with him and admires the picture. Though the duke presents his wife and his own behaviour in positive, conventionally sanctioned terms, it becomes quite clear that, despite his words, he has murdered his wife. In this case, the mere fact that the narrator tries to hide his former actions and that his tale ostensibly conforms to current moral principles highlights the divergence between the values the protagonist acts upon and those embodied in the story. Like many other modern novels using 'unreliable narrators,' Nabokov's *Lolita* is more difficult to deal with. Here the narrator is convinced that his actions as well as his behaviour are unexceptional, and he employs several narrative devices in order to persuade the readers that they should trust him. Nonetheless, a careful reading can distinguish several markers of 'unreliability,' which expose the narrator's opinions as precarious and point to the discrepancy between the evaluations and judgements and the values conveyed by the narrative. This serves to illustrate that the values and moral principles embodied in a fictional world cannot be reduced to the intentions, actions, opinions, beliefs, or characteristics of either characters or the narrator; they are constructed and conveyed by the narrative, by the interplay between the fictional facts and the way of telling the story. These examples also allude to another aspect of narratives which I will deal with in the following: the importance of genre conventions.

7. Genre conventions. Like the concept of 'species' in biology, the term 'genre' is extremely difficult to define; many scholars of literature and literary theory have spent much time on a host of explications of the concept (see, among others, Fowler; Hempfer; Herman, *Story Logic*; Todorov) or have come to use related terms like 'generic frames.' It is controversial, for example, whether genres can be determined on the basis of the features of a given body of texts which belong to a particular genre (which, however, would first of all have to be established) or whether we should base our explication on the concept of 'ideal types.' In spite of these difficulties, however, there seems to be widespread agreement that a knowledge of genres (which may be just as intuitive as our knowledge of what constitutes a narrative) is very important to the production and under-

standing of texts. As Fowler has it, genres are "of little value in classification," but relevant as "a communication system, for the use of writers in writing, and readers and critics in reading and interpreting" (256). This was already recognised by Virginia Woolf, who alerted us to the importance of genre conventions and devoted many essays to enhance our understanding of the change of conventions—and of readers' propensity to prefer traditional narrative modes, which impedes their understanding of contemporary texts, which are constructed according to different modes of writing.[7]

Woolf's endeavour may serve to illustrate the importance of narrative conventions, even as far as realist texts are concerned. As William Mitchell has stressed, "realism is simply the most conventional convention"; (27) a convention that is so convincing that it is not recognised as a mode of writing (or painting) at all. At the beginning of the twentieth century writers like Joyce, Woolf, Lawrence, Faulkner, and others believed that the old conventions of writing realist fiction were no longer adequate to convey a relevant representation of human beings in time: the experience of the First World War as well the insights of Freud and Einstein had changed their perception of reality to such a degree that the old "tools," as Woolf had it, "are not our tools [...]. For us those conventions are ruin, those tools are death" (103–4). Even though these writers still placed stories about contemporary characters centre stage, though they still wrote about human beings in time, about love, illness, and death, they used different genre conventions and thus changed the appearance of novels to such a degree that readers as well as critics were puzzled: they found it difficult to deal with this mode of writing, and they preferred the traditional ways. The Nobel Prize was given to John Galsworthy, not to any of the authors mentioned above. At the time, readers did not appreciate the concentration on the 'stream of consciousness,' the focus on the subjective perceptions and world views of characters instead of the 'objective' rendering of the fictional world, or the highlighting of the differences between 'mind time' and 'clock time.' Looking at the novels by Woolf, Joyce, and Faulkner, they recognised that they were completely different from the works they were used to. They recognised the importance of genre conventions.

One reason for the difficulty in defining genres may be that there are two different factors involved: On the one hand, the respective genre conventions shape the construction of fictional worlds; one can distinguish the novels of Joyce and Charles Dickens, for instance, by their different ways of describing the narrated worlds. To this extent, the

---

[7] See Woolf. Some of the following arguments about genre are more fully developed in Nünning, "The Relevance of Generic Frames."

definition of genres is related to intertextual relations, to those features a given body of texts has in common, and readers intuitively recognise this: they know after a few sentences whether the book has the characteristics they expect to find in a detective novel, a historical novel, a romance, a gothic novel or whatever. On the other hand, more than just textual features are part of these expectations, which are so important for the communication between readers and writers. As the example of modernist fiction shows, the cultural 'background' has to be taken into account; it does make a difference whether a narrative was published in the nineteenth century or after the First World War. The 'background knowledge' that readers need in order to understand a text not only embraces literary conventions, but it also contains models of the way human beings think and act (implicit personality theories) and of more general cultural knowledge (world views, beliefs concerning what is 'real,' hierarchies of values). The expectations of readers and writers concerning genres and ways of writing like 'realism' belong "not to a constrained 'literary' field, but to a cultural field" (Ermarth 1073).[8]

Though many features of the construction of narratives which have been mentioned so far are applicable to stories in general, the conventions that shape particular texts are quite specific, both as far as the construction of the story world and the features of the narrative discourse are involved. Most texts belong to a specific genre, and the conventions of this genre govern the production and the interpretation of these texts. It is not only narratives that we come to think of as 'natural' because they are ubiquitous; the same applies to different genres—though the degree of sophistication in producing and recognising these kinds of narratives differs according to the education and socialisation of readers. Perhaps there are nowadays more experts in the identification of media formats like 'thriller,' 'soap,' 'costume drama,' fantasy, 'talk show,' and others—which many viewers can recognise while zapping through the programmes—than the narratives which are mediated by language only.

It is not possible here to provide even a brief account of the different conventions of even the most common narrative genres. I would like to

---

8   When we want to explore the relevance of generic frames for the interpretation of novels, we therefore have to acknowledge that these sets of expectations are influenced by three aspects: Firstly, we have to take into account the relation between novels and their 'context'; fiction is intricately interwoven with other areas of culture, and sets of expectations are informed by hierarchies of values and numerous facets of our view of 'reality.' Secondly, we have to be aware of the textual properties of particular classes of texts such as Gothic novels, crime fiction or historical novels. Thirdly, we have to consider historical change: Both aspects – cultural concerns and the characteristics of specific classes of texts—are changing constantly, albeit not necessarily in unison (see Nünning "Generic Frames").

emphasise three points, however. First, generic conventions not only pertain to the selection and combination of the events and characters that constitute the story world. Of course, the appearance of a space ship will tell readers at once that there is some kind of science fiction involved—that is, if it is not a parody, or an embedded story (for instance a story a character reads, a dream, or an account of a film) or a new kind of hybrid genre. Genre conventions are not determined solely by the story world, but by its interrelation with the level of discourse and the values established in the narrative. Indeed, in many cases the style of narration is much more important than the mental model of the events that the reader can make of the story world: judged only with regard to 'what happens,' *Tristram Shandy* is a conventional autobiography—but anyone who has looked at it will know that this is a highly reductive view at best. Second, fictional narratives can supply models which influence the construction of reality in non-fictional works as well. Since many readers are neither aware of the way in which narratives shape our thought nor of the different types of narratives and ways of writing, it seems highly likely that people are not aware whether they came to know the conventions of a specific genre in fiction or in non-fiction. Thus fictional autobiographies shaped later life stories as well as non-fictional accounts (see also Bruner, "Self-making and World-making" 68). Many fictional and non-fictional genres share a common ground; especially as far as works of historiography are concerned, which up to the middle of the nineteenth century were influenced by the ways of writing in historical novels. Third, the narrative conventions in non-fictional texts seem to lag behind those written by authors of fiction, who are often more attuned to changes with regard to genres—both as far as new mental models of reality are concerned and with regard to the change of textual features. This may even hold true with regard to narrative psychologists: as far as I could gain insight into the field, they are highly conscious of the fact that the establishing of a life story and of the 'I' is dependent on the use of narrative, but they still seem to posit the nineteenth century model of autobiography, which closely resembles the bildungsroman, as the 'natural' way of representing a life, while there is no discussion of the fact that in a postmodern world other forms of life writing, which have been explored by contemporary writers of novels, might be just as adequate or perhaps even more appropriate today.

8. Perspectivisation and experientiality. Works of fiction, to use Virginia Woolf's words once again, "deal with character" (97), with agents who may appear in the form of animals or angels, but who still sport human-like attributes, who have intentions, and who are placed in a specific

spatio-temporal situation.⁹ What is more important in this context, however, is that these particular characters are depicted from a specific perspective. This aspect is therefore closely related to Bruner's feature of "particularity" which signifies that narratives "take as their ostensive reference particular happenings" ("Narrative Construction" 6) . It also encompasses, however, David Herman's concept of 'what it's like,' because narrative representation "also conveys the experience of living through this storyworld-in-flux, highlighting the pressure of events on real or imagined consciousness affected by the occurrences at issue" ("Narrative Ways of Worldmaking" 73). Experientiality, which has been said to be the most important feature of narratives by Monika Fludernik, therefore refers to the fact that narrative worlds not only convey particular characters and their lives and opinions, but also a subjective sense of their experiences: we are able to grasp what specific occurrences mean to a character or narrator. The importance of that aspect has been emphasised in an article by the psychologist McAdams, who discusses the difficulties of 'Heidi,' who was not able to react in this way even to her own story. Though she told a seemingly perfect narrative of her life, this tale was devised by her mother, and she herself lacked "the imagination necessary to make her story go beyond logical, causal coherence to a story rooted in subjectivity" (Josselson 112). Fictional narratives not only represent particular characters and events, but they also convey a sense of experiencing what is told on the level of the story.

I would like to differentiate this from a closely related, certainly not less important, aspect of fictional narratives: their inherent perspectivisation. The events and characters in fiction are always presented from a particular perspective—the seemingly 'objective' viewpoint of the 'omniscient,' 'heterodiegetic' narrator being just one case in point. Even such narratives, which by convention are understood to present a 'neutral' point of view which is not 'tainted' by the opinions and values of a particular character, offer a specific perspective upon the events that are related; they present the story from a particular point of view, which is important to the establishment of the values constructed by the narrative as a whole. The historical development of this narrative convention shows, moreover, that the more 'objective' these narrators became (that is when they refrained from expounding personal views and value judgements), the more they employed a convention called 'focalisation' by narratologists: they used characters on the level of the story world as 'reflectors' and presented the events in the way they appeared to a particu-

---

9   This may not be specified with regard to references to the real world—however, narratives place these agents in a particular spatio-temporal situation.

lar character. One might regard this inherent perspectivisation as a drawback in comparison to scientific worldmaking, which is not tinged with this kind of subjectivity. As Catherine Elgin has shown, however, literature may present us with 'facts' that are just as important as those distributed in scientific works:

> Works of fiction equip us to adopt alien perspectives, enabling us to see the world as others see it. Much epistemology favors an objective stance, according to which we see things correctly when we adopt what Nagel calls the 'view from nowhere.' But not all properties are disclosed from the view from nowhere. The property of 'looking red to George' is not an illusory property. It is a genuine property of certain things, even if a car has that property only because G's vision is somehow defective. [...] Sometimes an item's important properties are [...] the ones the view from some other perspective discloses. ("Laboratory of the Mind" 51)

This already hints at the functions that reading fictional worlds might fulfil.

4. Functions of Fictional Worlds

Engaging with fictional worlds, I hope to show, can have important effects. Since it depends on the individual reader, on one's knowledge and expertise in interpretation, one's predilections and one's willingness to 'let oneself into the story,' it is impossible to predict whether a particular function will be fulfilled. In this section I will therefore be concerned with the properties of fictional texts that allow them to have specific functions. Since the making of fictional worlds is part of the more encompassing activity of the narrative construction of reality, most of the functions which I will discuss in my brief sketch pertain to non-fictional stories as well. However, fictional narratives present a particularly rich world and provide more intricate and complex models for understanding our surroundings than non-fictional texts which are often less dense and less intricately structured than literary tales. A more advanced level of mastery of the production and interpretation of fictional stories may therefore yield more fruitful results with regard to all the functions that will be mentioned in the following.

As has been shown by several scholars, narrative works as a mode of thinking; it might be characterised as a "pattern-forming cognitive system that organises all sequentially experienced structure, which can then be operationalised to create tools for thinking" (Herman, "Stories as a Tool for Thinking" 171). Because of the radical difference between the two spheres of life and the chaotic experience which is part of our 'stream of consciousness' on the one hand, and language as well as narrative on the other hand, narratives do not just 'mirror' life; instead, they shape our perception and understanding of the world. Narratives enable us to select what we think memorable and to organise chaotic events into a meaningful spatio-temporal sequence. Since they invite readers to construct causal and temporal relationships, tellers "can safely leave things unstated that it would otherwise take far too much time and effort to spell out" (177); moreover, they help us to develop adequate expectations and to set them in relation to outcomes. The "narrative representation of anomalous or atypical events can in turn reshape a culture's [...] sense of what is normal or typical, and thereby help build new models for understanding the world" (179). As Bradd Shore points out, when confronted with anomalous or disturbing events, we tend to tell and retell them, "until the events are gradually domesticated into one or more coherent and shared narratives" (58). They provide patterns which allow us to sequence our behaviour during different types of interaction, and they "fill the breach when typification fails; [...] narrative is a means of redressing problems that arise when anticipated similar experiences do not materialize" (Herman, "Stories as a Tool for Thinking" 180). This is also recognised by Bruner, who states that narratives allow for "negotiability" and stresses that they are a "viable instrument for cultural negotiation" ("Narrative Construction" 16–17): we tend to be more permissive when we negotiate narratives than when we deal with "arguments of proofs" (17).

If narrative is indeed a primary tool for understanding the world we live in, and if our identity is created through narrative, then it becomes of paramount importance to provide knowledge about the construction of narrative worlds. As Catherine Elgin stresses with regard to Bruner's (and others') insights into the narrative construction of identity, "[w]hom one takes oneself to be [...] is a function of the categories available for self-description" ("What Goodman Leaves Out" 94). This implies that it is vital to establish instruments for (narrative) self-description that are as refined as possible. Our categories, our vocabulary and our understanding of the conventions of the narrative construction of reality should be refined as far as possible in order to enable us to choose between a vast array of tools in order to construct models of the self and the world that fit our individual propensities. This richness with regard to both language, the construction of mental models, and the presentation of different modes of narratives, I would argue, is characteristic of fictional worlds, the authors of which are interested in and aware of the importance of genre conventions.

Non-fictional as well as fictional narratives can serve both to multiply and detail the perspectives that can be adopted on the world, and they can also enrich the store of events that constitutes humans' knowledge base (see Herman, "Stories as a Tool for Thinking" 184). However, two features of fictional works render them particularly valuable in this respect. On the one hand, because of their fictionality, they invite a 'suspension of disbelief' and can develop alternative worlds that as yet are not part of the cultural knowledge of the time. On the other hand, they allow us insight into the characters' consciousness—something that is rare in non-fictional stories—and help to enlarge our store of knowledge about modes of perceiving, thinking and feeling as well as about the hierarchy of values and patterns of judgement that help or impede our understanding of others. By providing significant parts of the histories that result in a sometimes very idiosyncratic and extreme situation, they enable us to adopt the characters' perspectives and see some quality of a given, seemingly ordinary phenomenon that may have escaped our notice before.[10] As Elgin argues, this perspectivisation is an asset rather than a disadvantage. Thomas Hardy's novel *Tess of the D'Urbervilles: A Pure Woman* (1891) illustrates that even a desperate act like a murder may acquire very different meanings when one knows, for instance, that the murderer has been for years taunted and (sexually) abused by the victim.

The 'experientiality' pertaining to fictional narratives invites us to identify with or feel empathy for a particular character, to share his or her plight and adopt his or her point of view, without losing sight of the complexity of the overall situation which the character may be unaware of. This recognition of the state of mind and intentions of others is a condition of our development of a 'theory of mind,' which is of central importance to human cognition. Engaging with highly complex and 'experiential' narratives may help us to enlarge our store of knowledge as far as the relation between feelings, intentions, and actions is concerned, and it can provide us with models which can be used in dealing with human beings in face-to-face situations, when we do not have any direct access to the thoughts of others.[11]

---

10 I owe this insight into the importance of the storytelling capacity of fiction to a lecture by Peter Bieri which he held in the spring term in 2008 in Heidelberg (as part of the *Heidelberger Poetik-Vorlesungen*).

11 See Herrmann et al. In other theories concerning the development of human intelligence—like the "general intelligence hypothesis" and the "social intelligence hypothesis"—"theory of mind" is awarded an importance place, as well; see ibid. 1360; Roth and Dicke (254). The importance of empathy is due to the necessity of projecting the future behaviour of others and to develop "cognitive skills for understanding psychological states such as goals and perceptions" (Herrmann et al. 1361). A very good overview of the literature with re-

The function of providing a 'store of knowledge' both with regard to the interpretation of situations involving the viewpoints and intentions of others and with regard to genre conventions, however, may evoke a reductive view of fictional narratives. After all, producing and reading fiction involves a rather long process of concentrating on the fictional world, of following (and identifying with) characters' intentions, actions, and developments. They engage us in the narrative mode of thinking. This involves the processes of ordering as well as the interplay between the story world and the mode of narrative transmission discussed above, and, in connection with 'experientiality' and 'perspectivisation,' it is conducive to our refinement of 'theory of mind' (see Nünning, "Literatur als Lebenswissen" 165–66). It also involves the reconsideration of former insights in the light of new developments of the story; we have to revise our evaluation of the aristocratic narrator in Browning's "My Last Duchess," when we realise that he has murdered his wife—a feature that genres like detective novels have turned into a genre convention. This makes it necessary for readers to revisit and revise their former opinions and may be conducive to the acquisition of mental flexibility, which has been held to be an important indicator of intelligence (see Roth and Dicke). If we accept that narratives are "a tool for thinking," the mastery of complex narratives with a high degree of features like 'experientiality' and 'perspectivisation' may in turn refine our (narrative) mode of cognition.

Since fictional narratives establish moral values and invite us to feel empathy, they might be of importance with regard to our moral development, too.[12] The dense fictional rendering of selected events offers readers a way to orient themselves towards the characters and the values embedded in the work. In spite of the ambiguity of most fictional representations, discerning readers may recognise implicit criticism of some characters and actions, as well as the endorsement of others. By means of their selectivity, their fictional privileges and their use of narrative techniques, works of fiction can provide some reference points which invite us to adopt an ethical position to what is depicted. Instead of positing and argumentatively discussing the pros and cons of different kinds of actions,

---

gard to 'theory of mind' and 'embodied simulation' (which provides an alternative mode of explaining this human faculty) is provided by Kerr.

12 A whole approach to the study of fiction, 'ethical criticism,' is concerned with the ethics inherent in works of fiction. For a brief overview of ethical criticism see Heinze. In psychology, the importance of stories for moral development is controversial; see Vitz and Day. In a basic manner, narratives provide "templates for behaviour in physical as well as moral-cultural worlds" (Herman, "Stories as a Tool for Thinking" 182)—and a look at censorship debates or the ongoing discussion about the effects of the presentation of violence in Hollywood movies illustrates that the fictionality of stories does not impede this function.

they present actions in a way which has ethical relevance and asks readers to position themselves in relation to them. This, again, might refine our understanding of ethical issues and make it easier for us to orient ourselves in relation to others.

This does not imply, however, that it is easy to assign a clear-cut meaning to what we read. On the contrary, as a consequence of the complexity of the fictional signifying processes, a work of fiction usually does not present us with simple models of behaviour; as a rule, there are no clear-cut characters which are held up as wholeheartedly 'good' or 'evil.' Since fictional narratives are polyvalent, they invite us to tease out several layers of meaning. In dense descriptions, there are too many issues involved, too many causes to be considered, too many different points of view and evaluations of the same instance; intricate use of genre conventions often conveys a complex and 'multiperspective' view on what happens in the fictional world. Though one can discern some guiding lines within the text, there is no simple message even with regard to apparently simple phenomena. This may be one of the most important cognitive functions of literature: although we are provided with many, often convincing indicators which lead us to construct meaning in a specific way, and even though it is possible to discern salient facts and relations, these usually do not add up to a coherent point of view encompassing all the data we were given throughout the story. We are denied simple solutions. Instead, we have to deal with ambiguity, and we have to put up with the fact that it is not possible to assign specific meanings and evaluations which are able to cover all the aspects that are important. In contrast to (thought) experiments in the natural sciences, there are no conclusive deductions to be drawn. Instead, we are provided with a plethora of ways of interpreting and evaluating the events as well as their human costs and consequences. On the one hand, we acquire an understanding of the characters involved in the story, of their thoughts, feelings, intentions and actions which may enhance our ability to understand ourselves and others as well as quickly orient ourselves in similar situations in real life. On the other hand we have to accept the fact that there are no general answers even to seemingly simple questions, and that a deepening of our understanding does not provide us with the means to judge both the attitudes of others and their lives.

Fictional narratives are therefore more than just a "primary resource for building and updating models for understanding the world" (Herman, "Stories as a Tool for Thinking" 184);[13] they can also influence our cogni-

---

13 However, Herman refers to the properties of narratives in general—I think that this function is even more pronounced in fictional narratives.

tive faculties in that they enable us to refine our 'theory of mind,' invite us to feel empathy and adopt an ethical position to the story, require cognitive flexibility and expose us to polyvalence, denying simple closures. In addition to that, the self-reflexivity characteristic of fictional worlds can raise our awareness of the narrative conventions we use in our construction of reality. By reflecting upon an important mode of cognition, they show us to what extent our lives are shaped by narrative and illustrate the intricate connections between thinking, reading, and living.

References

Barth, John. "The Literature of Exhaustion." *Atlantic Monthly* 229 (1967): 29–39.
Barthes, Roland. "Introduction to the Structural Analysis of Narratives." 1966. *Image Music Text*. Trans. Stephen Heath. New York: Hill and Wang, 1977. 79–124.
Berensmeyer, Ingo. "Hermeneutische und neohermeneutische Methoden der Textinterpretation." *Methoden der literatur- und kulturwissenschaftlichen Textanalyse: Ansätze, Grundlagen, Modellanalysen*. Eds. Vera Nünning, and Ansgar Nünning. Stuttgart: Metzler, 2010.
Blagov, Pavel S., and Jefferson A. Singer. "Four Dimensions of Self-Defining Memories (Specificity, Meaning, Content, and Affect) and Their Relationships to Self-Restraint, Distress, and Repressive Defensiveness." *Journal of Personality* 72 (2004): 481–512.
Brontë, Charlotte. *Jane Eyre*. 1847. London: Penguin Classics, 2006.
Browning, Robert. "My Last Duchess." *Selected Poems* 1842. Ed. Robert Browning. London: Penguin Classics, 2001.
Bruner, Jerome. "The Narrative Construction of Reality." *Critical Enquiry* 18.1 (1991): 1–21.
—. "Self-making and World-making." *Journal of Aesthetic Education* 25.1. (1991): 67–78.
Conway, Martin, Jefferson A. Singer, and Angela Tagini. "The Self and Autobiographical Memory: Correspondence and Coherence." *Social Cognition* 22.5 (2004), 491–529.
Day, James M. "Narrative, Psychology, and Moral Education." *American Psychologist* 46.2 (1991): 167–68.
Defoe, Daniel. *Robinson Crusoe*. 1719. London: Penguin Classics, 2003.
Dickens, Charles. *Oliver Twist*. 1838. London: Penguin Classics, 2003.
Disraeli, Benjamin. *Sybil: Or Two Nations*. 1845. Oxford: Oxford UP, 2009.
Eakin, Paul John. *How Our Lives Become Stories: Making Selves*. Ithaca, NY: Cornell UP, 1999.
Elgin, Catherine Z. "The Laboratory of the Mind." *A Sense of the World: Essays on Fiction, Narrative, and Knowledge*. Eds. John Gibson, et al. New York: Routledge, 2007. 43–54.
—. "What Goodman Leaves Out." *Journal of Aesthetic Education* 25.1 (1991): 89–96.
Ermarth, Elizabeth D. "Realism." *Encyclopedia of the Novel*. Ed. Paul Schellinger. Vol. 2. Chicago, et al.: Fitzroy Dearborn, 1998. 1071–78.

Fielding, Henry. *Shamela*. 1741. Whitefish, MT: Kessinger Pub Co, 2004.
Fludernik, Monika. *Towards a 'Natural' Narratology*. London/New York: Routledge, 1996.
Fowler, Alastair. *Kinds of Literature: An Introduction to the Theory of Genres and Modes*. Cambridge, MA: Harvard UP, 1982.
Fowles, John. *The French Lieutenant's Woman*. London: Cape,1969.
Grice, H. Paul. "Logic and Conversation." *Syntax and Semantics* 3 (1975): 41–58.
Hardy, Thomas. *Tess of the D'Urbervilles: A Pure Woman*. 1891. London: Penguin Classics, 2003.
Heinze, Rüdiger. "'The Return of the Repressed': Zum Verhältnis von Ethik und Literatur in der neueren Literaturkritik." *Ethik und Moral als Problem der Literatur und Literaturwissenschaft*. Eds. Jutta Zimmermann, and Britta Salheiser. Berlin: Duncker & Humblot, 2006. 265–81.
Hempfer, Klaus W. *Gattungstheorie: Information und Synthese*. München: UTB, 1973.
Herman, David. *Story Logic: Problems and Possibilities of Narrative*. Lincoln, et al.: U of Nebraska P, 2002.
—. "Stories as a Tool for Thinking." *Narrative Theory and the Cognitive Sciences*. Ed. David Herman. Stanford: CSLI Publications, 2003. 163–92.
—. "Narrative Ways of Worldmaking." *Narratology in the Age of Cross-Disciplinary Narrative Research*. Narratologia 20. Eds. Sandra Heinen, and Roy Sommer, Berlin/New York: de Gruyter, 2009. 71–88.
Hermans, Hubert J.M. "Voicing the Self: From Information Processing to Dialogical Interchange." *Psychological Bulletin* 119.1 (1996): 31–50.
Herrmann, Esther, et al. "Humans Have Evolved Specialized Skills of Social Cognition: The Cultural Intelligence Hypothesis." *Science* 317 (2007): 1360–66.
Josselson, Ruthellen. "On Becoming the Narrator of One's Own Life." *Healing Plots: The Narrative Basis of Psychotherapy*. Eds. Amia Lieblich, Dan P. McAdams, and Ruthellen Josselson. Washington, DC: American Psychological Association, 2004. 111–27.
Joyce, James. *Ulysses*. 1922. London: Penguin, 2000.
Kerr, Catherine. "Dualism Redux in Recent Neuroscience: 'Theory of Mind' and 'Embodied Simulation' Hypotheses in Light of Historical Debates About Perception, Cognition, and Mind." *Review of General Psychology* 12.2 (2008): 205–14.
Lamarque, Peter, and Stein H. Olsen. *Truth, Fiction, and Literature: A Philosophical Perspective*. Oxford: Clarendon Press, 1994.
Leander, Niels Buch. "To Begin with the Beginning: Birth, Origin, and Narrative Inception." *Narrative Beginnings: Theories and Practices*. Ed. Brian Richardson. Lincoln/London: U of Nebraska P, 2008. 15–28.
Link, Jürgen. "Literaturanalyse als Diskursanalyse. Am Beispiel des Ursprungs literarischer Symbolik in der Kollektivsymbolik." *Diskurstheorien und Literaturwissenschaft*. Eds. Jürgen Fohrmann, and Harro Müller. Frankfurt a.M.: Suhrkamp, 1988. 284–307.
McAdams, Dan P. "Identity and the Life Story." *Autobiographical Memory and the Construction of a Narrative Self: Developmental and Cultural Perspectives*. Eds. Robyn Fivush, and Catherine A. Haden. Mahwah, NJ: Lawrence Erlbaum Associates, 2003. 187–207.

—. "The Problem of Narrative Coherence." *Journal of Constructivist Psychology* 19 (2006): 109–25.
Mitchell, William J.T. "Realism, Irrealism, and Ideology: A Critique of Nelson Goodman." *Journal of Aesthetic Education* 25.1 (1991): 23–35.
Nabokov, Vladimir. *Lolita*. 1955. London: Penguin, 2000.
Nelson, Katherine. "Narrative and Self, Myth and Memory: Emergence of the Cultural Self." *Autobiographical Memory and the Construction of a Narrative Self: Developmental and Cultural Perspectives*. Eds. Robyn Fivush, and Catherine A. Haden. Mahwah, NJ: Lawrence Erlbaum Associates, 2003. 3–28.
Nünning, Vera. "Literatur als Lebenswissen: Die Bedeutung von Literatur für menschliches Verstehen und Zusammenleben am Beispiel von Ian McEwans *Enduring Love*." *Literaturwissenschaft als Lebenswissenschaft: Programm – Projekte – Perspektiven*. Eds. Wolfgang Asholt, and Ottmar Ette. Tübingen: Narr, 2009. 145–68.
—. "The Relevance of Generic Frames for the Interpretation of Novels." *Genre and Interpretation*. Eds. Tintti Klapuri, Pirjo Lyytikäinen, and Minna Maijala, forthcoming (2010).
Orwell, George. *Animal Farm*. 1945. London: Penguin, 2000.
Richardson, Samuel. *Pamela, Or: Virtue Rewarded*. 1740. Oxford: Oxford UP, 2008.
Ricœur, Paul. *Time and Narrative*. Trans. Kathleen Blamey and David Pellauer. Vol. 1. Chicago: Chicago UP, 1984.
Roth, Gerhard, and Ursula Dicke. "Evolution of the Brain and Intelligence." *Trends in Cognitive Sciences* 9.5 (2005): 250–57.
Schmidt, Siegfried J. *Grundriß der Empirischen Literaturwissenschaft*. Frankfurt a.M.: Suhrkamp, 1991.
Shakespeare, William. "My mistress' eyes are nothing like the sun," Sonnet 130. 1609. London: Penguin, 1999.
__. *The Tempest*. 1623. Oxford: Oxford UP, 2008.
Shore, Bradd. *Culture in Mind: Cognition, Culture, and the Problem of Meaning*. Oxford: OUP, 1996.
Sterne, Laurence. *Tristram Shandy*. London: Wordsworth Classics, 1995.
Todorov, Tzvetan. "Literary Genres." *Current Trends in Linguistics*. Vol. 12. Ed. Thomas A. Sebeok. The Hague: Mouton, 1974. 957–62.
—. *Genres in Discourse*. Trans. Catherine Porter. Cambridge: Cambridge UP, 1990.
Vitz, Paul C. "The Use of Stories in Moral Development: New Psychological Reasons for an Old Education Method." *The American Psychologist* 46 (1990): 709–20.
Wells, H. G. *The War of the Worlds*. 1898. London: Penguin Classics, 2005.
Wilde, Oscar. *Plays*. Harmondsworth: Penguin, 1980.
Woolf, Virginia. "Mr. Bennett and Mrs. Brown." 1924. *The Captain's Death Bed and Other Essays*. London: Hogarth Press, 1950. 90–111.

Literary Worldmaking

Inger Østenstad

Literature is worldmaking not just in the conventional sense that literary works make fictive worlds, but also in Nelson Goodman's sense in which literature shapes worlds in the same way as all our descriptions of the world do. "We are confined to describe whatever is described," he writes (*Ways of Worldmaking* 3); "[a]ny notion of reality consisting of objects and events and kinds established independently of discourse and unaffected by how they are described or otherwise presented must give way to the recognition that these, too, are parts of the story" (*Of Minds and Other Matter* 67). Since both a fact and a fiction are made discursively, the difference between them is a difference in "referential distance" (63). In this way, Goodman's nominalism confronts preconceived ideas of reference, fictionality, and reality.

In addition to its fictional worlds, literary discourse, generally speaking, not only shapes the world of the writer and the worlds in which his work is read and evaluated, but it somehow also plays a crucial role in the shaping of our common world. Literature is a "constituting discourse," as the French linguist Dominique Maingueneau has put it; it is a discursive field with a specific status that claims to found other discourses without being founded by them.[1] The phenomenon of literary worldmaking thus calls attention to why and how a literary world shapes other worlds. Literature's power is a "symbolic power," according to Pierre Bourdieu, who maintains that the source of this power is extrinsic to the literary work (*Language and Symbolic Power* 170). On the other hand, the prominent Norwegian novelist Dag Solstad voices a view shared by many in the literary field when he claims that the writer is subservient to the literary work, which is spiritual and beyond any notion of power or ideology. Starting from the Goodmanian notion of worldmaking and using some of the later works of Solstad where these questions are addressed as my examples, this

---

1 See Maingueneau and Cossutta, and Maingueneau *Le discours littéraire*; in Maingueneau "Analysing Self-Constituting Discourses," the French term 'discours constituant' is translated into English as "self-constituting discourse." In the following, I use the notation "[self-]constituting discourse."

essay explores a third answer to the question of the source of literature's worldmaking power based on the theory of literary discourse analysis established by Maingueneau.

1. What About the World?

Goodman reduces the divide between the many worlds by conceiving them as versions of an already existing world: "World structure is heavily dependent on order of elements and on comparative weight of kinds; and reordering and weight-shifting are among the most powerful processes used in making and remaking facts and worlds" (*Of Minds and Other Matter* 121). If we, as Goodman states, "are confined to describe whatever is described," we have the liberty of innovation in our confinement. Worldmaking is a creative activity. Transferred from "descriptions" (in space) to "narratives" (in time)—the border between which intuitively seems blurred—a new world is made by a new "emplotment" (White). A new story is a new world or a new version of the world. The distinction between world and version is, however, elusive, according to Goodman (*Of Minds and Other Matter* 30); "Surely we make versions, and right versions make worlds" (42). To be right seems to have to do with being somehow convincing, to be false with being unbelievable; "A true version is true in some worlds, a false version in none" (31). Here the version is not a version *of* a world, but a version *in* a world. One problem with the Goodmanian terminology is that it is elusive itself.

The basis of a more consistent terminology could be sought, for example, in the investigations of the biological roots of human understanding performed by Humberto R. Maturana and Francisco J. Varela. This theory is uncompromising when it comes to the individuality of our perceived worlds since our nervous system does not operate with representations that are independent of us as individuals. Our experience of living in a shared world resides in the consensus arising from our social interactions and communications. By 'languaging' in interaction with one another, we not only make language and the distinctions and descriptions that form our individual worlds, but we shape a common world as well (see Maturana and Varela). The deeper explanation for the presence in every society of certain kinds of privileged discourses can well be found here; a society needs some sort of privileged 'languaging' to bind it together.

The etymology of the words 'world' in English, *Welt* in German, or *verden* in Norwegian can be tracked back to *wira-aldi*, meaning 'man-age,' 'life of man,' while *mundus*, the Latin source of *monde* in French, *mundo* in

Spanish or *mondo* in Italian, implies, in the same way as the Greek word *kosmos*, a superior perspective on the world order and on 'all there is.' The word 'world' thus carries the aspect of the individual perspective; every man has his life and therefore his world, while *mundus* is the universe of all things and living organisms from eternity to eternity. In this way, there is no contradiction between one *mundus* and many worlds. One world is not a more or less correct representation of *mundus*, and, as *mundus* is indescribable, it is not a pattern or a 'container' for the worlds, restricting their form and their number. All we think we know about *mundus* belongs to a world. The world engulfs *mundus*. The latest work by Dag Solstad, *Armand V: Fotnoter til en uutgravd roman* (*Armand V: Footnotes to an Unexcavated Novel* 2006) plays on this incompatibility of *mundus* and world. In the novel, the sixty-something protagonist Armand V. becomes aware of the remarkable fact that the History of the World in sixteen volumes standing on his bookshelf dedicates four of these volumes to the last sixty years of the twentieth century, thus exaggerating the importance of his world. After Armand V. has revised this chronology with "historical discipline," he achieves a perspective where the last of the 16 volumes of a History of the World covers the period from 1500 until 2000 AD (Solstad, *Armand V*. 136–37). In this perspective *mundus* engulfs the worlds.

This incompatibility of *mundus* and 'world' has been subsumed into literature as its paradoxical *sine qua non*. Since Romanticism, literature has been striving for 'absolute,' 'pure,' 'universal' works, and simultaneously biographical writing and the writers' subjective commentaries to their art have proliferated. The masterpieces of canonised literature can only come into being through the medium of the writer's world, but, because of this world's intrinsic subjectivity, literature is threatened with extinction together with its writer. "The vision of a Universe without life. Eternally silent—like a beautiful thought"[2] is Solstad's expression of the attractive thought of the disappearance of the world, and thereby the disappearance of subjectivity and the dependence of time. In this perfect space for pure art, however, literature cannot be.

2. "Writer's Power/Reader's Power"

In 2001, Dag Solstad gave a lecture at the Norwegian Literature Festival at Lillehammer. This lecture was later incorporated into his novel *16-07-41*

---

2 "Visjonen om et Univers uten liv. Endeløst taust—som en vakker tanke" (Solstad, *Armand V*. 174). Where there is no reference to a publication in English, the translation from Norwegian or French is mine.

(2002). The title of the lecture in the Festival programme, "Writer's power/reader's power,"[3] was the same as suggested to Solstad by the organisers of the event. However, as could have been foreseen, facing his audience the 59-year-old nationally acclaimed writer absolutely repudiated the relevance of any notion of power to the creation of literature "in the writer's workroom,"[4] or to the assignation of literary quality. Alternative notions that could have deserved his attention, he suggested, were literature's "spiritual power" and "the enlightened public." Thus, he evaded the discussion of the empowering of the writer, of potentially competing powers or of the relation between power and impotence within the field of literature by substituting an idealised notion of literature for the literature arising from the writer's world, and then allying it to an idealised notion of the public exposing itself to its enlightening spirit. To speak of power in connection with literature is wrong, Solstad told his audience, as it transfers this notion from the domain in which power is exercised to a domain where it does not belong. Worse, it also represents an attack on literature as spirit, opposed to any worldly power: "Spirit against power, art against state."[5] Not power, but solely literature's intrinsic quality gives it the right to claim recognition, although it has no guarantee of receiving it, except from people with a 'genuine relationship to literature,' presumably represented by the enlightened public he was facing. For everybody else, this notion of intrinsic quality is a nuisance as it hinders the publishers in making easy money, and encumbers the world of the media with unknown, worst-selling writers surrounded by an irritating nimbus. It is even a drag for academics because it makes them seem stuck-up in the eyes of the good people. While people with a 'genuine relationship to literature' form an exception, "the notion of quality is an almost provocative challenge to the majority of the book readers because it deprives them of the great democratic reader's power claimed by the media."[6] As I am now not submitting to Solstad's repudiation of the relevance of any notion of power to literature, but wish to discuss it further, I presumably belong to the "many inside academia who are in the process of shifting

---

3 "Forfattermakt/lesermakt."
4 "For selvsagt finnes makta, og sannsynligvis kan man også snakke om intellektuelle med makt, men da får man rette blikket, og pekefingeren, mot de steder der makta utøves, og si: Der, der er makta. Og det er ikke i forfatterens arbeidsrom, som er det stedet hvor romaner skapes" (Solstad, *16-07-41* 134–35).
5 "Ånd mot makt, kunst mot stat" (*16-07-41* 136).
6 "[K]valitetsbegrepet er en utfordring av nesten provokativ art for storparten av dem som leser bøker, fordi det fratar dem den store av media påståtte demokratiske lesermakt, ved å gjøre den illusorisk" (*16-07-41* 140). The wording is awkward in Norwegian.

sides,"[7] no longer aligning with spirit but with power. In this way, Solstad enacts his power by establishing a privileged consensus, while he rules out anyone holding conflicting views.

3. Spirit vs. Power

When Søren Kierkegaard in the beginning of *The Sickness Unto Death* asks what it means that the human being is spirit, he answers that the spirit of the human being is his self-consciousness that makes him a contradictory synthesis of the ideal and the concrete, and therefore it is not a self, but a derivate relationship to "that which established the entire relation" (351). Solstad, however, does not hold literature to be spirit in the context of any such philosophical speculation, but emphasises that literature is unique. Literature's spirit is something it expresses in addition to "dejection and misery, or self-contemplation and vitality;"[8] as "work of the spirit" literature is untouched by any human activity, and therefore it can only be judged by "the qualities of the work itself that decide whether it is an important work or not."[9] As he sees it, the spirit is both the unworldly legitimising source of the work, as well as its unique quality.

The ideas connecting spirituality to literature are deeply rooted in Western culture. The doxa of poetry's divine inspirational source lasted in various forms from Antiquity until Romanticism. With the secularisation of culture and the dignifying of profane literature, writers emerged as a new "secular priesthood" (Bénichou), first as the philosophers of the Enlightenment, then as the Romantic poets. Between 1830 and 1848, the poet-philosopher, a new kind of writer, emerged; at the same time an inspired bearer of modern enlightenment and of dark mysteries, he was a leader on the path to a pure future. By then, literature had become the conveyor of ideas, and not solely of aesthetic values. The long-lasting figure of the poet-philosopher should be examined as a historical phenomenon, as should the idea of "literature as spirit." In her study of the interdependence of literature and the writer's biography, Ann Jefferson points to the common source of these phenomena: "With the gradual consolidation of a field eventually known as 'literature,' and the concomitant decline of genre and poetics as its framework, it is possible to see the

---

7   "[K]valitetsbegrepet er en hemsko for akademia fordi det gjør dem blærete i godtfolks øyne, og derfor er mange innen for akademia i ferd med å skifte side" (*16-07-41* 140).
8   "[…] mismot og elendighet, eller selvbeskuelse og vitalitet" (*16-07-41* 137).
9   "Altså, det er egenskaper ved verket selv som avgjør om det er et betydningsfullt verk eller ikke, og ikke leserne, kritikerne, forlagene, akademia, mediene, eller for den saks skyld forfatteren" (*16-07-41* 136).

consecration of the writer described by Bénichou as a counterpart to this process" (39). All literature is however not spirit. In the last part of his lecture, while he identifies himself with "his" great writers, Solstad "cannot see that [he and most of his contemporary novelists] are working in the same line."[10] Someone familiar with Solstad's work knows the list of "his" writers by now, as he shares them with the protagonists of his novels. For example with Elias Rukla in *Shyness and Dignity* (2006; *Genanse og verdighet*, 1994): "He mostly read novels of the 1920s, which were a concept to him: Marcel Proust, Franz Kafka, Hermann Broch, Thomas Mann, and Musil were the authors he liked to read, and they were all authors of the 1920s to him" (*Shyness and Dignity* 135). Quite in line with what Ann Jefferson calls the "self-contesting character of the literary" (10), Solstad is identifying himself and his work with a certain canonised high modernism, while he is distancing himself from most other literary production. Literature as spirit is a privilege; only a few are chosen. Solstad's claim that literature is spirit is delimitative, not definitional.

If literature is to be characterised as spiritual in any descriptive or definitional sense, it must be in a rather restricted way. At the same time as it belongs to the realm of material things like books inscribed with both text and paratext, merchandise in a marketplace, and texts consisting of sequences of language signs with a communicative function, literature is spiritual in the sense that it creates mental images and ideas in the readers—and thus shapes their worlds. As the signifier and the signified belong together like the two sides of a sheet of paper (Saussure), both the material text and the mental ideas that this sequence of signs creates in the reader are necessary for literature to be literature. If Goodman is right about the difference between a fact and a fiction just being a difference in "referential distance," literature cannot be spiritual in the sense that this kind of discourse lacks informational value about the material world and has no tangible referent in reality. A 'fiction' can only be identified to the extent it does not refer to a 'fact' or 'reality,' is not 'veracious,' and so on.

It is also difficult to accept Solstad's rigid dichotomy between spirit and power. His denial of any relevance of power (*makt*) to the making of literature takes into consideration the complexities neither of the process of subjection in the literary creation, nor of the production of worlds by the means of language in an actual cultural surrounding, nor of the concept of power itself. His notion of power seems simplistic compared to

---

10 "Ja, de fleste romanforfattere står meg ytterst fjernt, jeg har vanskelig for å se at vi arbeider i samme genren. Men så er det unntakene da, mine store romanforfattere, med dem er det noe annet, fra dem har jeg mottatt dype, og livbestemmende inntrykk" (*16-07-41* 145).

Judith Butler's notion as she explores the duplicity of both the word and the phenomenon of subjection and its relation to power:

> We are used to thinking of power as what presses on the subject from the outside, as what subordinates, sets underneath, and relegates to a lower order. This is surely a fair description of part of what power does. But if, following Foucault, we understand power as *forming* the subject as well, as providing the very conditions of its existence and the trajectory of its desire, then power is not simply what we oppose but also, in a strong sense, what we depend on for our existence and what we harbour and preserve in the beings that we are. (2)

The root of the words *Macht* (German) and *makt* (Norwegian) is connected to "knowledge, aptitude" and to "access" (Bjorvand and Lindeman; Falk and Torp), while the modern word *makt* is synonymous to "power" and signifies (1) (bodily) force, aptitude, wealth; (2) violence, force; (3) mastery, authority, strong influence; (4) something holding power (in the meaning of [3]); (5) armed force; (6) a supernatural being (*Bokmålsordboka*). As Solstad was facing his audience, denying holding any power as a writer, his aptitude and access to speak in this way in this context, as well as his audience's receptivity to his words, nonetheless was granted to him because he as a writer is renowned for his mastery of literature. The discursive act of lecturing, in which one person is positioned apart from and often physically above the audience with the right to speak uninterrupted on his or her own terms, serves as an illustration of the uneven relationship between the writer and his readership. Lecturing, as does literature, conditions authority, and as Solstad is devoid of any representational or economic power, only his authority and power as a writer grant him the right to speak in this way.

As a public figure, Solstad is reputed to be unpredictable and full of surprises. In addition to the pleasure of seeing and hearing one of Norway's greatest living writers in the flesh and the attraction to fame, the best-informed members of the audience had reason to expect to see some flair of the next turn in Solstad's career during his public appearance at the beginning of a new millennium. He has always been obsessed with the passage of time and with numbers, counting his books and sectioning his career by decades. His modernist phase had lasted from his first book in 1965 until 1970, during which he impersonated the renegade writer threatening the evil, bourgeois society. In the 1970s, he converted to Marxism-Leninism and wrote social realist novels in the service of the working class. After having given a lecture to his fellow party members where he declared his return to bourgeois literature in 1980, he became the chronicler of his generation, writing novels replete with postmodern irony on the theme of his political experience during the 1970s. 1990 introduced a new, surprising break as he published the corporate history of Norway's largest industrial firm, written by him on commission, and called it a novel. His four highly acclaimed novels of the 1990s circled around the existential malaise of middle-aged man and were posed as a critique of culture. In 2001, he seemed predestined to set out in yet another direction. His audience did not know what to expect, but whatever happened was due to be significant and memorable. And he did not let his audience down. After having spent the first part of the lecture repudiating the theme proposed by the organisers, in the second part he turned to the subject of his choice. He elaborated on the fact that he was now entering the last part of his career as an active writer. With presumably only two or three novels left to write, his great routine and extensive experience as a novel writer were a danger to his writing rather than an asset; therefore his next novels were bound to be different than the ones he had been writing for the last decade. The lecture thus illustrates the dynamic between the writer's and the audience's worlds. The audience's expectations and the writer's fulfilment of these expectations reciprocally condition one another.

The lecture achieved a stronger, more lasting literary impact as it was incorporated into the novel *16-07-41*. One could dwell on the following paradox: while the person Dag Solstad, in his capacity as a renowned writer, stands facing his audience, the general ethics of the situation presupposes that he speaks candidly. This candour is no longer presupposed when the lecture is incorporated in an autobiographical text generically labelled 'novel' and presented as the words of the fictional character of "Dag Solstad," presumed lecturer at Lillehammer as well as the writer of the novel that the reader is in the process of reading. On the contrary, the playful, self-contradictory mode, which the members of his audience, "knowing" Solstad, probably expected in the actual lecture, but nevertheless found it difficult to identify, is enhanced by the meta-consciousness of the novel. "Dag Solstad," for example, comments on the way he is staging his official *persona* facing his audience at Lillehammer: „The lecture provoked immense applause, for which I thanked by bowing awkwardly, something which is partly due to nature, but which gradually must be said to belong to the props I use in the public staging of myself.[11] In apparent confidentiality with the reader, "Dag Solstad" here discloses the self-conscious role-playing of Dag Solstad in his public appearances. However, this candour about his lack of candour reflects back on the writer (controlling the disclosure of candour and lack of candour) and contributes to

---

11 "Foredraget frembrakte stor applaus, som jeg takket for med å bukke på en keitete måte, noe som delvis skyldes natur, men som etter hvert nok må sies å tilhøre de rekvisitter jeg benytter til den offentlige iscenesettelsen av meg selv" (*16-07-41* 151).

the construction of his ethos both as an enunciator of literary discourse and as a person staging himself in actual situations in the literary field. As this adds to the uncertainty of how to interpret Solstad's words and his works, and gives each and every reader a feeling of the uniqueness of his or her interpretation, it undoubtedly enhances Solstad's power as a writer and performer. Solstad's doubling thus resembles the elegant doubling in Borges' famous text "Borges and I," in which Borges is confused with the "I in the text" being confused with the "I outside the text" being of course identical to the "I in the text." The "Is inside and outside the text" sound in duet when the text concludes: "I do not know which of us has written this page" (Borges 339), while the whole confusion belongs to the reader's world and his or her mental representation of a textual scene in which the dramatist is Borges himself (having staged the doubling of "himself" in the text). In Borges' as in Solstad's case the stage of the confusion is not restricted to the text, but enlarged to include "reality." Poul Behrendt has labelled this "aesthetic innovation" of entanglement of fact and fiction that has become so widespread in contemporary literature "[t]he Double Contract" (my translations) between writer and reader.

4. The Writer's Symbolic Power

The opportunity to make one's world manifest in words and deeds and thus to expose it to the interest and the recognition of one's fellow beings is, of course, unevenly distributed. A person's capacity to produce understandable sentences can be wholly insufficient for his or her capacity to produce discourse that is actually listened to and considered significant (Bourdieu). Without a legitimate competence, a person is excluded from active participation in the social and cultural fields where individual worlds are formed and the common worlds shaped. Literary 'worldmaking' involves communicating something unexpected and new and reshaping the consensus; it requires a more specialised competence than the one necessary for communicating mere sensible sentences. Without "symbolic power" to back up the discursive production, no literary worldmaking can take place. As Bourdieu has conceived the notion of "symbolic power," it does not imply solely the ability of an individual or an institution to maintain a given "symbolic system," but also the authority of an agent to impose its own.

> Symbolic power—as a power of constituting the given through enunciating, of making people see and believe, of confirming or transforming the vision of the world and, thereby, action on the world and thus the world itself, an almost magical power which enables one to obtain the equivalent of what is obtained by

force (whether physical or economical), by virtue of the specific effect of mobilization—is a power that can be exercised only if it is *recognized*, that is, misrecognized as arbitrary. This means that symbolic power does not reside in the 'symbolic systems' in the form of an 'illocutionary force' but that it is defined in and through a given relation between those who exercise power and those who submit to it, i.e. in the very structure of the field in which *belief* is produced and re-produced. (170)

In the lecture hall, the audience has come to witness the manifestation of Solstad's symbolic power—his status as a nationally renowned writer, the power of his words to shape their worlds—, and it applauds as he is denying holding any power at all, enhancing his power by this act. This illustrates that symbolic power is an invisible power that can only be exercised "with the complicity of those who do not want to know that they are subject to it or even that they themselves are exercising it" (Bourdieu 164). Bourdieu claims that language's power to maintain or subvert the social order—its worldmaking power—resides in "the belief of the legitimacy of words and of those who utter them. And words cannot create this belief" (Bourdieu 170; translation modified).[12] What Bourdieu here maintains is that the discourse itself has no bearing upon its symbolic power as the power does not reside in the "symbolic system," but in the social field where the symbolic system is at work. Thus symbolic power is a delegated power endowed to certain discourses by a social system. This radical assertion has great implications, at least for the academic study of literature. It is also situated at the other extreme of Solstad's idealism on behalf of literature's intrinsic quality and its legitimate claim to recognition and authority regardless of any human activity.

5. Does It Matter Who the Writer Is?

If Solstad is right in his idealism, it does not really matter who the writer is: literature's authority and its symbolic power are of a supreme kind, and the writer is a depersonalised medium:

> Everything in my life is written words. The writing, the poetry. It is I[,] not Dag Solstad from Sandefjord. There I am someone else. What concerns Dag Solstad,

---

12 "Ce qui fait le pourvoir des mots et des mots d'ordre, pouvoir de maintenir l'ordre ou de le subvertir, c'est la croyance dans la légitimité des mots et de celui qui les prononce, croyance qu'il n'appartient pas aux mots de produire" (*Language et pouvoir symbolique* 210).

is not significant to me, even the things to which I am attached. Everything in my life is writing.[13]

This disappearance of the writer into the writing seems to fulfil T. S. Eliot's ideal in *The Sacred Wood*: "The progress of an artist is a continual self-sacrifice, a continual extinction of personality" (53). Seventy-five years after Eliot, Solstad also reaches back to Romantic ideas dating back to the end of the eighteenth century, when the Romantics transformed the 'I' into a creative medium for a universal, absolute Idea combining Liberty, Beauty, Truth, and Goodness, and assigned a higher value to poetry in the intellectual and social hierarchy. One answer to the question of why Solstad finds it necessary to repeat this step towards a universalising idealism at the beginning of the twenty-first century might well be found in Stephen Toulmin's theory of the two phases of modernity. For Toulmin, modernity's first phase was the tolerant and sceptic humanism of the sixteenth century. This was the time of Erasmus, Rabelais, Montaigne, and Shakespeare, and it was marked by "Urbane open-mindedness and sceptical tolerance" (Toulmin 25). The transition from modernity's first to its second phase is a transition from the accepted coexistence of many worlds to the primacy of an idealised *mundus*. It went from Montaigne's axiom, "I decide nothing—I don't understand—I hold myself in the doubt—I examine,"[14] to Descartes' "Cogito ergo sum" and was achieved with the seventeenth century's search for certainty and authoritative rationalism: "17th-century philosophers set aside the long-standing preoccupations of Renaissance humanism. In particular, they disclaimed any serious interest in four dif-ferent kinds of practical knowledge: the oral, the particular, the local, and the timely" (Toulmin 30).

As philosophical thought sought to ground aesthetic judgment in universal, timeless and non-contextual validity shared by all rational beings in the universe, it did not break with the universalising tendency of its time; it only chose the other side of the dichotomy reason/feeling. At the transition from the twentieth to the twenty-first century, however, there seems to be a renewed interest for the plurality of individual worlds and "urbane open-mindedness and sceptical tolerance" (Toulmin 25), exemplarily represented by the Goodmanian concept of "worldmaking." In this context, it is tempting to see Solstad's return to Romantic idealism

---

13 "Alt i mitt liv er skrift. Skrivingen, diktningen. Det er jeg[,] ikke Dag Solstad fra Sandefjord. Der er jeg en annen. Det som har med Dag Solstad å gjøre, betyr ikke nok for meg, selv ikke ting jeg har et kjært forhold til. Alt i mitt liv er skrift" (*16-07-41* 164).

14 "Je ne décide rien. — Je ne comprends pas. — Je me tiens dans le doute. — J'examine" (Montaigne LXXII; the quotations inscribed in the roof beams of Montaigne's workroom were taken from Sextus Empiricus, *Hypotyposes,* I. 22, 23, 26).

as a reaction to the threat to literature's privileged status that constructivist's relativism seems to imply.

If Bourdieu is right, not Solstad, and "authority comes to language from outside" (Bourdieu 109), it means that questions regarding the social identity and positioning of the author and the source of his or her worldmaking power are essential questions to ask. The so-called intrinsic qualities of the literary work, its "genuinely novelistic" qualities, its "indissoluble, epic element," the "possible magic of the novelistic art" or the "necessity of art,"[15] are of no definitive significance. The contest for literature's power is fought by means of the writer's position in a social field where he or she competes for some delegated authority along with other writers.

The symbolic power of a writer with Solstad's kind of fame and recognition, acquired in the course of a long career, seems self-evident, legitimate and, so to speak, natural. Solstad has not only been remarkably successful in shaping his own world to fit his claim of literary greatness, but also in transforming the worlds of his fellow Norwegians to fit. It can therefore be useful to bear in mind that four decades earlier, in his first years as a writer, he recurrently elaborated on the topic of power and literature in a quite different mode, promoting modernist literature as an agent of change. As Solstad then saw it, bourgeois society, by canonising literature and assigning prophetic authority to the writer, in fact neutralised his power by assigning him the role of an inoffensive curator of the legitimate order. In defence of literature, the 'real' writer then had an obligation to regain literature's power to provoke change. Never questioning by which authority a young person at the beginning of his career gains this competence and the right to call himself a writer, Solstad dealt with the *aporia* of the recognition of the writer's work being a precondition for the writer's power to make an impact on his reader's worlds, and presented himself as a subversive writer of great importance from his very first words.

Compared to Bourdieu's view on authority as something that necessarily comes to language from without, and the older Solstad's view on literature's intrinsic quality and authority, the view of the young Solstad that the writer has to claim literature in order to conquer worldmaking power represents a third view. These seemingly contradictory perspectives are combined in the notion of literature as a "self-constituting discourse." Proposed by Dominique Maingueneau and Frédérique Cossutta, this no-

---

15 "Det genuint romanmessige ved enhver roman" (Solstad, *16-07-41* 143); "Romankunstens mulige magi" (143); "romanens uoppløselige episke element" (147); "kunstens nødvendighet" (148).

tion, at least partly, agrees with Bourdieu in his view that authority comes to language from without. The authority of [self-]constituting discourses, however, is not delegated or conquered in the social field of literature, but claimed in the discursive production itself as literature connects itself with its source:

> To found other discourses without being founded by them, [self-constituting discourses] must set themselves up as intimately bound with a legitimizing Source and show that they are in accordance with it, owing to the operations by which they structure their text and legitimate their own context, the way they emerge and develop. (Maingueneau "Analysing Self-Constituting Discourses" 183)

Thus, when Solstad is talking of "literature as spirit," he is not stating an unconditioned truth, but invoking a transcendent source which empowers him with symbolic power as he invokes it in this way. In this kind of self-confirming movement of legitimisation, literature, together with discourses such as philosophy, science, and religion, is set apart from the majority of society's discursive production. It becomes a special kind of privileged discourse which founds other discourses and thus contributes to the constitution of a society—of its values, its memory, its authority, and so on. It is in the very process of using language at a certain aim in a certain way in a certain situation that a [self-]constituting discourse acquires its elevated status. Thus the notion of [self-]constituting discourse also supports the younger Solstad's view that the writer conquers literature's worldmaking capacity by uncompromisingly setting himself apart from his forerunners and imposing his alternative worldview. And it supports the older Solstad view on literature's intrinsic authority; nevertheless this authority does not belong to the dehumanised word of the idealised spirit, but is generated by literature as human activity in a discursive field where the writer's and the reader's worlds are confronted with each other and their shared worlds. The notion of [self-]constituting discourse makes the question of writer's power versus reader's power a legitimate question to ask as recognised authors are

> perceived as delivering not just any message, but one authorized by their privileged acquaintance with 'ultimate' discourses: discourses upon which others are based—that have a particular relationship with the foundations of society and with the signification of human destiny. ("Analysing Self-Constituting Discourses" 183)

Symbolic power might be seemingly magical; it is nevertheless exercised by an agent upon those who submit to it. Every world is made by someone, and the bare fact that a world is made manifest and public raises the question of the source of the legitimacy and recognition of its maker.

6. The 'Impossible' Author

A doubling similar to the self-conscious doubling or splitting of the author in "Borges and I" takes place in several of Solstad's novels. In this kind of literary game, which has become a widespread practice in contemporary literature, the identity of the speaker matters, but is impossible to pin down as the conventional distinction between writer and narrator is adeptly destroyed. According to a long-lasting literary doxa, the historical person at the origin of the literary work is completely external to the text, while the notion of the narrator refers to an act of telling internal to the text. As modern literature undermines this doxa by transgressing the boundaries between reality and fiction and displaying shifting subjectivities and discursive strategies, it still depends on it. In Solstad's case, where the game resides in the essential difference between "Dag Solstad," the character given this name in some of Dag Solstad's novels, with the actual writer Dag Solstad, it presupposes that a literary writer has access to two distinct modes of autographical discourse.[16] In some types of literary discourse, such as fictional prose or poetry, the writer, by convention, is not bound by reality. If the author utters 'I,' this 'I' is without a 'real' referent. In other kinds of literary discourse, such as a lecture, an interview or an essay, the border between a truth and a lie is essential, clear, and binding. If the author utters 'I,' it refers to his 'real' person. This nice distinction seems, however, to be without bearing in experience. Besides Goodman's claim that the difference between a fact and a fiction represents a mere difference in referential distance, it is also essential to keep in mind that truth and untruth are fluid categories in the ongoing, human shaping of the self. Undoubtedly, the truth of the self as a unique and changing physical and spiritual being is inaccessible to others. The world of one person can never be transparent or shared. Nevertheless, the self as social reality comes into being as the subjectivity that utters 'I' differentiates itself from 'you.' The author who utters "'I'" in a fictional tale differentiates this "'I'" from the 'real' 'I,' that is the 'I' that utters "'I.'" It is of no relevance whether the expression of the self is 'true' or 'false,' 'real' or 'fictive,' yet what is relevant is how it constructs the self—as it acts and its acts are interpreted and met by others. "'Ego' is the one who says 'ego,'"

---

16 To avoid the distinction between 'autobiography' and the neologism 'auto fiction,' I prefer the term 'autography,' or 'self writing,' proposed by Pascale Delormas.

according to Benveniste.[17] As expression of the self, subjectivity is productive, and it is not possible to identify the subject that expresses itself in discourse before discourse; the subject is shaped by discourse and social interplay.

In his famous paper "What is an author?", Foucault's starting point is a sentence from Beckett's *Text for Nothing*: "'What does it matter who is speaking,' someone said, 'what does it matter who is speaking.'"[18] Foucault's claim in the paper's last paragraphs is that the image of the author dominating any discourse with author-function is "the ideological figure by which one marks the manner in which we fear the proliferation of meaning" ("What is an Author?" 209).[19] With its disappearance, discourses will "develop the anonymity of the murmur" (210) and be met with other questions than the recurrent questions about the human subject at the source of the discourse. This is a development Foucault favours as he foresees that the interpretation of fictional discourse then will happen more freely and a more analytic approach to the variety of discursive practices will come into being as questions about their mode of existence and the conditions of their circulation and appropriation move to the forefront.

In response to the conclusion of Foucault's paper, one can ask whether a development towards the "anonymity of the murmur" would not also lead to the collapse of discourse, as any answer regarding what is said then would echo the indifference of Beckett's *Text for Nothing*, "What difference does it make who is speaking?" If it is of no importance who is speaking, of what importance can it then be what is said? If speech is both productive and a product of subjectivity, can dehumanised speech then be possible? If all that can be heard is uttered in "the anonymity of the murmur," it seems that either the shaping of the common world is no longer going on, or that the individual worlds have become totally alike.

While the "image of the author," according to Foucault, is an "ideological figure" which is imposed on texts from the outside, texts with author-function are produced from the inside by a "plurality of self" ("What is an Author?" 205). For example, the "I"s of a mathematical

---

17 "Est 'ego' qui *dit* 'ego'" (Benveniste 265).
18 Quoted after Foucault, "What is an Author?" 210.
19 The first version of Foucault's paper was presented to the "Société française de philosophie" in 1969. In 1970, Foucault presented a slightly modified version in English at the State University of New York at Buffalo. This version was published in the USA in 1979. The English version adds three paragraphs towards the end of the essay elaborating on the author as an ideological product. Foucault subsequently gave permission to reproduce either of the two versions (see Foucault, "Qu'est-ce qu'un auteur?" 789, 811).

treatise refer to three selves that can be differentiated from one another and described quite precisely. "The author-function," Foucault concludes,

> is not assumed by the first of these selves at the expense of the other two, which would then be noting more than a fictitious splitting in two of the first one; on the contrary, in these discourses the author-function operates so as to effect the dispersion of these three simultaneous selves. ("What is an Author?" 205)

A "text with author-function" seems to be Foucault's label for what Maingueneau has named "self-constituting discourse," and in Maingueneau's theory of literary discourse analysis, we find the same triadic splitting of the enouncing subjectivity as in Foucault's paper. But unlike Foucault, who does not identify a discursive principle at the base of the splitting, Maingueneau identifies what he calls the "paratopic" positioning of the enunciator of a [self-]constituting discourse as the force that splits his or her subjectivity into three instances and assembles them in the "impossible" figure of the author. Not unlike Foucault's taxonomy, the three instances of the subjectivity are labelled the "person," referring to the actual man or woman; the "writer," referring to the way he or she plays the role of the writer in the literary field; and the "inscriptor," designating the instance which assumes responsibility for the text in its singularity and its genre, and as in Foucault's model, there is no hierarchy between these instances since they generate each other in a dynamic of differentiation and convergence. Together they form a paradoxical, indeterminate and multiple image of the author that is "larger" than each of the three instances that produces it and different from the sum of them. The metaphor Maingueneau proposes to visualise this model is the "Borromean knot," a figure consisting of three rings that are linked in such a way that removing one ring results in the unlinking of the two other rings, while he designates "paratopia" as "the clinamen which renders this knot possible and which is rendered possible by this knot."[20] Here "clinamen" refers to Lucretius' notion of the tiny deviation of the atoms that allows them to meet and matter to form, while "paratopia" is the notion proposed by Maingueneau to designate the

> paradoxical relation of inclusion and exclusion in a social space that follows from the special status of a text belonging to literature. [...] This paradoxical status is a result of the distinct character of these discourses that can only *authorize* themselves: If the speaker has a *topic* position he cannot speak on behalf of a transcen-

---

20 "le clinamen qui rend possible ce nœud et que ce nœud rend possible" (*Le discours littéraire* 108).

dence, but if he does not in any way write himself into the social space, he cannot spread a receivable message.[21]

By way of his or her paratopic positioning and the paradoxical tension it creates, the author becomes simultaneously an integrated member and a marginal dissident to 'his' or 'her' community. (To visualise how this paratopic positioning works, it can be useful to think of the prophet's withdrawal into the desert to distance himself from 'his' people and their wrongdoings, while he draws them out in the desert with him with his words.)

Maingueneau's concepts and the model of the "Borromean knot" contribute significantly to the understanding of literary worldmaking and the discursive dynamic that generates literature's symbolic power. Since there exists in a society a certain kind of discourse with a privileged status and role in the shaping of the common worlds, the founding characteristics of these discourses have to be analysed according to the special dynamics of self-legitimising and appropriation of symbolic power by which they come into being and acquire their force. Their attribution to a productive subjectivity, and the more or less literal concretisation of this subjectivity into the figure of the author, does not happen from the "outside" as an ideological contamination to hinder the free interpretation of the text, as Foucault claims. As a world is always the world of someone, literature's worldmaking power would be impossible if the reader did not have some idea about its enunciator. It is by understanding how the image of the author that emerges from the text becomes "impossible" that one also can understand the privileged status of literature and other [self-]constituting discourses and the special role they have to play in the shaping of the shared worlds that binds us together in cultures and societies.

References

Amossy, Ruth. *Images de soi dans le discours: La construction de l'éthos.* Lausanne: Delachaux et Niestlé, 1999.
Behrendt, Poul. *Dobbeltkontrakten: En æstetisk nydannelse.* Copenhagen: Gyldendal, 2006.

---

21 "[…] la relation paradoxale d'inclusion/exclusion dans un espace social qu'implique le statut de locuteur d'un texte relevant des discours constituants […] Ce statut paradoxal découle de la spécificité de ces discours qui ne peuvent *s'autoriser* que d'eux-mêmes : si le locuteur occupe une position *topique*, il ne peut parler au nom de quelque transcendance, mais s'il ne s'inscrit pas en quelque façon dans l'espace social, il ne peut proférer un message recevable" (Maingueneau in Charaudeau and Maingueneau 420).

Bénichou, Paul. *Le sacre de l'érivain 1750–1830: Essai sur l'avènement d'un pouvoir spirituel laïque dans la France moderne*. Paris: Librairie José Corti, 1973.
Benveniste, Émile. "De la subjectivité dans le langage." *Problèmes de linguistique générale*. Vol. 1. 1985 Paris: Gallimard, 1979. 258–66.
Bjorvand, Harald, and Fredrik Lindeman. *Våre arveord: etymologisk ordbok,* rev. and ext. edition. Oslo: Novus, 2007.
Bokmålsordboka. April 2009 <http://www.dokpro.uio.no/ordboksoek.html>.
Bourdieu, Pierre. *Language and Symbolic Power*. Trans. Gino Raymond and Mathew Adamson. Cambridge: Polity Press, 1991. Trans. of *Language et pouvoir symbolique*. Paris: Éditions du Seuil, 2001.
Borges, Jorge Luis. "Borges and I." Trans. James E. Irby. 1957. *Authorship: From Plato to the Postmodern: A Reader*. Ed. Seán Burke. Edinburgh: Edinburgh UP, 1995. 339.
Butler, Judith. *The Psychic Life of Power: Theories in Subjection*. Stanford: Stanford UP, 1997.
Charaudeau, Patrick, and Dominique Maingueneau. *Dictionnaire d'analyse du discours*. Paris: Seuil, 2002.
Delormas, Pascale. "L'image de soi dans les « autographies » de Rousseau et le recours à la rhétorique traditionnelle."*Argumentation et Analyse du discours* 1 (2008): Eds. Ruth Amossy and Roselyne Koren. April 2009 <http://aad.revues.org/index171.html>.
Eliot, T.S. *The Sacred Wood: Essays on Poetry and Criticism*. 1920. London: Methuen, 1960.
Falk, Hjalmar, and Alf Torp. *Etymologisk ordbog over det norske og det danske sprog: Ord, røtter og opprinnelige betydning*. 1903–1906. Oslo: Bjørn Ringstrøms Antikvariat, 1994.
Foucault, Michel. "What is an Author?" 1969. *Modern Criticism and Theory: A Reader*. Ed. David Lodge. London: Longman, 1991. 196–210.
—. "Qu'est-ce qu'un auteur?" *Dits et écrits*, Vol. 1. Eds. Daniel Defert and Francois Ewald. 1969. Paris: Gallimard, 1994. 789–821.
Goodman, Nelson. *Ways of Worldmaking,* Hassocks: Harvester Press, 1978.
—. *Of Minds and Other Matter*. Cambridge, MA: Harvard UP, 1984.
Jefferson, Ann. *Biography and the Question of Literature in France*. Oxford: Oxford UP, 2007.
Kierkegaard, Søren. "The Sickness unto Death, a Christian Psychological Exposition for Upbuilding and Awakening by Anti-Climacus." 1849. *The Essential Kierkegaard*. Eds. Howard V. Hong and Edna H. Hong. Princeton: Princeton UP, 2000.
Maingueneau, Dominique. "Analysing Self-Constituting Discourses." *Discourse Studies*. Vol. 1.2. London: Sage (1999): 175–99.
—. *Le discours littéraire: Paratopie et scène d'énonciation*. Paris: Armand Colin, 2004.
Maingueneau, Dominique, and Frédéric Cossutta. "L'analyse des discours constituants." *Langages* 117 (1995): 112–25.
Maturana, Humberto R., and Francisco J. Varela. *The Tree of Knowledge: The Biological Roots of Human Understanding*. Trans. Robert Paolucci. 1987. London: Shambhala, 1992.
Montaigne, Michel de. *Les essais : Edition de Pierre Villey*. 1580–1595. Paris: Presses Universitaires de France, 1999.
Saussure, Ferdinand de. *Cours de linguistique générale*. 1916. Paris: Payot, 1995.

Solstad, Dag. "Spilleren." *Moderne prosa: Arbeidsbok frå eit litteraturseminar.* Eds. Tor Obrestad and Einar Økland. Oslo: Samlaget, 1968.
—. *16-07-41. Roman.* Oslo: Oktober, 2002.
—. *Armand V.: Fotnoter til en uutgravd roman.* Oslo: Oktober, 2006.
—. *Shyness and Dignity.* Trans. Sverre Lyngstad. 1994. London: Harvill Secker, 2006.
Toulmin, Stephen. *Cosmopolis: The Hidden Agenda of Modernity.* 1990. Chicago: U of Chicago P, 1992.
White, Hayden. "The Historical Text as Literary Artifact." *Clio* 3 (1974): 277–303.

Writing Lives and 'Worlds': English Fictional Biography at the Turn of the 21st Century

Caroline Lusin

> There can be magic in a name. A name can conjure up a world, and 'a world' can be a story.
>
> (C.K. Stead, *A Secret History of Modernism* 16)

1. Biography, Worldmaking, and Narrative

In his fictional autobiography *A Secret History of Modernism* (2001), C.K. Stead sums up the connection between biography, worldmaking, and narrative in a few words: A person's name evokes his or her life and 'world,' and this 'world' can be turned into a story. In reality, however, this process is far more complex and richer than it appears to be in Stead's simple statement. Today, numerous forms of (auto-)biography—and therefore numerous versions of what Nelson Goodman called 'ways of worldmaking'—are available to the biographer. They range from the classic factual biography to what Ansgar Nünning ("Von der fiktionalen Metabiogarphie"; "Fictional Metabiographies") has called 'biographical metafiction' or 'fictional metabiography.'[1] The former—the factual biography—concentrates on facts, tends to follow the traditional pattern of beginning, middle, end, and focuses on a straightforward development of character. The fictional metabiography, in contrast, discards factual reality in favour of metafictional reflections on problems of reconstruction and representation. In fictional metabiographies, the emphasis is thus placed on the indeterminacy of biographical knowledge as well as on the epistemological uncertainties involved in the representation of biographical facts (see A. Nünning, "Fictional Metabiographies" 196ff.). Fictional metabiographies such as Julian Barnes's *Flaubert's Parrot* (1984) or A.S. Byatt's *The Biographer's Tale* (2000) show that the biographer's search for dependable facts and disambiguation must invariably be in vain, as there is no

---

[1] For a more comprehensive and detailed survey of the other subgenres see A. Nünning, "Fictional Metabiographies" (199; 210ff.).

such thing as a single, definite truth (see Maack 173).[2] Instead of presenting one, definitely 'true' story, Barnes, Ackroyd, and Byatt "juxtapose several stories that present the reader with highly self-reflexive intertextual, or rather intermedial, biographical quests for the respective biographee" (A. Nünning "Fictional Metabiographies" 196).

In an article published in *The Guardian* in 2006, the novelist and critic David Lodge points out that another biographical subgenre has gained popularity since the 1990s. Combining certain conventions of the novel and of biography, the so-called 'fictional biography' centres on a historical person and his or her life.[3] The narrative strategies of this hybrid genre do not primarily aim at the presentation of 'hard' facts, but encourage authors to take recourse to the imaginative possibilities of fiction in order to close gaps in factual information (see Lodge). According to a definition by Ina Schabert, "FICTIONAL BIOGRAPHY is engaged in the comprehension of real historical individuals by means of the sophisticated instruments of knowing and articulating knowledge that contemporary fiction offers." (Schabert 4) In fictional biographies, the straightforward discourse of the classic factual biography, which is based more or less exclusively on documentary sources, thus merges with the devices of fiction. These characteristics of fictional biographies also affect the strategies as well as the functions of worldmaking pertaining to this genre.

Biography—be it factual or fictional—involves what Nelson Goodman has called 'worldmaking' in a very literal sense. According to Nelson Goodman's constructivist theory, worlds are always made from other worlds:

> The many stuffs—matter, energy, waves, phenomena—that worlds are made of are made along with the worlds. But made from what? Not from nothing, after all, but *from other worlds*. Worldmaking as we know it always starts from worlds already at hand; the making is a remaking. (Goodman 6)

Consequently, according to Goodman there is no such thing as an 'aboriginal reality' (Bruner 96), but only other, previously constructed world versions. In other words, "world making involves the transformation of worlds and world versions already made" (Bruner 96). Writing a biography conforms to this theory perfectly. First of all, in order to fulfil his or her primary task of recreating the individual world of a historical person, he or

---

2   See A. Nünning ("How Do We Seize the Past?"; "Fictional Metabiographies"; "Fiktionale Auto/Biographien") for an analysis of the metabiographical aspects of these novels.

3   Lodge uses the term 'biographical novel' synonymously with 'fictional biography,' whereas Ina Schabert (31–32) draws a clear distinction between the two, pointing out that the biographical novel goes back to the 19th century, particularly to Edward Bulwer-Lytton.

she has to rely primarily on documents such as letters, diaries, or other biographies. From these documents, which can be considered as 'worlds' in themselves, the biographer reconstructs the biographee's world. The entire narrative 'world,' i.e. the text of a biography, is therefore made from other 'worlds,' mainly other texts or oral narratives. Consequently, for the biographer there really is "no unique 'real world' that pre-exists and is independent from human mental activity and human symbolic language" (Bruner 95). Second, the process of composing a (fictional) biography includes exactly the same steps as Goodman's worldmaking. As Goodman maintains, "the making of one world out of another usually involves some extensive weeding out and filling—actual excision of some old and supply of some new material" (14). Correspondingly, the biographer has to choose the sources and facts to be included and, particularly in fictional biographies, to complement them with fictive facts and conjectures. Apart from this step of deletion and supplementation, writing a (fictional) biography, just like worldmaking, also encompasses processes of composition and decomposition, weighting, ordering, and deformation, the latter meaning that material is reshaped to better fit into the whole. These components of worldmaking are closely related to the narrative strategies involved in writing a biography.

As far as the reconstruction of a biographee's world is concerned, narrative comes into play on various levels. Just like historiography, biography is an intrinsically narrative genre, which continues the nineteenth-century tradition of mimetic narration (see Maack 169). Just like the process of composing a novel, writing a history book or a biography comprises questions of selection, structure, and perspective. As Ira Bruce Nadel puts it, "[b]iography is fundamentally a narrative which has as its primary task the enactment of character and place through language—a goal similar to that of fiction" (8).[4] Moreover, a large part of the informative material available to the biographer is written in the narrative vein, too: Biographical documents like letters or diaries are themselves forms of the narrative processing of the world. The task of the biographer, therefore, is not simply to reproduce random facts, but to organise them as a narrative text, drawing back on the conceptions of plot, character, and narrative perspective (see Maack 169). Particularly in fictional biography, facts may be restructured, rearranged, reinterpreted and supplemented by fiction.

The opposition of the 'truth of fiction' and the 'truth of fact' has always figured prominently in discussions about the faults and merits of worldmaking in fictional (auto-)biography. In newer examples of the

---

4 Similarly, Phyllis Rose states that "artful biography, composed and not compiled biography […] aspires to the condition of the novel" (11).

genre, for example David Lodge's *Author, Author* (2004) and Colm Tóibín's *The Master* (2004), the issue of worldmaking, more precisely: the quest for the biographical subject as well as the tension between 'fact' and 'fiction,' play a crucial and complex role. A closer look at these two fictionalised lives of Henry James not only helps to identify crucial characteristics of English fictional biography at the turn of the twenty-first century, but also sheds light on some more general tendencies of contemporary fiction in English

2. 'The Supreme Novelist': Worldmaking in David Lodge's *Author, Author* (2004) and Colm Tóibín's *The Master* (2004)

In their fictional biographies about Henry James, David Lodge, and Colm Tóibín proceed in an exemplary way according to the five 'acts' of narrative worldmaking Ansgar Nünning identifies in his article in this volume. The authors must choose those incidents of James's life that are to become the events of their respective stories. Integrating these separate events into a narrative, i.e. a story, involves a great deal of selection, deletion, abstraction, and prioritisation. The differences between the two biographies prove that, as Nünning points out, there is "a plurality of stories, narratives, texts and other media products that can be generated about any event" (A. Nünning in this volume), in this case about certain events in the life of Henry James.

2.1 Perspective and the Biographical Subject

Focusing on Henry James' life, both Lodge and Tóibín try to fulfil what James's friend Edmund Gosse demanded from a good biography: that it draws "the faithful portrait of a soul in its adventures through life" (952). The strategies they employ in order to achieve this aim, however, are quite different from those Gosse must have had in mind. David Lodge centres *Author, Author* (*AA*) on James's failed attempts to become a playwright and his efforts to come to terms with the public humiliation this entailed, whereas Colm Tóibín gives a linear account of James's middle years from 1895 to 1901, which is interrupted by frequent flashbacks. The charm and quality of *Author, Author* and *The Master* (*TM*) are due precisely to their lack of any fixed or one-sided judgments concerning either the subject of art or the life of Henry James, which results above all from the narrative perspective the authors have chosen. Both use James as a focaliser, which not only gives better insight into his life, but encourages readers more strongly to sympathise or identify with him and to perceive the world through his "ideological perspective," i.e. "his [...] values and norms," as Ansgar Nünning puts it in this volume. To some degree, though, both authors introduce other perspectives, too, particularly Lodge in *Author, Author*. In this novel's crucial section, which describes the failure of *Guy Domville* on the stage, Lodge draws on multiperspective presentation in order to give a more multifaceted, balanced and lively account of his biographee.[5] Although Tóibín, in contrast, persistently sticks to just one focaliser, he also introduces other points of view. More specifically, Tóibín incorporates dialogues between James and his friends or acquaintances, which provide readers with different, even contrasting perspectives on him. Different as the two novels seem, a closer look at their strategies of emplotment therefore reveals that they have much in common concerning both the narrative techniques and the topics they explore.

But why have Lodge and Tóibín chosen Henry James as their subject? Is this interest in Henry James just, as one critic stated with reference to Lodge's *Author, Author*, a new way "to pay homage to the nineteenth-[or twentieth-]century novel" (Guignery 171)? In his satire *Mensonge* (1987), Malcolm Bradbury whimsically defines the intricacy of the overarching genre as follows: "Biographies are said to be fictions revealing more about the biographer than they do about their subjects, who, of course do not exist anyway" (29). Ironical and highly exaggerated as it is, this statement nevertheless gets to the core of the matter: due to the nature of their subject, fictional biographies, above all those about authors, lend themselves perfectly to self-projection, self-reflexivity, and metafiction (see A. Nünning "Fictional metabiographies" 196). In this respect, Henry James, who was frequently praised as "the supreme example in English of the novelist's novelist" (Saunders 127), is a particularly fitting subject, for he allows his biographers to thematise several crucial issues concerning authorship: the various links between authorship and literary worldmaking, authorship and ethics as well as authorship and memory.[6]

---

5   Moreover, this method enables Lodge to describe the performance of the play which James did not attend himself.

6   Similarly, Olsson states that *The Master* "is a text about literature and writing, about the conditions of literature, and the relation of literature to life" (140). Saunders gives a matter-of-fact background explanation of the interest in James, asserting that "the way for these novels was prepared by very specific developments in James biography and criticism. They didn't come out of nowhere, or out of a generalised 'Zeitgeist,' but out of recent rethinking of James' friendships with men and women" (125). Similarly, Harvey expounds that "in the year 2000, the name 'Henry James' is synonymous with Literature—high literature, the genuine difficult article" (76).

2.2 Authorship and Literary Worldmaking

Neither Lodge nor Tóibín take any trouble to disguise the self-projection and self-reflexivity involved in their accounts of Henry James. In an article published two years after *The Master*, Tóibín consciously stylised himself as Henry James's doppelganger. Tóibín describes himself during a stay in Florence, where he embarked on writing the novel, as follows: "I was in my mid-forties, bald, unattached, bookish. I liked company and I liked being alone. This meant that the house at Santa Maddalena worked wonders for me. There was company for lunch and supper, but my own quarters were sacrosanct" (Tóibín, "Henry James for Venice" 194). In this description, Tóibín not only looks like Henry James, but also shares his need for undisturbed solitude. The parallels between the two authors even pertain to the novel's existential dimension. For instance, in the same article Tóibín (196–97) traces his claustrophobic description of James's failure as a playwright back to his own experience of not having been awarded the Booker Prize for his shortlisted novel *The Blackwater Lightship* in 1999. Parallels between Lodge and his James can easily be found, too: like James, Lodge also tried to write for the stage (see Guignery 169), and just like the James he depicts in his novel, he is already a famous author in his later years. Even the novelists' choices concerning weighting or emphasis seem to conform to personal interests or predispositions: whereas Lodge concentrates mainly on questions of fame, integrity, and 'sellability,' the Irish Tóibín, who has written a monograph on homosexual artists (*Love in a Dark Time: Gay Lives from Wilde to Almodóvar*, 2001/02), quite strongly foregrounds James's Irish origins as well as his presumed latent homosexuality.

In both novels, however, self-projection and self-reflexivity go far beyond the merely personal. According to Tóibín, it is impossible to identify "the amount of the secret self that goes into any book" (198) and to define the narrow line between invention and autobiography. Tóibín's intention in baring this autobiographical dimension, though, is to demonstrate how fiction works:

> I am pointing this out—much of it is obvious—merely to show that my own method of merging the deeply personal with the imagined, matters which come deliberately and also unwillingly and unconsciously, belongs to the main method by which novelists work and by which James himself, the supreme novelist, also worked. (Tóibín, "Henry James for Venice" 200)[7]

---

7   In the novel itself, though, any traces of the author should, according to Tóibín, disappear entirely. As he writes about his experiences in reading James: "I never once thought about

While Tóibín has kept any such statements out of his fiction, Lodge makes his protagonist think the very same: "Writing fiction, however artful, was inevitably to some degree an exposure of the author's own self, his own soul" (*AA* 63). In other words: *The Master* and *Author, Author* are by no means only designed to depict the life of a famous novelist or to mirror the idiosyncrasies of their authors, but are meant to illustrate certain aspects of authorship and narrative worldmaking in general. The title *Author, Author* refers primarily to the fatal call with which James was lured onto the stage after the complete failure of *Guy Domville*. It also draws the reader's attention to the author and his subject: another author.[8] Similarly, the title *The Master* refers less to Henry James as an individualised person than to his outstanding achievements as an author. In this way the issue of writing, authorship and thus creative 'worldmaking' is foregrounded in both novels from the beginning.

Obviously, fictional biographies like *Author, Author* and *The Master* are determined not only by their respective author's ways of shaping the world. They also stage the corresponding strategies of their author-subjects. In these novels it is therefore the author who really comes to the fore as an agent of worldmaking: Authors sketch the worlds of authors who were in turn engaged in fictional worldmaking. Negotiating the tension between 'fact' and 'fiction,' the biographies' authors try to evoke the lives and 'worlds' of other authors. Thus, 'worldmaking' here involves a many-layered process. In *Author, Author*, David Lodge tends to deviate from his own usual way of writing to imitate the elaborately elegant style of Henry James instead, just as Tóibín does in *The Master*.[9] In that respect, the term 'ways of worldmaking' fits these works of art perfectly: They really are "culturally shaped world models or versions" (A. Nünning in this volume) in the most literal sense of the term. However, the two novels are 'fictional biographies' not only by genre. Both authors shift the meaning of the term 'bio-graphy,' which is composed of the Greek words for 'life' ('bios') and 'writing' ('graphia'), to a more general, metafictional plane: They show how 'life' becomes 'literature,' how 'reality' becomes 'narrative.' In other words: They describe how the real world becomes a fictional world.

As far as this connection of life, literature, and worldmaking is concerned, Henry James proves a particularly fitting subject. Since James is known for modelling the topics or plots of his stories on real-life inci-

---

Henry James himself. He seemed beautifully absent from his own novel, which was another aspect of his power" (Tóibín, "Henry James for Venice" 193).

8 For a whole range of further explanations of this title see Guignery 163–64.

9 For details as well as a critical evaluation of their respective stylistic experiments see Saunders (128–29).

dents, he meets the demands of illustrating the fortunes and hazards of literary worldmaking very well. Due to this habit of turning real-life material into stories, he gives his biographers the perfect opportunity to address the complex relationship of literature and reality. At the beginning of *Author, Author*, for instance, the dying master mumbles significant scraps of one of his most famous mature stories, "The Beast in the Jungle": "It's the beast in the jungle, and it's sprung" (*AA* 11). The full meaning of this sentence becomes clear only in the course of the novel. In the frame story, the reader is only told the plot of that story, which centres on unrequited love, on the inability to love, and on death. In the middle section, Lodge then elaborates on the story's possible origins: James's intimate, but at the same time distanced and platonic relationship with the American expatriate writer Constance Fenimore Woolson, which ended with her committing suicide. Vice versa, Lodge also refers to a number of Woolson's stories, which are in turn modelled on her experiences with Henry James. In order to stress the connection of life and literature further, Lodge even provides some kind of a 'real life example' for this story, which he inserts as *mise en abîme* into the frame: the relationship between two of James's servants not only resembles that of James and Woolson, but perfectly corresponds to the pattern described in "The Beast in the Jungle." In *The Master*, Tóibín proceeds similarly, connecting different levels of fiction and reality. He refers to the real-life implications of "The Beast in the Jungle," too, for he makes his protagonist begin the story at the novel's end. Moreover, in his account of James's life Tóibín blends his fiction, James's fiction and biographical documents. This is best illustrated by a scene from *The Master* (199ff.) in which young Henry walks with his father on a beach. This scene, in which James senior stares at a bathing woman, goes back to an event in the year 1857 which he recorded in a letter to Anne Ward. Years later, James junior wrote a strikingly similar scene in chapter 30 of his novel *What Maisie Knew*. Tóibín in turn incorporates this scene as a memory of young Henry into his novel, repeating parts of *What Maisie Knew* word by word. Due to this complex and entangled structure, it is impossible to detect a really 'aboriginal reality' behind these scenes. Even the supposedly 'factual' account James senior gave of it in his letter was presumably to some degree 'fictionalised,' since it must have been shaped by numerous social and cultural conventions. To put it more generally: The fictional world of the novel mirrors another fictional world which in turn seems to mirror 'reality.' In fact, this 'reality' is for us—as well as for Tóibín and Lodge—only composed of narrative accounts in the form of letters, diaries or biographies written by other authors (which, of course, are in turn based on other narrative accounts). By mentioning Woolson's stories, Lodge even introduces different fictional interpretations of that reality, to which readers may add still others. Consequently, any definite reality disappears in a *regressus ad infinitum* of fictional accounts. As in Goodman's theory of worldmaking, it becomes apparent in *Author, Author* and *The Master* that there is no 'aboriginal' reality, but only other culturally pre-shaped worlds.

While Lodge and Tóibín thus illustrate the ambiguous results and implications of James's literary worldmaking, they also demonstrate his worldmaking in progress. In the course of their novels, both authors frequently show how James stores up experiences and how he jots down stories he was told by friends or acquaintances for future literary use. Particularly Tóibín's novel contains such a wealth of intertextual references to James's work, that, as one critic put it, "readers of James can amuse themselves in playing 'spot the novel' within the novel" (Lowdon 10). This includes both novels written within the time frame *The Master* depicts, like *What Maisie Knew*, and later novels, for Tóibín also invents the origin of images which James would use in his later novels. For instance, an antique dealer the fictional James meets in 1897 is to become the antique dealer who figured in the author's 1904 novel *The Golden Bowl* (see Tóibín "Henry James for Venice" 201). The fact that James thus often made shameless use of people as 'material' for his art raises a number of ethical questions both Lodge and Tóibín address quite explicitly.

2.3 Authorship and Ethics

The problematic relation of authorship and ethics, which is crucial to both novels, originates mainly from the contrast between 'public' and 'private' as well as from the connection between the worlds of 'life' and 'literature.'[10] In *Author, Author*, Lodge establishes this relation within the first few pages. He parallels James's death in 1916 with history—the simultaneous death of countless soldiers in Flanders—and compares the young men's unlived lives to unwritten books, to "blank pages that will never be filled" (*AA* 3). In *The Master*, the fictional James thinks something strikingly similar: "He lived, at times, he felt, as if his life belonged to someone else, a story that had not yet been written, a character who had not been fully imagined" (*TM* 118). These images convey a whole range of ambiguous ideas concerning literature. On the one hand, they equate life and literature, implying that life is being determined by an author or at least

---

10   Hannah also stresses the importance of the contrast between 'public' and 'private,' but focuses primarily on "figures of exposure and concealment" (72) concerning James's alleged homosexuality.

certain narrative patterns; on the other hand, they foreground the existential value of literature as something holistic that provides experience and fulfilment. Finally, these comparisons imply that literature—particularly, but not only, for James—depends on life for its plots and themes. As Lodge writes about James's fictional method in *Author, Author*: "[H]e depended on friends for human interest and input, for the stimulus of other minds, for the occasional anecdote that might be the 'germ' of a new piece of fiction" (92). In its most extreme, this method results in people being reduced to mere material for fiction, which—from an ethical point of view—comes close to exploitation.[11]

As the most prominent example for James's fictional method, both authors give a detailed account of his platonic, but close and intimate relationship with Constance Fenimore Woolson, which he kept secret for fear of being suspected of an amorous adventure. In *Author, Author*, Lodge distinctly identifies the literary 'value' which this relationship had in store for James: "He felt something of the excitement and sense of risk that he imagined must attend real assignations, and stored up the experience for future literary use" (*AA* 73). In *The Master*, Tóibín lets one of the characters utter precisely the same idea, making Woolson, who appears to have been a rather mediocre writer, but a very sharp and insightful judge of people, reproach James with this literary habit herself. Having been introduced to two of James's friends in Florence who obviously served him as models for characters in one of his books, Woolson openly suspects him of intending to 'use' her, too, in a sequel to the novel. As the fictional James's supposed thoughts show, she is right:

> He was doing, he understood, what Constance had suggested—placing her close to his other characters, the father and daughter from *The Portrait of a Lady*, to see what would happen. He put the idea for the story aside, not wishing to satisfy her speculation as to why he might have introduced her to the Bootts […]. (*TM* 236)

For the purposes of the novel, it is irrelevant whether this actually occurred or not. Assuming that authors—as Tóibín and Lodge state—always proceed at least to some degree from some kind of real-life experience, this incident illustrates the ethical hazards not only of Henry James's fictional method, but of writing in general.

In both *Author, Author* and *The Master*, the ethical impasse of people being used as material is shown to go hand in hand with another potentially problematic aspect of writing: being creative necessarily involves a certain amount of egotism. In *Author, Author* (272), Henry James re-

---

11 As Saunders points out, Lodge and Tóibín rely upon the ability of their readers "to recognise an idea or a situation as the germ of a later story" (130).

proaches himself with having used Woolson and Alice as confidantes, counsellors and supporters, without having supported them adequately in turn. In *The Master*, some of his friends and acquaintances even hold him responsible for the death of three women to whom he had a close relationship: Constance Fenimore Woolson, James's invalid sister Alice, and his consumptive cousin Minnie Temple, who had begged him to take her with him to Italy for a cure. Both authors, however, imply that James's neglect of those women who were close to him is not due to any senseless egotism, but was ultimately caused by his profession. As Lodge explicitly states in *Author, Author*:

> He needed to be free, free to be selfish—that is to say, selflessly committed to his art. Free to travel, free to seek new experiences, and free, when his muse beckoned, to shut himself up for hours and days at a time to write, without bothering about the needs, emotional and economic, of a wife and children. (*AA* 54)

The thoughts which Tóibín ascribes to James in *The Master* with respect to Alice's death imply the same need for independence: "He did not want his invalid cousin. [...] He needed then to watch life, or imagine the world, through his own eyes. Had she been there, he would have seen through hers" (*TM* 122). Being a writer, Lodge and Tóibín insinuate, at times necessitates a certain solitude and reclusion.[12]

Neither *Author, Author* nor *The Master*, though, depict the conception of authorship and literature that the distinguished Henry James stands for—demanding, innovative works written in an elegant, increasingly elaborate and complex style—as the only ideal. On the contrary, both authors introduce other forms of art and creative worldmaking. Out of fear and excitement, James did not attend the premiere of his own drama *Guy Domville* in 1895, but went to see the first performance of Oscar Wilde's *An Ideal Husband* instead. This gives Lodge and Tóibín the opportunity to contrast two entirely different conceptions of art, James's own reflections about them (to say he did not like Wilde's play would be a tremendous euphemism) as well as the differing reactions of the public. While Wilde's innovative comedy was an enormous success, James' highly refined, but old-fashioned tragedy fell through. After the failed performance, James was lured onto the stage by the public and—to his dumbfounded terror—booed. To make things worse, *Guy Domville* was quickly put off again and, as Tóibín mentions in his account of the affair, succeeded by Wilde's *The Importance of Being Earnest*, which would become

---

12 In *The Master*, Woolson is granted at least some kind of satisfaction posthumously. After the funeral, James feels as though everything were happening according to her authorial directions: "They were her characters; she had written the script for them" (259).

another great success. This contrast between James's failure and Wilde's huge popularity raises various questions concerning worldmaking: in the case of James, the strategies of worldmaking were, as the *Domville*-tragedy shows, fatefully incongruent with the expectations of the public, whereas Wilde's far more superficial and simplistic play obviously met the public's taste perfectly. James's plight is the dilemma of the artist who has to choose between keeping up his own standards or adapting them for the sake of being commercially successful. The ideal would be, as Lodge writes in *Author, Author*, "to make sufficient amounts of money *and* to advance the art of fiction" (95). Again, this is a choice every artist may at some stage have to face.[13] Thus, Lodge remarked in an interview with *The Independent*: "'Novels are business and they are art, […] and they have always been both. I always say that you've got to be an artist when you write a novel, and a businessman when you publish it—but it's quite difficult to keep that separation'" (Tonkin). The artistic value of a work of art, however, has its foundations at least partially in the relation between authorship and memory.

2.4 Authorship and Memory

The connection of authorship and memory concerns both the creative process and the completed work of art. Due to James's method of turning real-life incidents and characters, experiences he made or stories he was told into fiction, his works become a reservoir of the past and of his past self. In his essay on James, Tóibín points to the mnemonic quality which James's works achieve in that way: "We presume that James' novels are peppered with […] raids on the real as a way of anchoring them in time, as a way of restoring what is lost to the publicity of the printed page" ("Henry James for Venice" 200). In *The Master*, Tóibín even shows how this pertains to other people's lives, too. For instance, James has obviously 'prolonged' his dead cousin's life by giving her another life in his fiction: "In *Poor Richard*, he had sent her to Europe where she did not marry. In *Daisy Miller*, in which he had emphasised her brashness and bravery and careless attitude to conventions, she had died in Rome. In *Travelling Com-*

---

13 In order to dramatise this aspect of authorship even further and to stress its relevance, both Lodge and Tóibín introduce another artist figure which may be seen as a contrast or complement to Henry James. In *Author, Author*, this is James's artist friend and caricaturist George Du Maurier, who not only lived with a very lively and blossoming family, but also achieved tremendous success with his popular novel *Trilby*. In *The Master*, the young, egotistical and highly ambitious sculptor Hendrik Andresen—whom James befriends in Rome—fulfils a similar function.

panions, he had invented a marriage for her" (*TM* 113). Thus, both novels draw back on the age-old topos of art as a means to realise lost possibilities and, above all, to achieve immortality.

However, Lodge and Tóibín evoke another kind of immortality inextricably linked to consciousness and the life of the mind. In his preface, Lodge states with regard to the novel's structure: "It begins at the end of the story, or near the end, and then goes back to the beginning, and works its way to the middle, and then rejoins the end, which is where it begins …" (preface). The frame story of *Author, Author* is devoted to the last days of James's life, his death and—to some extent—his afterlife. However, the end does not just rejoin the novel's beginning in describing James's death; it also constitutes the beginning of his posthumous fame. In quite an unexpected recourse to a postmodernist device, the novel's author now enters the discourse. Drawing on one of James's essays, Lodge completes the novel with general thoughts on art and immortality as such. Before, Lodge had made James confess his modernist artistic credo: "'Consciousness is my religion, human consciousness. Refining it, intensifying it—and preserving it'" (91). Functioning as a mediator between James and the reader, Lodge now links this credo to immortality, when he says about his biographee, incorporating James's own writing in regular print:

> So what gives him any confidence in the possibility of personal immortality? Simply 'the accumulation of the very treasure itself of consciousness,' an accumulation heightened and refined by the circumstance of being an artist: It is in a word the artistic consciousness and privilege in itself that thus shines as from immersion in the fountain of being. Into that fountain [...] our spirit dips—to the effect of feeling itself, qua imagination and aspiration, all scented with universal sources. [...] [H]ow can we after it hold complete disconnection likely? (*AA* 381)

Although *The Master* does not have such a marked circular and therefore 'preserving' structure as *Author, Author*, Tóibín achieves a closure similar to Lodge's. While the first lines of *The Master* include a dream about the dead, the novel's final sentence mentions life and the world being "remembered and captured and held" (359).[14] On a more abstract level, both authors thus start with death and end with some kind of immortality. Moreover, at the end of *The Master* Tóibín describes a discussion between Edmund Gosse and Henry's brother William James, one of the most renowned scientific specialists in consciousness:

---

14 For a closer reading of the "memory structure" of *The Master* see Olsson 142ff.

> The world beyond the sense, in which a sphere of life more powerful and larger than ourselves exists, may be continuous with our consciousness and we may know this and this may cause us to believe or have religious feeling, however vague, in a more satisfying way than we have religious argument. (*TM* 354)

While Tóibín does not connect this kind of immortality to literature as explicitly as Lodge does, he links it to the process of engaging in something outside one's consciousness, too. After all, this is precisely what a writer whose work is devoted to consciousness and to the mind does. What is seen as the gateway to immortality appears in both cases to be not just, as in Horace's 'Exegi monumentum,' the work of art itself, but the imaginative process involved in creating it. In other words, both Lodge and Tóibín here do not foreground the world that is made, but the process of 'worldmaking' in itself, the fact of being creatively active. At the same time, though, both authors also reflect on their own present literary, i.e. biographical activity, investigating into the relationship between literature and reality.

2.5 The 'Truth of Fiction' and the 'Truth of Fact'

Addressing themselves to the contrast between the 'truth of fiction' and the 'truth of fact,' Lodge and Tóibín in a final self-reflexive turn simultaneously investigate the specious opposition of 'fiction' and 'biography.' In *Author, Author*, Lodge lets James intone a bitter strike against conventional biography, in which the voice of the author himself is hardly disguised: "There is no privacy, no decency any more. Journalists, interviewers, biographers—they're parasites, locusts, they strip every leaf. The art we lavish—the pains we take—to create imaginary worlds—is wasted on them. They care only for trivial fact" (*AA* 87).[15] While James caricatured the biographer's unquenchable thirst for sensational facts in his novella *The Aspern Papers*, to which *Author, Author* and *The Master* make generous reference, James' 'biographers' Lodge and Tóibín evade sensationalist pitfalls by highlighting the 'truth of fiction.' As far as worldmaking, biography, and fiction are concerned, they adopt a stance that strongly resembles those of both Nelson Goodman and C.K. Stead. James's self appears to be composed and supplemented by his fiction, because, as Tóibín muses in *The Master*, "each book he had written, each scene described or character created, had become an aspect of him, had entered into his driven spirit and lay there much as the years themselves" (287). For conclusions

---

15 Ironically of course, Lodge in this novel functions as a biographer himself.

concerning James's life and personality, both 'biographers' therefore not only rely on documentary sources, but do at least the same degree draw on James's fiction.

As a prime example for the intricate link between the author and his work, Lodge and Tóibín refer to James's late story "The Beast in the Jungle." *Author, Author* practically begins with that story being mentioned, whereas *The Master* ends with James planning to write it. The story's plot, as Tóibín sums it up, is quite simple: the Protagonist "tells a woman of his unknown catastrophe and she becomes his greatest friend, but what he does not see is that his failure to believe in her, his own coldness, is the catastrophe, it has come already, it has lived within him all along" (*TM* 355). This strongly autobiographical story, which deals with the failure to love and really engage in human relationships, represents the very core of both novels. Tóibín links this failure, which he illustrates with James's flawed relationship to Alice James, Minnie Temple, and Constance Fenimore Woolson, to James's professional need for solitude. Lodge stresses the connection between art and human failure even more strongly, when he quotes Madame Flaubert writing to her son: "'*Your mania for sentences has dried up your heart*'" (*AA* 211). In the guise of his fiction, James thus seems to have given a more truthful account of himself than in his carefully phrased and reticent letters, many and probably the most intimate of which—those to Woolson—he destroyed anyway.

Still, neither Lodge nor Tóibín attempt to reconstruct a single 'true' version of James's world. To phrase it in Nelson Goodman's terms: They simply build up different world-versions which, within the frame of reference provided by existing biographical documents, are all 'true.' They enforce the 'truth of fiction' not only by writing fictional biographies, but also by insinuating that a work of fiction, "The Beast in the Jungle," gives the 'truest,' if very compressed and abstract, account of James' life. In *The Master*, the 'truth of fiction' has even found both a colourful and powerful emblem in an ancient, but artificially restored tapestry in which James admires "the pure delicacy of the colouring, the bright threads working against the faded, the texture suggesting a vast realm long gone" (139). Acknowledging the self-sufficient and beautiful 'truth' of this restored and therefore 'fictionalised' work of art, he buys it against the better advice of an expert who looks for 'the real thing': "'It was made to fool us all,' Lady Wolseley said. 'It's quite striking, quite beautiful,' Henry said" (*TM* 139). As far as the truth of biography is concerned, David Lodge and Colm Tóibín therefore conform perfectly to the credo A.S. Byatt has her fictional poet Randolph Ash state in her novel *Possession*: "Art tells a truth, sweet girl, though all her tales/Are lies i'the law-court, or the chemist's phial—/We must be artful for the spirit's truth" (409). Ultimately, all these authors thus reiterate what Goodman argued regarding the validity of different 'ways of worldmaking': that "in a poem or novel, metaphorical or allegorical truth may matter more, for even a literally false statement may be metaphorically true [...] and may mark or make new associations and discriminations, change emphases, effect exclusions and additions" (18). The vogue which fictional (auto-)biographies currently enjoy in English-speaking countries sustains the validity of Goodman's insight.

3. English Fictional (Auto-)Biographies at the Turn of the 21st Century

The renewed interest in biography and fictional (meta-)biography has been variously linked to the author's stubborn resistance against death. In fact, as a literary subject, the author is sprightly alive, since many of the more recent fictional biographies characteristically focus on writers (see Harvey 75). For instance, J.M. Coetzee's *The Master of Petersburg* (1994) depicts the life of Fyodor Dostoevsky in the year 1869, C.K. Stead's *Mansfield* (2004) concentrates on the famous writer from New Zealand, and within only a few years, four authors have chosen Henry James as their biographical subject.[16] *Author, Author* and *The Master* as well as *The Master of Petersburg* and *Mansfield* are not written in the same vein as prototypical fictional metabiographies like Barnes's *Flaubert's Parrot* or Ackroyd's *Chatterton*, which are characterised by a high degree of metabiographical reflection. Still, they contain metafictional elements in the widest sense. Rather than raising issues concerning the writing of biographies, though, all of them pose vital questions linked to the condition of authorship. Coetzee's *The Master of Petersburg* depicts Dostoevsky in a critical phase of his life, when he is pursued by his creditors while struggling with his next novel. C.K. Stead's novel describes Mansfield's complicated and difficult personal life during the First World War and shows her finding her own style as an artist. *The Master* and particularly *Author, Author*, finally, both incorporate two very difficult stages of Henry James's life as an author: his failure at establishing himself as a dramatist and his complex relationship

---

16 In addition to the two novels discussed here, these are Emma Tennant in *Felony* (2002) and the South-African Michiel Heyns in his still unpublished "The Typewriter's Tale" (see Saunders 121). As further examples of recent fictional biographies dealing with writers, Lodge names Emma Tennant's *The Ballad of Sylvia and Ted* (2001), Penelope Fitzgerald's *The Blue Flower* (1996), Michael Cunningham's *The Hours* (1999), Malcolm Bradbury's *To the Hermitage* (2000), Beryl Bainbridge's *According to Queeney* (2001), Edmund White's *Fanny: A Fiction* (2003), Kate Moses's *Wintering* (2003), Alberto Manguel's *Stevenson Under the Palm Trees* (2004), Andrew Motion's *The Invention of Doctor Cake* (2004) and Julian Barnes's *Arthur & George* (2005).

with Constance Fenimore Woolson. In short, all of these fictional biographies show their author-subjects in situations where they are at odds with their personal and their professional world.

With respect to biography, metafictional self-reflexivity therefore seems to have shifted from meta-biographical towards more general aesthetic and authorial questions in recent years. A significant number of contemporary fictional biographies do not engage in postmodernist play with different versions of the reconstructed world, but assert the 'truth of fiction' and stage the condition of authorship as such. It might therefore be adequate to apply the term 'biographical metafiction' specifically to fictional biographies which do not address metabiographical, but purely metafictional problems. Since these are closely linked to the condition and functioning of authorship, they might even be referred to as 'meta-authorial' problems.

In spite of their abstract focus, though, novels like *Author, Author* and *The Master* allow various readings. The ideal reader of fictional biographies should be able to weigh the tension between what is 'fact' and what is 'fiction' and to identify the intertextual references that are embedded in the texts. Still, the general appeal of these novels consists precisely in the fact that they provide their readers with different ways of 'worldmaking.' They can be read on an abstract level as a reflection on what authorship means, but they are also compelling page-turners. In other words: They are adaptable to different subjectivities. The pronounced interest in (fictional) biography over the last couple of years, which has prompted Justin Kaplan to state that we live in a 'Culture of Biography,' may be due to the fact that this genre allows its readers to witness and imaginatively live other, allegedly real lives and to experience other ways of 'worldmaking' in the sense of understanding the world. To some degree, fictional biography even satisfies a need similar to that of reality TV. It provides its readers with an account of other subjectivities. It seems that being confronted with different cognitive preconditions and ethical standards is an integral part of self-construction. Particularly internal focalisation makes readers experience 'life' from a different angle, virtually through the eyes of another person. The exploration of 'the other' which this method entails is only one of several characteristics recent fictional biographies share with the contemporary novel in English.

Many recent English novels are a blend of factual and fictional discourse, whether it be fictional biographies like those named above, fictional diaries (Zoë Heller, *Notes on a Scandal*, 2003; M.J. Hyland, *Carry Me Down*, 2006), confessions (A.L. Kennedy, *Paradise*, 2004; Graham Swift, *Tomorrow*, 2007) or memoirs (J.M. Coetzee, *Youth*, 2002; John Banville, *The Sea*, 2005; James Robertson, *The Testament of Gideon Mack*, 2006). As Ansgar Nünning remarks, the "proliferation of hybrid genres located on the borderline between factual and fictional biography bears witness to the fact that the conventional dichotomy between 'fact' and 'fiction' has of late been called into question" ("Fictional Metabiographies" 198). More specifically, all of these hybrid, in the widest sense of the word '(auto-)biographical' works bear witness to a heightened interest in subjectivity, ways of worldmaking, perception and 'truth,' which points towards a revival of modernist aesthetics in contemporary English fiction in both form and content. While the recourse to factual genres underlines their claim on 'truth,' many of these novels are told by highly unreliable first-person narrators. In accordance with the premises of modernism, the issue of epistemological and ethical 'truth' is thus at once foregrounded and questioned (see A. Nünning "Fictional Metabiographies" 244–45; 254–55; V. Nünning "Experiments with Ethics," "How can you say?", "Ethics and Aesthetics"). Obviously, this renewed interest in modernism is part of a more widespread cultural phenomenon. For instance, the question "Is Modernity Our Antiquity?" was the first of the designated leitmotifs of the documenta 12 in 2007.[17] Therefore, it does not come as a surprise that this revival of modernist aesthetics and concerns characterises not only the contemporary English novel, but also many recent fictional (auto-)biographies: Characteristically, the majority of the latter focus on writers who are directly or indirectly concerned with modernism, whether it be Henry James in *Author, Author*, *The Master*, and *Felony*, Sir Arthur Conan Doyle in *Arthur & George*, Fyodor Dostoevsky in *The Master of Petersburg* or Katherine Mansfield in *Mansfield* (see Bauder-Begerow and Lusin 243–44).

A reading of twenty-first-century English fictional (auto-)biographies from the point of view of Nelson Goodman's 'ways of worldmaking' foregrounds the most interesting aspects of this genre. Goodman's theory draws attention to the ways in which fictional (auto-)biographies, particularly those about authors, illustrate and examine the many-layered process involved in the worldmaking power of narrative. In C.K. Stead's *The Secret History of Modernism*, another hybrid novel, this powerful capacity of narrative worldmaking comes clearly to the fore:

> Life, more like a very long novel […], falls into discrete but interlocking narratives, and narratives break into scenes. That's how we hold on to 'what happens,' how we process it, extracting and ordering the essentials and ridding ourselves of the copiousness of impression and sensation. Memory, if we didn't contain it, would destroy us. (18)

---

17 See the documenta's official website for the year 2007: <http://www.documenta12.de/leitmotive.html?&L=1>.

The hybrid novels mentioned in this article thus highlight the epistemological and ethical qualities of narrative, negotiating the tension between the 'truth of fact' and the 'truth of fiction.' Ultimately, they show their authors seeking to achieve knowledge via the very process of narrative worldmaking. Consequently, they imply, one might even say enact, the answer to one of Goodman's central concerns, the question: "how is worldmaking related to knowing?" (Goodman 1) Pursuing this question, David Lodge and Colm Tóibín have impressively proved that a single name can, as C.K. Stead put it in *The Secret History of Modernism*, really conjure up a whole multifarious world.

References

Ackroyd, Peter. *Chatterton*. London: Hamish Hamilton, 1987.
Banville, John. *The Sea*. London: Picador, 2005.
Bauder-Begerow, Irina, and Caroline Lusin. "Der englische Roman zu Beginn des 21. Jahrhunderts: Ian McEwan." *Der zeitgenössische englische Roman: Genres - Entwicklungen - Modellinterpretationen*. Eds. Vera Nünning, and Caroline Lusin. Trier: WVT. 243–59.
Barnes, Julian. *Flaubert's Parrot*. London: Jonathan Cape, 1984.
—. *Arthur & George*. 2005. London: Vintage, 2006.
Bradbury, Malcolm. *Mensonge*. 1987. Harmondsworth: Penguin, 1993.
Bruner, Jerome, ed. "Nelson Goodman's Worlds." *Actual Minds, Possible Worlds*. Cambridge, MA/London: Harvard UP, 1986. 93–105.
Byatt, Antonia S. *Possession*. London: Vintage, 1990.
—. *The Biographer's Tale*. London: Chatto & Windus, 2000.
Coetzee, John M. *Youth*. London: Secker & Warburg, 2002.
—. *The Master of Petersburg*. London: Secker & Warburg, 1994.
Documenta12: "Leitmotifs." Ed. Roger M. Buergel. 2005. 18 March 2010 <http://www.documenta12.de/leitmotive.html?&L=1>.
Goodman, Nelson. *Ways of Worldmaking*. 1978. Indianapolis: Hackett Publishing, 1992.
Gosse, Edmund. "Biography." *The Encyclopaedia Britannica*. 1910–1911.
Guignery, Vanessa. "David Lodge's *Author, Author* and the Genre of the Biographical Novel." *Études Anglaises* 60.2 (2007): 160–72.
Hannah, Daniel. "The Private Life, the Public Stage: Henry James in Recent Fiction." *Journal of Modern Literature* 30.3 (2007): 70–94.
Harvey, John. "Lessons of the Master: The Henry James Novel." *Yearbook of English Studies* 37.1(2007): 75–88.
Heller, Zoë. *Notes on a Scandal*. London: Penguin, 2003.
Hyland, Maria J. *Carry Me Down*. Edinburgh: Canongate, 2006.
Kaplan, Justin. "A Culture of Biography." *The Literary Biography: Problems and Solutions*. Ed. Dale Salwak. Houndsmills/Basingstoke/London: Macmillan, 1996. 1–11.
Kennedy, Alison L. *Paradise*. London: Jonathan Cape, 2004.
Lodge, David. *Author, Author*. 2004. London: Penguin, 2005.

Lowdon, Claire. "Screwing Henry James (Into a Novel)." *The Owl Journal* 6 (2005): 8–10.

Maack, Annegret. "Die Weiterentwicklung der fiktiven Biographie bei A.S. Byatt." *Radikalität und Mäßigung: Der englische Roman seit 1960*. Eds. Annegret Maack, and Rüdiger Imhof. Darmstadt: Wissenschaftliche Buchgesellschaft, 1993. 183–87.

McEwan, Ian. *Saturday*. 2005. London: Vintage, 2006.

Nadel, Ira Bruce. *Biography: Fiction, Fact and Form*. London/Basingstoke: Macmillan, 1984.

Nünning, Ansgar. "'How do we seize the past?' Julian Barnes' fiktionale Metabiographie *Flaubert's Parrot* als Paradigma historiographischer und biographischer Metafiktion." *Literatur in Wissenschaft und Unterricht* 31.2 (1998): 145–71.

—. "An Intertextual Quest for Thomas Chatterton: The Deconstruction of the Romantic Cult of Originality and of the Paradoxes of 'Life-Writing' in Peter Ackroyd's Fictional Metabiography *Chatterton*." *Biofictions: The Rewriting of Romantic Lives in Contemporary Fiction and Drama*. Eds. Martin Middeke, and Werner Huber. Rochester, NY: Camden House, 1999. 27–49.

—. "Von der fiktionalen Metabiographie zur biographischen Metafiktion: Prolegomena zu einer Theorie, Typologie und Funktionsgeschichte eines hybriden Genres." *Fakten und Fiktionen: Strategien fiktionalbiographischer Dichterdarstellungen in Roman, Drama und Film seit 1970*. Ed. Christian von Zimmermann. Tübingen: Gunter Narr, 2000. 15–36.

—. "Fictional Metabiographies and Metaautobiographies: Towards a Definition, Typology and Analysis of Self-Reflexive Hybrid Metaagenres." *Self-Reflexivity in Literature*. Eds. Werner Huber, Martin Middeke, and Hubert Zapf. Würzburg: Königshausen & Neumann, 2005. 195–209.

—. "Fiktionale Auto/Biographien und Metabiographien: Peter Ackroyds *Chatterton*." *Handbuch zeitgenössischer englischer Roman: Gattungen – AutorInnen – Modellinterpretationen*. Eds. Vera Nünning, and Caroline Lusin. Trier: WVT, 2007. 83–100.

Nünning, Vera. "Experiments with Ethics in Contemporary British Fiction: The Lack of a Stable Framework." *The Ethical Component in Experimental British Fiction since the 1960s*. Eds. Susan Onega, and Jean-Michel Ganteau. Newcastle: Cambridge Scholars Publishing, 2007. 210–31.

—. "'How can you say they're like you and me?' Ethics and Unreliability in Contemporary British Fiction." *'On the Turn': The Ethics of Fiction in Contemporary Narrative in English*. Eds. Bárbara Arizti Martín, and Silvia Martínez Falquina. Newcastle: Cambridge Scholars Publishing, 2007. 327–41.

—. "Ethics and Aesthetics in British Novels at the Beginning of the 21st Century." *Ethics in Culture: The Dissemination of Value through Literature and Other Media*. Eds. Astrid Erll, and Herbert Grabes. Berlin/New York: De Gruyter, 2008. 369–92.

Olsson, Anders. "The Broken Place: Memory, Language, Tradition, and Storytelling in Colm Tóibín's Texts." *Recovering Memory: Irish Representations of Past and Present*. Eds. Hedda Friberg, and Irene Gilsenan Nordin. Newcastle upon Tyne: Cambridge Scholars, 2007. 128–48.

Robertson, James. *The Testament of Gideon Mack*. London: Hamish Hamilton, 2006.

Rose, Phyllis. "Biography as Fiction." *Tri-Quarterly* 55 (1982): 111–24.

Saunders, Max. "Master Narratives." *Cambridge Quarterly* 37.1 (2008): 121–31.

Schabert, Ina. *In Quest of the Other Person: Fiction as Biography*. Tübingen: Franke, 1990.

Stead, Christian K. *The Secret History of Modernism: A Novel*. 2001. London: Vintage, 2003.
—. *Mansfield: A Novel*. London: Vintage, 2004.
Tennant, Emma. *Felony*. London: Jonathan Cape, 2002.
Tóibín, Colm. *The Master*. 2004. London/Basingstoke/Oxford: Picador, 2005.
—. "Henry James for Venice." *The Henry James Review* 27.1 (2006): 192–201.
Tonkin, Boyd. "Artist in the Goldfish Bowl." *The Independent* 27 Aug. 2004. 18 Mar 2010 <http://www.independent.co.uk/arts-entertainment/books/features/david-lodge-artist-in-the-goldfish-bowl-557874.html?cmp=ilc-n>.

Fictional Narratives and Their Ways of Spiritual Worldmaking: (De-)Constructing the Realm of Transcendence in *City of God* by Way of Metafiction and Multiperspectivity

HANNA BINGEL

1. Introduction: Religious Faith and Its Narrative Expression

The analysis of literary ways of worldmaking is an intricate undertaking as readers of fiction are faced with an overwhelming diversity of realities. The construction of spiritual worlds, however, surely poses a challenge as one tries to get a grip on the literary imagination of the invisible realm of transcendence, a realm that is truer for some than for others. The theme of religion and faith in God has always been prominent in literature. Numerous novels portray a search for God, the divine, or ultimate meaning, thus posing a challenge to a postmodernist rejection of religious belief in a form of being that reaches beyond the human world. In recent literature, however, we encounter a rather hesitant and uncertain engagement with religious thought and assumptions.[1] Rather than striving for a nostalgic 'enchantment' with reality, contemporary texts undermine an outright affirmation of faith. Many of them draw attention to the constructed nature of religion by raising questions of how transcendental worlds are manifested within and created through the stories of God we tell in order to articulate and clarify the sense of our lives. Revising, and often demystifying the old categories of ontotheology, these literary texts redirect our attention from timeless truth to the centrality of language and narrative. They thus seem to correspond closely with Nelson Goodman's claim that

---

[1] It is important to stress, however, that uncertainty of faith and unbelief are by no means a specificity of postmodern literature. In the modern period, many writers in the US-American tradition "treated religious belief as something that was either 'lost' or rendered irrelevant" (Lundin xx). Among the most famous 19th-century authors whose writings give expression of their grappling with God and religious heritage are Herman Melville, Emily Dickinson, and Nathaniel Hawthorne.

there is no pure or given world but only world versions generated within the symbolic activities of the subject in a particular time and place.[2] And this, of course, has an effect on the formal and aesthetic appearance of fiction writing and its investigation of religious worlds.

This essay pursues the question of how literary texts, as highly condensed narratives, are at work in forming, ordering, valuing and negotiating sets of belief. Whereas Goodman discusses at length how different types of activities create different versions of the world, little has been said about the narrative and literary processes that go into spiritual worldmaking. As Jacob A. Belzen,[3] Wesley A. Kort, and Paul Ricœur among others have stressed, narrative is not merely one symbolic form among others for the expression of the religious, but a primary mode of bringing home what is presumed to lie outside the human world. Surely, from a religious perspective, God is not a mere narrative. For the believer the supernatural is, in fact, associated with ultimate reality that reaches beyond discursive constructions. Given that narratives can never fully cover what is felt to be religious, they certainly play a central part in establishing culturally admissible forms of matters of faith and transcendence. They are, as is repeatedly stressed throughout this volume, a very powerful way of worldmaking.

There are essential features of narrative that make it particularly relevant to religious beliefs. To begin with, it is apparent that, unlike abstract theology, narratives do not primarily contain speculative metaphysical thought or theological argumentation. As Jerome Bruner states "[n]arratives are about people acting in a setting, and the happenings that befall them must be relevant […] to their beliefs, desires, theories, values, and so on" (7). The significance of narratives, then, lies in the ability to give expression to the so-called religious experience enabling the human being to give an account of his or her feelings of awe, fear, love, and dependency on 'something beyond.' It is imperative to stress, however, that narratives neither simply represent the religious experience, nor can they be regarded as a neutral container of some religious or theological content. Rather, they generate versions of the self's world in most productive ways. By couching events, states, feelings, and thoughts in causal-teleological order with a beginning, a middle, and an end, narratives impose order and meaning on contingent experience and establish meaningful connections,

---

2   This thesis is, of course, most comprehensively conducted in his famous book *Ways of Worldmaking*.

3   In his essay, Belzen points out: "For, whatever religion may be besides this, it is in any case also a reservoir of verbal elements, stories, interpretations, prescriptions and commandments which in their power to determine experience and conduct and in their legitimization possess narrative character" (241–42).

which renders reality intelligible to the subject (see Ricœur 241). Much of narrative worldmaking, then, derives from this configurational act of narrating where temporally and thematically diverse elements are gathered and joined together to form a meaningful whole (see Neumann).

Moreover, what makes narrative attractive as a mode for religious world construction is that they offer a place where subjective experience and the self's imagination of God is joined to overarching sacred stories that are particular of a specific religion. This aspect is well expressed by Stephen Crites who points out that "the sacred story forms the very consciousness that projects a total world horizon" (70). In this world of consciousness the self that is oriented to it creates in turn its own story. The performative force of sacred stories is notably exerted by narrative devices such as schemata, scripts, images, or plot which serve as a frame of reference for individual and communal storytelling. Consider, for example, the close connection between the self's narrative and the biblical stories in the spiritual autobiography. Here, the narrator envisages and identifies with figures from the bible, handling his own situation by re-enacting essential parts of the saints' stories (see Lerner). The self-narration is thus performed in the light of sacred stories that prefigure reality for the believer and shape the way s/he constructs a meaningful world.

In view of this transformation into narrative and language, therefore, the 'religious experience'—whatever this controversial notion may be in its essence[4]—finally has an aesthetic dimension: emplotment, tropes, metaphors, and genre patterns are essential aesthetic characteristics of religious narratives, which operate within a culture and determine the way the individual and collective think and speak of the 'divine,' the 'transcendental,' or the 'ultimate.'

It is this interdependence of narrative, aesthetic, and the religious, which is most consciously explored in literature. Against assumptions that literary narratives merely imitate existing versions of spiritual worldmaking, one should assert that they themselves originate essential aspects that cannot be expressed by other symbolic modes or activities, such as art, film, or theatrical performance. Literary texts closely interact with other stories of faith, weaving together narratives already in circulation and

---

4 Paul Ricœur points out the possibilities and limits of interpreting the spiritual by investigating its textual expression. He emphasises that analysing the discourse of religion does not say "that language, that linguistic expression, is the only dimension of the religious phenomenon; nothing is said—either pro or con—concerning the controversial notion of religious experience, whether we understand experience in a cognitive, a practical, or an emotional sense. What is said is only this: whatever ultimately may be the nature of the so-called religious experience, it comes to language, it is articulated in a language, and the most appropriate place to interpret it on its own term is to inquire into its linguistic expression" (35).

imaginatively configuring them into new concepts of religious reality. The close relation of religion, narrative, and literature raises the question of how exactly literary texts create transcendental worlds and how their role within a culture and its overarching belief horizons can be defined. I will address this subject matter on a basic level, trying to pinpoint the distinctive features of the fictional text that specifically contribute to construing the religious. These features, as will be shown, distinguish the fictional expression of the religious from other kinds of religious narratives (in a narrow sense). The examination of the fictional discourse and its narrativisation of sacred universe has become even more urgent, given that since 'the narrative' has become the focus of interest of both the literary scholar and the theologian, the notion has become an umbrella term for a great variety of different types of texts. This has resulted in confusing methodological and terminological interferences in analyses of narrative articulations of religious belief (see Stroup 424), which fail to grasp the discourse-specific modes and functions of texts mediating the religious.

The essay comes in three parts: First, I will review the current state of research concerning the relation of narrative and religious experience, which will involve a short excursion into theology and religious studies. I will then turn to the literary discourse illustrating the unique potential of the fiction text to construe innovative models of faith in God. Finally, I will analyse the novel *City of God* by Edgar L. Doctorow (2001 [2000]) illustrating some of the literary discourse strategies the novel exploits to explore the interdependence of narrative, religious experience, and world construction in an experimental manner.

2. Narrative and Religious Experience in Current Theories and Research

It is one of the leading premises of social studies and religious criticism that religion—like any other cultural phenomena—does not simply happen or merely exist, but finds its shape in social and cultural contexts. In their examination of the faith-constituting mechanisms, which shape and produce religious beliefs and attitudes, scholars have predominantly put the focus on institutional factors such as congregations, hierarchies, special interests, academies, and public rituals. In these studies, the category of narrative as an essential mode for representing and construing the religious has been largely ignored (see Belzen; Yamane).

The relationship between narrative and religious experience has been examined in greater detail by representatives of theology. It is here that the two disparate research areas of narrative and religion have been recently brought together: over the last few decades, theologians have entered into a productive exchange with literary and linguistic studies increasingly engaging with the assumption that religious faith may be identified on the basis of the narrative structure employed. Acknowledging the narrative form in which religious faith is proclaimed, and indeed constructed, theology has shifted its focus away from Christology, ecclesiology, or systematic metaphysical thinking to the narrative representation of faith, from a concept-oriented and systematic approach to theological questions to the language of the religious (see Eisen 14). This approval of the concept of narrative has been encouraged by a growing uneasiness concerning the academic norm of a detached speaking and writing of God. The postmodern era, with its "valuing of multiple ways of knowing" (McMinn and Hall 251), has fostered this turn away from 'solid' theological analysis, based on rationality, logic, and proposition, towards an interpretative and experiential understanding of religion and faith in a divine being as proposed by narrative and stories (see McMinn and Hall).

The narrative paradigm has given birth to a branch of what has become known as 'narrative theology,' a field that is rather diverse (see Stroup). The common interest, however, is the literary exegesis of religious narrative, in particular the biblical text collection. Whereas formerly the focus was put on an historical-critical analysis, bible exegetes have started to study the bible as a poetic text, a narrative which figures God and spiritual worlds by way of literary and rhetoric devices. Many of these studies emerging at the interface of literary criticism, narratology, and bible exegesis offer insightful analysis as they have reached an interpretative understanding of how texts generate spiritual worlds by identifying their rhetorical and grammatical characteristics. However, given that these studies show no particular interest in other kinds of literature than the biblical texts, their connectivity is limited.

The study of religious narratives has been given new impetus by the philosopher and theologian Paul Ricœur. In giving a brief summary of his approach I wish to show those interfaces of theology and literary studies that are also relevant for transcendental worldmaking in fictional narrative. Ricœur renders more complex phrases such as 'the narrative construction of God' by introducing discourse analysis into the interpretation of texts dealing with the religious phenomenon. He distinguishes between different literary genres such as prophecies, hymns, prayers, liturgies, legislative texts, proverbs, wisdom sayings and liturgical formula. Ricœur is not so much concerned with genre as a mode of classification, but as a means of production and of creating order. In order to emphasise their "*generative* function" (Ricœur 37–38), he therefore prefers to apply the notion of discourse to these different texts arguing that the theological content of each of it is determined by the literary form employed to mediate religious understanding. By way of genre-specific linguistic and literary codes each discourse produces a particular theology: "Throughout [them] God appears differently each time, sometimes as the hero of a saving act, sometimes as wrathful and compassionate, sometimes as the one to whom one can speak in a relation of an I-Thou type" (Ricœur 41). The scriptural figuration of the divine thus fundamentally depends on the genre employed by the biblical writers. Each discourse is a component within a manifold net of significations referring to 'God,' the 'transcendental,' or the 'religious.' In this net each of the discourses fulfils a specific function within the bible as a whole.

By applying discourse analysis to the bible, Ricœur opens up the examination of how texts create models of religious realities for a study of contemporary literature. He draws attention to the fact that each mode of discourse works in specific ways in their reference to the divine while following its own structural and epistemic logic. In this dynamic relationship of content, form, and context, each discourse has specific potentials to signify the religious. The subsequent enquiry into spiritual worldmaking in literature is thus led by the question of how the literary discourse transforms the religious experience into narrative text according to discourse-specific rules allotted to it in the contemporary context in which it is produced.

3. The Literary Negotiation of God and Transcendence

The contemporary discourse of literature differs in its various forms and functions from other types of religious narratives. It engenders versions of the religious on its own terms, as it operates within a specific symbolic system. As Hubert Zapf puts it, literature is a powerful agent in a culture not primarily because of its contents, but because it generates "a distinctive form of textuality, which only gains its specific, culturally indispensable function through its aesthetic transformation of cultural experience"[5] ("Das Funktionsmodell der Literatur" 67, my translation). However, surprisingly little research has been dedicated to examining fiction writing and its religious world construction. This is even more curious when we consider that the narrative turn has not only brought about significant changes in the theories and methods of theology, but also to the status of

---

5   "[L]iteratur [stellt] eine ökologische Kraft innerhalb ihrer Kulturwelt nicht primär aufgrund ihrer Inhalte [dar...], sondern aufgrund ihrer Herausbildung als einer unverwechselbaren Form der Textualität, die erst in ihrer ästhetischen Transformation kultureller Erfahrung ihre besondere, kulturell unverzichtbare Funktion gewinnt" ("Das Funktionsmodell der Literatur" 67, my translation).

fictional texts in questions of God and transcendence. How, then, can the intricate relationship between narrative, literature, and the religious be captured in order to understand the productive quality of literary discourse for the making of transcendental worlds?

In what follows, emphasis will be placed on the observation that the twentieth century—with its turn away from overarching metaphysical systems of thought to individual narrative and storytelling—has produced a mode of fiction writing that very consciously explores this interdependence of narrative patterns and the human imagination of the sacred, with some representatives of this mode vigorously writing against any established scripting of the religious imagination. Novels make use of a broad range of literary strategies to (de-)construct, rearrange, or affirm narrative schemes that lie underneath the human stories about God and kinds of belief. I wish to show some specific aspects of literary discourse dealing with the religious in order to highlight its potential to schematise novel relationships between the common experience and the narrative expression of religious imagination. I consider three aspects to be decisively relevant to an analysis of spiritual world construction in fictional texts. These aspects are depragmatisation, self-reflexivity, and interdiscursiveness. The elaboration of these criteria not only forms the basis for the subsequent analysis of the novel *City of God*, but also highlights crucial differences between religious texts and fiction texts dealing with the spiritual, which, as will be explained further on, may be usefully called 'fictions of spirituality.'

To begin with, the literary exploration of the religious differs from other narratives in that the fictional text is not primarily bound to pragmatic purposes. It is released from any assertive, didactic, and descriptive relation to the extra-literary world. Rather than depicting the world in a straightforward, descriptive manner, the text is enabled to configure reality under the guidance of the imaginary and the possible. Hubert Zapf in "Literature as Cultural Ecology" has coined the term of 'depragmatisation' in order to define the structural conditions that allow the fictional text to investigate a given reality in an explorative and speculative way. Depragmatisation "enables the aestheticising distancing of real-world experiences and at the same time makes possible their imaginative exploration" ("Literature as Cultural Ecology" 87). In a similar vein, Paul Ricœur argues that "it is this distanciation of the real from itself […] that fiction introduces into our apprehension of reality" (43). According to Ricœur, the explorative and imaginary aspect of fiction writing may obtain a religious dimension when the literary imagination generates new metaphors which become a viable tool for the imagination of God. Here, the metaphorical imagination of fiction is made an ally for the understanding and articulation of faith. Ricœur claims that the textual figuration of the world has the potential to reveal dimensions of the human condition not understood before. He attributes a revelatory power to fiction, which unfolds when the 'world of the text' engages with the 'world of the reader.' This encounter may cause a productive clash when the world figured by the text runs against the reader's own understanding of self and the world. The reader might inhabit the world proposed projecting her "'ownmost' possibilities" into it. This is why through fiction "new possibilities of being-in-the-world" (42) are opened up; it is the reality of the 'possible.'

A second implication of the aspect of depragmatisation may be described with what Jerome Bruner has called the "'breach' component of the narrative" (12). Whereas religious narratives such as the sermon or confessional texts function to build consensus among the religious group, a fictional text may subvert the patterns the religious community has chosen as a common ground and thus rupture common assumptions about the nature of 'God,' the 'transcendental,' or the 'sacred.' The aspect of depragmatisation allows the text to go beyond the conventional and to offer new expressions of the religious. Through breaches of the canonical, literary storytelling may therefore challenge the content of sacred texts and problematise the implicit rules that construct official narrative (see also Disch 6). Bruner explains that the 'breach' component of the narrative is what makes storytelling an innovative activity. Quoting Tzvetan Todorov, he goes on to argue that to engage in the literary invention of a new reality is, indeed, not so much to propose new plots as to challenge and problematise the previously familiar and to confront the reader with fresh interpretative activities (Bruner 12–13).

Alternative realities in fiction are not only constituted by way of breaches in canonicity. The imaginative creation of spiritual worlds is also essentially linked with the function of the literary text as 'reintegrative inter-discourse' (see Link, "Literatur als Interdiskursanalyse"). Michael Titzmann describes a discourse as a mode of organising domains of knowledge in specific social contexts. The separation of the scientific and the theological discourses is characteristic of the modern era, each of them holding a specific set of premises, questions, and rules of thinking and speaking. Deliberate attempts to cross these discourse borders create clashes and irritation within the coordination system of the post-enlightenment era, as the US-American debate on intelligent science and creation theory demonstrates. Whereas the formation of different kinds of discourse is constitutive for creating the symbolic order in a culture, the discursive configuration of cultural reality may result in conflicting ways of worldmaking: For the specialist, to demand full authority is to claim that his world is not only one version among others, but the only real one. The doctrine of the scientist and that of the theologian thus sound alike, both claim their own version of the world as the only one correct (see also Goodman 20–21).

The conflict between religion and science is a major theme in US-American fiction. Literature, however, is free to explore the God question in various discursive contexts and can thus work against the specialist's tendency to fabricate his world by objectivising data and reducing it to a one-dimensional explanation. As Link emphasises, literature does not represent specialised knowledge, but integrates different kinds of logic by means of inter-discursive elements, ranging from stereotyped characters, to collective symbols, to narrative schemata (e.g. myth), to themes, problems, or arguments in the widest sense (Link, "Diskursive Ereignisse, Diskurse, Interdiskurse" 154–55). The function of such elements not only lies in generalising and integrating selective knowledge for subjects in everyday life context (Link, "Diskursive Ereignisse, Diskurse, Interdiskurse" 155), but they also allow the text to select and edit postulations a culture considers mutually exclusive. Consider, for instance, Updike's *Roger's Version* (1986). The plot of the novel revolves around a dispute between Roger Lambert, a professor of theology, and Dale Kohler, a student of computer sciences, who by means of technology wants to prove that God created the world, no less. The choice of character allows the novel to integrate the specialised discourse of the theologian as well as of that of the scientist. Unlike an intellectual treatise, however, Updike's novel does not simply elaborate on the tension-loaded confrontation of science, theology, and religious faith. It is one of the salient characteristics of the text that the theme of search for the 'right' version of the world is ridiculed by the way the story is mediated through the unreliable first-person narrator. The medium-specific device of unreliable narration brings to the fore the role of subjective imagination in the processes that constitute reality. The novel thus creates a fictive world where the culturally given boundaries between 'subjective belief' and 'scientific objective knowledge' are undermined. In doing so, it self-consciously reflects on the possibilities and limits of the human quest for truth, highlighting the way that truth eludes human rationality no matter how many interpretations and theories attempt to approach the God question.

In view of their inter-discursive construction of fictional worlds, literary texts thus have the potential to (re-)articulate a perception of reality that at a given time cannot be grasped though other forms of discourse, and requires equally that the reader as well probes the borders between a given and an imaginary reality. It is in this sense that one can understand Goodman's claim that "the arts must be taken no less seriously than the sciences as modes of discovery, creation, and enlargement of knowledge in the broad sense of advancement of the understanding, and thus that the philosophy of art should be conceived as an integral part of metaphysics and epistemology" (102).

Thirdly, fiction has the potential to reflect on itself to be a work of fiction, which is a discursive metamorphosis of reality rather than a deposit of some truth propositions. The self-reflexive dimension is unique to literary discourse and makes the fictional text fundamentally distinctive from other documents of faith. Documents of faith function to stabilise a community's belief in a reality more valuable and more reliable than the everyday world and advise people to depend on this reality. In contrast, self-reflexive fiction poses questions about the believers' reality, their religious commitment and trust in the 'other' world. The mode of aesthetic self-reflexivity is therefore a privileged tool of fiction to *un*make established worlds. In contemporary fiction dealing with religious subject matters, self-reflexivity tends to be aligned with a wish to expose how spiritual worlds are mediated and constituted in linguistic and literary expression (see also Detweiler 227). In drawing attention to its own constructivity a text may reveal that the relation between the text and the extra-textual world is not descriptive but inventive and transformative and that its construal of God is likewise the creative artefact of a storyteller. Accordingly, self-reflexive fiction encourages the reader to distanciate from an apprehension of reality s/he has grown accustomed to by drawing attention to the discursive forms and narrative processes that are conditional for his or her religious imagination. It is this shift in attention from the world 'behind' the text to the world *of* the text that can prompt a reconsideration of a given reality.

According to the insights gleaned from these reflections I can now clarify the genre term 'fictions of spirituality' introduced above. 'Fictions of spirituality' refer to these narratives that, over the last few decades, have increasingly turned to matters of faith and transcendence while tapping the full potential of the privileges of fiction writing in their construal of the religious, many of them very consciously exploring the interdependence of narrative processes, aesthetic devices, and faith in God. In 'fictions of spirituality,' the search for sense and meaning tends to be accompanied by a self-reflexive dimension: Novels such as *City of God* by E.L. Doctorow (2001), *Roger's Version* by John Updike (1986), *A Prayer for Owen Meany* by John Irving (1989), or *Gilead* by Marylinne Robinson (2004) explore religious subject matters on a meta-level drawing attention to how religious faith is constructed and unfolds in mutual exchange with a culture's stories of God and the sacred. In such literary narratives religious reality cannot be signified in an especially conclusive manner. And yet, in integrating, synthesising and rethinking prevalent religious ideas, experience, beliefs, and assumptions, they take part in the formation and restructuring of a culture's belief systems, and, in this engagement, educe new versions of religious imagination. It is in this sense that their role as both worldmakers and critics of transcendental worldmaking may be understood. Given the great variety in the content, forms and functions of contemporary literary narratives dealing with the God question, the term 'fictions of spirituality' seems to be decidedly useful as it covers the range from the religious novel at one end of the spectrum, to the novel that finally denies any transcendentally oriented world construction at the other. Hence, their defining feature is by no means a specifically religious world view, but rather lies in their extensive reference to and dynamic dialogue with the current discourses of the prevalent debates about 'God,' the 'spiritual,' and the 'sacred.'

4. Metafiction and Multiperspectivity in *City of God*

City of God (*CG*), published in 2000, is a remarkable example for the genre of 'fictions of spirituality.' It makes use of highly innovative narrative techniques in order to critically engage with the question of God while constructing its very specific theology. Like many representatives of US-American fiction, *City of God* shows a strong intertextual relationship with biblical narratives, the constitutive text collection of the Jewish and Christian faith traditions. The novel confirms the thesis that the exploration of biblical concepts of God in US-American literature is implicit or marginal, but often in a decidedly explicit and upfront way. The scholar of US-American religion and culture Mark Noll similarly states that the centrality of the Christian religion in US-American literature "has become even sharper and more powerful over the course of the 20th century, at the same time that the general culture has slipped more obviously beyond the control of Christian institution" (408). In their negotiating of the spiritual US-American novels oscillate between a reinforcement of the nation's religious heritage, deeply rooted in the biblical faith tradition, and an aspiration to achieve a new understanding of the spiritual in view of cultural change and development. This very presence of religious subject matters in US-American literature corresponds to the significant role of the Jewish and Christian religion in the United States, but also interrelates with a range of major, troublesome issues that are openly discussed and commented on, not only by representatives of the church, but also within the sphere of education, politics, and business: the validity of the bible, the linkage of science and religion, the role of the church in the political realm are repeatedly debated and ensure ongoing controversies between believers and non-believers, as well as within the great variety of the particular Jewish and Christian communities.

City of God reads as an experimental novel, in that ambiguity and self-reflexivity are the foundations of its negotiation of religious faith and God. In its spiritual search, the novel takes the reader through the last one hundred years of European and US-American history. In opening a vast window on a range of major events past and present, developments, and occurrences, the novel sets up the background of a vibrant US-America, which at the beginning of the twenty-first century is characterised by a vaster number of different world views, lifestyles, religions, and denominations than ever before in its history. The main plot of the novel revolves around main protagonist Thomas Pemberton, an Anglican reverend of a small Episcopal Church in New York. The reverend suffers from an intense crisis of faith, considering the conservative protestant faith tradition to be no longer compatible with reason. One day, Pemberton realises that the cross of his church has been stolen. The loss of the cross leads the troubled clergyman to Sarah Blumenthal und Joshua Gruen, a rabbinical couple of a Synagogue of Evolutionary Judaism on the Upper West Side. The Evolutionary Judaist teaching strives for an integration of newest scientific theories into faith in God and submits the bible to the historical-critical bible exegesis. The academic-theological discussions with the Jewish rabbis leave a deep impression on Pemberton and help him to find new spiritual ground, where he feels that mind, heart, and intellect are brought together. Finally, the Anglican preacher decides to convert from Christianity to Judaism.

The novel presents the storyline described above in a non-linear and fragmented way. The reader is required to navigate through the variety of themes and stories in order to recognise the plot of Pemberton's search for God that unfolds among the different chapters. The lack of a coherent configuration of a plot results from the novel's multiperspective structure that applies to the narrative situation as well as to the thematic and formal structure.[6] The novel contains a great number of first-person narrators and focalising characters, all of whom connect with the novel's underlying spiritual theme by pursuing these questions that lie at the heart of the human quest for sense and meaning: what is the purpose of life? What can be said about the origin of existence? Is there a world beyond our reality? And if there is a God, how do we understand God's role in our culture and history? The protagonists, each of them symbolising specific religious

---

6   For an introduction into the theory of multiperspectivity see Nünning and Nünning (39–78).

or theological standpoints, appear as representatives of different disciplines, as artists, historical witnesses, or simply as observers of everyday life occurrences. In addition to the multitude of narrators and characters, the novel holds many different types of text genres such as songs, tape recordings, historical documents, diary entries, emails, or official papers. The incorporation of the heterogeneous text material adds to the complexity of the perspective structure as the reader is not only challenged to follow the change of perspectives, but also to switch between different genres.

The unmediated juxtaposition of different perspectives creates a microcosm of independent worlds, all of them following a different logic in dealing with mankind's "wrecked romance with God" (*CG* 217). Since the individual standpoints swiftly alternate and hectically run one after the other, the novel does not offer any firm and positive statement about God. In contrast, the individual viewpoints relativise and at times undermine each other and hence leave the reader with a multi-angled evaluation of the question of God. In view of the rapid change of contrastive perspectives, the reader is held off from sympathising with an individual statement of belief but forced to engage with a multiperspective and highly controversial negotiation of theological and religious subject matters.

In addition to the plurality of standpoints the novel orchestrates the religious theme by placing the characters and narrators on different time levels. In diachronically distributing the perspectives over a time scale of about one hundred years the novel depicts the historical and socio-cultural background that has led to the theological predicaments that the main protagonists, Pemberton and Sara, are faced with. The novel incorporates revolutionary changes in the field of science such as the theory of relativity and evolutionary theory, as well as world-shattering events, such as the horrors of two world wars, the slaughters during the Nazi regime, and the Vietnam War.

The method of perspectivisation in *City of God* is constitutive of its textual representation of spirituality and faith in God. The selection and combination of perspectives enables the narrative to negotiate different kinds of beliefs, drawing attention to the fact that the human point of view can never be universal, objective, or absolute, but that the individual interprets and experiences the sacred from within a specific spatial and temporal placement. Accordingly, *City of God* is not concerned with a 'right' version of the world. By means of a synchronic and diachronic multiperspectivity it makes the question of God a leitmotif of its various chapters and configures a 'transcendental' dimension that lies underneath the fictional world. In connecting the theme of spirituality with recent US-

American and European history, the narrative depicts a world that is shaped by a spiritual drive and imbued with the question of a reality beyond the human world. In view of the kaleidoscopic diversity of voices and the lack of a God's-eye point of view, however, the narrative abandons any synthesising and monological answer to the question of God. Instead, by means of multiperspectivity, the novel distorts any religious discourse that claims to be true by foregrounding the perspectivity of any kind of religious belief, and demands that the reader similarly engages in a spiritual search in which belief and scepticism are intrinsically interwoven, shaping and conditioning each other.

City of God not only explores the God question by means of multiperspectivity. The novel also questions any propositional truth claims, be they religious or scientific, by drawing attention to the rhetorical and narrative patterns that govern scientific as well as religious discourse in their organisation and interpretation of the world. The text plays freely with the conventions of theological, historical, and scientific discourse and consequently violates the culturally sacred borders of narrative fabulation, spiritual questioning, and scientific reasoning. The theories of the fictional Einstein are not written in the style of the scientific treatise (e.g. *CG* 48–52). His thoughts are interspersed with childhood memory and intimate self-exposure. They vacillate between playful exploration of ideas, melancholic contemplation of the universe, and reflections on how to imagine God. The intermingling of scientific, religious and literary discourse results in a merging of fictional construction and what is customarily taken to be reality. The reader who wants to know what is historically 'accurate' and what is 'made up' is disconcerted, as s/he is never sure when the novel provides him or her with historical information and when s/he is reading pure fabulation. This happens most obviously when the novel parodies its characters, in particular Wittgenstein, who presents himself as an egocentric loner: "I was aware that to the degree they [the students] were awed was the extent they would make fun of me behind my back. Professor Ludwig Wienerschnitzel. Arguing with himself, lapsing into his German, hearing what he had just said aloud as if someone else had said it, and then disagreeing vehemently" (*CG* 174–75).

Moreover, the novel eradicates the boundaries of storytelling and scientific explanation in depicting the theory of evolution in the manner of an experimental science fiction story. In so doing, the novel foregrounds the narrative patterns that lie underneath a theory that has turned into an all-embracing formula in the twentieth century, and are likewise integrated by Pemberton and Sara as a central concept for their new theology. The anonymous first-person narrator in the novel, who gives a short introduction to the beginning of the world, compensates for his lack of technical vocabulary and knowledge with unorthodox comparisons and metaphors, revealing his scepticism towards the grand theory by ridiculing it:

> Uncounted billions of years idle away as this single-cell organism, this speck of corruption, this submicroscopic breach of nonlife, evolves selectively through realms of slime and armor-plated brutishness, past experimental kingdoms of horses two feet tall and lizards that fly, into the triumphant dominions of the fury self-improving bipeds, those of the opposed thumb and forefinger, who will lope out of prehistory to sublime into a teenage nerd at the Bronx High School of Science. (CG 13)

Hence, whereas Pemberton and Sara optimistically aim to "recast" (*CG* 290) God by harmonising science and theology, the textual structure of *City of God* deeply relativises the theologians' vision, laying bare the constructed and selective character of the basis that serves Pemberton and Sara as a starting point for their reformulation of God.

By blurring the line between scientific, religious, historical and literary discourse and by discharging the distinction of 'imagination' and 'reality,' the novel shows the reader the world as a tightly woven web of stories and draws attention to the fine line between fact and fiction, and between mythology and truth. As a consequence, *City of God* poses a profound challenge not only to Pemberton's and Sara's specific religious vision, but also to faith in God in general as it leaves open the question as to whether God is merely a chimera within mankind's creative and productive interpretation of the world. In this sense, one may conclude that the novel suggests that all ideas of God defy the categories of absolute truth and bare reality, but instead are indistinguishably interwoven within a combination of fabulation and reality and intrinsically depend on mankind's need to fabricate and imagine his world through and within stories.

To sum up: By way of multiperspectivity and metafiction, the novel keeps the reader constantly on the move between perspectives as well as between different levels of textual reality. The structural framework, within which the characters' search for God unfolds, renders the reading process uncertain and ambiguous. In disconnecting the spiritual search from a particular perspective, the novel requires that the reader simultaneously sustains the two conflicting postulations of the existence and the non-existence of God. What the novel exemplifies, then, is a drastic reorganisation of familiar ways of thinking and perceiving, since it combines diverging versions of the world that, in fact, present mutually exclusive truths. It develops a narrative form that escapes from the familiar dictum that there is only one world and depicts instead a multidimensional universe. In this respect, *City of God* seems to share Goodman's conviction that there is no 'real' world but only versions of it. However, the novel also shows that the God question finally exceeds any philosophical or literary inquiry. It investigates possibilities for a 'new being in the world' (see Ricœur 43) in that it invites us to theological inquiry and the religious search for the numinous while illustrating that the religious can never be separated from its human expression in narrative. Debunking attempts to fabricate a sacred universe that define religious assumptions as certain and unmistakable, it reveals the quest for God as unsettling and challenging; that is, as a quest that does not result in confident belief, but remains a tentative and heuristic undertaking, and inscribes into its very structure the kind of belief the doubtful character Pem puts his hope in: "a longing, a navigating principle, redemptive not on arrival, but in never quite getting here" (*CG* 281).

5. Conclusion

How, then, may we finally answer the introductory question of how to define the role of literature that deals with the spiritual within a culture and its overarching belief horizons? What is the potential of literary texts to depict fictional worlds shaped by religious and theological ideas, beliefs, and feelings? First, if Goodman (21–22) is right in claiming that advancing insight and understanding is not first and foremost a matter of formulating a proposition or of discerning what is true, but of learning "to see or hear or grasp features and structures we could not discern before," then 'fictions of spirituality' are certainly able to contribute insight into the multilayered reality of religion and belief in divine being. In making concrete, selecting, focusing upon, exhibiting, and raising awareness of essential aspects constitutive of the theme of God and the human search for ultimate meaning, fiction provides patterns and schemata that help to integrate and interact with conflicting ways of worldmaking. Literature, however, not only helps us to deal with a multifaceted reality, but it can also serve to provide models for how we as readers interpret our experience in the search for what goes beyond perceivable reality. Novels such as *City of God* introduce religious imagination into our apprehension of reality; thus, they have the potential to challenge familiar ways of perceiving. They recreate reality through the modality of imagination while transgressing simple dualities such as 'worlds of fiction and worlds of fact,' of 'belief and knowledge,' or of 'faith and reason.' In this vein, *City of God* serves as an ideal example of literature that seeks to create new avenues for religious exploration. It both depicts the human quest for a world that pervades human explanation and self-consciously draws attention to the processes that go into spiritual worldmaking. In this dialectic of a religious search and analytic interpretation—or, as Ricœur puts it, of distanciation and appropriation—, fiction may exhibit new dimensions of reality challenging both the critic's and the believer's tendency to reduce one's world to a single base.

Second, always bearing in mind that literature's world-creation does not work as a closed system but interacts with other signifying processes and engages with a culture's prevalent stories of God, an analysis of fiction allows insight into a culture while, at the same time, providing answers to ideological challenges and problems posed in particular times and places. In fact, in view of the close intertwinement of literature with prevailing discourses, one has to stress the potential of literature not only to elaborate and expand on cultural imaginations of ultimacy and transcendence, but also to confront the ideological power that can never be divorced from such visions. Thus, *City of God* addresses the current situation in contemporary US-America, which is characterised by fundamental changes and a reshuffling of the religious landscape. Undoubtedly, the Christian religion continues to play a significant role in the United States. However, the religious has also appeared with an unforeseen vengeance outside these familiar boundaries and has taken a vast variety of forms and contents. US-America can no longer be called a Christian nation, given the radical pluralism of ideologies, religions, beliefs, and lifestyles. The processes of pluralisation and secularisation are accompanied by deepening gaps between different cultural groups, religions, and world views, a situation which enflames and intensifies controversies between a scientific materialism and religious fundamentalism and, in its worst manifestation, gives rise to terrorist deeds such as the event of 9/11.

One can hardly fail to notice that *City of God* forcefully tackles the God question within a historical context characterised by antagonistic cultural and religious forces. On the one hand, it turns against the truth claims inherent in both logical positivism and religious discourse. The novel rejects any ontological certainty and thus embraces the ideal of a postmodern de-hierarchisation. On the other hand, *City of God* does not construct a world of disorder and emptiness, but it investigates the possibility of shared beliefs and a common ground of cultural experience. This search for commonality and integration is based on the idea of God, the nation's most powerful master-story. *City of God* affirms this master-story by employing God as a unifying metaphor, a positive kernel of the eclectic scenery of the text; yet it reformulates it while shifting it from transcendence to radical immanence by depicting it within the human discursivisation of the world. In the reformulation from the transcendental to the immanent, the novel renders this construct 'God' spiritually mobile, yet proposes it as a place from which the negotiation of universal values and ethical norms within a postmodern culture may proceed. This 'God,' then, is resemantisised and reconceptualised as a result of being disconnected from the concept of mimesis and reconstructed within the process of narration and storytelling. It evolves within a discursive and multifaceted reality which defies any definite categories of true and false. By evoking this simultaneousness of sacred absence and presence, *City of God* centres the fictional world around a middle, which is extremely instable and fluid, yet which still holds it together and provides a foundation for reintegration.

It is clear that the term 'fictions of spirituality' is useful in discussions of spiritual world construction as a means of paying tribute to a broad range of the fictional expressions of God and the spiritual, which cannot necessarily be called religious in a narrow sense. *City of God* can thus hardly be called a religious novel, provided that one is convinced that faith is always "more than a mere imaginative leap into a[...] possible world" (Wolf 118). Rather than affirmatively building religious assumptions into the fictional world, contemporary novels such as *City of God* foreground the constructed and indeed fictitious nature of religious narratives, and depict the search for meaning as a playful, creative and imaginative activity. They thus offer sceptical resistance to an unyielding belief in religious or theological truth positions demonstrating that sacred worlds are as much made as found. However, regardless of whether *City of God* is interested in the God question as an innately religious question, the novel engages with the extra-literary discourses of religion and the spiritual and hence partakes in forming and shifting our imagination and experience of it while moving as one voice within the polyphonic net of significations referring to 'God,' the 'transcendental,' or the 'religious'—a net which in its totality creates the asymmetrical intertext of a culture's God-talk.

References

Bellah, Robert N. *Beyond Belief: Essays on Religion in a Post-traditional World*. 1970. Berkeley: U of California P, 1991.

Belzen, Jacob A. "The Cultural Psychological Approach to Religion: Contemporary Debates on the Object of the Discipline." *Theory and Psychology* 9.2 (1999): 225–29.

Bruner, Jerome. "The Narrative Construction of Reality." *Critical Inquiry* 18.1 (1991): 1–21.

Crites, Stephen. "The Narrative Quality of Experience." *Why Narrative? Readings in Narrative Theology*. Eds. Stanley Hauerwas, and L. Gregory Jones. Grand Rapids: Eerdmans, 1989. 65–88.
Detweiler, Robert. "Theological Trends of Postmodern Fiction." *JAAR* 44.2 (1976):225–37.
Disch, Lisa. *Hannah Arendt and the Limits of Philosophy*. Ithaca/London: Cornell UP, 1994.
Doctorow, E.L. *City of God*. 2000. London: Abacus, 2001.
Eisen, Ute E. *Die Poetik der Apostelgeschichte: Eine narratologische Studie*. Göttingen: Vandenhoeck/Ruprecht, 2006.
Fluck, Winfried. *Theorien amerikanischer Literatur*. Konstanz: Universitätsverlag Konstanz, 1987.
Goodman, Nelson. *Ways of Worldmaking*. Indianapolis: Hackett Publishing, 1978.
Griffin, David Ray. "Introduction: Postmodern Spirituality and Society." *Spirituality and Society: Postmodern Visions*. Ed. David Ray Griffin. Albany, NY: State U of New York P, 1988. 1–31.
Gymnich, Marion, Birgit Neumann, and Ansgar Nünning. *Kulturelles Wissen und Intertextualität: Theoriekonzeptionen und Fallstudien zur Kontextualisierung von Literatur*. Trier: WVT, 2006.
Irmer, Thomas. *Metafiction, Moving Pictures, Moving Histories: Der historische Roman in der Literatur der amerikanischen Postmoderne*. Tübingen: Narr, 1995.
Irving, John. *A Prayer for Owen Meany*. New York: William Morrow, 1989.
Kort, Wesley A. "Narrative and Theology." *Journal of Literature and Theology* 1.1 (1987): 27–38.
Lerner, Laurence. "Puritanism and the Spiritual Autobiography." *Hibbert Journal* 55.4 (1957): 373–86.
Link, Jürgen. "Literaturanalyse als Interdiskursanalyse." *Diskurstheorien und Literaturwissenschaft*. Eds. Jürgen Fohrmann, and Harro Müller. Frankfurt a.M.: Suhrkamp, 1988. 284–307.
—. "Diskursive Ereignisse, Diskurse, Interdiskurse: Sieben Thesen zur Operativität der Diskursanalyse, am Beispiel des Normalismus." *Das Wuchern der Diskurse*. Eds. Hannelore Bublitz et al. Frankfurt a.M.: Campus, 1999. 148–61.
Luckmann, Thomas. "Shrinking Transcendence, Expanding Religion?" *Sociological Analysis* 51.2 (1990): 127–38.
Lundin, Roger. "Introduction." *There Before Us: Religion, Literature, and Culture from Emerson to Wendell Berry*. Michigan: Eerdmans/Grand Rapids, 2007. x–xxii.
McClure, John A. "Postmodern/Post-Secular: Contemporary Fiction and Spirituality." *Modern Fiction Studies* 41.1 (1995): 141–63.
McMinn, Mark R., and Todd W. Hall. "Christian Spirituality in a Postmodern Era." *Journal of Psychology and Theology* 29.4 (2000): 251–53.
Neumann, Birgit. "Narrating Selves, (De-)Constructing Selves? Fictions of Identity." *Narrative and Identity: Theoretical Approaches and Critical Analyses*. Eds. Birgit Neumann, Ansgar Nünning, and Bo Pettersson. Trier: WVT, 2008. 53–69.
Noll, Mark. *A History of Christianity in the United States and Canada*. Grand Rapids: Eerdmans, 1992.

Nünning, Ansgar, and Vera Nünning. *Multiperspektivisches Erzählen. Zur Theorie und Geschichte der Perspektivenstruktur im englischen Roman des 18. bis 20. Jahrhunderts.* Trier: WVT, 2000.

Ricœur, Paul. *Figuring the Sacred: Religion, Narrative, and Imagination.* Minneapolis: Augsburg Fortress Press, 1995.

Robinson, Marilynne. *Gilead.* New York: Farrar, Straus and Giroux, 2004.

Schunack, Gerd. "Neuere literaturkritische Interpretationsverfahren in der anglo-amerikanischen Exegese." *Verkündigung und Forschung* 41(1996): 28–55.

Sternberg, Meir. *The Poetics of Biblical Narrative: Ideological Literature and the Drama of Reading.* Bloomington: Indian UP, 1985.

Stroup, George. "Theology of Narrative or Narrative Theology? A Response to *Why Narrative?*" *Theology Today* 47.4 (1991): 424–32.

Surkamp, Carola. *Die Perspektivenstruktur narrativer Texte: Zu ihrer Theorie und Geschichte im englischen Roman zwischen Viktorianismus und Moderne.* Trier: WVT, 2003.

Titzmann, Michael. "Kulturelles Wissen – Diskurs – Denksystem. Zu einigen Grundbegriffen der Literaturgeschichtsschreibung." *Zeitschrift für französische Sprache und Literatur* 99 (1989): 47–61.

Updike, John. *Roger's Version.* New York: Fawcett Crest, 1986.

Wolf, Werner. "Migration Towards a Rewarding Goal and Multiculturalism with a Positive Centre: Yann Martel's *Life of Pi* as a Post-Postmodernist Attempt at Eliciting (Poetic)Faith." *Canada in the Sign of Migration and Trans-Culturalism.* Eds. Klaus Dieter Ertler, and Martin Löschnigg. Canadiana/Frankfurt a.M.: Lang, 2004. 107–24.

Yamane, David. "Narrative and Religious Experience." *Sociology of Religion* 61 (2000): 171–89.

Zapf, Hubert. "Literature as Cultural Ecology: Notes towards a Functional Theory of Imaginative Texts with Examples from American Literature." *Literary History/Cultural History: Forcefields and Tensions* (= REAL 17). Ed. Herbert Grabes. Tübingen: Narr, 2001. 85–100.

—. "Das Funktionsmodell der Literatur als kultureller Ökologie: Imaginative Texte im Spannungsfeld von Dekonstruktion und Regeneration." *Funktionen von Literatur: Theoretische Grundlagen und Modellinterpretationen.* Eds. Marion Gymnich, and Ansgar Nünning. Trier: WVT, 2005. 55–78.

Narrating Life: Early Modern Accounts of the Life of Queen Christina of Sweden (1626–1689)

Elisabeth Wåghäll Nivre and Maren Eckart

> The Poets (men, who in their brains comprise A Mint, where Fancy can coine Histories, And feign Creations) have so loudly prais'd The beauties of a Venus, that they rais'd Her person up to heaven, and gave her there The glories of a Goddess, and a Star: But there was no one such, nor could she ever Attain those beauties which the Poets give her....
>
> (de Harst and G. L. Gent)[1]

In 1656, a Mr. G. L. Gent addressed his translation of a panegyric to "Mrs. R. G." The text was originally published in French and is dedicated to Queen Christina of Sweden (1626–1689), but Gent's translation is interesting since it includes a number of additions; letters/poems that reflect upon the narration of lives—on how to tell the life of a person and his or her place in the world. The seventeenth-century text indicates the use of a life story to express how someone or something should or could be understood and that there is more than one way to tell the life of a person. The story itself thus becomes a way of "worldmaking," to bring into play the expression used both in the title of this volume and by Nelson Goodman in his 1978 publication *Ways of Worldmaking*. Goodman is concerned with investigating "the processes involved in building a world out of others" (Goodman 7) in a different and much more complex way than the translator of the seventeenth-century panegyric, but Gent's translation, as well as other similar texts, point toward a growing interest in using (in)famous people for creating new worlds that can be experienced by a reading public which, at that time, did not yet have a sense of literature as 'fiction,' or of 'fiction' as a matter of genre. The absolutist regimes emerging in Europe no doubt fostered an interest in the leading mon-

---

1 *A panegyric of the most renowned and serene Princess Christina, by the grace of God, Queene of Swedland, Goths and Vandals* Written originally in French, by the learned pen of Mr. de Harst, and now translated into English by W. L. Gent London, 1656. The copy used here has been made available to me through Early English Books Online and is stamped 'Museum Britannicum' at the end.

archs, whose distance to the 'common man' or woman was great. The printing press paved the way for the 'mass consumption' of written texts on cheap paper. New media such as the newspaper-made events and occurrences taking place far away known to ever-growing numbers of people, as is discussed by Knut Ove Eliassen in his essay on the historicity of media concepts. The circulation of information and knowledge in Europe increased as more people travelled long distances and scientists made new discoveries that widened and deepened the knowledge of the world and the human being. At the same time, men and women in power re-enacted their own lives. Stephen Greenblatt's "Renaissance self-fashioning" figures in a Shakespearean England (Greenblatt), and the concept of a *theatrum mundi*—the theatre of the world—point in the same direction: at an interest in (re-)writing and enacting human life and discovering, as well as setting limits and borders for what can be done and told. Queen Christina of Sweden is thus only one—albeit an important—example of a person whose life was widely debated, told, and circulated all over Europe. Christina was also an avid writer and very careful about staging her own appearances. She acted and re-enacted her life,[2] thus contributing to the image of herself as a multi-headed Hydra, a queen in her own right whose womanhood was questioned. In the figure of Christina it becomes clear that 'being famous' is an act performed by an agent or a subject while also being a construction of those surrounding that same subject/agent. It is something that is transmitted by word of mouth as well as in written discourse. "Being famous" seems to include the duplication of one's life in long narratives that are printed and distributed in a way that was impossible before the invention of the printing press. In the case of Christina, the gossip concerning her own sex, her sexual preferences, and her religious and political preferences made way for speculations that often seem closely related to questions regarding gender. Not only Christina herself tried to create her own world order and express her own world view; there were many people who, just like Mr. Gent, wanted to make her fit into their textual world, thus contributing to rewriting life and making the world appear anew. This can be seen in the light of the plurality of stories and narratives that Ansgar Nünning in his essay ties to any given 'event,' but here we also seem to be dealing with a plurality of 'figures' in one and the same person, as will be discussed below.

Early modern Europe experienced a number of female regents of great dignity, such as Catherine de Medici (France 1519–1589), Elizabeth I (England 1533–1603), Mary Stuart (Scotland 1542–1587), and Christina (Sweden 1626–1689). The interest in these women, in their lives as well as

---

2   For the autobiographical writings of Queen Christina, see Haettner Aurelius.

in their deeds quickly resulted not only in court gossip but also in a number of written accounts of their lives. Texts were published, translated, edited, and republished, thus often changing their shape but also preserving the rumors that circulated. At a time when the *querelle des femmes* and the reformation movements were focusing on 'woman,' and learned men around Europe wrote extensively on the nature of woman, on her place in the family and in society—and some women wrote in her defence—,the interest in writing about female regents is rather obvious. Stories about their lives circulated all over Europe—also in the German-speaking lands that only had experience with ruling women in the separate states of the "Empire."[3] Translations, editions and original works in German on early modern female rulers can be found in archives and libraries both inside and outside of the German-speaking countries, but for a long time there has been greater interest among scholars in investigating autobiographical texts by women rather than narratives on their lives written by others. There has also been a clear stress on 'lives,' while less attention has been directed towards the narration itself. The focus on what has thus overshadowed the how, in other words, the person described has been of greater importance than her literary representation.

The growing circulation of texts can be assumed to have contributed to development and change, to new ways of 'telling lives' for new audiences. In *The Rhetoric of Life-Writing in Early Modern Europe,* Thomas F. Mayer and D. R. Woolf claim in their discussion of the development of the biography that

> Undoubtedly, keeping the web [the narrative, EWN] seamless became steadily more difficult in the Renaissance, as writers became adept at (and aware of) more self-consciously rhetorical forms of constructing texts. Thus, the taken-for-granted purpose of most life-writing, exemplarity, became increasingly problematic as later humanism began to appreciate that ancient examples could, in fact, be 'less than exemplary,' either frustratingly inapplicable or embarrassingly inappropriate. (3)

Even though Europe saw increasing literacy rates in the seventeenth century and different kinds of texts circulated in growing numbers and editions, we have to keep in mind that very much was written about the very few—and that the texts appear very disparate yet at the same time bound to convention. In the case of female rulers, the attention that could be projected onto their lives in the early modern period can consequently be

---

[3] Since the German emperor was elected, the question of the (female) inheritance of the throne was a matter of less significance than in kingdoms such as England and France.

linked to the traditional notion of woman as unsuitable for a position of power.

This contribution intends to investigate the making of a queen in texts that develop a textual world with little or no similarity to the everyday world of the Swedish Queen.[4] The real or lived lives of Christina will be of no significance in our discussion; rather, the focal point will be the concept of biographical writing—of the making or narration of a life that appears true within the textual world that is depicted. Within the field of gender studies it has been shown that genre is closely connected to gender in many early modern texts (see Schnell, "Text und Geschlecht" 9–46, *Frauendiskurs, Männerdiskurs, Ehediskurs* 11–21, 282ff.; Wåghäll Nivre). When creating and shaping a world governed by a powerful woman, the aspect of gender thus seems as important as that of class or power. The author needs to find ways of expressing himself—to find a genre—that allows him[5] to tell his story of the life he has chosen to write about and to place it in the world he wants to depict. Below we will look at questions regarding genre and gender, the position of the biographer/narrator in the text and the possible relation to the author, editor, or translator. In the following, we will hence use Queen Christina of Sweden as an example of life narratives on early modern female rulers. The first part of the article will discuss the theoretical and methodological problems of early modern biographical writing seen in the light of gender. The (re-)construction of the life of women in power seems to be an important part of early modern history writing. The need to tell and retell their life stories is a crucial part of mapping the world and 'correcting' history as it could otherwise be perceived. Because of the importance of 'telling' lives, we have chosen to focus on the narratological aspects of biographical writing in the seventeenth and eighteenth centuries, on the discrepancy between factual knowledge and the need to tell a story—an exciting life story. After a brief introduction to some of the earliest biographical texts on Christina, the second part of the article will go into greater depth in its textual analysis of the German version of Johann Arckenholtz's (compilation) biography of the Queen (1751–1760) and will investigate the performative power of narrative as discussed by Ansgar Nünning in his contribution.

"A biography, typically, is a chronological narrative which tells a story of a life. Its defining concern is with being, with the nature of ontological existence as seen within the exemplar of the life investigated and discussed," says Liz Stanley in her 1992 article "Process in Feminist Biogra-

---

[4] This article is part of a larger research project on early modern biographical writing. Elisabeth Wåghäll Nivre and Maren Eckart are working together on this project.

[5] Very few biographical accounts of the kind discussed here seem to have been written by women in the seventeenth and eighteenth centuries.

phy and Feminist Epistemology" (120). Her definition of the writing of lives, of life stories, is one of many that try to make sense of a genre as disparate as the people it tries to portray. Christian Klein has even asserted biography to be "the bastard of the humanities" (Klein 1, our translation), but the interest in reading and writing about the lives of people other than oneself—living or dead—does not seem to be in conflict with the formal and structural differences and difficulties of the genre. With its roots in Antiquity, in genres such as the encomium and the epitaph, early forms of life narratives were developed to praise the lives of great men. Medieval hagiographies, on the other hand, told the stories of men and women—of the saints who had suffered for their faith—while the Renaissance, with its interest in ancient times, again turned to older sources when praising the prominent and the learned. Even though these texts narrate lives, they mainly appear as biographies in scholarly works dealing with the history of the biography. They are biographical but not necessarily 'biography'—the term proper to Post-Enlightenment texts. Stanley uses her definition for discussing contemporary women's writing on other women's lives, but it seems to serve the purpose of an overall preliminary definition for early modern life narratives. One could, however, claim with Mayer and Wolf that:

> Lack of terms is no certain proof of the absence of things, but the fact that no society prior to the middle of the seventeenth century developed a word for 'biography' supports our argument about the instability of genre [...] just as *biography* appears only in eighteenth-century English. (Mayer and Woolf 7; see Buck 3)

It is nevertheless difficult to talk of a 'women's biography' from this time, despite the number of texts written in late medieval and early modern Europe that focus thematically on 'woman' and also on the more formal aspects of genre. Medieval hagiography portrayed the lives of female saints as well as male ones. The *Exempelliteratur* was prescriptive rather than narrative, as were all didactic texts. They told the reader what one should be or not be, what one should do or not do. These texts had no interest in the 'ontology' of a single person since they were written in a tradition focusing on the communal rather than the individual. It should be stressed further that both male and female rulers were the target of biographical accounts and that these narratives cannot simply be split into typically male or female biographies. First and foremost they are written about people in power. The gender aspect is only one of many and needs further investigation before claims about clear distinctions can be made. The biographical accounts were written as examples of good and bad, depicting good and evil rulers, as people in charge living up to conventional norms or breaking all rules, and it can be assumed that the transgression of norms as is described in texts about Christina and others of the European nobility was only possible because of their outstanding social status. Their power allowed them to create a world of their own. Sheila ffolliott questions whether there are "distinctive issues regarding the rhetoric employed by the writers of early modern lives of women," stating:

> From the early Middle Ages when the genre arose, the writing of queens' biographies [...] assumed a didactic exemplary purpose transcending the recording of individual lives. For the most part, exemplary life-writing occurred only after the subject's death, and concerned itself with locating the subject in the narrative continuum of history, a moral enterprise that at the same time reflected particular—and polemical—positions. Employing rhetoric appropriate to their desired ends, medieval authors fit individuals into one of two polarized versions of queenship, in both of which gender was always at the fore. The praiseworthy model of queenship illustrated what such exemplary biographies continued to reproduce as the best that could be expected from the acknowledged inferior sex. Such a representation largely conflated queenship with female sainthood for it de-emphasized the queen's public—what might be called political—role in favour of what was advocated as more appropriate female conduct. [...] The negative queenly exemplar, on the other hand, was she who involved herself, inappropriately for her gender, in politics. (ffolliott 321–22)

ffolliott's hesitation elucidates the dangers of turning biography into a pure matter of gender. However, biographical writing among some scholars is considered a "male" genre (Barry 33). The biography, according to Barry, focuses on men's lives and it reflects a society determined by patriarchal norms since it is often written in a narrative tradition of historiography—a literary genre long dominated by male authors. It can therefore be useful to focus on life narratives of women and to investigate them separately if wanting to include early modern women in biographical writing. The woman in power can be assumed to have challenged traditional genres and thus indirectly encouraged authors to rewrite her life and make a narrative universe that would fit conventional thinking and norms. The life of a woman in power is neither exemplary nor possible to ignore. Her life story combines the typical with the untypical, the public (her role as ruling queen) with the private (her domestic role), as has been discussed widely in gender/women's studies at least since Joan Kelly-Gadol's "Did Women Have a Renaissance?" (Kelly-Gadol 1977). The female regent can at the same time be mother and wife or widow, being at the top of the secular hierarchy while inferior and required to submit to male norms as expressed in Christian theology and social convention. Her life in the 'real' or lived world and that which is depicted in written discourse generally overlap and clash but are cultural constructs dependent on a given world view or world order.

When applying a male-dominated genre to women in power, the biographers find themselves in conflict with the expected loyalty towards the legitimate authority, as Merry Wiesner-Hanks has pointed out: "In all three cases—rulers, wives, and widows—women had not only power, but also authority, that is, power that was supported by legal, political, and religious institutions and by cultural norms" (Wiesner-Hanks 28). The male biographers thus had to accept the legitimacy of female regency, even though they seem simultaneously to be eager to point out the dangers of female rule and to pronounce the ruling woman an exception to the common norm. Deviations obviously needed to be arranged to fit into familiar patterns and general stereotypes. Anette Dixon claims in the same volume that "[f]emale leaders were threatening because they upset, at a state level, the established male-female power balance in society, unleashing angst about uppity wives, dangerous seductresses, and female warriors gaining the upper hand in the domestic sphere" (Dixon 22).

Considering the great number of texts depicting the woman at the top as symbolising a world turned upside down, ffolliott's description of ruling women's biographies as either stressing exemplary goodness or focusing on the evils in woman makes sense. There is, however, the need for a more detailed study of early modern biographical writing on ruling women, since the lack of coherence among the texts indicates that there is more to these texts than a simple separation of good from evil. The woman in power cannot be solely evil if portrayed in her lifetime—unless from the point of view of the enemy, as was the case with Christina (see below). She is, furthermore, an exception with few connections to 'woman' in general. Her biographers are, in a legal sense, always her inferiors since they are rarely as high up in the social hierarchy as she is herself. This relationship between biographer and biographee is clearly important and also difficult when studying biographies from the sixteenth, seventeenth and eighteenth centuries. The use of stereotypes in rhetoric and narrative, and of gender roles, of mythological as well as allegorical figures may at times say more about the biographer or rather his view of the world and his moral and ethical standards than about the person being portrayed. The biographer brings his own values, interests, and prejudices into the narrative, thus making contextualisation necessary. When translated or edited—as were so many early modern biographies—the narrated life changes its shape, as will be shown below. A great many early modern biographers typically legitimise their texts by referring to eyewitness accounts that cannot be verified or to their own experiences. On the level of discourse they create "systems of truth," as discussed by

Frederik Tygstrup in his contribution. In the Christina biographies, certain parts are told and retold while other parts are added loosely to the story. The author/editor/translator at times refers to "secret but reliable" sources, and at times questions sources while claiming his own story to be true or at least truthful. He sometimes emerges with his own comments while at other times he disappears, hiding behind the story, allowing documents to speak for themselves, or he overtly states his own position. He could perhaps be termed an unreliable biographer if using modern terminology, but in several of the texts published on the life of Christina we can also trace the voice of a narrator who appears in the text to tell her life story—this narrator writes himself into the text as her biographer.

Dale Spender has noted that the authors of life stories need to get close to their object of study and to make them fit into their own understanding of the world. The author of biographies can only write from his or her own perspective and thus becomes central to the life depicted—the biography cannot be anything but a construction of a life—of life in context (Spender viii–ix). The relationship between biographer and biographee can hence be regarded as ideologically determined and bound by genre. The choice of subject and the choice of what to tell about the subject are crucial factors for the representation of a person in the narrative. In cases where conventional norms are turned upside down the biographer finds himself in a difficult position. He has to write about something as true—the reigning woman—while at the same time stressing the extraordinary situation in order to restore order. The female sovereign can thus only exist as deviant. Kathleen Barry alludes to the image of the woman as evil, almost monstrous, a creature to tame if diverging from the general norm:

> Patriarchal society will not accept any woman who refuses to be dominated. If she persists thus, it rewrites her history and reshapes her character, punitively twisting her will, bending her image, and distorting her identity; her defiance appears as a deformity—an aberration of nature. (24)

Women who were officially appointed to rule in early modern Europe—in their own right or as consort rulers—belong to a small group of women who are too outstanding for a general comparison with other women or groups of women. It is nevertheless important to look at their biographies and biographers since they belong to the few early modern women who were given personal attention and whose lives were turned into written narratives. Looking into the German publications on Queen Christina, it becomes evident that many of them claim to focus on her life but that they do not primarily tell her life story. They do not solely engage with her "being" but rather with the turbulence that characterised her lifetime in

Europe.[6] Their interest in explaining Christina to the reader—whether positively or negatively—nonetheless demonstrates their ontological concerns with the person portrayed. Here only a few textual examples will be presented to illustrate the interdependence between gender and genre when narrating the life of an early modern queen and making a world to fit her.

Hardly any other female European ruler has attracted as much attention up to the present day as Queen Christina, even though her reign lasted a mere ten years (1644–1655). Hundreds of monographs have been written about her, not to mention other genres such as historical novels, plays, books for children etc. (see Grage 35n2). Throughout her lifetime, the queen broke with a number of conventional expectations; she was a controversial central figure in the politics of the time, and as a result the opinions about her varied widely. Until the middle of the eighteenth century most of the texts depicting Christina seem to have been ideologically coloured and depended on the political camp and religion of the individual author. The presentations of her life were either warped through slanderous satire or transfigured by panegyrics. Early modern accounts of Queen Christina generally prove the didactic intentions of the author/biographer/editor who wants more than to just tell the story of her life. The reader should not be led astray and think of Christina as anything other than an extreme exception from the common norm. The queen ruling in her own right becomes reality only when there is no other option—when the family line has to be saved.

The officially sanctioned image of Christina doubtlessly plays an important role in the literary interpretation of her life. In the panegyrical representations, which were manifested in hymns praising the sovereign, on coins, engravings and medals, three factors are especially evident, namely Christina's role as Gustavus Adolphus's daughter; as the "Queen of Peace"; and as an intellectual ruler interested in art and culture. From her very birth Christina acquired an exceptional position as daughter and heir to the throne of her father Gustavus Adolphus, the Protestant hero-king revered as the "Lion of the North." This was a role that entailed specific expectations, virtues, and duties (see Falkdalen 117ff.). Gustavus Adolphus was the precondition for her legitimacy and position as monarch; it was he who bestowed authority upon her reign. This positioning of a woman through the man is characteristic of a gender-related pattern

---

6 "[T]he epistemological challenge to biography has been intensified by poststructuralist and postmodernist critiques of language, selfhood, and historical narrative. If language cannot transparently convey reality, if the self is a fictive construct or mere multiplicity of subject positions, if narrative itself imposes a false coherence on events, then no biographical account of someone's life can be in any sense 'true'" (Hoberman 109ff.).

that was the rule for female monarchs. The identification of Christina through her father was emphasised in allegorical representations, often symbolised by the phoenix. The genealogical iconography marks her not only as the legitimate successor but also as the trustee of the legacy of her father's spirit. One of many examples, an engraving from the year 1653, shows Gustavus Adolphus in the figure of Jupiter/Zeus flying on an eagle and handing the male symbols of Hercules's club and lion skin to his daughter (see Baumgärtel 107, Dixon 117). In this apotheosis of the ruler, both the sovereigns are rendered mythical, even represented as ancient gods. Another part of the official Christina iconography is the picture of her as a ruler committed to peace, mainly because it was during her reign that the Peace of Westphalia was ratified in 1648, thus ending the Thirty Years' War. The most common allegorical representation of Christina shows her as Minerva or Pallas Athena with the attributes of erudition and of the art of war. This mythologisation, not unusual for female rulers of this era, became almost a synonym for Christina (see Haak 44). No other woman of the seventeenth century was depicted so often as the goddess of wisdom and of peace and as protector of the arts. People paid homage to her as the Minerva of the North, as the true Pallas, as Pallas Suecia and as the tenth muse. In addition, she was also represented as Diana, since—like the virgin goddess of the hunt—Christina remained unmarried all her life (see Haak 70). In sum, one can say about the official panegyrical texts and images that a royal mythography was constructed in order to emphasise the extraordinary nature of her personality and her position (see also Kajanto, *Christina Heroina* and "Queen Christina in Latin Panegyrics"). "Queen Christina of Sweden" is used metaphorically and the narratives of her life become representations of a new world power—Sweden. By telling the magnificent life of the Queen a glorious world in the North is made up. The worldmaking that takes place in the texts written in Christina's honour helps to put the Swedish nation state and its history (far removed and long marginalised) on the European map. It goes without saying that those aspects which did not fit the image were suppressed or remained unmentioned.

Official historiography had a significant influence on the biographical writing about Christina. The scholarly writing of the Finnish-Swedish court historiographer Samuel Pufendorf, in particular, plays an important role. Pufendorf's magnificent epoch-making 26-volume work about the military and political events of the seventeenth century in Sweden and Germany appeared in German in 1688, and in Latin somewhat earlier.[7] It

---

7   *Commentariorum De Rebus Suecicis ab Expeditione Gustavi Adolphi in Germaniam ad Abdicationem usque Christinae (1686)*. The German title (1688) reads *Herrn Samuel von Pufendorf Sechs vnd*

also depicts Christina's reign, albeit without addressing her as a person. Nonetheless, all biographies use Pufendorf as a reference. In a remarkable way, early modern biographies about Christina wish to differ from the official writing about the Queen and still aim to create a kind of historiography of the private. The earliest original accounts of Christina in German can be found in *Zeitungen* ('newspapers') that were published in Europe in the seventeenth century, but these texts neither gave their readers comprehensive descriptions of her life, nor did they seek to capture the Queen's character. An interesting book by Liselotte von Reinken with the title *Deutsche Zeitungen über Königin Christine 1626–1689* (1966) shows that very few of the news reports were interested in the Queen as a person; they focused instead on the impact her decisions and actions had on other European countries. Reinken gives many textual examples of brevity and clarity, as well as of the need to tell news but not a story.[8] The readers of the newspapers are given information but it is up to each reader to put together his or her image of what is depicted—to draw his or her own conclusions and to make up his or her own image of a world that seems to be in constant wars—by using one or several of the news reports. Few interpretations are provided by the reporter who, in the seventeenth century, is generally bound to a neutral tone and to seemingly objective reporting.

One of Christina's first biographers was the French deputy in Sweden, Pierre Chanut. His writings about the Queen are an exception among the early texts published in France. Even though he did not write an actual biography of Christina he included his—very positive—impressions of the Queen when relating his experiences in Sweden in the middle of the seventeenth century. According to Martin Weibull, Chanut's work was completed and published by one of his successors in Sweden, Picques, a man much less favourably disposed to the Queen.[9] This explains why the text at times appears contradictory to the reader. Chanut was the person who encouraged Christina to write her *auto*biography but it was never completed. Parts of the autobiography were, however, later published in Arckenholtz's multivolume work. Chanut's accounts of the Queen are mostly

---

zwantzig Bucher der Schwedisch- und Deutschen Kriegs- Geschichte von König Gustav Adolfs Feldzuge in Deutschland an, bisz zur Abdanckung der Königin Christina [. . .]. Grauert, who himself wrote a Christina biography, praises the "great clearness, considerateness and the antique way of presentation" ["große Klarheit, Besonnenheit und antike Darstellung" (Grauert VIII)] in Pufendorf's work.

8 See Wåghäll Nivre, "Eine Königin in den Zeitungen" on Queen Christina in the newspapers.

9 Weibull presented his research on Chanut and Picques in an article that explained the discrepancies in Chanut's work and uncovered the changes that Picques had undertaken (see Weibull).

known for having been used and misused in almost all published biographies of Christina.

Early biographical writing about the Swedish Queen is primarily based on French lampoons which were first and foremost politically motivated. The pamphlet literature basically amounted to accusations regarding the Queen's alleged inconstancy, atheism, and libertinism in the sense of being sexually dissolute and harbouring free-thinking attitudes (see Grage 40; Wortmann). This propaganda literature laid the foundation for French-language *intrigue biographies*, primarily polemical accounts of the period after Christina's abdication which reported anecdotes and rumours about her life and her court whilst they were in Rome. The most famous of them was *Histoire des intrigues galantes de la Reine Christine de Suède et de sa cour, pendant son séjour à Rome*, which was published in 1697 in Amsterdam and written as a *chronique scandaleuse*.[10] The French text was translated into English,[11] Dutch,[12] and German[13] at the end of the seventeenth and the beginning of the eighteenth century.[14] In contrast to the official propaganda, these texts gave rise to a mythography *ex negativo* which cemented the Christina myth reflected in subsequent biographies into the twentieth century. The two German-language biographies from 1705 which elaborate on the French sources have certain characteristics in common and they clearly show that the narrative and rhetorical constructions do not yet correspond to the narrative patterns of a modern biography.[15] The course of the Queen's life forms a framework for anecdotal narratives about the people who come into contact with her. Facticity is evoked through an

---

[10] A 1697 text was published anonymously but is often attributed to a man named Christian Gottfried Franckenstein. It has not been possible to confirm Franckenstein as the author but we have chosen to list the text under his name in the bibliography. A question mark has been added in parentheses (?). The name of Christian Steiff can be found in a 1705 Leipzig edition, but it is another unverifiable name. For the *chronique scandaleuse* see Ballaster, *Seductive Forms* 56ff.

[11] *The history of the intrigues & gallantries of Christina, Queen of Sweden, and of her court whilst she was at Rome*. London, 1697.

[12] *Het leven en bedryf van Christina, koniginne van Sweeden, &.c. sedert geboorte tot op des zelvs dood.* Leyden, 1697.

[13] The anonymous German translation of the *Histoire des intrigues galantes* was published in 1705 in Rome as *Leben der Schwedischen Königin Christina und Ihres Hofes/(seit sie nach Rom begeben/) Nebst einigen Anmuthigen Staats- und Liebesintriguen. Von einem Ihrer Domestiquen in Französischer Sprache zusammen getragen/ und anitzo wegen der dabey vorgefallenen Curiositäten ins hochteutsche übersetzt.* In the same year, another German biography about Queen Christina was published in Leipzig, probably by Christian Stieff: *Leben der Weltberühmten Königin Christina von Schweden und denen geheimesten intrigven und merckwürdigsten umständen mit möglichstem fleiße entworffen.*

[14] Odier and Morelli refer to the German translation as "senza interpolazioni" (9) and call it a "traduzione è letterale" (11).

[15] See Eckart.

authorial-omniscient biographer, who personally attests to the truth of what is depicted and shows the reader a degenerating courtly world. The transitions between fiction and historically verifiable reconstruction are indistinct. The *delectare* aspect—wanting to entertain the readers by repeating court gossip—is at least as important as the reliable characterisation of a historical person. The texts explicitly distance themselves from the rhetoric of panegyrics on rulers, from newspapers and official historiography. Christina's life is used to exemplify the moral degeneracy and the unbridled plotting and scheming at court, just as these traits are taken to characterise Christina. Her inconstancy, in turn, makes her a representative of her sex. It is not the political achievements of the Queen, but rather her private life that is placed in focus. Even though the two texts deal differently with the source material, they are both close to being popular fiction. In both texts the biographers add what they find important and tell stories from her court that are not always based on true or real occurrences. They mix gossip with historiography and fact with fiction in a way that suits the overall aim of their narrative—telling the story of an extraordinary person whose life and lifestyle should not be copied. "Christina," as depicted in these texts, oscillates between a world made up of "historical facts" and another—fictional—world constituted through gossip, prejudice, and a fear of social, religious and political change.

It thus can and should be questioned whether the narratives on early modern ruling women are biographies in the strictest sense of the word; however, some of the texts on Christina indicate that it would be wrong not to call them biographical—and we would argue here that they are the biographies of their time. The tendency among historians as well as literary scholars to locate the origins of modernity in the Enlightenment often reduces the importance of the time that came before that which, in the development of literary genres, we like to claim as being 'modern.'

In what follows we would like to discuss a way of representing Christina which is, in many respects, a counter-reaction to the preceding biographies and could thus indicate a changing view of the world. Johan Arckenholtz, librarian in Kassel, published four volumes in French[16] between 1751 and 1760, comprising a biography, a collection of sources and a first edition of Christina's writings. At the same time, the German translation appeared under the title *Historische Merkwürdigkeiten, die Königinn*

---

16 Arckenholtz, Johan. *Memoires concernant Christine reine de Suede, pour servir d'Eclaircissement a l'Historie de son Regne et Principalement de sa Vie priée, et aux Evenements de l'Histoire de son tems ci vile et litéraire: Suivis de deux Ouvrages de cette savante Princesse, qui n'ont jamais été imprimés. Le tout fondé sur ses Lettres, & recueilli des Historiens & des Monuments les plus Auhtentiques, tant manuscrits qu'imprimés, accompagné de Remarques Historiques, politiques, Chritiques & Litéraires; avec des Medailles & un Appendice de Piéces Justificatives ou Instructives.* 4 vol. 1751–1760.

Christina von Schweden betreffend (*Noteworthy Historical Information Related to Queen Christina of Sweden*). In Arckenholtz's text the characteristic feature of biographical writing—its location between literature and scholarship—is handled differently than in its predecessors. The work is primarily distinguished through its comprehensive collection of material. In addition to over one thousand letters by the Queen, as well as some of her other writings, Arckenholtz gathered as much source material as possible about Christina—everything from letters, reports and panegyrical texts to inscriptions and coins. In addition, there are subject and name indices. On account of this extensive collection of material, the Christina volumes were considered the standard by historians and biographers for a good hundred years. The actual biography is only a fraction of the documentation about Christina forming a framework which is filled with source material. There might be pages of text referring to documents before the author returns to the narrative.

Arckenholtz draws a much more positive picture of Christina than the preceding biographies. The text is a defence of the discredited Queen, paying particular tribute to her intellectual abilities. As Pufendorf had already provided a detailed description of the public affairs of Sweden, Arckenholtz wrote, he would like to report on "the private life of the queen and her particular activities"(8).[17] Here, biography becomes a part of historiography, the text being a counterpart to Pufendorf's on the level of the non-public. This narrative intention corresponds to that of previous biographies. Privateness as a characteristic of early biographies of female sovereigns is not only genre- but also gender-related. Male subjects of biographies and their deeds belong to the public sphere. In the descriptions of women's lives, biographers direct their attention to the women's non-public activities, regardless of their historical importance.[18] It is a paradox of early biographical writing about female rulers that although these women assume traditionally male roles and act as public persons, as objects of biographies they are located in the private sphere.

Arckenholtz explains his decision to write about Christina through the need for an impartial representation, as he feels none of the previously published works is reliable. His sharp criticism of existing biographies is directed particularly at their blending of fact and fiction, their subjective and biased style of writing, and their historical inaccuracies. Arckenholtz, who views himself as a chronicler, wants to completely revise the picture of Christina. Authenticity is no longer generated through reference to the author as a contemporary or an eyewitness, but instead through the direct

---

17 "[…] von dem Privatleben der Königin und ihren besonderen Handlungen" (8).
18 See Falkdalen about female rulers in early modern times and their male roles.

citation or review of sources which are not arranged according to historical relevance. In turn, these are then annotated, primarily in the footnotes. Like Pufendorf's encyclopedic work, the text is chronological and includes marginalia listing key terms from the main text as well as dates. This structure admittedly detracts from the literary quality of the text. Arckenholtz defends his chosen narrative structure by saying that the reader should use the sources to independently "draw conclusions and form judgments."[19] In other words, the biographer here withdraws from his authorial and judgmental role. Arckenholtz's biography is not intended as such in the strict sense of the word, he writes, but such a one might follow later.[20] Here, he touches on the fundamental narrative weakness in his text, namely the problem of readability. Those with a different motivation for reading the work are given the pragmatic advice to simply skip over the many quotations from the source material.[21] On the border between literature and scholarship, Arckenholtz's aim clearly leans toward the latter. The *delectare* aspect of wanting to entertain has become unimportant.

In Arckenholtz's description, Christina appears incomparable in her gender identity as a woman, particularly with reference to her intelligence and culture. In the second volume, Arckenholtz increasingly emphasises her religious convictions. His praise culminates at the end of the biography, where he writes "that it would take entire centuries to bring forth another person of her sex who would be equal to her."[22] In contrast to earlier biographies, which primarily reproach the Queen for her female inconstancy, Arckenholtz's text thematises the gender aspect only when he wants to emphasise her superb character. Christina's historically documented ambiguous gender behaviour is largely disregarded in order to create a positive image which evidently required her being clearly attributed to the female sex. However, he also explains that she was not proclaimed Queen but rather King, which picks up the idea of a ruler—male or female—having two bodies: the natural and the political (see Baumgärtel 97). The fact that Christina never married represents a political problem. Arckenholtz' account of the public debate about her successor to the throne and possible marriage fills several pages. Ultimately, Arck-

---

19 "Folgerungen ziehen und Urtheile ziehen" (20).
20 "Da man übrigens dieses alles nur gleichsam als Stoff und Baugeräthe angesehen haben will, daraus einst einmal eine förmliche Lebensgeschichte dieser durchlauchten Königinn aufgeführt werden könnte" (preface 20–21).
21 "Endlich kann man denenjenigen, die von gar zu kützlichen Geschmacke seyn möchten, keine besseren Rath geben, als dass sie sich an den Text gegenwärtigen Werkes selbst halten, und thun, als ob sie die eingerückten Stellen, Anmerkungen und Verweise auf fremde Verfasser, die auch zu dem Ende auf jeder Seite unten stehen, nicht sähen" (preface 20).
22 "[…] daß ganze Jahrhunderte dazu gehören, um in ihrem Geschlechte noch eine Person hervorzubringen, die ihr gleich komme" (vol. 2: 392).

enholtz explains Christina's behaviour by suggesting that "probably one of her loves had made her abhor the idea of matrimony."[23] Arckenholtz here simply makes use of reduction and leaves out what does not fit his purposes.

As a biographer Arckenholtz explains more than he judges. He foregoes novella-like anecdotes and court gossip. However, in the footnotes one does find sub-plots, in which rumours are repudiated, adversaries of the Queen criticised, and sources corrected or supplemented. As already mentioned, the focus is on the representation of the Queen's intellectual superiority. Her abdication and conversion are dealt with in great detail. Using a wide variety of sources, Arckenholtz illustrates the different opinions that flourished in Europe at the time. The motive he provides for Christina's renunciation of the throne is that after her decision to remain unmarried and not have any children there was no reason for her to burden herself with the troubles of governing.[24] That Christina, after her abdication, often appeared in men's clothes is mentioned (see 471) but not discussed. Arckenholtz cites such departures from conventional gender behaviour without providing any commentary. Instead, the sources depict the way in which Christina was regarded by her contemporaries. For example, one report describes how Italian women were taken aback upon Christina's entry into Rome (523n). Despite the narrative intention to let the sources speak for themselves, Arckenholtz does evaluate the few sources penned by women differently from the eyewitness reports by male authors. Christina's entry into Paris is documented in two detailed reports by ladies-in-waiting, the Duchesse de Montpensier and Madame de Motteville (see 563).[25] The texts describe, from a female perspective, how people reacted to Christina. The ladies-in-waiting are first astonished by Christina's unfeminine manner. However, once they have gotten over their shock over her appearance, they are fascinated by her personality. What Arckenholtz criticises in these women's texts is that the French ladies should have the audacity to be so contemptuous towards women of other nations, especially as Christina's appearance was the result of a lack of both money and interest (see 572–73n). The women's reports are also

---

23 "Es muß nothwendig wohl einer von ihren Lieblingen ihr den Ehestand zuwider gemacht haben" (163–64).

24 "Denn da Christina einmal für allemal sich fest und steif entschlossen hatte niemals zu heirathen, so wollte sie die übrige Lebenszeit für sich zubringen. Und da sie keine Kinder erwartete, so fiel auch die Nothwendigkeit sich mit Regierungssorgen zu plagen weg. Zumahl da ihr sowohl die Ehre als die Mühseligkeiten und Unruhen des königlichen Standes zur Last wurden. Da sie einen erhabenen Geist besaß, so schmäuchelte sie sich bey den mittäglichen Völkern unbekannte Reize anzutreffen, und versprach sich neues Vergnügen, wenn sie in dem schönen Italien leben [...] könnte" (421).

25 See even Wortmann 192.

trivialised: although Arckenholtz states that one cannot cast doubt on the sources, he polemicises that they are just an expression of female envy.[26] As compensation he includes a positive description of Christina by a Duc de Guise, who stresses that Christina sees herself as an Amazon and is just as wild and proud as her father.[27] Male witnesses do not criticise unfeminine gender behaviour; on the contrary, they emphasise her masculine spirit and mentality. From a male perspective, masculinity is applied as a positive norm, even for a female sovereign. Arckenholtz's further vindication of the Queen's honour is provided *ex negativo* with the conclusion that there would undoubtedly have been talk about her illicit sexual practices, had proof of such behaviour ever existed (see Vol. 2: 25).

Besides the many written documents, Arckenholtz comments on coins which mirror central events in Christina's life. This is noteworthy insofar as coins are a part of the official visual language. This in turn gives rise to the question of what Arckenholtz understands in general by his narrative intent of presenting the Queen's private sphere. The sources do describe and document the Queen's nature, but much of that which Arckenholtz represents belongs in the realm of political events and juridical reflections, or explains particular issues such as the university system in Sweden. Arckenholtz's work ushers in a new phase in the biographical writing about Christina. He records Christina's life using collected documents but does not create popular fiction, and he leaves it to the reader to (re-)construct the life of the Queen. The collection of material resembles a puzzle that the biographer does not put together to form a coherent picture, which may be labelled as the retreat of the interpreting biographer. The narrative intention is to depict the private sphere, yet the work focuses *de facto* not on Christina as a private person but is instead an account of individual statements about her and correspondence with her.

The life stories of Queen Christina show the complexity characterising early modern biographical writing. The biographical accounts of the

---

26 "Man würde zwar unrecht handeln, wenn man die Erzählungen dieser beyden Hofdamen von Christinens ersten Aufenthalte in Frankreich überhaupt in Zweifel ziehen wollte. Allein es fragt sich nur, ob man allen und jeden kleinen und besonderen Umständen ihres Berichtes kecklich trauen darf, oder ob man nicht vielmehr sagen müsste, die dem schönen Geschlechte so sehr eigene Eifersucht habe ihrer Feder die anzüglichen Ausdrücke wieder Christinen eingeflößet, und solche Unordnungen ihr aufbürden und solche Fehler an ihr finden lassen, die wenigsten denen großen Eigenschaften, die ihr niemand streitig machen konnte, die Wage hielten" (574–75).

27 "Sie ist ein Weiser, der vom weiblichen nichts als die Geschlechtsglieder hat. Ihr Geist ist dergestalt zur Offenherzigkeit geneigt, daß sie sich niemals den Blicken und Geberden, die zu Spielung der weiblichen Rolle erfordert werden, unterziehen, auch nicht einmal in der Absicht, Weibertracht anlegen können. Sie betrachtet die Welt mit der gesetzten und männlichen Entschließung, die ihr Scepter und Ueberfluß verachten" (578).

Queen remind the contemporary reader that twenty-first-century genre categorisation is not applicable to these kinds of texts. Furthermore, it is not possible to identify a 'poetics of biography' out of the textual material presented here. We would, however, claim that the authors of the texts discussed above were well aware of many of the possibilities, options, and traps surrounding life-writing. They pick and choose in their search for 'their' presentation of the biographee, while almost always relating to the sex/gender of the Swedish monarch—directly or indirectly. They make new (narrative) worlds by remaking an important historic figure in their narratives. Personal characteristics of the Queen are mixed with events linked to her life. There seems to have been an ongoing exchange of ideologically, politically, and religiously charged ideas between Christina biographers in Europe already during her lifetime. They wanted to tell the right or true story, to entertain, or to stress moral values and chose to write in different traditions and genres. Their common goal—to generate a life from the parts selected by (and available to) them—shows different ways of worldmaking, but the Christina biographers of the seventeenth and eighteenth centuries were writing with a desire to create a 'whole' world, a Christian world of good and evil with clear boundaries and limits. In his essay "An Introduction to Radical Constructivism" (1984), Ernst von Glasersfeld states:

> [I]t seems to me that the resistance met in the eighteenth century by Giambattista Vico, the first true constructivist, and by Silvio Ceccato and Jean Piaget in the more recent past is not so much due to inconsistencies or gaps in their argumentation as to the justifiable suspicion that constructivism intends to undermine too large a part of the traditional view of the world. (17)

Glasersfeld, in his discussion of Goodman's theories, not only points out the conservatism inherent in the human being and the fear of new worlds and world orders. He ultimately refers to the narration of life stories, since human life to us is what makes our world 'the world.'[28] With the example of Queen Christina we have seen that she is allowed eccentric traits as long as they do not conflict with convention, question gender norms, or threaten institutions of power such as the papacy or absolutist monarchy. As soon as the Queen transgresses the boundaries so closely connected with her social position and her sex—as is described in almost all the texts written about her—her biographers have to adjust the textual world to fit their purposes. A world then takes shape that more often than not stresses values of tradition and convention that typically carry male connotations.

28　See also Steven Connor's contribution in this volume. Connor talks about the world as "an open necessity" to the human being.

References

Arckenholtz, Johan. *Historische Merkwürdigkeiten, die Königinn Christina von Schweden betreffend; zur Erläuterung der Geschichte ihrer Regierung und insonderheit ihres Privatlebens, wie auch der Civil- und Gelehrtenhistorie ihrer Zeit; nebst zwyen noch nie gedruckten Werken dieser gelehrten Prinzesinn. Durchgehends auf deren Briefe gegründet, und aus den bewährtesten Geschichtschreibern, beglaubten Handschriften und gedruckten Urkunden zusammengetragen, mit historischen, politischen, kritischen und gelehrten Anmerkungen, wie auch mit Gedächtnißmünzen erläutert. Nebst einem Anhange einiger Stücke zu fernerer Belehrung und Rechtfertigung.* 4 vols. Trans. Johann Friedrich Reiffstein. Leipzig/Amsterdam: Mortier, 1751–1760.

Ballaster, Ros. *Seductive Forms: Women's Amatory Fiction from 1684 to 1740.* Oxford: Oxford UP, 1998.

Barry, Kathleen. "Toward a Theory of Women's Biography: From the Life of Susan B. Anthony." *All Sides of the Subject: Women and Biography.* Ed. Teresa Iles. New York: Teachers College Press, 1992.

Baumgärtel, Bettina. "Is the King Genderless? The Staging of Female Regent as Minerva Pacifera." *Women Who Ruled: Queens, Goddesses, Amazons in Renaissance and Baroque Art.* Ed. Annette Dixon. London: Merrell, 2002. 97–117.

Buck, August. *Biographie und Autobiographie in der Renaissance.* Wiesbaden: Harrossowitz, 1983.

Chanut, Pierre. *Mémoires de ce qui s'est passé en Suède, et aux provinces voisines, depuis l'année 1645 jusques en l'année 1655. Ensemble le demêlé de la Suède avec la Pologne. Tirez des depesches de monsieur Chanut ... par P. Linage de Vauciennes.* Paris: n.p., 1675.

De Harst, and G. L. Gent. *A panegyrick of the most renowned and serene Princess Christina, by the grace of God, Queene of Swedland, Goths and Vandals Written originally in French, by the learned pen of Mr. de Harst, and now translated into English by W. L. Gent.* London: n.p.,1656. 29 Sept. 2009 <http://eebo.chadwyck.com/home>.

Dixon, Anette, ed. *Women who Ruled: Queens, Goddesses, Amazons in Renaissance and Baroque Art.* London: Merrell, 2002.

Eckart, Maren. "Erzählstrategien in frühneuhochdeutschen Biografien über Königin Christina." *Am Rande im Zentrum: Beiträge des VII. Nordischen Germanistentreffens Riga 2006.* Eds. Thomas Taterka, Dzintra Lele-Rozentāle, and Silvija Pavīdis. Berlin: SAXA, 2009. 23–31.

Falkdalen, Karin Tegenborg. *Kungen är en kvinna. Retorik och praktik kring kvinnliga monarker under tidigmodern tid.* Umeå: Institutionen för historiska studier, 2003.

ffolliott, Sheila. "Exemplarity and Gender: Three Lives of Catherine de Medici." *The Rhetorics of Life-Writing in Early Modern Europe: Forms of Biography from Cassandra Fedele to Louis XIV.* Eds. Thomas F. Mayer, and D.R. Woolf. Ann Arbor: U of Michigan P, 1995. 321–40.

Franckenstein, Christian Gottfried. *Histoire des intrigues galantes de la Reine Christine de Suède et de sa cour, pendant son séjour à Rome.* Amsterdam: n.p., 1697.

—. *The History of the Intrigues & Gallantries of Christina, Queen of Sweden. And Of her Court, whilst she was at Rome. Faithfully Render'd into English, from the French Original.* 1697. Trans. Philipp Hollingworth. London: n.p., 1927.

—. *Leben der Schwedischen Königin Christina und Ihres Hofes/(seit sie nach Rom begeben/) Nebst einigen Anmuthigen Staats- und Liebesintriguen. Von einem Ihrer Domestiquen in*

Französischer Sprache zusammen getragen/ und anitzo wegen der dabey vorgefallenen Curiositäten ins hochteutsche übersetzt. Rome: D.G. Nescher, 1705.

—. *Istoria degli intrighi galanti della regina Christina di Svezia e della sua corte durante il di lei soggiorno a Roma.* Eds. Jeanne Bignami Odier, and Giogio Morelli. Rome: Fratelli Palombi Editor, 1979.

Glasersfeld, Ernst von. "An Introduction to Radical Constructivism." *The Invented Reality.* Ed. Paul Watzlawick. New York: Norton, 1984. 17–40.

Goodman, Nelson. *Ways of Worldmaking.* Indianapolis: Hackett Publishing, 1978.

Grage, Joachim. "Entblößungen: Das zweifelhafte Geschlecht Christinas von Schweden in der Biographik." *Frauenbiographik: Lebensbeschreibung und Porträts.* Eds. Christian von Zimmermann, and Nina von Zimmermann. Tübingen: Narr, 2005. 35–59.

Grauert, Wilhelm Heinrich. *Christina Königin von Schweden und ihr Hof.* 2 vols. Bonn: Weber, 1837–42.

Greenblatt, Stephen. *Renaissance Self-Fashioning: From More to Shakespeare.* Chicago: U of Chicago P, 1980.

Haak, Christina. Commentary to the pictures in the catalogue: *Christina: Königin von Schweden. Katalog der Ausstellung im Kulturgeschichtlichen Museum Osnabrück 23. November 1997–1. März 1998.* Ed. Ulrich Hermanns. Bramsche: Rasch, 1997.

Haettner Aurelius, Eva. *Inför lagen: Kvinnliga svenska självbiografier från Agneta Horn till Fredrika Bremer.* Lund: Lund UP, 1996.

Hoberman, Ruth. "Biography: General Survey." *Jolly* 1: A-K (2001): 109–12.

Kajanto, Iiro. *Christina heroina: Mythological and Historical Exemplification in the Latin Panegyrics on Christina Queen of Sweden.* Helsinki: Suomalainen tiedeakatemia, 1993.

—. "Queen Christina in Latin Panegyrics." *Acta Conventus Neo-Latini Hafniensis: Proceedings of the Eighth International Congress of Neo-Latin Studies. Copenhagen, 12 August to 17 August 1991.* Medieval and Renaissance Texts and Scribes Vol. 120. Eds. Rhoda Schnur et al. Binghampton, NY: Medieval & Renaissance Texts & Studies, 1994. 43–59.

Kelly-Gadol, Joan. "Did Women Have a Renaissance?" *Becoming Visible: Women in European History.* Eds. Renate Bridenthal, and Claudia Koonz. Boston: Houghton Mifflin, 1977. 148–52.

Klein, Christian. *Grundlagen der Biographik: Theorie und Praxis des biographischen Schreibens.* Stuttgart: Metzler, 2002.

Mayer, Thomas F., and D. R. Woolf. *The Rhetoric of Life-Writing in Early Modern Europe: Forms of Biography from Cassandra Fedele to Louis XIV.* Ann Arbor: U of Michigan P, 1995.

Pufendorf, Samuel von. *Sechs und zwanzig Bücher Schwedisch und Deutschen Kriegs-Geschichte von König Gustaf Adolfs Feldzuge in Deutschland an, biss zur Abdanckung der Königin Christina.* Trans. Johan Joachim Möller v. Sommerfeld. Franckfurt am Mayn, 1688. Trans. of *Commentariorum De Rebus Suecicis Libri XXVI. Ab expeditione Gustavi Adolfi Regis in Germaniam ad abdicationem usque Christinae.* Utrecht: n.p., 1686.

Reinken, Liselotte von. *Deutsche Zeitungen über Königin Christine 1626–1689: Eine erste Bestandsaufnahme.* Münster: C. J. Fahle, 1966.

Schnell, Rüdiger. "Text und Geschlecht: Eine Einleitung." *Text und Geschlecht: Mann und Frau in Eheschriften der Frühen Neuzeit.* Ed. Rüdiger Schnell. Frankfurt a.M.: Suhrkamp, 1997.

—. *Frauendiskurs, Männerdiskurs, Ehediskurs: Textsorten und Geschlechterkonzepte in Mittelalter und Früher Neuzeit.* Frankfurt a.M.: Campus, 1998.
Sidén, Karin. *Den ideala barndomen: Studier i det stormaktstida barnporträttets ikonografi och funktion.* Stockholm: Raster, 2001.
Spender, Dale. "Foreword." *All Sides of the Subject: Women and Biography.* Ed. Teresa Iles. New York: Teachers College Press, 1992.
Stanley, Liz. 1992. "Process in Feminist Biography and Feminist Epistemology." *All Sides of the Subject: Women and Biography.* Ed. Teresa Iles. New York: Teachers College Press, 1992.
Stieff, Christian. *Leben der Weltberühmten Königin Christina von Schweden und denen geheimesten intrigven und merckwürdigsten umständen mit möglichstem fleiße entworffen.* Leipzig: Thomas Fritschen, 1705.
Weibull, Martin. "Om Mémoires de Chanut." *Historisk tidskrift.* 7 (1887): 49–80, 151–92.
Wiesner Hanks, Merry. "Women's Authority in the State and Household in Early Modern Europe." *Women who Ruled: Queens, Goddesses, Amazons in Renaissance and Baroque Art.* Ed. Anette Dixon. London: Merrell, 2002. 27–59.
Wortmann, Anke. "Das Bild der Königin Christina im zeitgenössischen Frankreich." *Christina: Königin von Schweden. Katalog der Ausstellung im Kulturgeschichtlichen Museum Osnabrück 23. November 1997–1. März 1998.* Ed. Ulrich Hermanns. Bramsche: Rasch, 1997. 183–96.
Wåghäll Nivre, Elisabeth. *Women and Family Life in Early Modern German Literature.* Rochester, NY: Camden House, 2004.
—. "Eine Königin in den Zeitungen: Königin Christina von Schweden als Beispiel frühneuzeitlicher Nachrichtenvermittlung." *Daphnis* 37:1 (2009): 301–32.

Seeing a World Unmade, and Making a World (Out) of Remains: The Post-Apocalyptic Re-Visions of W. S. Merwin and Carolyn Forché

RENÉ DIETRICH

> Tell me what you see vanishing and I
> Will tell you who you are
>
> (W. S. Merwin, "For Now" 74)

1. Made by the End: Post-Apocalypse and World(un)making

An often-quoted review of W. S. Merwin's possibly best-known volume of poetry, *The Lice*, published in 1967, states that this book "has perfectly captured the peculiar spiritual agony of our time, the agony of a generation which knows itself to be the last" (Liebermann qtd. in Perloff 122). These words place the work not only in a particular cultural situation defined by the social upheavals of the 1960s and the Vietnam War. They also assign an apocalyptic sensibility to it that often times has been regarded as a characteristic feature of the 1960s "generation," and which several critics have found prominent in Merwin's poetry of this decade.[1] However, Merwin's relation to the end is not as straightforwardly apocalyptic as, for instance, Barry McGuire's song "Eve of Destruction," nor is the sense of doom that pervades his poetry characterised by a simple proclamation of the last days.[2] Instead of serving as a prophet of the end, Merwin complicates the relation to the end, and our entire notion of it, by "bearing witness to a world already in mid-apocalypse" (Ramsey 22), and

---

1   See for instance Ramsey's assertion (22): "As all the reviewers of *The Lice* have declared, its first premise is an intuition of apocalypse," a paradigmatic instance in "a decade of writing that will be remembered for its apocalyptic obsessions." Note also the devotion of an entire chapter in Hix's *Understanding W.S. Merwin* (43–60) to "Apocalypse."

2   Indeed, such a reading would justify Harold Bloom's critique (more than Merwin's work itself does) that "Merwin's litanies of denudation will read very oddly when a fresh generation proclaims nearly the same dilemma [of being the last generation], and then yet another generation trumpets finality" (Bloom qtd. in Perloff 125).

even creating a "postapocalyptic situation" (Frazier 49). The quote at the beginning of the essay illustrates that the world, as seen by Merwin's "you," is already vanishing, which, for the speaker, clearly implicates this "you" in the process of ending. Taken from one of the last poems in *The Moving Target* (1963), these lines indicate what is at stake in the post-apocalyptic vision developed fully in the *The Lice*: "When the forests have been destroyed their darkness remains" (*TL* 118).[3] In the first line of the Vietnam poem "The Asians Dying," the world has vanished, is un-made, shattered by a historical catastrophe, and what is left to be seen is that what can no longer be seen. Paradoxes such as this abound in a post-apocalyptic vision, and will inform the discussion of W. S. Merwin's *The Lice* and Carolyn Forché's *The Angel of History* (1994) in this essay.

These works both engage in the poetic mode of the post-apocalyptic, which has been central to the works of a number of American poets since 1945 and especially since the 1960s until today. Such poetry approaches the end of the world from a post-apocalyptic perspective, presenting the world as already having come to an end, composed of nothing but fragments, ruins, and remains. This is not to say that there is no world anymore, but that the world is no longer the one as we knew it. Instead it has been transformed by an utterly destructive and possibly unnameable and undateable event into a state after its own end. Consequently, the world seen by the post-apocalyptic vision is one unmade and in a creative effort remade (out) of remains.

In bringing to the fore what it means for the world to end, to be unmade, such poetry thus highlights what is at stake in "worldmaking," and develops its own particular way of worldmaking. For the representation of a world already ended illustrates how the concept of "worldmaking" extends beyond a constructivist dimension to issues of specific cultural-historical situations and to ultimately personal-existential concerns. In arguing what worlds are made of, Goodman states: "Not from nothing after all, but from other worlds. Worldmaking as we know it always starts from worlds already on hand; the making is a remaking" (6). This aspect of remaking in the processes of worldmaking, however, can be charged with the specific urgency of a personal-existential concern when confronted with a cultural-historical situation in which the world, as one knew it, and the grounds on which this world was made, have in fact come to nothing, have to be remade because they were utterly destroyed. In such a situation, the remaking of worlds starts inside of ruins, ruins of a world made, and ruins of ways of worldmaking. In the aftermath of a catastrophe of such devastation, "remaking" and "nothing" become charged with

---

3   All of Merwin's poetry is quoted from *The Second Four Books of Poetry*.

new layers of meaning, shift from abstract terms of construction to the personal-existential challenges faced in a concrete cultural-historical situation of loss. Remaking becomes necessary in order to counter the threat of nothingness experienced in the historical catastrophe. Although the processes of remaking in such a situation clearly do not start from nothing, they are nevertheless imbued with a concrete sense of nothingness which in the twentieth century has found its most drastic expression in the nuclear ground zeros of Hiroshima and Nagasaki, and the Nazi death camps. The ways of worldmaking which reflect the effect of such catastrophes are always to a certain extent themselves "Ways of Nothingness," as John Gery (1996) has argued for poetry engaged with the possibility of nuclear annihilation. Similarly, post-apocalyptic poetry partakes in the personal-existential challenge of remaking after historical catastrophe, but does so in a way that highlights the persistence of destruction. The remaking processes of post-apocalyptic poetry themselves are charged by the obliterating forces of the unmaking; what the poetry remakes in its writing is the moment and aftermath of the unmaking. The way of worldmaking in post-apocalpytic poetry remakes through depicting worlds unmade.

In the same manner, the idea of vision, which assumes a prominent place in both of Merwin's poems quoted above, conveys and combines several pertinent aspects in the discussion of world(un)making, (post-)apocalypse, and poetry. It is evidently a central aspect of worldmaking on a personal dimension, for it is our ability to see, both in the meaning of a physical sense, and as an imaginative capacity, that is vital to our access to and our making of our world. Furthermore, vision is deeply embedded in various aspects of poetic creation. The visionary poet, *poeta vates*, has enjoyed a long tradition that can be traced back to Homer. Additionally, the poetic world is made and determined through the perspective of the speaker, that means through how and what he or she sees, and comes into being through language noted for its imagery.[4] Thus, through claiming a specific vision of the world, the world altered by vision is re-created in poetry in word images. Finally, the concept of vision has been closely linked to apocalypse, since the prophet of the end is gifted with a power of sight unavailable to 'normal people'—a point of convergence with the figure of the visionary poet, or prophet-poet, that has received considerable critical attention, foremost in the figure of Blake.[5] A failing

---

4   For the interrelation of the speaker's perspective and the world depicted, see Müller-Zettelmann (134).

5   Blake's position in the apocalyptic canon of writing can be traced back to Northrop Frye's interpretation in *Fearful Symmetry*. See Robinson's analysis ("Literature and Apocalyptic" of the "romantic or visionary" (373) Blakean apocalypse, and Frye's "Blakean apocalyptic man" as analysed by Robson (171).

of vision, then, as well a shift from vision to re-vision, transports exactly what is implied in a change from an apocalyptic to a post-apocalyptic perspective of the end, a shift that in Merwin and Forché has to be read in relation to the particular cultural-historical situation of the United States in the latter half of the twentieth century. Accordingly, the post-apocalyptic sensibility of their poetry combines a historical awareness, a concern for poetic form and tradition, as well as a personal dimension. Although these three aspects cannot be neatly separated, their discussion in the following paragraphs is both to theoretically frame the readings of their poetic vision and to sketch the questions that are at the heart of world (un)making and post-apocalyptic poetry.

2. Seeing That the End has Already Come: The Post-Apocalyptic Re-Visions of a World Unmade

In many ways, World War II can still be argued to be the event that divides the twentieth century and makes it possible to talk about its 'latter half,' in that it has been conceived of as a catastrophe of a truly world-shattering apocalyptic impact:

> Both at the time and subsequently, World War II has been understood to signify a moment of rupture that permanently devalues the principles and aspirations associated with Euro-American tradition. The war signifies the end of the great narratives that have shaped Western civilization for the past two hundred years. (Dellamora, "Introduction" 2)

In addition to having signified an ending to the "great narratives that have shaped Western civilization," WW II has also become a pivotal landmark for our contemporary understanding of the end of the world. In the destruction that was wrought by the genocide of the European Jews and the annihilation of Hiroshima and Nagasaki through atomic bombs, mankind has proven capable of bringing the end on itself, and in order to imagine it, these images need only to be remembered and reproduced. Their nothingness cannot be enhanced, and instead of a movement forwards, they only signal "Ways of Nothingness" (Gery) as possible further routes for humanity. Additionally, sites of absolute destruction such as Auschwitz and Hiroshima present us with images of what the world after the end would look like, and thus make it possible to view the moment after the moment of our own extinction.[6]

---

[6] See Schwenger on the experience of Hiroshima survivors, "the instant after the blast the internal perceptions of the victims was that absolutely nothing remained of the reality

Such a post-apocalyptic vision has been prominently captured in the midst of World War II by Walter Benjamin in his image of "The Angel of History," interpreting the painting *Angelus Novus* by Paul Klee. Just as Lyotard leads us through "the end of the great narratives" to the postmodern heterogeneity of the many little narratives and finalities (see Dellamora, "Introduction" 2; Lyotard), so does Benjamin's vision of continuing destruction open up a specific dimension of postmodern historicity of the retrospect:

> This is how one pictures the angel of history. His face is turned toward the past. Where we perceive a chain of events, he sees one single catastrophe which keeps piling wreckage and hurls it in front of his feet. The angel would like to stay, awaken the dead, and make whole what has been smashed. But a storm is blowing in from Paradise; it has got caught in his wings with such a violence that the angel can no longer close them. The storm irresistibly propels him into the future to which his back is turned, while the pile of debris before him grows skyward. This storm is what we call progress. (Walter Benjamin, "Theses on the Philosophy of History, IX"; qtd. in the epigraph to Forché's *The Angel of History*)

This image singularly combines the post-apocalyptic situation of revision and a specific postmodern view of history characterised by the cataclysmic events that precede and shape the present. The angel, gifted with a specific vision, is able to see catastrophes of ongoing endings, but only in retrospect. Such a reversal is constitutive of the post-apocalyptic vision: with the gaze directed towards the ruinous past, the future becomes inaccessible and recedes instead of progresses. The angel still serves as a messenger, but instead of a prophet of the apocalypse as a witness of the end.[7]

The status of the witness puts the "angel of history" in a position akin to the one occupied by the speaker in much of post-apocalyptic poetry, combining in the term 'witness' the special capacity to see, the ultimate powerlessness of the position, and the implication in the catastrophic history itself. With the shift from prophet to witness, post-apocalyptic representations become less concerned with prophecy than with trauma. In the post-apocalyptic vision, the signs of the end become symptoms of

---

around them" (49), and Gery: "For one who has survived atomic war, nothingness is not only an absence and a void, it has also become a way of life" (3). For a larger sense of the post-apocalyptic, see Berger: "It seems significant that in the late twentieth century we have had the opportunity [...] to see after the end of our civilization—to see in a strange prospective retrospect what the end would actually look like: it would look like a Nazi death camp, or an atomic explosion, or an ecological or urban wasteland" (xiii).

7   See the excellent analysis of Benjamin's 'angel of history' in Kalaidjan (*The Edge of Modernism* 97ff.); see also Dellamora ("Introduction" 3).

destruction—and the speaker is not exempt from that state of ruins.[8] Just like the "angel of history," the speaker in post-apocalyptic poetry is captured by the end he means to capture, caught in revising the end he cannot change. Thus, the speaker himself appears traumatised by the ending he views after the fact. Equally, blown away by the storm of progress, the angel of history does not remain unaffected by the catastrophes whose results only he can see. His position is one of constant retrospection, and he is as much propelled into the future as projected by Benjamin into a post-apocalyptic future that presents itself as a "complex form of stasis" (Berger xiii) always after each world-shattering and transforming catastrophe. This situation of the permanent aftermath is the defining feature of post-apocalyptic poetry: the end is all there is to know but at the same time always beyond grasp, unknowable in itself and knowable only through its remainders and ruins. These ruins can be read metaphorically as well as literally, and indeed the post-apocalyptic sensibility is intimately linked to actual historical catastrophes. These in turn have been conceived of as traumatic ruptures, have been remembered apocalyptically as standing for the end of the world as we know it, and have henceforth shaped our understanding of that end—most prominently for the latter half of the twentieth century, World War II.

With the ending of the great narratives in a world-shattering catastrophe, any concept of totality, which was still a touchstone for much of modernism, became questionable and, indeed, suspect. The idea of totality itself was increasingly conceived of as apocalyptic, since such an ideology was the main condition for any meta-narrative running towards some great imaginary end—leaving real damage in its wake. For American postwar post-apocalyptic poets, fragmentation presented itself in two different ways: it appeared both as a given, an inevitable historical condition to struggle with, and was actively created through poetic techniques as a means of critical reflection. Objects of such criticism were specific present conflicts that were apocalyptically coloured, e.g. the Vietnam War, the general dominance of the apocalyptic sensibility in the American cultural imaginary, and an unflinching progressivism that has been apocalyptically charged since the first settlers.[9] Such an embedding of post-apocalyptic

---

8   The psychoanalytic vocabulary that 'symptoms' evokes is not incidental. For the link between (post-)apocalypse and trauma, see Berger: "Apocalypse and trauma are congruent ideas, for both refer to shattering of existing structures of identity and language, and both effect their own erasures from memory and must be reconstructed by means of their traces, remains, survivors, and ghosts: their symptoms" (19).

9   See for poetic reactions to the Vietnam War Chattarij, for its apocalyptic significance in US culture, O'Leary ("Popular Culture and Apocalypticism" 416–17). For the apocalyptic sensibility in American culture from the Puritan settlers to the beginning of the 21st century, see for instance the relevant chapters in volume III of Collins, McGinn and Stein. For the

poetry in its socio-cultural situation attaches a political significance to the term 'witness' and elucidates its position towards central tenets of postmodernism.

It must first of all be clearly stated that 'post-apocalyptic' cannot be equated with 'postmodernist.' Instead, by maintaining a special relation to central tenets of postmodernism such as fragmentation, disunity, and dissociation, it takes a conflicted stand towards it: since the post-apocalyptic vision historicises the postmodern condition in relation to world-shattering catastrophes of the twentieth century, it does not unequivocally salute it as an unproblematic liberation of former constraints. However, through its historical consciousness, a prior state of imaginary totality does not appear desirable either, and in many ways, an embrace of fragmentation is necessary in order to address its problematic. In much of post-apocalyptic poetry, one finds an urgency, a sense of necessity in its poetical innovation, an awareness that this historical notion of fragmentation extends to the poetic traditions, to form and to language itself. If such poetry does not want to pretend that it can un-do the unmaking, it has to work with (and possibly work through) fragmentation, dissociation, and destruction as central tenets of its poetics. Postmodern post-apocalyptic poets thus have to formulate their own artistic responses to the experience of fragmentation and endings, just as modern poets engaged in apocalyptic discourses and struggled with notions of totality. Besides William Carlos Williams and T. S. Eliot, Wallace Stevens is a very prominent example, whose relation to the end is always a complex and conflictual one—we find in his poetry the "ideal of nothingness" as strongly as his resistance to the apocalyptic desire for total destruction.[10] However, this resistance also stems from the desire to preserve a form of totality from destruction, and thus entails either a resistance against the loss of, or a mourning of a lost totality. Woodland's argument (xi) that the questions whether Stevens should be regarded as a modernist or a postmodernist poet and whether he should be conceived of as an apocalyptic

---

latter half of the 20th century, especially see Boyer, for a comparison between apocalyptic rhetoric in the 19th and 20th centuries, O'Leary (*Arguing the Apocalypse*), for a collection of insightful essays on apocalyptic and millennial discourses from the 17th to the 19th century Engler, Fichte, and Scheiding. Robinson (*American Apocalypses*) provides a comprehensive discussion of the relation between the apocalypse and American literature, and convincingly argues for a differentiated apocalyptic hermeneutic.

10 See for an insightful discussion of Stevens's relation to the apocalypse Woodland: "These earlier engagements with apocalyptic discourse have more in common with the optimistic, early modernist use of apocalypse as a way of troping modernism's desire to break with the past [...]. This later version of apocalypse threatens to end the era that the earlier version helped inaugurate, and Stevens' resistance to this end tells us a great deal about his aesthetics and his place in literary history" (xvii).

or anti-apocalyptic poet are related to each other, furthermore point out that in the specific relation to the apocalypse one can maintain a shift of emphasis from modernism to postmodernism. One reason for such a shift might be found in the changed relation to the world's end in the wake of World War II's end-of-the-world scenarios. In the atomic age, poems on nothingness take on a historical urgency and currency that Stevens's "the nothing that is not there" (Ramazani, Ellmann and O'Clair 247) in his "Snowman" from 1921 simply did not possess to the same degree. Whereas Stevens highlights the possibility or impossibility of the ideal of absence, post-apocalyptic poetry focuses on what has actually been lost and destroyed in a moment of nothingness.[11] Such poetry thus becomes the remnant of a world that is gone, and the instant of a present world in ruins.

In that the study of the post-apocalyptic is a study of the aftermath, it is also a study of the remainder and transformation of the remainder (Berger 7). Due to these processes of transformation, a certain degree of formal self-reflexivity, complexity, and difficulty is necessary for a post-apocalyptic mode of expression. Any artistic representation consequently has to work out its own implication in these processes of transformation. More than a post-apocalyptic poem simply being a creation after the destruction, and standing for the possibility of creation in the face of destruction, the processes of creation and destruction are intricately linked in it. The creative processes by which the poem is formed are transformed by the destruction of the world that the poem captures, and to which the poem puts itself in a position of the retrospect, the aftermath. This aftermath paradoxically includes the apocalypse itself—in a post-apocalyptic world, this concept of the ultimate and defining catastrophe has become obsolete, part of the ruins of the past. Since the apocalypse has to be ultimate, it is indeed destroyed by a catastrophe that leaves nothing but ruins. In such a world of remains, in which all is opened up, but nothing revealed, revelation itself is obliterated. In Derrida's famous post-

---

11 See for the distinction between absence and loss, LaCapra's salient essay "Trauma, Absence, Loss." One finds a similar argument in the distinction between structural and historical trauma in Berger (22–23). Gery discusses this distinction in relation to the changed concept of nothingness in a pre- and post-Hiroshima world in a comparative analysis of "The Snowman" and Thom Gunn's "The Annihilation of Nothing" "The difference between them reveals, I believe, a paradigm of how ideas of nothingness have changed in the nuclear age: While Stevens' poem is highly seductive in the way it imagines nothingness, Gunn's poem [...] provides a more realistically (or 'extrinsically') grounded expression of nothingness, as we have come to think of it since Hiroshima" (151). Gery continues to argue: Whereas Stevens' "poem approaches an almost ideal expression of nothingness" (154), Gunn imbues nothingness with the "concept of *present* annihilation" (Gery 158). For a discussion of the importance of the nuclear age to poetry, see the chapters in Bruner: "Noir Poetics" (183) and "Nuclear Family" (218).

structuralist deconstruction of apocalyptic thought/tone, this state is captured through aporetic constructions, "an end without end," "the apocalypse of the apocalypse," indeed "the apocalypse without apocalypse, an apocalypse without vision, without truth, without revelation" ("Of an Apocalyptic Tone" 94–95)—an apocalypse *sous rature,* under erasure.

The consequent implications of such processes of erasure for the poetic form are analysed by Brian McHale in the context of his discussion of postmodern "Poetry under Erasure": "When the semantic building blocks of the poem fall under erasure, its world oscillates or flickers—between one state of affairs and another, even between being and non-being, something and nothing" (290). Hence, such poetry, he continues, "problematizes world-*making.* [...] Projected worlds, or parts of worlds, are susceptible of being placed under erasure retrospectively—*un*made" (293). McHale does not explicitly link such "poetry under erasure" to notions of apocalypse or post-apocalypse, but the way in which he historicises it, between "the erasure of the European Jews [and] the mass erasure, sometime in the indeterminate future, of us all" (297), echoes Berger's (6–7) theorisations of the post-apocalyptic that is positioned between two catastrophes, a real one in the past and an imagined one projected onto the future. Equally, the flickering between something and nothing captures the intricate relationship of creation and destruction one finds at the heart of post-apocalyptic poetry.

McHale's assertion that such poetry "problematizes world-making" additionally highlights that poetry presenting the world "*un*made" brings to attention the existential and personal dimension that is actually at stake in worldmaking and, respectively, world-unmaking. For Goodman's dictum that it is *we* who make our worlds, remaking them out of other worlds, should not be taken too lightly. This statement of radical constructivism carries with it a note of existential concern that is not to be overlooked. Understood in this manner, "worldmaking" does not liberate us from confronting the world as it is. Even more so, it is not a creative option we have, or an arbitrary act of our choice, but something we need to do in order to exist in the world as such. Accordingly, it does not make our actions any less inconsequential that we cannot access the world other than through the very capacities of the self that make our subjective world. Instead, this undeniable link between our self and our world can make us realise how very fragile our world, the world of each one of us, in fact is—the world we make and by which we, in turn, are made. What is at stake in this making, and what it means for one's world to be unmade, Elaine Scarry has pointed out with admirably painstaking clarity in dissecting the phenomena of war and torture: for it means precisely the destroying of voice, space and self of someone.[12] These are indeed the very aspects of human existence that we live by, which additionally are essential concepts to our making of the world in the sense of creating a civilisation, of 'culture-making.'[13] What is unmade, then, are not merely the elements or parts a world is made of, but the very structure of making itself in that it is "being reversed or uncreated or deconstructed" (Scarry 20). Accordingly, Scarry has termed both war and torture processes of "unmaking of civilization," "uncreating of the created world," "world unmaking" (45). In these actions, everything that makes our world, including the very structures that make such making possible, is unmade by "the structure of unmaking" (Scarry 20). Beyond the standard assumption that "torture and war are acts of destruction (and hence somewhat the opposite of creation), that they entail the suspension of civilization (and are somehow the opposite of that civilization)," investigating their "structure of unmaking" reveals that they are "in the most literal and concrete way possible, an appropriation, aping and reversing of the action of creating itself" (Scarry 21). The reversal, which figures so importantly in a post-apocalyptic vision, constitutes for Scarry the destruction that is the unmaking of the world.

Furthermore, a redirection of the focus, with Scarry's help, to what it means to unmake someone's world, and which instances do this in the most persisting way, also highlights the necessity of our worldmaking in relation to the world at large. For, as her historical references to dictatorships, wars, and the Holocaust demonstrate: the uncaring destruction of someone's world is echoed in the destruction of the world at large; the objectification of people finds its equivalent in regarding the world without any connection to human life. In fact, the world-shattering catastrophes of World War II which have shaped our image of the end of the world do not merely present endings to the philosophical and social 'great narratives.' They can equally be regarded as the unmaking of the worlds of millions of people—whether they died or survived, in actual ruins and/or traumatised in a state of *Death in Life*[14]. In the same respect, the horror of

---

12 See for the interrelatedness of these phenomena, her analysis of intense pain in torture: "It is the intense pain that destroys a person's self and world, a destruction experienced spatially as either the contraction of the universe down to the immediate vicinity of the body or as the body swelling to fill the entire universe. Intense pain is also language-destroying: as the content of one's world disintegrates, so the content of one's language disintegrates, so that which would express and project the self is robbed of its source and its subject" She goes on to summarise: "World, self, and voice are lost, or nearly lost, through the intense pain of torture" (Scarry 35).

13 The extent of their importance to poetry-making and its critical analysis will be demonstrated in the readings of Merwin and Forché.

14 So the title of Robert-Jay Lifton's famous study on Hiroshima survivors.

ecological disasters that spurn apocalyptic fears today is also the horror vision of a world that can no longer be made by us, of a world we have unmade and ended by making it hostile to human habitation.

In tying the after-the-end-of-the-world state to the perspective of a speaker, whether explicitly or implicitly present, post-apocalyptic poetry brings to the fore the personal dimension of the experience and effects of world destruction. Not simply an all-seeing and strangely disconnected "angel of history," the post-apocalyptic speaker reflects the traumatised position of someone from whom the world has been taken away, and the post-apocalyptic poem represents the position of something that has been wrestled from a world that is gone, and, equally traumatised, now exists after its end. Through the unmaking, uncreating, of the very structures of making, the concept of worldmaking is problematised to the point of its reversal. Thus, the poetic form reflects the speaker's need to struggle with the properties of voice, self, vision, space and time in order to recreate something of a—rephrasing the title of Kermode's seminal study on the modern apocalypse—sense of an after-the-ending situation in the poem. Post-apocalyptic poetry then demonstrates that the depiction of a world unmade, or shattered into fragments, does not only entail a historical and a formal dimension, but also a very personal-existential one, and that any apocalyptic vision or post-apocalyptic revision is about the end of the world as we know it, but also about the end of the world that we have made for us by our very senses. As Merwin stated at the outset of the essay: "Tell me what you see vanishing and I / will tell you who you are." Since the eye/I tells you who you are by what you see vanishing, you literally see what you are: and the less you see, the less you are. For the speaker in post-apocalyptic poetry, his or her special capacity to see is constantly questioned and compromised by the struggles with the ending that is also the ending of seeing. The post-apocalyptic vision is thus permanently caught in between revision and blindness, in between a past ending that cannot be seen, but from which one cannot avert the gaze, and a present state after-the-end in which seeing is no longer possible.

In which intricate ways the various dimensions of world-unmaking find expression in American post-apocalyptic poetry of the latter half of the twentieth century will be analysed in respect to two examples: W. S. Merwin's 1960s post-apocalyptic poetry of the "deep image" in *The Lice* (1967), in which surreal imagery is connected to a critique of American apocalyptic progressivism, and Carolyn Forché's poetry of the post-apocalyptic witness in *The Angel of History* (1994), an epic work of fragmented poetic speech that depicts a contemporary "wasteland" in reference to historical catastrophes of the twentieth century.

3. "You Saw not Darkness but Nothing": Blindness and Seeing the End of America in W. S. Merwin's *The Lice*

W. S. Merwin's poetry of the 1960s is regularly grouped with, among others, the poetry of Robert Bly and James Wright under the heading "Deep Image." Influenced by French and Spanish surrealism, their imagery of depth aimed at capturing a reality beyond the everyday visible one by creating poetic landscapes of an archetypal subconscious quality (see the introduction in Ramazani, Ellmann, and O'Clair lii). "Deep image" poetry thus highlighted the importance both of imagery and of vision for the making of poetry: particular images were created to represent that what remains ordinarily hidden, to reveal the unfamiliar and the uncanny in the world around us, and thus to let the reader see the world anew.[15]

In Merwin's *The Lice*, the world of deep images is characterised by its disappearances and absences—both in the depiction of a deserted world and in its poetic form without punctuation and regular metre. Merwin's post-apocalyptic vision catches the world in the constant process of fading away after what appears as an ultimate but inaccessible catastrophe. His poetry evokes images of a world that is gone in the very sense that it can no longer be seen or that the inhabitants of that world are struck by blindness. Absence of sight is both linked to the absence of light as well as to the end of being: Blindness, darkness, blackness characterise the visible landscape of *The Lice*, which in fact appears as a landscape robbed of everything visible: "This is the waking landscape / Dream after dream after dream walking away through it / Invisible invisible invisible" ("The Widow," *TL* 102). This invisibility is partly imaged by a loss of light, partly by a failing vision. "Today the sun is farther than we think" ("Is That What You Are," *TL* 82). The source of light, the sun, is evoked as far from the earth in that it is not merely setting, but either abandoning the world that revolves around it or dying itself: "The sun goes away to set elsewhere" ("A Scale in May," *TL* 112), "Where dying a sun rises" ("In a Clearing," *TL* 124). With the loss of light, darkness becomes both an ubiquitous phenomenon and an active agent in that world: "The darkness began to dance" ("Unfinished Book of Kings," *TL* 91), "Darkness gathered on the money" ("Pieces for Other Lives," *TL* 93), "Darkness moves up the nail" ("The Moths," *TL* 95), "Offering snow to the darkness" ("Whenever I Go There," *TL* 96). Through its constantly moving presence, darkness seems to have a reign over this world. This reign of dark-

---

15 For the importance of vision and the visible in the conception of the new surrealism see also Libby: "they work a direct magic on ordinary vision, suggesting hidden patterns in the visible world, inevitably moving toward the creation of myth" ("W. S. Merwin and the Nothing that Is" 28).

ness, however, is not uncontested. To some degree, the idea of an invisible world finds its strongest expression in the moment of nothingness in which darkness, too, loses all substance: "you / Saw not darkness but / Nothing" ("Pieces for Other Lives," *TL* 94). In the absence of everything describable by categories of visibility, it is nothing, and not darkness, which becomes the quality associated with blindness: "My blind neighbor has required of me / A description of darkness" ("The Gods," *TL* 99). Merwin's world is then not merely one which cannot be seen due to absence of light, but in which only "nothing" can be seen, and hence, exists. The loss of sight thus implicates the inhabitants of the world in the processes of vanishing surrounding them. Merwin's imagery of the eye demonstrates how literally, and physically, he understands the end of seeing in blindness: "The eyes disappeared" ("Pieces for Other Lives," *TL* 95), "he will have fallen into his eyes" ("The River of Bees," *TL* 100), "The extinct animals are still looking for home / Their eyes full of cotton" ("In Autumn," *TL* 107). Whether this impossibility of seeing prefigures the world's disappearance, or whether it is a result of this process, is hard to determine. Yet, with the "extinct animals" who are blinded by "the eyes full of cotton," it is clear that more is at stake than the end of sight. The end of seeing is linked to the world's end, to the disappearance of everything existing, particularly everything in nature. Similarly, a herd of sheep is pictured "Like a light in the light / And when it goes out they vanish" ("In a Clearing," *TL* 124). The invisible world made in Merwin's poetry is in fact the world un-made by apocalyptic catastrophe. Merwin's past apocalypse is revealing insofar as it is revealing a blind world having reduced itself to nothing. The blindness of the after-the-end state reflects the blindness of man acted out in the extinction of the animals and, following from that, their own species ("For a Coming Extinction," *TL* 122–23). The world reduced to nothing is the logical outcome of political and economical processes whose underlying world view reduces everything via the cold rationale of power and progress to its sheer utility—robbing it of any ungovernable and uncommodifiable excess, in short, any life. The result is a world both silenced, as Ed Folsom has pointed out, and blinded—his observation is applicable to sight as much as to voice: "This self becomes voiceless, as the things he would use his voice to describe disappear; a barren landscape is all that remains, and the poet's stripped barren words to reflect it" (235).

Merwin's post-apocalyptic vision of a "barren landscape" can also be read as a revision in two senses: first of all, it revises the visionary or romantic apocalypse found in Blake, and secondly, it puts under critical revision the apocalyptic narrative of end and renewal dominant in US culture. Both senses of revision are related to the fact that the post-apocalyptic situation Merwin creates seems to exist in a temporal limbo: it is both a projection into an unspecified future, and a representation of the present world. The final passages of "The Gods" illustrate this clearly:

> I
> am all that became of them
> Clearly all is lost
>
> The gods are what has failed to become of us
> Now it is over we do not speak
>
> Now the moment has gone it is dark
> What is man that he should be infinite
> the music of a deaf planet
> The one note
> Continues clearly this is
>
> The other world
> These strewn rocks belong to the wind
> If it could use them (*TL* 98)

Lazer observed of the poem that in it "our present day earth and the future planet of extinction are indistinguishable" (277).[16] Merwin's poetry creates a collapse of borders between one world and "[t[he other world," implicating the collapse of basic dimensions of human existence: "Once, distinctions among past, present and future, and between life and death, were clear. Now, they are not" (Lazer 281).[17] Such a loss of distinctions in the post-apocalyptic vision seems to echo the processes of unveiling in the "romantic or visionary" (Robinson, *American Apocalypse* 373) apocalypse as analysed in respect to William Blake sixty years ago by Northrop Frye in *Fearful Symmetry*. The poet's specific vision reveals the true nature of the world, which is "an already existing paradisal reality, which we already live in if we could but see it" (Frye 371). The heavenly world of oneness is not placed in an indeterminate future, but is already with us, sensed and, at the same time, created by the poetic act of seeing itself—an act of seeing in which the boundaries and limitations of the old, ordinary world are un-

---

16 Equally, Ramsey describes "The Gods" as a poem "whose mood and imagery [...] may be properly called postapocalyptic" (32).

17 Lazer's reading echoes Berger's commentary on the temporal confusion caused in writing the post-apocalypse, through which the living are perceived as already dead.

made, "consumed in fire" of infinity (Blake qtd. in Robinson "Literature and Apocalyptic" 39). Merwin's post-apocalypse both radicalises and negates such a Blakean outlook on the end in the present. Equally emphasising the act of seeing in his poetry for the making of a world, the dominating imagery of blackness and blindness demonstrate that the reality "which we already live in if we could but see it" is the one in which there is nothing to see because everything is already gone. Additionally, instead of a unitarian oneness, Merwin's loss of distinctions creates a world of fragments, ruins, remains, and ghosts. Giving up the sense of linear temporal progression for "cyclical or intersecting time" does not result in offering an opening up towards timeless infinity: "What is man that he should be infinite / The music of a deaf planet" (Lazer 280). On the contrary, all temporal dimensions become inaccessible, and man is exiled into the temporal post-apocalyptic aftermath of "complex stasis" (Berger xiii), in which time somehow continues beyond itself: "In turn, the present becomes a moment wedged between the past, which cannot be remembered, and in the future, which, if it will exist, will exist without us." And even that moment of the present is always already gone, lost in darkness: "Now the moment has gone it is dark" (Lazer 282).

Depicting the end of time is for Merwin clearly motivated by the spirit of his own historical time and place. Thus, *The Lice* can be read, as has been noted by various critics, as an outcry against man's arrogance and ignorance in dealing with the natural world, and, to a lesser degree, those victimised by political power struggles. The outcry is muted, however, in that it offers no alternative perspective.[18] Such a failure of seeing 'a way out' for humanity have led some to criticise the work for its tenets of a "basic anti-humanism" (Libby, "W. S. Merwin" 36). One might argue, though, that in post-apocalyptic poetry, written from the projected aftermath of an ultimate catastrophe, such an alternative perspective cannot find expression, since it has no place in that poetic universe and has indeed been destroyed along with everything else. Nevertheless, whether effectively or ineffectively, critics have agreed that W. S. Merwin's poetry accuses especially Western humanity of its self-destructive behaviour (see also Ramsey 20). It has, though, largely gone unnoticed that in the few

---

18 The following quote from Libby may serve as representative for such an assessment: "For ecological as well as more traditional political reasons (Vietnam) Merwin felt by 1970 that the civilization which culminated in America was in a terminal phase of moral and cultural entropy. [...] When *The Lice* revealed him as fully the poet of nothingness, of the continuing apocalypse that fails to bring revelation, it was clear that his perspective had darkened well beyond the limits of political protest. Protest assumes the possibility of an alternative, and for Merwin by the end of the sixties it seemed to late for alternatives. Man the destroyer as cut off from any natural or spiritual centers of value; in a richly deserved exile he waited in darkness for the end of the End" ("Merwin's Planet" 50–51).

topical poems that address the causes of the world's destruction depicted in the poetry, Merwin wages a heavy critique specifically against certain aspects of American culture that are driven by the apocalyptic narrative of progressing for the sake of a great end. "The Last One" (*TL* 86–88), for instance, launches an attack against American expansion regardless of consequence, in whose march across the continent the nation followed its 'manifest destiny' in a heavenly predetermined history of progress. "The Asians Dying" (*TL* 118), and "When the War is Over" (*TL* 119), with the Vietnam War as backdrop, take up the topic of American imperialism as a history of creating 'good wars' which become apocalyptically metaphorised into end-battles of good vs. evil.[19] Merwin's imagery of devastation, the abstraction of the Americans into "possessors" who "move everywhere under Death their star" (*TL* 119), and his scathing remarks that "we will all enlist again" (*TL* 119) after "the War is Over" make clear that these end-battles create no new beginning but simply death, destruction, and their continuation in another war. In Lazer's analysis (271; see also Libby, "W.S. Merwin" 23), Merwin's seemingly general use of "we" and "man" becomes tied to the US in that he takes up the motif of "America's importance as an example to mankind" dating back to Winthrop's "city upon a hill" and twists it upon itself: "In Merwin's eyes our American political, ecological and industrial example becomes a thoroughly negative one" (Lazer 272). One might radicalise such an argument in suggesting that Merwin criticises the very idea that America should regard itself as a "city upon a hill," a redeemer nation, from which other nations should take their example on the way to a heavenly kingdom. Focusing on the outcome of political and economical instrumentalisations of this ideology of self-importance, his poetry depicts the results of such an unfailing belief in one's rightness and progress towards some great imaginary 'End,' with the results being real destruction left in its wake.

The destruction of Merwin's "burned out landscape" (Libby, "W.S. Merwin" 23) is reflected both in the poetry's stark imagery and the poetic form without punctuation and regular meter. The reprint of "The Gods" above displays the effect of such a "stripped barren" page (Folsom 235): The "I," "The one note," "The other world," are depicted both as singular and isolated. The line breaks signify both openings to various meanings but also actual ruptures, disconnecting words and meanings from their surroundings, dislodging them from text and context (see also Ramsey 25). In "Whenever I Go There," such a break becomes the formal mani-

---

19 This tendency can be noted in the "axis of evil" and "evil empire" rhetoric of recent US presidents. However, such a conception can be traced back to very beginning of the American nation in the apocalyptic charging of the War of Independence (see Boyer 68–79, 219–230).

festation of the content: "the beginning // is broken" (*TL*, 96) while in "The Asians Dying," "Remains" (*TL* 119) is all that remains from one line—again opening up the line to readings extending beyond what its context suggests ("Pain the horizon / Remains" (ibid.)). Additionally, *The Lice* has to be understood as post-apocalyptic poetry in that it appears as having been written "after the end" (Gross qtd. in Libby, "W.S. Merwin" 20). From the perspective that the poetry itself is projected into a post-apocalyptic moment, punctuation and regular metre signify a past order, a fixed structure of unities that is both lost and actively abandoned in the aftermath. Merwin's irregular broken lines demonstrate both aspects of the post-apocalyptic: through them we witness the processes of regaining poetic speech after a world- and language-shattering catastrophe, and they testify to the fact that one cannot revert to the poetic form of old in order to capture the impact of apocalyptic catastrophes, that in doing so one would in fact avoid what one appears to address. The catastrophic rupture after which *The Lice* places itself has to implicate poetic form and tradition as well as language and the production of text as such.[20] Merwin's poetry can then be read as a quintessential post-apocalyptic text. Whereas the apocalyptic text is motivated by a desire for total destruction, impossibly including the desire for its own destruction (Woodland 17), the post-apocalyptic text becomes its mirror in that it is led by the impossible desire to signify its own destruction, and the destruction of language itself, in its writing. For Merwin, employing sparse speech, losing punctuation, and breaking his verse into the lines of open forms become ways of combining the need for poetic innovation with the conveyance of the post-apocalyptic situation.

Thus, Merwin's post-apocalyptic vision and revision combine several layers of destruction and negation in *The Lice*. First, Merwin depicts in his verse a world of destruction and disappearances, makes through his poetry a world already unmade in which sight is lost and little remains to be seen. Secondly, his poetry destroys American founding myths in revealing them as narratives that affirm power structures, exploit the powerless and cause devastation. Thirdly, the making of poetry itself is implicated in the processes of destruction with the abandoning of regular lines and meter, and a revisionary treatment of traditions of apocalyptic-romantic poetry. Finally, the work of poetry appears as much as collected remnants of a destroyed imagination as it depicts a world of vanishings and endings. The speaker, who generally acts both as a presence in the poetic world and as its origin,

---

20   Derrida ("No Apocalypse" 28) argues in reference to a nuclear explosion that an ultimate catastrophe "would irreversibly destroy the entire archive and all symbolic capacity" (see Gery 33; Robson 72; Schwenger xvi). In terms of this essay, such a world-unmaking catastrophe would unmake the very structures by which we make meaning.

"appears as chief among the ghosts" (Ramsey 35).[21] The speaker is then not only one among many in the world after the end, but, according to the logic of poetry, has also generated this world himself (see Müller-Zettelmann 107ff., esp. 110). All that is left for the speaker is the destroyed world he sees outside of him but that finds its origin inside of him. All that is left for the reader is the depiction of endings and the question whether this represents an inner or an outer state. In Merwin's collapsing of boundaries, however, this no longer matters. As the speaker wanders among the dead he appears to have created, the distinction between inside and outside disappears. Whether there is no world anymore, or no other world available to the speaker anymore—either way there is nothing else left in this poetic universe: "I/am all that became of them/Clearly all is lost." With the speaker being "all," "all is lost." The "I," that becomes "all" in a poetry in which nothing else can be ascertained, is "lost," dwindles to nothing—and out of its own vanishing generates the poetic vision of a world continually fading out.

4. "Where Once the World Had Been": Revisiting Ruins as a Witness of the End in Carolyn Forché's *The Angel of History*

Poetry is generally regarded as the most 'private' of literary genres, and debates about the status of political poetry have surfaced regularly among poets and critics. In the introduction to her anthology *Against Forgetting: 20th Century Poetry of Witness*, Carolyn Forché takes a stand by arguing for a "third term, one that can describe the space between the state and the supposedly safe havens of the personal," and suggesting to "call this space 'the social'" (*Against Forgetting* 31). Such an argument for poetry's social space also infers that poetry always exists in the social sphere whether a specific poem makes this explicit or not.[22] Similar to the concept of post-apocalyptic poetry suggested in this essay, Forché's "poetry of witness" stands in direct interaction with historical events, particularly those with the effect of a traumatic rupture. Such poetry, in reaction to the World Wars, the Armenian Genocide, or the social upheavals of the 1960s, bears "the trace of extremity within them" (Forché, *Against Forgetting* 30) which "demands new forms or alters older modes of poetic thought. It also breaks forms and creates forms from these breaks" (42). In the first major

---

21 See also Lazer (284). See Berger (50ff.) for the position of ghosts as subjects in the post-apocalypse.

22 See Kalaidjian (*Languages of Liberation*), Stein, and Brunner for recent considerations on the social text in American poetry. See also the section on "Poetry as Social Act" in Finck and Scheiding (129).

work to depict the relation between American poetry and historical trauma, *The Edge of Modernism,* Kalaidjian proposes a particular relation between poetry and testimony in arguing that poetry can take on a special role in "staging traumatic histories" (11), claiming that it "provides a formal medium for giving testimony to trauma across the generations otherwise separating primary and secondary witness" (9). In both of these conceptions, formal considerations place an emphasis on the fragmentation and disruption of poetic language, "invoked interruptions of absence and silence, [...] non sequiturs and shifting patterns of syntax" (11). And although, as Forché argues, the "fragment is not new to poetry" and is indeed "a standard feature of literary modernism," its impact must also be read in relation to the object of its representation: "But the fragment gains urgency in the aftermath of extremity" (Forché, *Against Forgetting* 42).

In *The Angel of History* (*AH* 1994), Forché presents her own space of fragments that gain urgency in that they signal the amassed ruins of the twentieth century in a form which she describes herself as "polyphonic, broken, haunted, and in ruins, with no possibility of restoration" (notes to *Angel of History,* n. pag.). Bearing as the title Benjamin's image for a history destructive beyond redemption or healing and featuring his "Ninth Thesis on the Philosophy of History" as an epigraph, Forché's volume becomes a paradigmatic example of a "poetry of witness" of the end. In Forché's post-apocalyptic vision, the status of the "angel of history" as witness becomes central, and is, as Kalaidjian convincingly argues, directly associated with the visual power of the angel's gaze. In his Lacanian analysis, the angel's gaze itself is represented in Forché's poetry through the disruption of the world's visual characteristics. It is less that the "angel of history" figures as a speaker in the volume than that the world depicted is the one as seen by the angel, and affected by its gaze: "Positioned as historical witness, rather than messenger, Benjamin's angel assumes a special agency through the testimony of his gaze" (Kalaidjin, *The Edge of Modernism* 104). The angel's retrospect vision, its revision, affects the significance of the visual in the poem:

> Forché's visual landscape disperses a uniformly overexposed depth of field. Illumination no longer connotes the redemptive qualities of metaphysical values. Instead, it returns like an intrusive trauma of memory inflected by the fire imagery of Nazi death camps and the nuclear flash of Hiroshima. (105)

The meaning and the quality of the visual itself bears witness to the world's traumatisation, just as Forché's fragmented poetic speech bears witness to the changed status of language in such a traumatised world. Neither language nor the visible remain exempt from "the world-historical rupture of the Holocaust" (99). The consequence of that rupture for language, especially for poetic speech, found a direct and didactic expression directly in its aftermath that still merits close attention today. "Theodor Adorno's famous slogan that 'to write poetry after Auschwitz is barbaric' tacitly assumes a temporality locating us 'after' the Holocaust rather than within the deferred action of its unfolding event." (5). Adorno's radical statement, which he of course later modified, can however also be read in the way that poetry which places itself securely "after Auschwitz" instead of "within the deferred action" of the Holocaust, is indeed barbaric since it fails to acknowledge the lasting impact of traumatic rupture, or even actively erases it from memory. In this sense, Adorno's statement becomes of vital importance to Forché's post-apocalyptic poetry of witness, since it explicitly places itself within the "deferred action" of historical traumas. The poetry of *Angel of History* painfully attempts to work through their shattering impact by letting this impact shatter its own poetic voice into ruins, and by testifying to the "crisis in visuality" the world suffered after the Holocaust (49). It comments not only on the changed conditions of poetic representation, but also on the change that has affected the quality of the visual by which the world presents itself to us.

The Angel's gaze follows the Holocaust's "visible trace on the visual field of postmodernity" (105) and its textual traces in the interplay of various voices by revisiting specific sites of apocalyptic destruction in the twentieth century. "The Testimony of Light" (*AH* 72), a poem at the end of the volume on the nuclear devastation of Hiroshima, demonstrates her dismantling of the single poetic voice into a polyphony of fragments, and her world-unmaking into a blazing light of emptiness and erasure.

> Outside everything visible and invisible a blazing maple.
> Daybreak: a seam at the curve of the world. The trousered legs of the women shimmered.
> They held their arms in front of them like ghosts.
>
> The coal bones of the house clinked in a kimono of smoke.
> An attention hovered over the dream where the world had been.
>
> For if Hiroshima in the morning, after the bomb has fallen,
> is like a dream, one must ask whose dream it is.
>
> Must understand how not to speak would carry it with us.
> With bones put into rice bowls.
> While the baby crawled over its dead mother seeking milk.
>
> Muga-muchu: without self, without center. Thrown up in the sky by a wind.
>
> The way back is lost, the one obsession.

The worst is over.
The worst is yet to come. (*AH* 72)

In the place in which the "visible and invisible" collapse and are signified by "a blazing maple," any matter of substance is called into question. Whereas Merwin portrayed his world as one robbed of almost everything visible, the visual motives in Forché's poetry describe a world robbed of its substance, evaporating before one's eyes. The objects of the world are replaced, even erased by their visual impressions in the moment of destruction: "legs of the women shimmered," "coal bones," "kimono of smoke." A passage in the "Recording Angel" states this even more directly: "in light pulsing through ash, light of which the coat was made / Light of their brick houses" (*AH* 55). The resulting impression is a world of weightlessness, which signals not liberation, but a suspension of reality and life in a dream state of ghosts: "the dream where once the world had been." In Forché's "uniformly overexposed depth of field" the visual act of bleaching out is akin to the erasure of matter: the erasure of the visual surface is the destruction of matter itself. As the world appears "in the eerie, ghostlike shading of a photographic negative" (Kalaidjian, *The Edge of Modernism* 106), the world is nothing more but its own shade, ghost, smoke and ash after the fire: "Thrown up in the sky by a wind."

While the poem conjures up a visual representation of the world's aftermath, its use of poetic speech is characterised by fragmentation and erasure, even in the quoting of others. In a syntax that becomes broken and subjectless ("Must understand how not to speak would carry it with us. / With bones put in rice bowls"), Forché develops a poetry of ruins that seems to struggle with an artistic rendering of *Death in Life,* the title of Robert Jay Lifton's study of Hiroshima survivors. Its quotation in the poem sums up the poem's erasures, paradoxically in the absence of the poet's voice: "*Muga-muchu*: without self, without center." With a second quote placed in the middle of the poem, an excerpt taken from Peter Schwenger's work of nuclear criticism, *Letter Bomb: Nuclear Holocaust and the Exploding Word*, "Testimony of Light" demonstrates in miniature the intertextual method that runs throughout the volume. Through both incorporating and visually marking texts by others, cast in italics throughout the book, the volume turns its polyphony of voices into textual traces of historical trauma's aftermath. These intertextual traces haunt Forché's poetry in a paradoxical combination of silence and expression: the poet's voice is silenced while voices are given to others. Just as the fragment, the phenomenon of intertextuality is, of course, also not new and is in fact a standard feature of postmodernism. However, in Forché's post-apocalyptic poetry of witness, one can detect a sense of urgency, rather than of play.

Her quotations in different languages from interviews, diaries, critical texts, other poets and philosophers do not just signify and enact the dialogical relationships of all texts, but also populate the text with the ghostly voices of a devastated past, more fragments and leftovers of the catastrophic history that the angel records. Reading Forché's poetry through the perspective of the post-apocalyptic retrospect which makes the future of the catastrophic aftermath its present, every quote is infused with such a quality of the aftermath, appearing as a remnant of speech and civilisation now lost and destroyed.

Finally, the ghostly voices that run through the text also stand in for the voices of those that have been completely erased from the polyphony, have been ultimately silenced: "The page is a charred field where the dead would have written" ("Elegy," *AH* 69). As any other witness, the speaker in the post-apocalyptic poetry of witness, "attempt[s] to speak for the dead" (Berger 70), relating not only the experience of their death, but also giving a voice to those who no longer possess one. Furthermore, the speaker erases not only the boundary between primary and secondary witnessing, as Kalaidjian has argued, but also between the living and the dead. Placing oneself in the moment of destruction, of nuclear ground zero, "Testimony of Light" becomes also an attempt "to speak *as* the dead" (ibid.), "without self, without center." The recording of the 'angel of history' is a recording of erasures, with the speaker erasing herself (or himself) from the page by giving voice to others, speaking from the place of those erased. Paradoxically, this erasure which Forché's poetry constantly depicts relates in the last instance to the threat of the erasure from memory. The struggle with an artistic rendering of erasures and remains is the struggle of her poetry of witness against such processes of memory erasures. Writing itself then takes on a special form of agency. The "Testimony of light" testifies to the fact that the moment of absolute destruction needs to be captured in order not to be erased in the same light of extinction. The white light of erasure is countered by a writing that is figured as an intruding blackness, so that the whiteness of the empty page, on which the dead would have written, needs to be charred by her own writing. The white flash of extinction that characterises the visual landscape of Forché's post-apocalypse finds its reflection in the whiteness of the 'innocent' empty page, until she inscribes in it the "coal bones" of remains.

5. What Remains: (Un-)Making the Disappearing and Emerging Worlds of Post-Apocalyptic Poetry

Separated by nearly thirty years and drawing on different poetical traditions, Merwin's and Forche's poetry alone demonstrate the diversity post-apocalyptic expression has taken in American poetry in the last fifty years. These examples furthermore testify to the endurance of post-apocalyptic expression in the late twentieth century, and clarify that an occupation with the world's end is by no means restricted to the apocalyptic decade of the 1960s and continues to find repercussions in a post-Cold War world whose current anxieties (global terrorism, global warming) informs its after-the-end scenarios. Apocalyptically charged, 9/11 becomes for Native American poet and activist Joy Harjo the day "When the World as We Knew It Ended" (198). In the Pulitzer Prize winning *The Road* from 2006, Cormac McCarthy veers far beyond an ultimate catastrophe to depict a world barely recognisable as our own but that is nevertheless answering the greatest fears of, as one reviewer had it, "the globally warmed generation" (McCarthy back cover).

These various visions and revisions of the end transport diverse visualisations of the end, offering responses to the way seeing the end is related to the end of seeing. Whether fading away into the oblivion of darkness and blindness, or flashing in a white light of extinction and erasure, against which the "coal bones" of testimonial writing come into relief, post-apocalyptic vision regularly draws on visual extremes of reduction in depicting the end. Merwin's darkness and Forché's whiteness become both stand-ins for the nothingness of the aftermath and emblems for the remains beyond the end. What is left after everything has been taken away? The poetic processes of world-unmaking constantly face this question of what remains in the moment of and after nothingness, and how an imagined world of remains can be rendered into a poetic world made out of remains.

Intertwining unmaking and remaking in that manner, post-apocalyptic poetry comments through the perspective of reversal generally on the forces inherent in making a world, and specifically on the quality of poetry as a way of worldmaking. Through the interplay of the speaker's voice, the figurative language, the evocation of a setting and a particular moment, poetry creates the presence of a world in the moment of reading. The result of poetic worldmaking can solely be the glimpse into one consciousness at one instant, the brief overhearing of a voice, a specific view of one single thing—and due to this concentration on one aspect it might appear to be limited, weak, and ineffectual. But at the same time, poetic worldmaking works closely connected to the ways—thinking, hearing, seeing—by which we make our world on an everyday basis, and has the ability to make us aware of the everyday processes so that we re-recognise them in their singularity and strangeness. Thus, the world that poetry can make affects us strongly by being familiar and unfamiliar, common and singular, and is particularly vivid because of this irresolvable ambiguity which is actualised in every reading and re-reading. Even if the world made through the various levels of poetic writing is characterised mainly by its lack, its desolation, its unmadeness, it still highlights the specific vivid quality of poetic worldmaking by refusing to be fixed to a single meaning. The unmade world of post-apocalyptic poetry remains alive due to the shifting ambiguities and paradoxes through which it is constantly remade by various readings and varying re-readings, finally enabling the poetic world to go on despite depicting the moment after the end of everything.

A world, then, captured in the moment of darkness and whiteness can be read both as caught in the moment of complete disappearance and just in the moment of emerging from absolute nothingness. The strange limbo that the post-apocalyptic visions of Merwin and Forché create is an effect of their creative effort which produces a world appearing absolutely lost and, at the same time, oddly saved by their poetic making that projects unmade worlds both of and out of darkness, whiteness, nothingness. The post-apocalyptic reversal produces a circle from which it cannot escape. Its unmaking shows what the world is finally made of (McCarthy 293), and in depicting what can be made of and out of nothingness, it is a testimony to creation in all its ambiguous and paradoxical nature, to seeing a world of the imagination come alive which is made by the very remains that bear witness to the world's devastation.

> Perhaps in the world's destruction it would be possible to see at last how it was made. Oceans, mountains. The ponderous counterspectacle of things ceasing to be. The sweeping waste, hydroptic and coldly secular. The silence.

References

Berger, James. *After the End: Representations of Post-Apocalypse.* Minneapolis: U of Minnesota P, 1999.
Boyer, Paul S. *When Time Shall Be No More: Prophecy Belief in Modern American Culture.* 7. printing. Cambridge, MA: Belknap Press of Harvard UP, 1992.
Brunner, Edward. *Cold War Poetry: The Social Text in the Fifties Poem.* Urbana: University of Illinois Press, 2001.
Chattarij, Subarno. *Memories of a Lost War: American Poetic Responses to the Vietnam War.* Oxford: Clarendon Press, 2001.

Collins, John Joseph, Bernard McGinn, and Stephen J. Stein. *The Encyclopedia of Apocalypticism.* New York: Continuum, 1998.
Dellamora, Richard, ed. *Postmodern Apocalypse: Theory and Cultural Practice at the End.* Philadelphia: U of Pennsylvania P, 1995.
—. "Introduction." *Postmodern Apocalypse: Theory and Cultural Practice at the End.* Ed. Richard Dellamora. Philadelphia: U of Pennsylvania P, 1995. 1–17.
Derrida, Jacques. "Of an Apocalyptic Tone Recently Adopted in Philosophy." *Derrida and Biblical Studies.* Spec. issue of *Semeia* 23 Trans. John P. Leavey, Jr. (1982): 63–95.
—. "No Apocalypse, Not Now (Full Speed Ahead, Seven Missiles, Seven Missives)." *Diacritics* 14.2 Trans. Catherine Porter & Philip Lewis. (1984): 20–31.
Engler, Bernd, Georg O. Fichte, and Oliver Scheiding, eds. *Millennial Thought in America: Historical* and *Intellectual Contexts, 1630–1860.* Trier: WVT, 2002.
Finck, Diana von, and Oliver Scheiding. *Ideas of Order in Contemporary American Poetry.* Würzburg: Königshausen und Neumann, 2007.
Folsom, Ed. "'I Have Been a Long Time in a Strange Country': W. S. Merwin and America." *W. S. Merwin: Essays on the Poetry.* Eds. Cary Nelson and Ed Folsom. Urbana: U of Illinois P, 1987. 224–49.
Forché, Carolyn, ed. *Against Forgetting: 20th Century Poetry of Witness.* New York/London: Norton, 1993.
—. *The Angel of History.* Newcastle upon Thyne: Bloodaxe Books, 1994.
Frazier, Jane. *From Origin to Ecology: Nature and the Poetry of W. S. Merwin.* Madison, NJ: Fairleigh Dickinson UP, 1999.
Frye, Northrop. *Fearful Symmetry: A Study of William Blake.* Princeton: Princeton UP, 1947.
Gery, John. *Nuclear Annihilation and Contemporary American Poetry: Ways of Nothingness.* Gainesville: UP of Florida, 1996.
Goodman, Nelson. *Ways of Worldmaking.* 1978. Indianapolis: Hackett, 1992.
Harjo, Joy. *When We Became Human.* New York/London: Norton, 2002.
Hix, Harvey Lee. *Understanding W. S. Merwin.* Columbia, SC: U of South Carolina P, 1997.
Kalaidjian, Walter B. *Languages of Liberation: The Social Text in Contemporary American Poetry.* New York: Columbia UP, 1989.
—. *The Edge of Modernism: American Poetry and the Traumatic Past.* Baltimore, MD.: Johns Hopkins UP, 2006.
Kermode, Frank. *The Sense of an Ending: Studies in the Theory of Fiction.* London: Oxford UP, 1967.
LaCapra, Dominick. "Trauma, Absence, Loss." *Critical Inquiry* 25.2 (1999): 696–727.
Lazer, Hank. "For a Coming Extinction: A Reading of W.S. Merwin's *The Lice.*" *ELH* 49.1 (1982): 262–85.
Libby, Anthony. "W. S. Merwin and the Nothing that Is." *Contemporary Literature* 16.1 (1975): 19–40.
—. "Merwin's Planet: Alien Voices." *Criticism* 24.1 (1982): 48–63.
Lifton, Robert-Jay. *Death in Life: Survivors of Hiroshima.* New York: Basic Books, 1967.
Lyotard, Jean-François. *The Postmodern Condition : A Report on Knowledge.* Manchester: Manchester UP, 1989.
McCarthy, Cormac. *The Road.* London: Picador, 2006.

McHale, Brian. "Poetry under Erasure." *Theory into Poetry: New Approaches to the Lyric*. Eds. Eva Müller-Zettelmann and Margarete Rubik. Amsterdam/New York: Rodopi, 2005. 277–302.

Merwin, W.S. *The Second Four Books of Poems*. Port Townsend, WA: Copper Canyon Press, 1993.

Müller-Zettelmann, Eva. *Lyrik und Metalyrik: Theorie einer Gattung und ihrer Selbstbespiegelung anhand von Beispielen aus der englisch- und deutschsprachigen Dichtkunst*. Heidelberg: Winter, 2000.

Nelson, Cary, and Ed Folsom. *W. S. Merwin: Essays on the Poetry*. Urbana, IL: U of Illinois P, 1987.

O'Leary, Stephen D. *Arguing the Apocalypse: A Theory of Millennial Rhetoric*. New York: Oxford UP, 1994.

—. "Popular Culture and Apocalypticism." *The Encyclopedia of Apocalypticism*. Eds. John Joseph Collins, Bernard McGinn and Stephen J. Stein. 3 vols. New York: Continuum, 1998. 392–427.

Perloff, Marjorie: "Apocalypse Then: Merwin and the Sorrows of Literary History." *W. S. Merwin: Essays on the Poetry*. Eds. Cary Nelson and Ed Folsom. Urbana, IL: U of Illinois P, 1987. 122–44.

Ramazani, Jahan, Richard Ellmann, and Robert O'Clair, eds. *The Norton Anthology of Modern and Contemporary Poetry*. New York/London: Norton, 2003.

Ramsey, Jarold. "The Continuities of W.S. Merwin: 'What Has Escaped Us We Bring with Us.'" *W. S. Merwin: Essays on the Poetry*. Eds. Cary Nelson and Ed Folsom. Urbana, IL: U of Illinois P, 1987. 19–44.

Robinson, Douglas. "Literature and Apocalyptic." *The Encyclopedia of Apocalypticism*. Eds. John Joseph Collins, Bernard McGinn and Stephen J. Stein. 3 vols. New York: Continuum, 1998. 360–92.

—. *American Apocalypses: The Image of the End of the World in American Literature*. Baltimore/London: John Hopkins UP, 1985.

Robson, David. "Frye, Derrida, Pynchon, and the Apocalyptic Space of Postmodern Fiction." *Postmodern Apocalypse: Theory and Cultural Practice at the End*. Ed. Richard Dellamora. Philadelphia: U of Pennsylvania P, 1995. 61–79.

Scarry, Elaine. *The Body in Pain: The Making and Unmaking of the World*. New York: Oxford UP, 1985.

Schwenger, Peter. *Letter Bomb: Nuclear Holocaust and the Exploding Word*. Baltimore, MD: Johns Hopkins UP, 1992.

Stein, Kevin. *Private Poets, Worldly Acts: Public and Private History in Contemporary American Poetry*. Athens, OH: Ohio UP, 1996.

Woodland, Malcolm. *Wallace Stevens and the Apocalyptic Mode*. Iowa City: U of Iowa P, 2005.

Notes on Contributors

Hanna Bingel writes her doctoral thesis in English studies at the International Graduate Centre for the Study of Culture at the University of Giessen, Germany. Her thesis examines spirituality and religion in American literature. Research interests and teaching areas include American literature and culture, literary and cultural theory, narratology, and religious studies. She has published on Marilynne Robinson ("Scouring the Unsettled Self: Identity and Spiritual Quest in Marilynne Robinson's Fictional Autobiography *Gilead*," 2008) and on the American novel from 1980 onwards ("Zwischen Realismus und Experiment: Entwicklungstendenzen und Erscheinungsformen des Amerikanischen Romans von 1980 bis Heute," 2010). She is currently working as a research assistant at the Teaching Centre for Academic Instruction at the International Graduate Centre for the Study of Culture.

Steven Connor is Professor of Modern Literature and Theory at Birbeck College, London and Academic Director of the London Consortium, a Graduate Programme in Humanities and Cultural Studies taught in collaboration between Birkbeck College, London, the Architectural Association, the Institute of Contemporary Arts, Tate and the Science Museum. He is a writer and broadcaster for radio and the author of books on Dickens, Beckett, Joyce and topics in literary theory, including *Postmodernist Culture* (Blackwell, 1989, ²1996). His most recent books are *Dumbstruck: A Cultural History of Ventriloquism* (Oxford University Press, 2000), *The Book of Skin* (Reaktion, 2003), *Fly* (Reaktion, 2006), *The Matter of Air: The Science and Art of the Ephemeral* (Reaktion, 2010) and *Paraphernalia: The Secret Magic of Ordinary Things* (Profile, 2010). His website at www.stevenconnor.com includes lectures, broadcasts, unpublished work and work in progress.

Benjamin Dawson is a PhD candidate at Birkbeck (London Consortium) working on cultural history and the philosophy of science in the Romantic period. He has published essays on *Frankenstein* and on techniques of self-experimentation developed in the study of 'galvanic' phenomena. In 2010-11, he will be undertaking post-doctoral research at the Berlin Institute for Cultural Inquiry.

René Dietrich is a PhD student at the English department of the Justus-Liebig-University Giessen. He works as a research assistant and as a coordinator of the International PhD Program "Literary and Cultural Studies." His main research interests include the theory and representation of apocalypse and post-apocalypse, trauma studies and cultural memory, twentieth-century American poetry and drama, postmodernist fiction, crime fiction, and film noir. Together with Daniel Smilovski and Ansgar Nünning he is the editor of *Lost or Found in Translation: Interkulturelle/ Internationale Perspektiven der Geisteswissenschaften* (WVT, forthcoming).

Maren Eckart is Assistant Professor of German literature at Högskolan Dalarna, Sweden. Her main fields of interest are medieval and early modern German literature, narratology, and gender studies. She is currently working together with Elisabeth Wåghäll Nivre in a research project on early modern German biographies about female rulers. Publications include *Ob ich ein ritter wäre: Genderrelatierte Erzählstrategien im Nibelungenlied* (diss. Uppsala, 2001), "Von tugendhaften Königinnen und neugierigen Ehefrauen: Weibliche Genderentwürfe in deutsch- und schwedischsprachigen Schachzabelbüchern" (2005), "Erzählstrategien in frühneuhochdeutschen Biografien über Königin Christina" (2009); in print: "Königin Elisabeth I. und Königin Christina im Totengespräch" (2010).

Ulrik Ekman is Associate Professor at the Department of Arts and Cultural Studies, University of Copenhagen. Ekman's main research interests are in the fields of cybernetics and ICT, the network society, new media art, critical design and aesthetics, as well as recent cultural theory. He is currently the head of the Nordic research network "The Culture of Ubiquitous Information" with more than 150 participating researchers. Ekman's publications include the editing of *Throughout: Art and Culture Emerging with Ubiquitous Computing* (MIT Press, forthcoming), the co-editing with Anders Michelsen of the special issue "Interaction Designs for Ubiquity" of the *fibreculture* journal (forthcoming), the editing of the special issue "The Body: Beyond Posthumanity" of the *Turbulens* journal (2008), the co-editing with Frederik Tygstrup of *Witness: Memory, Representation, and the Media in Question* (Museum Tusculanum Press, 2008), and individual research articles and chapters such as "Of the Untouchability of Embodiment: Rafael Lozano-Hemmer" (*C-Theory*, 2010) and "Re: Touching Spatially – Living On Weakly with Open Machines" in *No Place to Hide: Interactive Media Art Exhibition* (Thaning and Appel, 2009).

Knut Ove Eliassen is Professor of Comparative Literature at the Norwegian University of Science and Technology, Trondheim, Norway. His main fields of interest are eighteenth-century literary and cultural history, French philosophy, aesthetic theory, media theory, and literature and technology studies. Recent publications include *Ledeord* (with Knut Stene-Johansen, Cappelen Damm, 2007), *Fabrikken* (with Håkon With Andersen et al., Spartacus, 2004), essays on a wide range of subjects as well as translations into Norwegian of Michel Foucault, Friedrich Kittler, and Jean Baudrillard.

Herbert Grabes is Professor Emeritus of English and American Literature at the Justus-Liebig-Universität Giessen, Germany. He has published widely on literary theory, Renaissance English literature and twentieth-century American literature and is the author of *The Mutable Glass: Mirror-Imagery in Titles and Texts of the Middle Ages and the English Renaissance* (Cambridge University Press, 1982, ²2009), *Das amerikanische Drama des 20. Jahrhunderts* (Klett, 1998), *Einführung in die Literatur und Kunst der Moderne und Postmoderne: Die Ästhetik des Fremden* (UTB, 2004), *Making Strange: Beauty, Sublimity, and the (Post)Modern 'Third Aesthetic'* (Francke, 2008). He is founder and co-editor of the yearbook *Research in English and American Literature (REAL)*. The most recent of the many books he has edited are *Writing the Early Modern English Nation* (Rodopi, 2001), *Literary History / Cultural History: Force-Fields and Tensions* (Narr, 2001), and *Literature, Literary History, and Cultural Memory* (Narr, 2005), and he has co-edited *Ethics in Culture: The Dissemination of Values Through Literature and Other Media* (de Gruyter, 2008); *Literature and Values* (WVT, 2009) and *Das neuere amerikanische Drama* (WVT, 2009).

Caroline Lusin is Assistant Professor ('Akademische Mitarbeiterin') at the English Department of the University of Heidelberg, Germany. Her main fields of interest are British literary and cultural history, particularly modernism and the contemporary British novel, (auto-)biography and intertextuality. Publications include the monograph *Virginia Woolf und Anton Čechov: Die Semantisierung von Raum und Zeit* (WVT, 2007) and articles on Ian McEwan, John Banville, J.M. Coetzee, and Matthew Kneale as well as on Lyudmila Petrushevskaya, Yuri Mamleev, and Miroslav Krleža. Currently she is working on a post-doctoral project on "Anglo-Indian Life-Writing from 1818 to the Present: The Narrative Construction of Personal and Collective Identities."

Birgit Neumann teaches English Literature and Culture at the Justus-Liebig-University Giessen, Germany as well as cultural theory at the International Graduate Centre for the Study of Culture (GCSC) in Giessen where she also has been Principal Investigator since 2006. She is the author of *Fictions of Memory* (de Gruyter, 2005), *Die Rhetorik der Nation in Literatur und Medien des 18. Jahrhunderts* (*The Rhetoric of Nation in 18th-century Literature*, WVT, 2009) and of an *Introduction to the Study of Narrative Fiction* (with Ansgar Nünning, Klett, 2008). She has also co-edited volumes on genre theory, cultural knowledge and intertextuality as well as on narrative and identity. Together with Jürgen Reulecke she is general editor of the series *Formen der Erinnerung* (*Forms of Memory*). Her current research topics include the relationship between literature and imperialism in seventeenth- and eighteenth-century England, the literary and cultural construction of space as well as gender and nation in English travelogues.

Ansgar Nünning has been Professor of English and American Literature and Culture at the University of Giessen, Germany since 1996. He is the founding director of the Giessen Graduate School for the Humanities (GGK) and of the International Graduate Centre for the Study of Culture (GCSC) as well as the academic director of the International PhD Program (IPP) "Literary and Cultural Studies" and a member of the Collaborative Research Centre "Memory Cultures." In 2007, he was awarded the "Excellence in Teaching" Prize of the Ministry of Higher Education, Research and the Arts of the state Hessen and the Hertie Foundation. He has published widely on English and American literature, cultures of memory, narratology, and literary and cultural theory. His most recent publications include *Metzler Lexikon Literatur- und Kulturtheorie* (Metzler, ^{4}2008), *Introduction to the Study of Narrative Fiction* (with Birgit Neumann, Klett, 2008), *Einführung in die Kulturwissenschaften* (edited with Vera Nünning, Metzler, 2003), *Metzler Handbuch Promotion: Forschung – Förderung – Finanzierung* (edited with Roy Sommer, Metzler, 2007), *An Introduction to the Study of English and American Literature* (with Vera Nünning, Klett, ^{4}2007), *Kulturwissenschaftliche Literaturwissenschaft* (edited with Roy Sommer, Narr, 2004), and *Erzähltextanalyse und Gender Studies* (edited with Vera Nünning, Metzler, 2004). He is editor of the series *Uni Wissen Anglistik /Amerikanistik, Uni Wissen Kernkompetenzen, WVT-Handbücher zum literaturwissenschaftlichen Studium* and *ELCH: English Literary and Cultural History* (both with Vera Nünning), *MCM: Media and Cultural Memory / Medien und kulturelle Erinnerung* (with Astrid Erll), and *WVT-Handbücher zur Literatur- und Kulturdidaktik* (with Wolfgang Hallet)

Vera Nünning is Professor of English Literature at Ruprecht-Karls-University Heidelberg, Germany. From 2006 to 2009 she acted as vice rector for international affairs in Heidelberg, yet continued to teach as guest professor at the universities of Zaragoza, Helsinki, or Catolica at Lisbon. She has published widely on British and American history as well as on English literature and culture from the eighteenth to the twentieth century. Her works include *Die Ästhetik Virginia Woolfs* (Peter Lang, 1990), *Der englische Roman des 19. Jahrhunderts* (Klett, 2000), *Grundkurs anglistisch-amerikanistische Literaturwissenschaft* (with Ansgar Nünning, Klett, 2001) and *Der amerikanische und britische Kriminalroman* (WVT, 2008). She also edited some collections of essays, among them three volumes on narratology and *Einführung in die Kulturwissenschaften* (with Ansgar Nünning, Metzler, 2003), and is associate editor of the journal *English Studies* and co-editor of the book series ELCH and Handbücher zum literaturwissenschaftlichen Studium.

Inger Østenstad is a lecturer at the Department of Literature, Area Studies and European Languages at the University of Oslo, Norway, and an author, translator and editorial director of the online journal barnebokkritikk.no. She is chairperson of the society God Kritikk and, in 2007, was awarded the Dalgard Critic Award for literature. Her research interests focus on discourse analysis, literary theory, and notions of authorship with publications on Dag Solstad (Unipub, 2009) or the staging of the literary authorial persona in "Quelle importance a le nom de l'auteur?" (*Argumentation et Analyse du Discours*, 2009).

Stephen Sale is a PhD student at the London Consortium where he is researching the relationship between technology and culture, with a particular focus on German media theory. Additional research interests include contemporary trends in telecoms and media, specifically the phenomenon known as web 2.0. Stephen Sale teaches at Birkbeck, University of London and Central St. Martins College of Art and Design. In 2008, Stephen curated a symposium on the work of Friedrich Kittler at Tate Modern. Publications include "Mobilisation or Distraction: Friedrich Kittler's Media Theoretical Reading of Ernst Jünger" (*Journal of War and Culture Studies*, 2010).

Matthew Taunton teaches English Literature (and related subjects) at Goldsmiths, Central St. Martins and the Open University and is admissions tutor at the London Consortium. His interests are in English and French literature from 1850 to the present, cities, film, and media history. His first book was *Fictions of the City: Class, Culture and Mass Housing in London and Paris* (Palgrave Macmillan, 2009). He was a major contributor to the *Dictionary of Nineteenth Century Journalism* (British Library, 2009) and has publications forthcoming on Julian Barnes, J.G. Ballard, and H.G. Wells. His present research has two main and sometimes interconnected strands: firstly, an inquiry into the impact of Bolshevism on the British literary intelligentsia between the wars, and secondly, the literature and politics of G.K. Chesterton. He is associate editor of *Critical Quarterly* and regularly contributes to the *New Statesman* and the *Times Literary Supplement*, among other publications.

Frederik Tygstrup is the Director of the Copenhagen Doctoral School in Cultural Studies and an Associate Professor of Comparative Literature at the University of Copenhagen. His primary specialisation is in the history and theory of the European novel (*Fictions of Experience: The European Novel 1615-1857*, 1992; and *In Search of the Real: Essays on the 20th Century Novel*, 2000, both in Danish). He has published widely in Scandinavian, English, French and German on topics in literary and cultural theory and analysis, with particular focus on the intersections of artistic practices and other social practices, including urban aesthetics, the history of representations and experiences of space, literature and medicine, literature and geography, literature and politics.

Elisabeth Wåghäll Nivre is Professor of German Literature at Stockholm University, Sweden. In her research she is above all concerned with the construction of gender and genre in early modern literature. She is currently working in a research project together with Maren Eckart on early modern biographies. She is general editor of the two series Stockholmer Germanistische Forschungen and Schriften des Germanistischen Instituts der Universität Stockholm. Publications include *Dargestellte Welt – Reale Welt: Freundschaft, Liebe und Familie in den Prosawerken Georg Wickrams* (Peter Lang, 1996); *Reformationstiden: Kultur och samhällsliv i Luthers Europa* (with Olle Larsson, Lund Studentlitteratur, 2001); *Women and Family Life in Early Modern German Popular Literature* (Boydell and Brewer, 2004); *Points of Arrival: Travels in Time, Space, and Self – Zielpunkte: Unterwegs in Zeit, Raum und Selbst* (with Marion Gymnich, Ansgar Nünning, and Vera Nünning, Francke, 2008); "Writing Life – Writing News: Representations of Queen Christina of Sweden (1626–1689) in Early Modern Literature" (*Journal for Renaissance Studies*, 2009).

Martin Zierold is Manager and Principal Investigator of the International Graduate Centre for the Study of Culture (GCSC) at Justus-Liebig University in Giessen, Germany. Among his fields of interest are cultural memory studies, digital media and communication theory, cultural theory, and arts management. Publications include *Gesellschaftliche Erinnerung* (de Gruyter, 2006), *Kommunikationskompetenzen* (with Ansgar Nünning, Klett, 2008) and a number of articles on communication theory, media cultures and modern media and memory. He is co-editor of special issues of the magazines *SPIEL* and *medien & zeit* on issues of memory and popular culture (2008, 2009). Together with the other members of GCSC's Executive Board he acts as general editor of the newly initiated series *Giessen Contributions to the Study of Culture*.

www.ingramcontent.com/pod-product-compliance
Lightning Source LLC
Chambersburg PA
CBHW061930220426
43662CB00012B/1857